Solutions Manual

Financial Accounting:
An Introduction to Concepts, Methods, and Uses

Fourteenth Edition

Roman L. Weil
University of Chicago
University of California, San Diego

Katherine Schipper
Duke University

Jennifer Francis
Duke University

SOUTH-WESTERN
CENGAGE Learning

Australia • Brazil • Japan • Korea • Mexico • Singapore • Spain • United Kingdom • United States

SOUTH-WESTERN
CENGAGE Learning

For product information and technology assistance, contact us at **Cengage Learning Academic Resource Center, 1-800-423-0563**.

For permission to use material from this text or product, submit all requests online at **www.cengage.com/permissions**. Further permissions questions can be emailed to **permissionrequest@cengage.com**.

ISBN-13: 978-1-133-37249-3
ISBN-10: 1-133-37249-X

South-Western Cengage Learning
5191 Natorp Boulevard
Mason, OH 45040
USA

Cengage Learning is a leading provider of customized learning solutions with office locations around the globe, including Singapore, the United Kingdom, Australia, Mexico, Brazil, and Japan. Locate your local office at: **international.cengage.com/region**.

Cengage Learning products are represented in Canada by Nelson Education, Ltd.

For your course and learning solutions, visit **www.cengage.com**.

Purchase any of our products at your local college store or at our preferred online store **www.CengageBrain.com**.

READ IMPORTANT LICENSE INFORMATION

Printed in the United States of America
1 2 3 4 5 6 7   16 15 14 13

PREFACE

This book presents answers and solutions for the questions, exercises, and problems contained in each chapter of the textbook *Financial Accounting: An Introduction to Concepts, Methods and Uses* Fourteenth Edition. We do not attempt to give all possible ways to work a problem, showing the multiple paths to the correct solution. We do not even try to give the most commonly chosen one, even if we know what that is, which is rare. Our students often ask the equivalent of, "Why can't I work the problem this way?" or "Is it OK to work the problem this other way?" In a word, yes. You can work most problems in several different ways. If you get the right final answer, then do not worry if you reached it via a path different from the one we show.

If you have any suggestions as to how this book might be improved in subsequent editions, please feel free to bring them to our attention.

R.L.W.

K.S.

J.F.

CONTENTS

CHAPTER 1

INTRODUCTION TO BUSINESS ACTIVITIES AND OVERVIEW OF FINANCIAL STATEMENTS AND THE REPORTING PROCESS

Questions, Exercises, and Problems: Answers and Solutions

1.1   The first question at the end of each chapter asks the student to review the important terms and concepts discussed in the chapter. Students may wish to consult the glossary at the end of the book in addition to the definitions and discussions in the chapter.

1.2   *Setting Goals and Strategies*: Although a charitable organization must obtain sufficient resources to fund its operations, it would not pursue profits or wealth increases as goals. A charitable organization would direct its efforts toward providing services to its constituencies.

Financing: A charitable organization may obtain some or all of its financing from donations (contributions). A charitable organization does not issue common stock or other forms of shareholders' equity, nor does it have retained earnings.

Investing: Similar to business firms, charitable organizations acquire productive capacity (for example, buildings) to carry out their activities.

Operations: A charitable organization might prepare financial statements that compare inflows (for example, contributions) with outflows. While these statements might appear similar to income statements, there would be no calculation of net income because the purpose of the charitable organization is to provide services to its constituents, not seek profits.

1.3   The balance sheet shows assets, liabilities and, shareholders' equity as of a specific date (the balance sheet date), similar to a snapshot. The income statement and statement of cash flows report changes in assets and liabilities over a period of time, similar to a motion picture.

1.4   The auditor evaluates the accounting system, including its ability to record transactions properly and its operational effectiveness, and also determines whether the financial reports prepared by the firm's managers conform to the requirements of the applicable authoritative guidance. The auditor provides an audit opinion that reflects his professional conclusions. For most publicly traded firms in the U.S. the auditor also provides a separate opinion on the effectiveness of the firm's internal controls over financial reporting.

1.5   Management, under the oversight of the firm's governing board, prepares the financial statements.

1.6   Employees and suppliers of goods such as raw materials or merchandise often provide the services or goods before they are paid. The firm has the benefit of consuming or using the goods or services before it transfers cash to the employees and suppliers. The length of the financing period is the number of days between when the employees and suppliers provide goods and services and when the firm pays cash to those employees and suppliers.

1.7   Accounts receivable represent amounts owed by customers for goods and services they have already received. The customer, therefore, has the benefit of the goods and services before it pays cash. The length of the financing period is the number of days between when the customer receives the goods and services and when the customer pays cash to the seller of those goods and services.

1.8   Both kinds of capacity represent investments in long-lived assets, with useful lives (or service lives) that can extend for several or many years. They differ in that land, buildings, and equipment represent physical capital, while patents and licenses represent intangible or intellectual capital.

1.9   A calendar year ends on December 31. A fiscal year ends on a date that is determined by the firm, perhaps based on its business model (for example, many retailers choose a fiscal year end that is close to the end of January). A firm can choose the calendar year as its fiscal year, and many do. Both calendar years and fiscal years have 12 months.

1.10   Most firms report the amounts in their financial statements using the currency of the country where they are incorporated and conduct most of their business activities. Some firms use a different currency.

1.11   A current item is expected to result in a cash receipt (assets such as accounts receivable) or a cash payment (liabilities such as accounts payable) within approximately one year or less. A noncurrent item is expected to generate cash over periods longer than a year (assets, such as factory buildings that will be used to produce goods for sale over many years) or use cash over periods longer than a year (liabilities such as long term debt). Users of financial statements would likely be interested in this distinction because the distinction provides information about short-term cash flows separately from long-term cash flows.

1.12   Historical amounts reflect the amounts at which items entered the firm's balance sheet, for example, the acquisition cost of inventory. Historical amounts reflect economic conditions at the time the firm obtained assets or obtained financing. Current amounts reflect values at the balance sheet date, so they reflect current economic conditions. For example, the historical amount for inventory is the amount the firm paid to obtain the inventory, and the current amount for inventory is the amount for which the firm could replace the inventory today.

1.13   An income statement connects two successive balance sheets through its effect on retained earnings. Net income that is not paid to shareholders as dividends increases retained earnings. A statement of cash flows connects two successive balance sheets because it explains the change in cash (a balance sheet account) from operating, financing, and investing activities. The statement of cash flows also shows the relation between net income and cash flows from operations, and changes in assets and liabilities that involve cash flows.

1.14   The U.S. Securities and Exchange Commission (SEC) is the government agency that enforces the securities laws of the United States, including those that apply to financial reporting. The Financial Accounting Standards Board (FASB) is the private-sector financial accounting standard setter in the United States. The International Accounting Standards Board (IASB) is a private-sector financial accounting standard setter that promulgates accounting standards. More than 100 countries require or permit the use of IFRS, or standards based on or adapted from IFRS, for some or all firms in those countries. Neither the FASB nor the IASB has any enforcement powers.

1.15   U.S. GAAP must be used by U.S. SEC registrants and may be used by other firms as well. International Financial Reporting Standards (IFRS) may be used by non-U.S. firms that list and trade their securities in the United States, and these firms may also use U.S. GAAP.

Solutions

1.16   The purpose of the IASB's and FASB's conceptual frameworks is to guide standard-setting decisions of the two Boards. For example, the conceptual framework specifies the purpose of financial reporting and the qualitative characteristics of financial information that would serve that purpose. FASB and IASB board members use this conceptual structure as they consider solutions to accounting issues.

1.17   The accrual basis of accounting is based on assets and liabilities, not on cash receipts and disbursements. It provides a better basis for measuring performance because it is based on revenues (inflows of assets from customers), not cash receipts from customers, and on expenses (outflows of assets from generating revenues), not cash payments. It matches revenues with the costs associated with earning those revenues and is not sensitive to the timing of expenditures.

1.18   (Palmer Coldgate, a consumer products firm; understanding the balance sheet.) (amounts in millions of US$)

   a.   Property, plant, and equipment, net = $3,015.2 million.

   b.   Noncurrent assets = $6,493.5 (= $3,015.2 + $2,272.0 + $844.8 + $361.5).

   c.   Long-term debt = $3,221.9 million.

   d.   Current assets – Current liabilities = $3,618.5 – $3,162.7 = $455.8 million.

   e.   Yes, the firm has been profitable since its inception. We know this because its Retained Earnings, $10,627.5 million, is positive. The firm may have had a loss in one or more prior years; cumulatively, it has had positive income.

   f.   Total Liabilities/Total Assets = $7,825.8/$10,112.0 = 77.4%.

   g.   Total Assets = Total Liabilities + Shareholders' Equity

        $10,112.0   = $7,825.8   + $2,286.2

1.19   (Capcion, a paper and packaging firm; understanding the income statement.) (amounts in thousands of euros)

   a.   Cost of goods sold = €1,331,292.1 thousand.

   b.   Selling and distribution expenses = €172,033.4 thousand.

   c.   Gross margin percentage = 23.4% (= €405,667.1/€1,736,959.2).

   d.   Operating profit = €169,418.2 thousand.

        Profit before tax = €170,863.9 thousand.

        Difference equals €1,445.7 thousand (= €169,418.2 – €170,863.9). The items that constitute this difference are nonoperating sources of income (expense).

   e.   Effective tax rate = €54,289.9/€170,863.9 = 31.8%.

   f.   Profit = €116,574.0 thousand.

1.20   (Seller Redbud, a retailer; understanding the statement of cash flows.) (amounts in thousands of US$)

   a.   Cash inflow from operating activities = $614,536 thousand.

   b.   Cash inflow from investing activities = $101,698 thousand.

   c.   Cash used in financing activities = $705,531 thousand outflow.

   d.   Net cash flow equals $10,703 thousand (= $614,536 + $101,698 – $705,531).

   e.   Change in cash balance equals $10,703 thousand (= $224,084 – $213,381). The increase was attributable to the net cash inflow during the year of the same amount, $10,703 thousand.

1.21   (EuroTel, a communications firm; balance sheet relations.) (amounts in millions of euros [€])

Current Assets	+	Noncurrent Assets	=	Current Liabilities	+	Noncurrent Liabilities	+	Share-holders' Equity
€20,000	+	€29,402	=	€15,849	+	?	+	€17,154

Noncurrent liabilities total €16,399 million.

1.22   (GoldRan, a mining company; balance sheet relations.) (amounts in millions of South African rand [R])

Current Assets	+	Noncurrent Assets	=	Current Liabilities	+	Noncurrent Liabilities	+	Share-holders' Equity
R6,085.1	+	R49,329.8	=	R4,360.1	+	R13,948.4	+	?

Shareholders' equity = R37,106.4 million.

1.23   (GrandRider, an automotive manufacturer; income statement relations.) (amounts in millions of pounds sterling)

Sales	£ 7,435
Less Cost of Sales	(6,003)
Gross Margin	1,432
Less Other Operating Expenses	(918)
Loss on Sale of Business	(2)
Net Financing Income	221
Profit Before Taxes	733
Less Tax Expense	(133)
Net Income	£ 600

1.24   (AutoCo, an automotive manufacturer; income statement relations.) (amounts in millions of US$)

Sales	$ 207,349
Cost of Sales	(164,682)
Other Operating Expenses	(50,335)
Net Financing Income	5,690
Net Loss	$ (1,978)

1.25   (Veldt, a South African firm; retained earnings relations) (amounts in millions of South African rand [R])

Retained Earnings at End of 2012	+	Income for 2013	−	Dividends Declared	=	Retained Earnings at End of 2013
R4,640.9	+	R2,362.5	−	?	=	R5,872.4

Dividends declared = R1,131.0 million.

1.26   (Delvico, an Indian firm; retained earnings relations.) (amounts in millions of Indian rupees [Rs])

Retained Earnings Start of Year	+	Net Income	−	Dividends Declared	=	Retained Earnings End of Year
Rs26,575	+	?	−	Rs3,544	=	Rs70,463

Net income for the year was Rs47,432 million.

1.27   (BargainPurchase, a retailer; cash flow relations.) (amounts in millions of US$)

Cash at Start of Year	+	Cash Flow from Operations	+	Cash Flow from Investing	+	Cash Flow from Financing	=	Cash at End of Year
$813	+	$4,125	+	$(6,195)	+	$3,707	=	?

Cash at end of year = $2,450 million.

1.28   (Buenco, an Argentinean firm; cash flow relations.) (amounts in millions of Argentinean pesos [Ps])

Cash at End of Year	+	Cash Flow from Operations	+	Cash Flow from Investing	+	Cash Flow from Financing	=	Cash at End of Year
Ps32,673	+	Ps427,182	+	?	+	Ps(21,806)	=	Ps101,198

The net cash outflow for investing for the year = Ps(336,851) million.

1.29   (Kenton Limited; preparation of simple balance sheet; current and noncurrent classifications.) (amounts in pounds sterling)

	January 31, 2013
Assets	
Cash	£ 2,000
Inventory	12,000
Prepaid Rent	24,000
Total Current Assets	38,000
Prepaid Rent	24,000
Total Noncurrent Assets	24,000
Total Assets	£ 62,000
Liabilities and Shareholders' Equity	
Accounts Payable	£ 12,000
Total Current Liabilities	12,000
Total Noncurrent Liabilities	—
Total Liabilities	12,000
Common Stock	50,000
Total Shareholders' Equity	50,000
Total Liabilities and Shareholders' Equity	£ 62,000

1.30 (Heckle Group; preparation of simple balance sheet; current and noncurrent classifications.) (amounts in euros)

	June 30, 2013
Assets	
Cash	€ 720,000
Total Current Assets	720,000
Property, Plant, and Equipment	600,000
Patent	120,000
Total Noncurrent Assets	720,000
Total Assets	€ 1,440,000
Liabilities and Shareholders' Equity	
Accounts Payable	€ 120,000
Total Current Liabilities	120,000
Note Payable	400,000
Total Noncurrent Liabilities	400,000
Total Liabilities	520,000
Common Stock	920,000
Total Shareholders' Equity	920,000
Total Liabilities and Shareholders' Equity	€ 1,440,000

1.31 (Hewston, a manufacturing firm; accrual versus cash basis of accounting.) (amounts in US$)

a. Net Income = Sales Revenue − Expenses

= $66,387 million− $62,313 million = $4,074 million.

Net Cash Flow = Cash Inflows − Cash Outflows

= $65,995 million− $56,411 million = $9,584 million.

b. Cash collections may be less than revenues for at least two reasons. First, customers may have purchased on credit and have not yet paid. Second, the firm may have collected cash from customers who purchased on credit last year, but cash collections remain less than cash collected on new credit sales.

c. Cash payments may be less than expenses for at least two reasons. First, the firm may have received goods and services from suppliers, but not yet paid for those items (i.e., the amounts are to be paid in the

1.31 c. continued.

next year). Second, the firm may have accrued expenses this year that will be paid in cash in future periods; an example would be the accrual of interest expense on a bond that will be paid the next year.

1.32 (DairyLamb, a New Zealand firm; accrual versus cash basis of accounting.) (amounts in millions of New Zealand dollars)

Calculation of net income:

Revenue	$ 13,882
Cost of Goods Sold	(11,671)
Interest and Other Expenses	(2,113)
Income Before Taxes	98
Tax Expense	(67)
Net Income	$ 31

Calculation of net cash flow:

Cash Receipts from Customers	$ 13,894
Miscellaneous Cash Receipts	102
Total Cash Receipts	13,996
Cash Payments to Employees and Creditors	(5,947)
Cash Payments to Milk Suppliers	(6,261)
Cash Payments for Interest Costs	(402)
Cash Payments for Taxes	(64)
Total Cash Payments	(12,674)
Net Cash Flow	$ 1,322

1.33 (ComputerCo, a Singapore manufacturer; balance sheet relations.) (amounts in millions of Singapore dollars [$])

The missing items appear in **boldface** type.

	2013	2012
Assets		
Current Assets	$ 170,879	$ 170,234
Noncurrent Assets	**28,945**	17,368
Total Assets	$ 199,824	$ **187,602**

1.33 continued.

Liabilities and Shareholders' Equity

Current Liabilities	$ 139,941	$ 126,853
Noncurrent Liabilities	7,010	**7,028**
Total Liabilities	146,951	133,881
Shareholders' Equity	52,873	53,721
Total Liabilities and Shareholders' Equity	$ 199,824	$ 187,602

1.34 (SinoTwelve, a Chinese manufacturer; balance sheet relations.) (amounts in thousands of US$)

The missing items appear in **boldface** type.

	2013	2012
Assets		
Current Assets	$ **4,705,366**	$ 3,062,449
Noncurrent Assets	2,494,481	**2,388,389**
Total Assets	$ **7,199,847**	$ 5,450,838
Liabilities and Shareholders' Equity		
Current Liabilities	$ 4,488,461	$ 3,527,504
Noncurrent Liabilities	1,098,123	**789,058**
Total Liabilities	**5,586,584**	**4,316,562**
Shareholders' Equity	**1,613,263**	1,134,276
Total Liabilities and Shareholders' Equity	$ 7,199,847	$ **5,450,838**

1.35 (EastonHome, a consumer products manufacturer; income statement relations.) (amounts in millions of US$)

The missing items appear in **boldface** type.

	2013	2012	2011
Sales	$ 13,790	$ **12,238**	$ 11,397
Cost of Goods Sold	**(6,042)**	(5,536)	(5,192)
Selling and Administrative Expenses	(4,973)	(4,355)	(3,921)
Other (Income) Expense	(121)	(186)	(69)
Interest Expense, Net	(157)	(159)	(136)
Income Tax Expense	(759)	(648)	(728)
Net Income	$ 1,738	$ 1,354	$ **1,351**

1.36   (Yankee Fashion, a clothing retailer; income statement relations.) (amounts in millions of US$)

The missing items appear in **boldface** type.

	2013	2012	2011
Net Revenues	$ 4,295.4	$ 3,746.3	$ 3,305.4
Cost of Goods Sold	(1,959.2)	(1,723.9)	(1,620.9)
Selling and Administrative Expenses	(1,663.4)	(1,476.9)	(1,377.6)
Operating Income	672.8	545.5	306.9
Other Income (Expense)	(34.0)	**(43.8)**	(2.7)
Interest Income (Expense), Net	**4.5**	1.2	(6.4)
Income Tax Expense	(242.4)	(194.9)	(107.4)
Net Income	$ 400.9	$ 308.0	$ **190.4**

1.37   (AB Brown, a Swedish firm; statement of cash flows relations.)

Statement of Cash Flows
(amounts in millions of Swedish kronor [SEK])

	2013	2012	2011
Operations:			
Revenues, Net of Expenses	SEK 19,210	SEK 18,489	SEK 16,669
Cash Flow from Operations	19,210	18,489	16,669
Investing:			
Acquisition of Property and Equipment	(4,319)	(3,827)	(3,365)
Acquisition of Businesses	(26,292)	(18,078)	(1,210)
Sale of Property and Equipment	152	185	362
Sale of Short-Term Investments	3,499	6,180	6,375
Other Investing Activities	(573)	663	(1,131)
Cash Flow from Investing	(27,533)	(14,877)	1,031
Financing:			
Proceeds from Borrowings	15,587	1,290	657
Repayment of Borrowings	(1,291)	(9,510)	(2,784)
Sale of Common Stock	94	124	174
Dividends Paid	(8,132)	(7,343)	(4,133)
Other Financing Activities	406	58	(288)
Cash Flow from Financing	6,664	(15,381)	(6,374)
Change in Cash	(1,659)	(11,769)	11,326
Cash, Beginning of Year	29,969	41,738	30,412
Cash, End of Year	SEK 28,310	SEK 29,969	SEK 41,738

1.38 (Jackson Corporation; statement of cash flows relations.)

JACKSON CORPORATION
Statement of Cash Flows
(amounts in millions of US$)

	2013	2012	2011
Operations:			
Revenues Increasing Cash...........	$ 19,536	$ 19,083	$ 17,233
Expenses Decreasing Cash..........	(16,394)	(18,541)	(18,344)
Cash Flow from Operations..............	3,142	542	(1,111)
Investing:			
Sale of Property, Plant, and Equipment................................	332	401	220
Acquisition of Property, Plant, and Equipment.........................	(3,678)	(3,640)	(1,881)
Other Investing Transactions......	71	(1,501)	268
Cash Flow from Investing................	(3,275)	(4,740)	(1,393)
Financing:			
Proceeds of Long-Term Borrowing...	836	5,096	3,190
Issue of Common Stock................	67	37	3
Repayments of Long-Term Debt .	(766)	(922)	(687)
Cash Flow from Financing..............	137	4,211	2,506
Change in Cash...............................	4	13	2
Cash, Beginning of Year..................	117	104	102
Cash, End of Year............................	$ 121	$ 117	$ 104

1.39   (JetAway Airlines; preparing a balance sheet and an income statement.)

a.   **JETAWAY AIRLINES**
                            Balance Sheet
                     (amounts in thousands of US$)

	Sept. 30, 2013	Sept. 30, 2012
Assets		
Cash	$ 378,511	$ 418,819
Accounts Receivable	88,799	73,448
Inventories	50,035	65,152
Other Current Assets	56,810	73,586
Total Current Assets	574,155	631,005
Property, Plant, and Equipment (Net)	4,137,610	5,008,166
Other Noncurrent Assets	4,231	12,942
Total Assets	$ 4,715,996	$ 5,652,113
Liabilities and Shareholders' Equity		
Accounts Payable	$ 157,415	$ 156,755
Current Maturities of Long-Term Debt	11,996	7,873
Other Current Liabilities	681,242	795,838
Total Current Liabilities	850,653	960,466
Long-Term Debt	623,309	871,717
Other Noncurrent Liabilities	844,116	984,142
Total Liabilities	2,318,078	2,816,325
Common Stock	352,943	449,934
Retained Earnings	2,044,975	2,385,854
Total Shareholders' Equity	2,397,918	2,835,788
Total Liabilities and Shareholders' Equity	$ 4,715,996	$ 5,652,113

1.39 continued.

b.

JETAWAY AIRLINES
Income Statement
(amounts in thousands of US$)

For the Year Ended:	Sept. 30, 2013
Sales	$ 4,735,587
Salaries and Benefits Expense..............................	(1,455,237)
Fuel Expense	(892,415)
Maintenance Expense	(767,606)
Other Operating Expenses	(1,938,753)
Interest Expense..	(22,883)
Interest Income...	14,918
Net Income..	$ (326,389)

c.	
Retained Earnings, September 30, 2012	$ 2,385,854
Plus Net Loss for 2013...	(326,389)
Less Dividends Declared During 2013 (Plug).................	**(14,490)**
Retained Earnings, September 30, 2013	$ 2,044,975

1.40 (Block's Tax and Bookkeeping Services; cash versus accrual accounting.) (amounts in US$)

a. **Income for July 2013:**

(1) **Cash Basis Accounting**

Sales Revenues..	$ 13,000
Rent (Office)..	(6,000)
Rent Equipment	(12,000)
Office Supplies Expense	(370)
Income (Loss)	$ (5,370)

(2) **Accrual Basis Accounting**

Sales Revenues..	$ 44,000
Rent (Office)..	(2,000)
Rent (Equipment)	(2,000)
Salaries Expense	(6,000)
Office Supplies Expense	(90)
Interest Expense..	(133)
Income (Loss)	$ 33,777

1.40 continued.

    b.   Cash on Hand:

Beginning Balance, July 1	$ 0
Financing Sources and (Uses):	
Jack Block Share Purchase	40,000
Bank Loan	20,000
Total Financing Sources	60,000
Operating Sources and (Uses):	
Cash Collected from Customers	13,000
Office Rent	(6,000)
Equipment Rental	(12,000)
Office Supplies Expense	(370)
Net Operating Uses	(5,370)
Ending Balance, July 31	$ 54,630

The ending balance in cash contains the effects of both operating activities, which have net cash flow of $(5,370), and financing activities, which have net cash flow of $60,000. The firm is financing its operating activities with a bank loan and with funds invested by its owner; both of these sources of funds represent claims on the firm's assets, not increases in net assets.

1.41   (Stationery Plus; cash basis versus accrual basis accounting.) (amounts in US$)

    a. **Income for November 2013:**

        (1) **Cash Basis Accounting**

Sales	$ 23,000
Cost of Merchandise	(20,000)
Rent	(9,000)
Salaries	(10,000)
Utilities	(480)
Income (Loss)	$ (16,480)

1.41 a. continued.

(2) Accrual Basis Accounting

Sales	$ 56,000
Cost of Merchandise	(29,000)
Rent	(1,500)
Salaries	(10,000)
Utilities	(480)
Interest	(1,000)
Income (Loss)	$ 14,020

b. **Income for December 2013:**

(1) Cash Basis Accounting

Sales Made in November, Collected in December	$ 33,000
Sales Made and Collected in December	34,000
Cost of Merchandise Acquired in November and Paid in December	(20,000)
Cost of Merchandise Acquired and Paid in December	(27,500)
Salaries	(10,000)
Utilities	(480)
Interest	(2,000)
Income (Loss)	$ 7,020

(2) Accrual Basis Accounting

Sales	$ 62,000
Cost of Merchandise	(33,600)
Rent	(1,500)
Salaries	(10,000)
Utilities	(480)
Interest	(1,000)
Income (Loss)	$ 15,420

1.42   (ABC Company; relations between net income and cash flows.) (amounts in US$)

a.

Month	Cash Balance at Beginning of Month	+	Cash Receipts from Customers	−	Cash Disbursements for Production Costs	−	Cash Balance at End of the Month
January	$ 875		$ 1,000		$ 750		$ 1,125
February	1,125		1,000		1,500		625
March	625		1,500		1,875		250
April	250		2,000		2,250		0

b. The cash flow problem arises because of a lag between cash expenditures incurred in producing goods and cash collections from customers once the firm sells those goods. For example, cash expenditures during February ($1,500) are for goods produced during February and sold during March. Cash is not collected from customers on these sales, however, until April ($2,000). A growing firm must generally produce more units than it sells during a period if it is to have sufficient quantities of inventory on hand for future sales. The cash needed for this higher level of production may well exceed the cash received from the prior period's sales. Thus, a cash shortage develops.

   The difference between the selling price of goods sold and the cost of those goods equals net income for the period. As long as selling prices exceed the cost of the goods, a positive net income results. As the number of units sold increases, net income increases. A firm does not necessarily recognize revenues and expenses in the same period as the related cash receipts and expenditures. Thus, cash decreases, even though net income increases.

c. The income statement and statement of cash flows provide information about the profitability and liquidity, respectively, of a firm during a period. The fact that net income and cash flows can move in opposite directions highlights the need for information from both statements. A firm without sufficient cash will not survive, even if it operates profitably. The balance sheet indicates a firm's asset and equity position at a moment in time. The deteriorating cash position is evident from the listing of assets at the beginning of each month. Examining the cash receipts and disbursements during each month, however, identifies the reasons for the deterioration.

1.42 continued.

    d. Strategies for dealing with the cash flow problem center around (a) reducing the lag between cash outflows to produce widgets and cash inflows from their sale, and (b) increasing the margin between selling prices and production costs.

        To reduce the lag on collection of accounts receivable, ABC might:

    (1) Provide to customers an incentive to pay faster than 30 days, such as offering a discount if customers pay more quickly or charge interest if customers delay payment.

    (2) Use the accounts receivable as a basis for external financing, such as borrowing from a bank and using the receivables as collateral or selling (factoring) the receivables for immediate cash.

    (3) Sell only for cash, although competition may preclude this alternative.

        To delay the payment for widgets, ABC might:

    (1) Delay paying its suppliers (increases accounts payable) or borrow from a bank using the inventory as collateral (increases bank loan payable).

    (2) Reduce the holding period for inventories by instituting a just-in-time inventory system. This alternative requires ordering raw materials only when needed in production and manufacturing widgets only to customer orders. Demand appears to be sufficiently predictable so that opportunities for a just-in-time inventory system seem attractive.

        To increase the margin between selling price and manufacturing cost, ABC might:

    (1) Negotiate a lower purchase price with suppliers of raw materials.

    (2) Substitute more efficient manufacturing equipment for work now done by employees.

    (3) Increase selling prices.

        Solutions

1.42 d. continued.

The cash flow problem is short-term because it will neutralize itself by June. This neutralization occurs because the growth rate in sales is declining (500 additional units sold on top of an ever-increasing sales base). Thus, the firm needs a short-term solution to the cash flow problem. If the growth rate were steady or increasing, ABC might consider obtaining a more permanent source of cash, such as issuing long-term debt or common stock.

1.43   (Balance sheet and income statement relations.)

a. Bushels of wheat are the most convenient in this case with the given information. This question emphasizes the need for a common measuring unit.

b.
IVAN AND IGOR
Comparative Balance Sheets
(amounts in bushels of wheat)

	IVAN		IGOR	
Assets	Beginning of Period	End of Period	Beginning of Period	End of Period
Wheat	20	223	10	105
Fertilizer.................	2	—	1	—
Ox....:....................	40	36	40	36
Plow	—	—	—	2
Land........................	100	100	50	50
Total Assets	162	359	101	193
Liabilities and Owner's Equity				
Accounts Payable	—	3	—	—
Owner's Equity	162	356	101	193
Total Liabilities and Owner's Equity................	162	359	101	193

Questions will likely arise as to the accounting entity. One view is that there are two accounting entities (Ivan and Igor) to whom the Red-Bearded Baron has entrusted assets and required a periodic reporting on stewardship. The "owner" in owner's equity in this case is the Red-Bearded Baron. Another view is that the Red-Bearded Baron

1.43 b. continued.

is the accounting entity, in which case financial statements that combine the financial statements for Ivan and Igor are appropriate. Identifying the accounting entity depends on the intended use of the financial statements. For purposes of evaluating the performance of Ivan and Igor, the accounting entities are separate—Ivan and Igor. To assess the change in wealth of the Red-Bearded Baron during the period, the combined financial statements reflect the accounting entity.

c.

IVAN AND IGOR
Comparative Income Statement
(amounts in bushels of wheat)

	IVAN	IGOR
Revenues	243	138
Expenses:		
Seed	20	10
Fertilizer	2	1
Depreciation on Ox	4	4
Plow	3	1
Total Expenses	29	16
Net Income	214	122

Chapter 1 does not expose students to the concept of depreciation. Most students, however, grasp the need to record some amount of expense for the ox and the plow.

d.

(amounts in bushels of wheat)	IVAN	IGOR
Owner's Equity, Beginning of Period	162	101
Plus Net Income	214	122
Less Distributions to Owner	(20)	(30)
Owner's Equity, End of Period	356	193

1.43 continued.

e. We cannot compare the amounts of net income for Ivan and Igor without adjustment because the Red-Bearded Baron entrusted them with different amounts of resources. We must relate the net income amounts to some base. The possibilities include the following:

	IVAN	IGOR
Net Income/Average Total Assets	82.2%	83.0%
Net Income/Beginning Total Assets	132.1%	120.8%
Net Income/Average Noncurrent Assets	155.1%	137.1%
Net Income/Beginning Noncurrent Assets	152.9%	135.6%
Net Income/Average Owner's Equity	82.6%	83.0%
Net Income/Beginning Owner's Equity	132.1%	120.8%
Net Income (in bushels)/Acre	10.70	12.20

The purpose of this question is to get students to think about performance measurement. The instructor may or may not wish to devote class time at this point discussing which base is more appropriate.

CHAPTER 2

THE BASICS OF RECORD KEEPING AND
FINANCIAL STATEMENT PREPARATION: BALANCE SHEET

Questions, Exercises, and Problems: Answers and Solutions

2.1   See the text or the glossary at the end of the book.

2.2   Accounting is governed by the balance sheet equation, which shows the equality of assets with liabilities plus shareholders' equity:

$$\text{Assets} = \text{Liabilities} + \text{Shareholders' Equity}$$

To maintain this equality, it is necessary to report every event and transaction in a dual manner. If a transaction results in an increase on the left-hand side (Assets), dual transactions recording requires that one of the following must occur to maintain the balance sheet equation: decrease another asset; increase a liability; increase shareholders' equity. Similarly, if a transaction results in an increase in a Liability account, then one of the following must occur to maintain the balance sheet equation: decrease another liability; decrease shareholders' equity; increase an asset.

2.3   Typically, the accountant records journal entries before transferring the amounts to T-accounts. A T-account is used to record the effects of events and transactions that affect a specific asset, liability, shareholders' equity, revenue, or expense account (which the text has not yet introduced). It captures both increases and decreases in that specific account, without reference to the effects on other accounts. It also shows the beginning and ending balances of balance sheet accounts. A journal entry shows all the accounts affected by a single event or transaction; each debit and each credit in a journal entry will affect a specific T-account. Journal entries provide a record of transactions, and T-accounts summarize the effects of transactions on specific accounts.

2.4   The distinction is based on time. Current assets are expected to be converted to cash (or used) within a year; for example, Accounts Receivable, converted to cash (or Advances for Insurance, used). Noncurrent assets are expected to be converted to cash over longer periods.

2.5   Contra accounts provide disaggregated information concerning the net amount of an asset, liability, or shareholders' equity item. For example, the account Property, Plant, and Equipment Net of Accumulated Depreciation does not indicate separately the acquisition cost of fixed assets and the portion of that acquisition cost written off as depreciation since acquisition. If the firm used a contra account, it would have such information. The alternative to using contra accounts is to debit or credit directly the principal account involved (for example, Property, Plant, and Equipment).   This alternative procedure, however, does not permit computation of disaggregated information about the net balance in the account. Note that the use of contra accounts does not affect the total of assets, or liabilities, or shareholders' equity, but only the balances in various accounts that comprise the totals for these items.

2.6   (Fresh Foods Group; dual effects on balance sheet equation.) (amounts in millions of euros [€])

Transaction	Assets	=	Liabilities	+	Shareholders' Equity
(1)	+ €678		+ €678		
(2)	− € 45		− € 45		
(3)	− €633		− €633		

2.7   (Cement Plus; dual effects on balance sheet equation.)   (amounts in millions of US$)

Transaction	Assets	=	Liabilities	+	Shareholders' Equity
(1)	+$14,300				
	−$ 2,300		+$12,000		
(2)	+$ 3,000				
	−$ 3,000				
(3)	+$ 6,500				+$ 6,500
(4)			−$12,000		+$12,000

2.8   (Balance sheet classification.)

a.	L	f.	L	k.	A
b.	SE	g.	A	l.	A (if purchased from another firm)
c.	A	h.	L		N/A (if created by the firm)
d.	N/A	i.	N/A	m.	N/A
e.	A	j.	L	n.	SE

2.9   (Balance sheet classification.)

a.	SE	h.	L
b.	A	i.	A
c.	N/A	j.	L
d.	A	k.	L
e.	SE	l.	A
f.	A	m.	L
g.	A (if purchased from another firm)	n.	SE (contra; subtract)
	N/A (if created by the firm)		

2.10   (Bullseye Corporation; dual effects of transactions on balance sheet equation and journal entries.) (amounts in millions of US$)

a.

Transaction Number		Assets	=	Liabilities	+	Shareholders' Equity
(1)		+ $ 960			+	+ $ 960
	Subtotal	$ 960	=			$ 960
(2)		+ 1,500		+ $ 1,500		
	Subtotal	$ 2,460	=	$ 1,500	+	$ 960
(3)		+ 3,200				
		+ 930				
		− 4,130				
	Subtotal	$ 2,460	=	$ 1,500	+	$ 960
(4)		+ 860	=	+ 860		
	Subtotal	$ 3,320	=	$ 2,360	+	$ 960
(5)		− 1,500		− 1,500		
	Subtotal	$ 1,820	=	$ 860	+	$ 960
(6)		− 430		− 860	+	+ 430
	Total	$ 1,390	=	0	+	$ 1,390

2.10 continued.

b. (1) Cash... 960.0
           Common Stock 1.7
           Additional Paid-In Capital........................... 958.3

Assets	=	Liabilities	+	Shareholders' Equity	(Class.)
+960.0				+1.7	ContriCap
				+958.3	ContriCap

Issue 20 million shares of $0.0833 par value common stock for $960 million. Different rounding convention might yield a different, correct answer.

(2) Merchandise Inventory 1,500
       Accounts Payable... 1,500

Assets	=	Liabilities	+	Shareholders' Equity	(Class.)
+1,500		+1,500			

Purchase $1,500 million of inventory on account.

(3) Building... 3,200
       Land... 930
       Cash.. 4,130

Assets	=	Liabilities	+	Shareholders' Equity	(Class.)
+3,200					
+930					
−4,130					

Acquires building costing $3,200 million and land costing $930 million, and pays in cash.

(4) Building Fixtures 860
       Accounts Payable... 860

Assets	=	Liabilities	+	Shareholders' Equity	(Class.)
+860		+860			

Acquires building fixtures costing $860 million on account.

2.10 b. continued.

     (5)   Accounts Payable..   1,500

              Cash...   1,500

Assets	=	Liabilities	+	Shareholders' Equity	(Class.)
−1,500		−1,500			

Pays suppliers in Transaction (2).

     (6)   Accounts Payable..   860.0

              Cash...   430.0

              Common Stock 0.7

              Additional Paid-In Capital.........................   429.3

Assets	=	Liabilities	+	Shareholders' Equity	(Class.)
−430.0		−860.0		+0.7	ContriCap
				+429.3	ContriCap

Pays suppliers of fixtures cash of $430 million in shares of common stock. Bullseye Corporation shares are trading at $50 per share, so it gave the supplier 8.6 million shares of common stock (= $430 million/$50 per share).

2.11   (Inheritance Brands; dual effects of transactions on balance sheet equation and journal entries.) (amounts in millions of US$)

a.

Transaction Number		Assets	=	Liabilities	+	Shareholders' Equity
(1)		+ $ 550			+	+$ 550
	Subtotal	$ 550	=			$ 550
		− 400				
(2)		+ 1,150		+ $ 750		
	Subtotal	$ 1,300	=	$ 750	+	$ 550
(3)		− 30				
		+ 30				
	Subtotal	$ 1,300	=	$ 750	+	$ 550
(4)		+ 400	=	+ 400		
	Subtotal	$ 1,700	=	$ 1,150	+	$ 550
(5)		− 400		− 400		
	Total	$ 1,300	=	$ 750	+	$ 550

2.11 continued.

b. (1) Cash.. 550.0
            Common Stock 31.25
            Additional Paid-In Capital........................... 518.75

Assets	=	Liabilities	+	Shareholders' Equity	(Class.)
+550.0				+31.25	ContriCap
				+518.75	ContriCap

Issue 10 million shares of $3.125 par value common stock for $55 per share.

(2) Land... 250
        Building.. 900
            Cash.. 400
            Notes Payable 750

Assets	=	Liabilities	+	Shareholders' Equity	(Class.)
+250		+750			
+900					
−400					

Gives $400 million in cash and promises to pay the remainder in Year 15 for land costing $250 million and a building costing $900 million.

(3) Prepaid Insurance... 30
            Cash.. 30

Assets	=	Liabilities	+	Shareholders' Equity	(Class.)
+30					
−30					

Pays $30 million in advance to insurance company for coverage beginning next month.

2.11 b. continued.

    (4)   Merchandise Inventory 400
             Accounts Payable 400

Assets	=	Liabilities	+	Shareholders' Equity	(Class.)
+400		+400			

Purchases merchandise costing $400 million on account.

    (5)   Accounts Payable 400
             Cash 400

Assets	=	Liabilities	+	Shareholders' Equity	(Class.)
−400		−400			

Pays cash to suppliers for merchandise on account.

2.12   (Winkle Grocery Store; journal entries for various transactions.) (amounts in US$)

    (1) Cash 30,000
          Common Stock 30,000

Assets	=	Liabilities	+	Shareholders' Equity	(Class.)
+30,000				+30,000	ContriCap

    (2) Cash 5,000
          Notes Payable 5,000

Assets	=	Liabilities	+	Shareholders' Equity	(Class.)
+5,000		+5,000			

    (3) Prepaid Rent 12,000
          Cash 12,000

Assets	=	Liabilities	+	Shareholders' Equity	(Class.)
+12,000					
−12,000					

2.12 continued.

(4) Equipment 8,000
      Cash 8,000

Assets	=	Liabilities	+	Shareholders' Equity	(Class.)
+8,000					
−8,000					

(5) Merchandise Inventory 25,000
      Cash 12,000
      Accounts Payable 13,000

Assets	=	Liabilities	+	Shareholders' Equity	(Class.)
+25,000		+13,000			
−12,000					

(6) Cash 4,000
      Advances from Customers 4,000

Assets	=	Liabilities	+	Shareholders' Equity	(Class.)
+4,000		+4,000			

(7) Prepaid Insurance 1,200
      Cash 1,200

Assets	=	Liabilities	+	Shareholders' Equity	(Class.)
+1,200					
−1,200					

(8) Prepaid Advertising 600
      Cash 600

Assets	=	Liabilities	+	Shareholders' Equity	(Class.)
+600					
−600					

(9) The placing of an order does not give rise to a journal entry because it represents a mutually unexecuted contract.

2.13 (Moulton Corporation; recording transactions and preparing a balance sheet.) (amounts in US$)

a. T-accounts.

Cash (A)				Merchandise Inventory (A)				Prepaid Insurance (A)		
(1)	800,000	500,000	(2)	(3) 280,000		5,000	(4)	(5) 12,000		
(6)	300,000	245,000	(4)							
		12,000	(5)							
	343,000				275,000				12,000	

Land (A)			Building (A)			Equipment (A)		
(2)	50,000		(2) 450,000			(7) 80,000		
	50,000			450,000			80,000	

Accounts Payable (L)				Note Payable (L)			Loan Payable (L)		
(4)	250,000	280,000	(3)		80,000	(7)		300,000	(6)
		30,000			80,000			300,000	

Common Stock (SE)		
	800,000	(1)
	800,000	

2.13 continued.

b.
MOULTON CORPORATION
Balance Sheet
December 31, Year 12

Assets

Current Assets:

Cash	$ 343,000
Merchandise Inventories	275,000
Prepaid Insurance	12,000
Total Current Assets	$ 630,000

Noncurrent Assets:

Land	$ 50,000
Building	450,000
Equipment	80,000
Total Noncurrent Assets	$ 580,000
Total Assets	$1,210,000

Liabilities and Shareholders' Equity

Current Liabilities:

Accounts Payable	$ 30,000
Note Payable	80,000
Total Current Liabilities	$ 110,000

Noncurrent Liabilities:

Loan Payable	$ 300,000
Total Liabilities	$ 410,000

Shareholders' Equity:

Common Stock	$ 800,000
Retained Earnings	0
Total Shareholders' Equity	$ 800,000
Total Liabilities and Shareholders' Equity	$1,210,000

2.14 (Patterson Corporation; recording transactions and preparing a balance sheet.) (amounts in US$)

a. T-accounts.

	Cash (A)				Marketable Securities (A)			Receivable from Supplier (A)	
(1)	210,000	5,400	(5)	(14)	95,000		(13)	1,455	
(11)	4,500	350	(6)						
		1,400	(8)						
		58,200	(9)						
		7,000	(12)						
		95,000	(14)						
	47,150				95,000			1,455	

	Merchandise Inventory (A)				Prepaid Rent (A)			Land (A)	
(4)	75,000	800	(7)	(8)	1,400		(2)	80,000	
		1,800	(9)						
		1,455	(13)						
	70,945				1,400			80,000	

	Buildings (A)			Equipment (A)			Patent (A)	
(2)	220,000		(2)	92,000		(3)	28,000	
(12)	60,000		(5)	5,400				
			(6)	350				
	280,000			97,750			28,000	

	Accounts Payable (L)			Advances from Customers (L)			Mortgage Payable (L)	
(7)	800	75,000 (4)			4,500 (11)			53,000 (12)
(9)	60,000							
		14,200			4,500			53,000

2.14 a. continued.

Common Stock Par Value (SE)		Additional Paid-In Capital (SE)	
	150,000 (1)		60,000 (1)
	280,000 (2)		112,000 (2)
	20,000 (3)		8,000 (3)
	450,000		180,000

(10) Because no insurance coverage has yet been provided and no cash has changed hands, the principle of mutual exchange suggests that no asset and no liability be recorded.

b.

PATTERSON CORPORATION
Balance Sheet
January 31, Year 13

Assets

Current Assets:

Cash	$ 47,150	
Marketable Securities	95,000	
Receivable from Supplier	1,455	
Merchandise Inventory	70,945	
Prepaid Rent	1,400	
Total Current Assets		$ 215,950

Property, Plant, and Equipment (at Acquisition Cost):

Land	$ 80,000	
Buildings	280,000	
Equipment	97,750	
Total Property, Plant, and Equipment		457,750

Intangibles:

Patent		28,000
Total Assets		$ 701,700

2.14 b. continued.

Liabilities and Shareholders' Equity

Current Liabilities:
Accounts Payable.. $ 14,200
Advances from Customers 4,500
   Total Current Liabilities .... $ 18,700
Long-Term Debt:
Mortgage Payable...................................... 53,000
   Total Liabilities .... $ 71,700
Shareholders' Equity:
Common Stock—$10 Par Value .... $ 450,000
Additional Paid-In Capital 180,000
   Total Shareholders' Equity 630,000
   Total Liabilities and Shareholders'
   Equity... $ 701,700

2.15 (Regaldo Department Store; recording transactions in T-accounts and preparing a balance sheet.) (amounts in thousands of Mexican pesos [$])

a. T-accounts.

Cash (A)				Merchandise Inventory (A)				Prepaid Rent (A)		
(1) 500,000	20,000	(2)		(5) 200,000	8,000	(6)		(4) 60,000		
	4,000	(2)			3,200	(7)				
	60,000	(4)								
	156,800	(7)								
	12,000	(8)								
247,200				188,800				60,000		

Prepaid Insurance (A)			Patent (A)			Accounts Payable (L)		
(8) 12,000			(2) 20,000			(6) 8,000	200,000	(5)
			(2) 4,000			(7) 160,000		
12,000			24,000				32,000	

Common Stock (SE)	
	500,000 (1)
	500,000

2.15 continued.

b.

Assets

Current Assets:

Cash	$ 247,200
Merchandise Inventory	188,800
Prepaid Rent	60,000
Prepaid Insurance	12,000
Total Current Assets	$ 508,000
Patent	24,000
Total Assets	$ 532,000

Liabilities and Shareholders' Equity

Current Liabilities:

Accounts Payable	$ 32,000
Total Current Liabilities	$ 32,000

Shareholders' Equity:

Common Stock	$ 500,000
Retained Earnings	0
Total Shareholders' Equity	$ 500,000
Total Liabilities and Shareholders' Equity	$ 532,000

2.16 (Whitley Products Corporation; recording transactions and preparing a balance sheet) (amounts in US$)

a. T-accounts.

Cash (A)				Raw Materials (A)			Prepaid Insurance (A)	
(1)	375,000	50,000	(2)	(10) 60,000	8,000 (11)		(6) 12,000	
(7)	1,500	125,000	(3)		1,040 (12)			
		2,800	(4)					
		3,200	(5)					
		12,000	(6)					
		50,960	(12)					
	132,540			50,960			12,000	

2.16 a. continued.

Land (A)		Buildings (A)		Equipment (A)	
(2) 25,000		(2) 275,000		(3) 125,000	
				(4) 2,800	
				(5) 3,200	
25,000		275,000		131,000	

Note Payable (L)		Accounts Payable (L)		Advances from Customers (L)	
	250,000 (2)	(11) 8,000	60,000 (10)		1,500 (7)
		(12) 52,000			
	250,000		0		1,500

Common Stock (SE)		Additional Paid-In Capital (SE)	
	250,000 (1)		125,000 (1)
	250,000		125,000

b.

WHITLEY PRODUCTS CORPORATION
Balance Sheet
April 30

Assets

Current Assets:
Cash .... $ 132,540
Raw Materials Inventory........................... 50,960
Prepaid Insurance................................. 12,000
   Total Current Assets............................. $ 195,500
Property, Plant, and Equipment:
Land .... $ 25,000
Buildings.. 275,000
Equipment 131,000
   Total Property, Plant, and Equipment ... 431,000
   Total Assets................................... $ 626,500

Solutions

2.16 b. continued.

Liabilities and Shareholders' Equity

Current Liabilities:

Advances from Customers	$ 1,500	
Total Current Liabilities		$ 1,500
Noncurrent Liabilities:		
Note Payable..	$ 250,000	
Total Noncurrent Liabilities..................		250,000
Total Liabilities		$ 251,500
Shareholders' Equity:		
Common Stock—$10 Par Value	$ 250,000	
Additional Paid-In Capital	125,000	
Total Shareholders' Equity		375,000
Total Liabilities and Shareholders' Equity...		$ 626,500

2.17   (Effect of recording errors on the balance sheet equation.) (amounts in US$)

Transaction Number	Assets	=	Liabilities	+	Shareholders' Equity
(1)	No		No		No
(2)	O/S $ 9,000		O/S $ 9,000		No
(3)	U/S $16,000		U/S $16,000		No
(4)	No[a]		No		No
(5)	U/S $ 1,500		U/S $ 1,500		No
(6)	U/S $12,000		No		U/S $12,000
(7)	No		No		No

[a]Also acceptable to show both O/S and U/S by $1,800, as one asset is overstated and another, understated.

2.18   (Effect of recording errors on the balance sheet equation.) (amounts in US$)

Transaction Number	Assets	=	Liabilities	+	Shareholders' Equity
(1)	U/S $ 8,000		U/S $ 8,000		No
(2)	O/S $ 3,000		O/S $ 3,000		No
(3)	U/S $ 800		U/S $ 800		No
(4)	O/S $ 1,000		O/S $ 1,000		No
(5)	U/S $ 2,500		No		U/S $2,500
(6)	O/S $ 4,900[a]		No		No
	U/S $ 4,900[a]				

[a]The response "No" is also acceptable here.

This page is intentionally left blank

CHAPTER 3

THE BASICS OF RECORD KEEPING AND
FINANCIAL STATEMENT PREPARATION: INCOME STATEMENT

Questions, Exercises, and Problems: Answers and Solutions

3.1   See the text or the glossary at the end of the book.

3.2   Temporary accounts are for recording revenues and expenses. These accounts are temporary in the sense that once they have served their purpose of accumulating specific revenue and expense items for an accounting period, they are closed, so that they begin the following accounting period with a zero balance, ready for the revenue and expense entries of the new period. Although it would be possible to record both revenues and expenses directly in the Retained Earnings account, doing so would suppress information about the components of net income. The temporary revenue and expense accounts accumulate the information that is displayed in the line items or rows on the income statement. This display provides information about the sources and amounts of revenues and the nature and amounts of expenses that net to earnings for the period.

3.3   The balance sheet and the income statement are linked (that is, they *articulate*) through the shareholders' equity account, Retained Earnings. Retained Earnings measures the cumulative excess of net income over dividends for the life of a firm; all undistributed earnings are aggregated in Retained Earnings. The following equation describes the articulation of the Retained Earnings:

Retained Earnings (beginning) + Net Income – Dividends = Retained Earnings (end).

3.4   The purpose of the income statement is to show the user of the financial statements the components of net income, that is, the causes of net income. A user of financial statements can calculate net income by analyzing the change in retained earnings, but this analysis does not reveal the specific factors that combine to produce the net income number.

3.5 An adjusting entry is used to record the effects of an event or transaction that was not previously recorded. Many adjusting entries result from the effects of the passage of time, for example, interest accrues on amounts owed over time. The accrual of interest at the end of an accounting period is an example of an adjusting entry. A correcting entry is a special case of an adjusting entry. A correcting entry is used to record properly the effects of an event or transaction that was improperly recorded during the accounting period.

3.6 (BrasPetro S.A.; analyzing changes in accounts receivable.) (amounts in millions of reals [R$])

Accounts Receivable, Beginning of Year 7	R$	1,594.9
Plus Sales on Account during Year 7		12,134.5
Less Cash Collections during Year 7		(?)
Accounts Receivable, End of Year 7	R$	1,497.0

Cash collections during Year 7 total R$12,232.4 million.

3.7 (BigWing Company; analyzing changes in inventory.) (amounts in millions of US$)

Inventory, Beginning of Year 7	$	8,105
Plus Purchases or Production of Inventory during Year 7		?
Less Cost of Goods Sold for Year 7		(45,375)
Inventory, End of Year 7	$	9,563

Purchases or production of inventory during Year 7 total $46,833 million.

3.8 (EkaPhone; analyzing changes in inventory and accounts payable.) (amounts in millions of Swedish kronor [SEK])

Inventory, Beginning of Year 7	SEK	21,470
Plus Purchases of Inventory during Year 7		?
Less Cost of Goods Sold for Year 7		(114,059)
Inventory, End of Year 7	SEK	22,475

3.8 continued.

Purchases during Year 7 total SEK115,064 million.

Accounts Payable, Beginning of Year 7	SEK	18,183
Plus Purchases of Inventory on Account during Year 7 from above		115,064
Less Cash Payments to Suppliers during Year 7		(?)
Accounts Payable, End of Year 7	SEK	17,427

Cash payments to suppliers during Year 7 total SEK115,820 million.

3.9   (Conima Corporation; analyzing changes in income taxes payable.) (amounts in millions of yen)

Income Taxes Payable, Beginning of Year 7	¥ 3,736
Plus Income Tax Expense for Year 7 (0.43 × ¥73,051)	31,412
Less Income Taxes Paid during Year 7	(?)
Income Taxes Payable, End of Year 7	¥ 14,310

Income taxes paid during Year 7 total ¥20,838 million.

3.10   (Ealing Corporation; analyzing changes in retained earnings.) (amounts in millions of US$)

Retained Earnings, Beginning of Year 7	$ 2,796
Plus Net Income for Year 7	?
Less Dividends Declared and Paid during Year 7	(251)
Retained Earnings, End of Year 7	$ 3,257

Net Income for Year 7 totals $712 million.

3.11   (Bayer Group; relations between financial statements.) (amounts in millions of euros)

a.   €5,868 + €32,385 − €5,830 = a; a = €32,423.

b.   €109 + b − €763 = €56; b = €710.

c.   €14,723 − c + €2,155 = €12,911; c = €3,967.

d.   €6,782 + €4,711 − d = €10,749; d = €744.

3.12   (Beyond Petroleum; relations between financial statements.) (amounts in millions of US$)

   a.   a + $288,951 − $289,623 = $38,020; a = $38,692.

   b. $2,635 + $10,442 − b = $3,282; b = $9,795.

   c. $42,236 + $15,162 + c = $43,152; c = $14,246.

   d. $88,453 + $21,169 − $8,106 = d; d = $101,516.

3.13   (Journal entries for inventories and accounts payable.) (amounts in millions of yen)

Merchandise Inventories... 1,456,412
    Accounts Payable 1,456,412

Assets	=	Liabilities	+	Shareholders' Equity	(Class.)
+1,456,412		+1,456,412			

Cost of Goods Sold (= ¥408,710 + ¥1,456,412 − ¥412,387)... 1,452,735
    Merchandise Inventories....................................... 1,452,735

Assets	=	Liabilities	+	Shareholders' Equity	(Class.)
−1,452,735				−1,452,735	IncSt → RE

Accounts Payable (= ¥757,006 + $1,456,412 − ¥824,825)... 1,388,593
    Cash... 1,388,593

Assets	=	Liabilities	+	Shareholders' Equity	(Class.)
−1,388,593		−1,388,593			

3.14 (Bonana Company; journal entries for insurance.) (amounts in millions of US$)

April 30, Year 8

Insurance Expense.. 12

   Prepaid Insurance 12

Assets	=	Liabilities	+	Shareholders' Equity	(Class.)
−12				−12	IncSt → RE

Adjusting entry required for prepaid insurance consumed during April, Year 8.

May 31, Year 8

Insurance Expense.. 12

   Prepaid Insurance 12

Assets	=	Liabilities	+	Shareholders' Equity	(Class.)
−12				−12	IncSt → RE

Adjusting entry required for prepaid insurance consumed during May, Year 8.

June 1, Year 8

Prepaid Insurance.. 156

   Cash.. 156

Assets	=	Liabilities	+	Shareholders' Equity	(Class.)
+156					
−156					

To record payment of insurance for next 12 months.

3.14 continued.

June 30, Year 8

Insurance Expense.. 13

    Prepaid Insurance... 13

Assets	=	Liabilities	+	Shareholders' Equity	(Class.)
−13				−13	IncSt → RE

Adjusting entry required for prepaid insurance consumed during June, Year 8 ($13 = $156/12 months).

July 31, Year 8

Insurance Expense.. 13

    Prepaid Insurance... 13

Assets	=	Liabilities	+	Shareholders' Equity	(Class.)
−13				−13	IncSt → RE

Adjusting entry required for prepaid insurance consumed during July, Year 8.

3.15   (EBB Group; journal entries for prepaid rent.) (amounts in millions of US$)

a.   **Journal Entries for January, Year 7:**
January 31, Year 7

Rent Expense 247

    Prepaid Rent.. 247

Assets	=	Liabilities	+	Shareholders' Equity	(Class.)
−247				−247	IncSt → RE

To record the adjusting entry for the consumption of the prepaid portion of rent expense for the month of January.

3.15 a. continued.

January 31, Year 7

Prepaid Rent.. 3,200

   Cash 3,200

Assets	=	Liabilities	+	Shareholders' Equity	(Class.)
+3,200					
−3,200					

To record the prepayment of rent for the next 12 months.

b. **Journal Entry in December, Year 7:**
December 31, Year 7

Rent Expense 2,933

   Prepaid Rent.. 2,933

Assets	=	Liabilities	+	Shareholders' Equity	(Class.)
−2,933				−2,933	IncSt → RE

To record the adjusting entry for the consumption of the prepaid portion of rent expense for the months of February through December.

Amount of Prepaid Rent consumed = [($3,200/12 months) × 11 months] = $2,933 million.

3.16   (SAPC Limited; journal entries for borrowing.) (amounts in millions of US$)

a.   SAPC repaid liabilities in fiscal Year 7, in the amount of $1,634 + $1,200 − $1,828 = $1,006 million. To record the repayment, SAPC made the following journal entry:

Date of Repayment, Fiscal Year 7

Noncurrent Financial Liabilities 1,006

   Cash 1,006

Assets	=	Liabilities	+	Shareholders' Equity	(Class.)
−1,006		−1,006			

3.16 continued.

b. **Journal Entries:**

Fiscal Year 7:
March 31, Year 7

Cash 1,200
    Bank Loan Payable   1,200

Assets	=	Liabilities	+	Shareholders' Equity	(Class.)
+1,200		+1,200			

To record the loan from the local bank.

September 30, Year 7

Interest Expense [= $1,200 Million × 0.075 ×
    (180/360)] 45
    Interest Payable   45

Assets	=	Liabilities	+	Shareholders' Equity	(Class.)
		+45		−45	IncSt → RE

Adjusting entry to record interest expense earned but
not yet paid at the end of fiscal Year 7.

Fiscal Year 8:
March 31, Year 8

Interest Payable.. 45
Interest Expense 45
    Cash   90

Assets	=	Liabilities	+	Shareholders' Equity	(Class.)
−90		−45		−45	IncSt → RE

To record payment of interest for the first year.

3.16 b. continued.

September 30, Year 8
Interest Expense [= $1,200 Million X 0.075 X
    (180/360)] 45
      Interest Payable 45

Assets	=	Liabilities	+	Shareholders' Equity	(Class.)
		+45		−45	IncSt → RE

Adjusting entry to record interest expense earned but
not yet paid at the end of fiscal Year 8.

Fiscal Year 9:
March 31, Year 9
Interest Payable.. 45
Interest Expense 45
      Cash 90

Assets	=	Liabilities	+	Shareholders' Equity	(Class.)
−90		−45		−45	IncSt → RE

To record payment of interest for the second year.

March 31, Year 9
Bank Loan Payable 1,200
      Cash 1,200

Assets	=	Liabilities	+	Shareholders' Equity	(Class.)
−1,200		−1,200			

To record repayment of the principal. No further
entries required as borrower has repaid note in full.

September 30, Year 9
None.

3.17 (JCM; journal entries related to the income statement.) (amounts in billions of yen)

Year 7

Accounts Receivable.. 22,670
   Revenues.. 22,670

Assets	=	Liabilities	+	Shareholders' Equity	(Class.)
+22,670				+22,670	IncSt → RE

To record product sales on account.

Cost of Goods Sold.. 18,356
   Inventories 18,356

Assets	=	Liabilities	+	Shareholders' Equity	(Class.)
−18,356				−18,356	IncSt → RE

To record the cost of sales.

Cash.. 22,670
   Accounts Receivable.. 22,670

Assets	=	Liabilities	+	Shareholders' Equity	(Class.)
−22,670					
+22,670					

To record the cash collected on sales made on account.

3.18 (IDC; journal entries related to the income statement.) (amounts in millions of US$)

Year 7

Accounts Receivable.. 9,408
   Revenues.. 9,408

Assets	=	Liabilities	+	Shareholders' Equity	(Class.)
+9,408				+9,408	IncSt → RE

To record product sales on account.

3.18 continued.

Cost of Goods Sold.. 6,531

    Inventories 6,531

Assets	=	Liabilities	+	Shareholders' Equity	(Class.)
–6,531				–6,531	IncSt → RE

To record the cost of sales.

Cash.. 2,659

    Accounts Receivable... 2,659

Assets	=	Liabilities	+	Shareholders' Equity	(Class.)
–2,659					
+2,659					

To record the cash collected on sales made on account.

3.19   (Bostick Enterprises; journal entries to correct recording error.) (amounts in millions of US$)

Entry Made:

Equipment Expense... 120,000

    Cash... 120,000

Assets	=	Liabilities	+	Shareholders' Equity	(Class.)
–120,000				–120,000	IncSt → RE

Correct Entries:

Equipment 120,000

    Cash... 120,000

Assets	=	Liabilities	+	Shareholders' Equity	(Class.)
–120,000					
+120,000					

3.19 continued.

Depreciation Expense (= $120,000/10) 12,000
    Accumulated Depreciation.. 12,000

Assets	=	Liabilities	+	Shareholders' Equity	(Class.)
−12,000				−12,000	IncSt → RE

Correcting Entry:

Equipment 120,000
Depreciation Expense... 12,000
    Equipment Expense... 120,000
    Accumulated Depreciation...................................... 12,000

Assets	=	Liabilities	+	Shareholders' Equity	(Class.)
+120,000				+120,000	IncSt → RE
−12,000				−12,000	IncSt → RE

3.20 (Callen Incorporated; preparing a balance sheet and an income statement.) (amounts in thousands of euros)

a.

CALLEN INCORPORATED
Balance Sheet

	Dec. 31, Year 8	Dec. 31, Year 7
Assets		
Cash	€ 30,536	€ 2,559
Merchandise Inventory	114,249	151,894
Other Current Assets	109,992	134,916
Total Current Assets............................	€ 254,777	€ 289,369
Property, Plant, and Equipment (Net).......	98,130	149,990
Other Noncurrent Assets............................	56,459	88,955
Total Assets..	€ 409,366	€ 528,314

3.20 a. continued.

Liabilities and Shareholders' Equity

Accounts Payable		€ 16,402	€	14,063
Notes Payable to Banks		15,241		43,598
Other Current Liabilities		84,334		109,335
Total Current Liabilities		€ 115,977	€	166,996
Long-Term Debt		31,566		38,315
Other Noncurrent Liabilities		19,859		27,947
Total Liabilities		€ 167,402	€	233,258
Common Stock		€ 72,325	€	72,325
Retained Earnings		169,639		222,731
Total Shareholders' Equity		€ 241,964	€	295,056
Total Liabilities and Shareholders' Equity		€ 409,366	€	528,314

b.

CALLEN INCORPORATED
Income Statement

For the Year Ended:	Dec. 31, Year 8
Sales	€ 695,623
Cost of Goods Sold	(382,349)
Selling Expenses	(72,453)
Administrative Expenses	(141,183)
Interest Expense	(2,744)
Income Taxes	(24,324)
Net Income	€ 72,570

c.	
Retained Earnings, December 31, Year 7	€ 222,731
Plus Net Income for Year 8	72,570
Less Dividends Declared during Year 8 (Plug)	(125,662)
Retained Earnings, December 31, Year 8	€ 169,639

3.21   (COC; preparing a balance sheet and an income statement.) (amounts in millions of US$)

a.   **China Oil Company**
                            Income Statement
                 For the Year Ended December 31, Year 8

Revenues:
 Net Operating Revenues .... $ 835,037
 Interest and Other Revenues.. 3,098
  Total Revenues .... $ 838,135
Less Expenses:
 Cost of Sales .... $ (487,112)
 Selling Expenses .... (41,345)
 General and Administrative Expenses....................... (49,324)
 Other Operating Expenses .... (64,600)
 Interest Expense .... (2,869)
 Income Taxes... (49,331)
  Total Expenses.. $ (694,581)
Net Income .... $ 143,554

3.21 continued.

b.

China Oil Company
Comparative Balance Sheet

	Dec 31, Year 8	Dec. 31, Year 7
Assets		
Noncurrent Assets:		
Intangible Assets	$ 20,022	$ 16,127
Oil and Gas Properties	326,328	270,496
Property, Plant, and Equipment—Net	247,803	231,590
Other Noncurrent Assets	163,711	132,214
Total Noncurrent Assets	$ 757,864	$ 650,427
Current Assets:		
Inventories	$ 88,467	$ 76,038
Other Current Assets	20,367	13,457
Advances to Suppliers	20,386	12,664
Accounts Receivable	18,419	8,488
Cash	88,589	54,070
Total Current Assets	$ 236,228	$ 164,717
Total Assets	$ 994,092	$ 815,144
Liabilities and Shareholders' Equity		
Noncurrent Liabilities:		
Long-Term Debt	$ 35,305	$ 30,401
Other Noncurrent Liabilities	42,062	36,683
Total Noncurrent Liabilities	$ 77,367	$ 67,084
Current Liabilities:		
Advances from Customers	$ 12,433	$ 11,590
Other Current Liabilities	84,761	90,939
Accounts Payable to Suppliers	104,460	77,936
Total Current Liabilities	$ 201,654	$ 180,465
Shareholders' Equity:		
Common Stock	$ 444,527	$ 354,340
Retained Earnings	270,544	213,255
Total Shareholders' Equity	$ 715,071	$ 567,595
Total Liabilities and Shareholders' Equity	$ 994,092	$ 815,144

3.21 continued.

c. Retained Earnings, December 31, Year 7 .... $ 213,255
   Plus Net Income for Year Ending December 31, Year 8......... 143,554
   Subtract Dividends for Year Ending December 31, Year 8
      (Plug) .... (86,265)
   Retained Earnings, December 31, Year 8 .... $ 270,544

3.22 (Moulton Corporation; analysis of transactions and preparation of income statement and balance sheet.) (amounts in US$)

a. T-accounts.

	Cash				Accounts Receivable (A)		
√	343,000			√	0		
(4)	1,400,000	950,000	(5)	(2)	2,000,000	1,400,000	(4)
		625,000	(6)				
		82,400	(7)				
√	85,600			√	600,000		

	Inventory (A)				Prepaid Insurance (A)		
√	275,000			√	12,000		
(1)	1,100,000	1,200,000	(3)			12,000	(9)
√	175,000			√	0		

	Land (A)			Building (A)	
√	50,000		√	450,000	
√	50,000		√	450,000	

	Equipment (A)			Accumulated Depreciation (XA)	
√	80,000			0	√
				34,000	(10)
√	80,000			34,000	√

3.22 a. continued.

Accounts Payable (L)				Note Payable (L)			
		30,000	√			80,000	√
(5)	950,000	1,100,000	(1)	(7)	80,000		
		180,000	√			0	√

Interest Payable (L)				Income Tax Payable (L)			
		0	√			0	√
		24,000	(8)			41,040	(11)
		24,000	√			41,040	√

Loan Payable (L)				Common Stock (SE)			
		300,000	√			800,000	√
		300,000	√			800,000	√

Retained Earnings (SE)				Sales Revenue (SE)			
		0	√	(12)	2,000,000	2,000,000	(2)
		61,560	(12)				
		61,560	√				

Cost of Goods Sold (SE)				Selling and Administrative Expense (SE)			
(3)	1,200,000	1,200,000	(12)	(6)	625,000	625,000	(12)

Interest Expense (SE)				Insurance Expense (SE)			
(7)	2,400			(9)	12,000	12,000	(12)
(8)	24,000	26,400	(12)				

Solutions

3.22 a. continued.

Depreciation Expense (SE)				Income Tax Expense (SE)			
(10)	34,000	34,000	(12)	(11)	41,040	41,040	(12)

(10) 34,000 = 450,000/25 + 80,000/5.

b.
MOULTON CORPORATION
Income Statement
For Year 13

Sales Revenue	$ 2,000,000
Expenses:	
Cost of Goods Sold	$ 1,200,000
Selling and Administrative Expenses	625,000
Insurance	12,000
Depreciation	34,000
Interest ($2,400 + $24,000)	26,400
Total Expenses	$ 1,897,400
Net Income before Income Taxes	$ 102,600
Income Tax Expense at 40%	(41,040)
Net Income	$ 61,560

c.
MOULTON CORPORATION
Comparative Balance Sheet

	Dec. 31, Year 12	Dec. 31, Year 13
Assets		
Cash	$ 343,000	$ 85,600
Accounts Receivable	0	600,000
Inventories	275,000	175,000
Prepaid Insurance	12,000	0
Total Current Assets	$ 630,000	$ 860,600
Land (at Cost)	$ 50,000	$ 50,000
Building	450,000	450,000
Equipment	80,000	$ 80,000
Less Accumulated Depreciation	0	(34,000)
Land, Building, and Equipment (Net)	$ 580,000	$ 546,000
Total Assets	$1,210,000	$1,406,600

3.22 c. continued.

Liabilities and Shareholders' Equity

Accounts Payable	$ 30,000	$ 180,000
Notes Payable	80,000	0
Interest Payable	0	24,000
Income Tax Payable	0	41,040
Total Current Liabilities	$ 110,000	$ 245,040
Loan Payable	300,000	300,000
Total Liabilities	$ 410,000	$ 545,040
Common Stock	$ 800,000	$ 800,000
Retained Earnings	0	61,560
Total Shareholders' Equity	$ 800,000	$ 861,560
Total Liabilities and Shareholders' Equity	$1,210,000	$1,406,600

3.23 (Patterson Corporation; analysis of transactions and preparation of income statement and balance sheet.) (amounts in US$)

a. T-accounts.

Cash (A)			
√	47,150		
(6)	1,206,000	2,400	(1)
		235,000	(5)
		710,000	(7)
√	305,750		

Marketable Securities (A)		
√	95,000	
√	95,000	

Accounts Receivable (A)			
√	0		
(3)	1,495,500	1,206,000	(6)
√	289,500		

Receivable from Supplier (A)		
√	1,455	
		1,455 (2)
√	0	

Merchandise Inventory (A)			
√	70,945		
(2)	1,050,000	950,000	(4)
√	170,945		

Prepaid Rent (A)		
√	1,400	
		1,400 (8)
√	0	

3.23 a. continued.

Prepaid Insurance (A)				Land (A)	
√	0			√	80,000
(1)	2,400	100 (11)			
√	2,300			√	80,000

Building (A)			Equipment (A)	
√	280,000		√	97,750
√	280,000		√	97,750

Accumulated Depreciation (XA)			Patent (A)		
	0	√	√	28,000	
	2,500	(9)			450 (10)
	2,500	√	√	27,550	

Accounts Payable (L)			Advance from Customer (L)		
	14,200	√		4,500	√
(7) 710,000	1,048,545	(2)	(3) 4,500		
	352,745	√		0	√

Interest Payable (L)			Income Tax Payable (L)		
	0	√		0	√
	265	(12)		124,114	(13)
	265	√		124,114	√

Mortgage Payable (L)			Common Stock (SE)	
	53,000	√		450,000	√
	53,000	√		450,000	√

Additional Paid-in Capital (SE)			Retained Earnings (SE)		
	180,000	√		0	√
				186,171	(14)
	180,000	√		186,171	√

3.23 a. continued.

Sales Revenue (SE)			
(14)	1,500,000	1,500,000	(3)

Cost-of-Goods Sold (SE)			
(4)	950,000	950,000	(14)

Selling and Administrative Expense (SE)			
(5)	235,000	235,000	(14)

Rent Expense (SE)			
(8)	1,400	1,400	(14)

Depreciation Expense (SE)			
(9)	2,500	2,500	(14)

Amortization Expense (SE)			
(10)	450	450	(14)

Insurance Expense (SE)			
(11)	100	100	(14)

Interest Expense (SE)			
(12)	265	265	(14)

Income Tax Expense (SE)			
(13)	124,114	124,114	(14)

3.23 continued.

b.

PATTERSON CORPORATION
Income Statement
For the Month of February, Year 13

Sales Revenue	$ 1,500,000
Expenses:	
Cost of Goods Sold	$ 950,000
Selling and Administrative Expenses	235,000
Rent	1,400
Depreciation	2,500
Amortization	450
Insurance	100
Interest	265
Total Expenses	$ 1,189,715
Net Income before Income Taxes	$ 310,285
Income Tax Expense at 40%	(124,114)
Net Income	$ 186,171

c.

PATTERSON CORPORATION
Comparative Balance Sheet

	January 31, Year 13	February 28, Year 13
Assets		
Cash	$ 47,150	$ 305,750
Marketable Securities	95,000	95,000
Accounts Receivable	0	289,500
Receivable from Supplier	1,455	0
Merchandise Inventories	70,945	170,945
Prepaid Rent	1,400	0
Prepaid Insurance	0	2,300
Total Current Assets	$ 215,950	$ 863,495
Land (at Cost)	$ 80,000	$ 80,000
Building (at Cost)	280,000	280,000
Equipment (at Cost)	97,750	$ 97,750
Less Accumulated Depreciation	0	(2,500)
Land, Building, and Equipment (Net)	$ 457,750	$ 455,250
Patent (Net)	28,000	27,550
Total Noncurrent Assets	$ 485,750	$ 482,800
Total Assets	$ 701,700	$1,346,295

3.23 c. continued.

Liabilities and Shareholders' Equity

Accounts Payable	$ 14,200	$ 352,745
Advance from Customers	4,500	0
Interest Payable	0	265
Income Tax Payable	0	124,114
Total Current Liabilities	$ 18,700	$ 477,124
Mortgage Payable	53,000	53,000
Total Liabilities	$ 71,700	$ 530,124
Common Stock	$ 450,000	$ 450,000
Additional Paid-In Capital	180,000	180,000
Retained Earnings	0	186,171
Total Shareholders' Equity	$ 630,000	$ 816,171
Total Liabilities and Shareholders' Equity	$ 701,700	$1,346,295

3.24   (LBJ Group; miscellaneous transactions and adjusting entries.) (amounts in millions of US$)

a. (1) Inventories 180,000
            Notes Payable... 180,000

Assets	=	Liabilities	+	Shareholders' Equity	(Class.)
+180,000		+180,000			

(2) Interest Expense [= $180,000 x 0.08 x (60/360)] 2,400
            Interest Payable 2,400

Assets	=	Liabilities	+	Shareholders' Equity	(Class.)
		+2,400		−2,400	IncSt → RE

b. (1) Cash 842,000
            Advances from Customers 842,000

Assets	=	Liabilities	+	Shareholders' Equity	(Class.)
+842,000		+842,000			

3.24 continued.

c. (1) Equipment 1,400,000
       Cash 1,400,000

Assets	=	Liabilities	+	Shareholders' Equity	(Class.)
+1,400,000					
−1,400,000					

(2) Depreciation Expense [= 3/12 × ($1,400,000
       − $160,000)/10] 31,000
       Accumulated Depreciation 31,000

Assets	=	Liabilities	+	Shareholders' Equity	(Class.)
−31,000				−31,000	IncSt → RE

d. (1) Accounts Receivable 565,000
       Revenues 565,000

Assets	=	Liabilities	+	Shareholders' Equity	(Class.)
+565,000				+565,000	IncSt → RE

(2) Cost of Goods Sold 422,000
       Inventory 422,000

Assets	=	Liabilities	+	Shareholders' Equity	(Class.)
−422,000				−422,000	IncSt → RE

e. (1) Prepaid Insurance 360,000
       Cash 360,000

Assets	=	Liabilities	+	Shareholders' Equity	(Class.)
+360,000					
−360,000					

3.24 e. continued.

(2)   Insurance Expense [= (4/12) × $360,000]......... 120,000

          Prepaid Insurance....................................   120,000

Assets	=	Liabilities	+	Shareholders' Equity	(Class.)
−120,000				−120,000	IncSt → RE

f.   (1)   Cash 1,040,000

          Common Stock Par Value..........................   40,000

          Additional Paid-in Capital   1,000,000

Assets	=	Liabilities	+	Shareholders' Equity	(Class.)
+1,040,000				+40,000	ContriCap
				+1,000,000	ContriCap

(2)   Accounts Payable.. 1,040,000

          Cash   1,040,000

Assets	=	Liabilities	+	Shareholders' Equity	(Class.)
−1,040,000		−1,040,000			

3.25   (Rybowiak's Building Supplies; journal entries, adjusting entries, income statement, and balance sheet preparation.) (amounts in US$)

a.   (1)   Accounts Receivable 85,000

          Sales Revenue...   85,000

Assets	=	Liabilities	+	Shareholders' Equity	(Class.)
+85,000				+85,000	IncSt → RE

Sales of merchandise on account.

(2)   Merchandise Inventory 46,300

          Accounts Payable.......................................   46,300

Assets	=	Liabilities	+	Shareholders' Equity	(Class.)
+46,300		+46,300			

Purchase of merchandise inventory on account.

3.25 a. continued.

(3)   Rent Expense 11,750
        Cash 11,750

Assets	=	Liabilities	+	Shareholders' Equity	(Class.)
−11,750				−11,750	IncSt → RE

Paid rent for July.

(4)   Salaries Payable... 1,250
        Salary Expense 19,350
        Cash 20,600

Assets	=	Liabilities	+	Shareholders' Equity	(Class.)
−20,600		−1,250		−19,350	IncSt → RE

Paid salaries during July.

(5)   Cash 34,150
        Accounts Receivable 34,150

Assets	=	Liabilities	+	Shareholders' Equity	(Class.)
+34,150					
−34,150					

Collected accounts receivable.

(6)   Accounts Payable... 38,950
        Cash 38,950

Assets	=	Liabilities	+	Shareholders' Equity	(Class.)
−38,950		−38,950			

Paid accounts payable.

3.25 a. continued.

(7) Insurance Expense.. 50
        Prepaid Insurance...................................... 50

Assets	=	Liabilities	+	Shareholders' Equity	(Class.)
–50				–50	IncSt → RE

Recognize insurance expense for July. $50 = $400/8. The Prepaid Insurance account has a balance of $400 on June 30, Year 12. Because the firm paid the one-year insurance premium on March 1, Year 12, we know that the policy has eight remaining months on June 30, Year 12.

(8) Depreciation Expense..................................... 1,750
        Accumulated Depreciation......................... 1,750

Assets	=	Liabilities	+	Shareholders' Equity	(Class.)
–1,750				–1,750	IncSt → RE

Recognize depreciation for July: $1,750 = $210,000/120.

(9) Salary Expense... 1,600
        Salaries Payable... 1,600

Assets	=	Liabilities	+	Shareholders' Equity	(Class.)
		+1,600		–1,600	IncSt → RE

Recognize unpaid salaries for July.

(10) Interest Expense... 25
        Interest Payable 25

Assets	=	Liabilities	+	Shareholders' Equity	(Class.)
		+25		–25	IncSt → RE

Recognize unpaid interest for July: $25 = $5,000 x 0.06 x 30/360.

3.25 a. continued.

(11) Cost of Goods Sold 36,500
       Merchandise Inventory 36,500

Assets	=	Liabilities	+	Shareholders' Equity	(Class.)
−36,500				−36,500	IncSt → RE

To recognize cost of goods sold for July: $36,500 = $68,150 + $46,300 − $77,950.

b. and d.
T-accounts for Rybowiak Building Suppliers

Cash

Bal.	44,200	11,750	(3)
(5)	34,150	20,600	(4)
		38,950	(6)
Bal.	7,050		

Accounts Receivable

Bal.	27,250	34,150	(5)
(1)	85,000		
Bal.	78,100		

Merchandise Inventory

Bal.	68,150	36,500	(11)
(2)	46,300		
Bal.	77,950		

Prepaid Insurance

Bal.	400	50	(7)
Bal.	350		

Equipment

Bal.	210,000	
Bal.	210,000	

Accumulated Depreciation

	84,000	Bal.
	1,750	(8)
	85,750	Bal.

Accounts Payable

		33,100	Bal.
(6)	38,950	46,300	(2)
		40,450	Bal.

Note Payable

	5,000	Bal.
	5,000	Bal.

Salaries Payable

(4)	1,250	1,250	Bal.
		1,600	(9)
		1,600	Bal.

Common Stock

	150,000	Bal.
	150,000	Bal.

3.25 b. and d. continued.

	Retained Earnings					Sales Revenue		
	76,650	Bal.	(12)	85,000	85,000	(1)
	13,975	(12)				
	90,625	Bal.				

	Rent Expense					Salaries Expense		
(3)	11,750	11,750	(12)	(4)	19,350		
				(9)	1,600	20,950	(12)
					20,950		

	Insurance Expense					Depreciation Expense		
(7)	50	50	(12)	(8)	1,750	1,750	(12)

	Interest Expense					Interest Payable		
(10)	25	25	(12)			25	(11)
						25 Bal.	

	Cost of Goods Sold		
(11)	36,500	36,500	(12)

c.

RYBOWIAK'S BUILDING SUPPLIES
Income Statement
For the Month of July, Year 12

Sales Revenue...		$ 85,000
Less Expenses:		
Cost of Goods Sold	$ 36,500	
Salaries Expense (= $19,350 + $1,600).....	20,950	
Rent Expense	11,750	
Depreciation Expense	1,750	
Insurance Expense	50	
Interest Expense	25	(71,025)
Net Income		$ 13,975

3.25 continued.

e.

RYBOWIAK'S BUILDING SUPPLIES
Balance Sheet
June 30 and July 31, Year 12

	June 30	July 31
Assets		
Current Assets:		
Cash	$ 44,200	$ 7,050
Accounts Receivable	27,250	78,100
Merchandise Inventory	68,150	77,950
Prepaid Insurance	400	350
Total Current Assets	$ 140,000	$ 163,450
Noncurrent Assets:		
Equipment—at Cost	$ 210,000	$ 210,000
Less Accumulated Depreciation	(84,000)	(85,750)
Total Noncurrent Assets	126,000	$ 124,250
Total Assets	$ 266,000	$ 287,700
Liabilities and Shareholders' Equity		
Current Liabilities:		
Accounts Payable	$ 33,100	$ 40,450
Note Payable	5,000	5,000
Salaries Payable	1,250	1,600
Interest Payable	--	25
Total Current Liabilities	$ 39,350	$ 47,075
Shareholders' Equity:		
Common Stock	$ 150,000	$ 150,000
Retained Earnings	76,650	90,625
Total Shareholders' Equity	$ 226,650	$ 240,625
Total Liabilities and Shareholders'		
Equity	$ 266,000	$ 287,700

3.26   (Hansen Retail Store; preparing income statement and balance sheet using accrual basis.) (amounts in US$)

a.

HANSEN RETAIL STORE
Income Statement
For the Year Ended December 31, 2013

Sales (= $52,900 + $116,100)...	$ 169,000
Cost of Goods Sold (= $125,000 – $15,400)	(109,600)
Salary Expense (= $34,200 + $2,400)	(36,600)
Utility Expense (= $2,600 + $180)	(2,780)
Depreciation Expense (= $60,000/30)	(2,000)
Interest Expense (= 0.10 × $40,000)................................	(4,000)
Net Income before Income Taxes.......................................	$ 14,020
Income Taxes at 40%...	(5,608)
Net Income	$ 8,412

b.

HANSEN RETAIL STORE
Balance Sheet
December 31, 2013

Assets

Cash (= $50,000 + $40,000 – $60,000 – $97,400 + + $52,900 + $54,800 – $34,200 – $2,600)......................	$ 3,500
Accounts Receivable (= $116,100 – $54,800)	61,300
Inventories	15,400
Total Current Assets..	$ 80,200
Building, Net of Accumulated Depreciation (= $60,000 – $2,000)	58,000
Total Assets..	$ 138,200

Liabilities and Shareholders' Equity

Accounts Payable (= $125,000 – $97,400)........................	$ 27,600
Salaries Payable..	2,400
Utilities Payable	180
Income Taxes Payable	5,608
Interest Payable..	4,000
Loan Payable	40,000
Total Current Liabilities	$ 79,788
Common Stock...	$ 50,000
Retained Earnings...	8,412
Total Shareholders' Equity	$ 58,412
Total Liabilities and Shareholders' Equity..............	$ 138,200

3.27 (Regaldo Department Stores; analysis of transactions and preparation of income statement and balance sheet.) (amounts in US$)

a. T-accounts.

	Cash (A)					Accounts Receivable (A)		
√	247,200				√	0		
(3a)	62,900	32,400	(4)		(3a)	194,600	84,600	(6)
(6)	84,600	2,700	(5)					
		205,800	(7a)					
		29,000	(7b)					
√	124,800				√	110,000		

	Inventory (A)					Prepaid Rent (A)		
√	188,800				√	60,000		
(2)	217,900	162,400	(3b)					
		4,200	(7a)				30,000	(11)
√	240,100				√	30,000		

	Prepaid Insurance (A)					Equipment (A)		
√	12,000	1,000	(12)		√	0		
					(1)	90,000		
√	11,000				√	90,000		

	Accumulated Depreciation (XA)					Patent (A)		
		0	√		√	24,000		
		1,500	(10)				400	(13)
		1,500	√		√	23,600		

	Accounts Payable (L)					Note Payable (L)		
		32,000	√				0	√
(7a)	210,000	217,900	(2)					
(7b)	29,000						90,000	(1)
		10,900	√				90,000	√

3.27 a. continued.

Compensation Payable (L)			
	0	√	
	6,700	(8)	
	6,700	√	

Utilities Payable (L)			
	0	√	
	800	(9)	
	800	√	

Interest Payable (L)			
	0	√	
	900	(14)	
	900	√	

Income Tax Payable (L)			
	0	√	
	5,610	(15)	
	5,610	√	

Common Stock (SE)			
	500,000	√	
	500,000	√	

Retained Earnings (SE)			
	0	√	
	13,090	(16)	
	13,090	√	

Sales Revenue (SE)			
(16)	257,500	257,500	(3a)

Cost of Goods Sold (SE)			
(3b)	162,400	162,400	(16)

Compensation Expense (SE)			
(4)	32,400		
(8)	6,700	39,100	(16)

Utilities Expense (SE)			
(5)	2,700		
(9)	800	3,500	(16)

Depreciation Expense (SE)			
(10)	1,500	1,500	(16)

Rent Expense (SE)			
(11)	30,000	30,000	(16)

3.27 a. continued.

Insurance Expense (SE)					Patent Amortization Expense (SE)			
(12)	1,000	1,000	(16)		(13)	400	400	(16)

Interest Expense (SE)					Income Tax Expense (SE)			
(14)	900	900	(16)		(15)	5,610	5,610	(16)

b.
REGALDO DEPARTMENT STORES
Income Statement
For the Month of February Year 8

Sales Revenue	$ 257,500
Expenses:	
Cost of Goods Sold	$ 162,400
Compensation (= $32,400 + $6,700)	39,100
Utilities (= $2,700 + $800)	3,500
Depreciation	1,500
Rent	30,000
Insurance	1,000
Patent Amortization	400
Interest	900
Total Expenses	$ 238,800
Net Income before Income Taxes	$ 18,700
Income Tax Expense at 30%	(5,610)
Net Income	$ 13,090

3.27 continued.

c.

REGALDO DEPARTMENT STORES
Comparative Balance Sheet

	January 31, Year 8	February 28, Year 8
Assets		
Cash	$ 247,200	$ 124,800
Accounts Receivable	0	110,000
Inventories	188,800	240,100
Prepaid Rent	60,000	30,000
Prepaid Insurance	12,000	11,000
Total Current Assets	$ 508,000	$ 515,900
Equipment (at Cost)	$ 0	$ 90,000
Less Accumulated Depreciation	0	(1,500)
Equipment (Net)	$ 0	$ 88,500
Patent	24,000	23,600
Total Noncurrent Assets	$ 24,000	$ 112,100
Total Assets	$ 532,000	$ 628,000
Liabilities and Shareholders' Equity		
Accounts Payable	$ 32,000	$ 10,900
Notes Payable	0	90,000
Compensation Payable	0	6,700
Utilities Payable	0	800
Interest Payable	0	900
Income Tax Payable	0	5,610
Total Liabilities	$ 32,000	$ 114,910
Common Stock	$ 500,000	$ 500,000
Retained Earnings	0	13,090
Total Shareholders' Equity	$ 500,000	$ 513,090
Total Liabilities and Shareholders' Equity	$ 532,000	$ 628,000

3.28   (Zealock Bookstore; analysis of transactions and preparation of income statement and balance sheet.) (amounts in US$)

a.   T-accounts.

	Cash (A)					Accounts Receivable (A)	
(1)	25,000	20,000	(3)	(8)	148,200	142,400	(10)
(2)	30,000	4,000	(4)				
(8)	24,600	10,000	(5)				
(10)	142,400	8,000	(6)				
(13)	850	16,700	(11)				
		139,800	(12)				
	24,350				5,800		

	Merchandise Inventory (A)					Prepaid Rent (A)	
(7)	160,000	140,000	(8)	(3)	20,000	10,000	(15)
		14,600	(9)				
	5,400				10,000		

	Deposit with Suppliers (A)			Equipment (A)	
(6)	8,000		(4)	4,000	
			(5)	10,000	
	8,000			14,000	

Accumulated Depreciation (XA)				Note Payable (L)	
	400	(16)		30,000	(2)
	1,500	(17)			
	1,900			30,000	

	Accounts Payable (L)				Advances from Customers (L)	
(9)	14,600	160,000	(7)		850	(13)
(12)	139,800					
		5,600			850	

3.28 a. continued.

Interest Payable (L)			Income Tax Payable (L)	
	900	(14)		1,320	(19)
	900			1,320	

Common Stock (SE)			Retained Earnings (SE)	
	25,000	(1)		1,980	(20)
	25,000			1,980	

	Sales Revenue (SE)				Cost of Goods Sold (SE)	
(20)	172,800	172,800	(8)	(8)	140,000	140,000	(20)

	Compensation Expense (SE)				Interest Expense (SE)	
(11)	16,700	16,700	(20)	(14)	900	900	(20)

	Rent Expense (SE)				Depreciation Expense (SE)	
(15)	10,000	10,000	(20)	(16)	400	1,900	(20)
				(17)	1,500		

	Income Tax Expense (SE)	
(19)	1,320	1,320	(20)

3.28 continued.

b.
ZEALOCK BOOKSTORE
Income Statement
For the Six Months Ending December 31, Year 4

Sales Revenue	$ 172,800
Less Expenses:	
Cost of Goods Sold	$ 140,000
Compensation Expense	16,700
Interest Expense	900
Rent Expense	10,000
Depreciation Expense	1,900
Income Tax Expense	1,320
Total Expenses	$ 170,820
Net Income	$ 1,980

c.
ZEALOCK BOOKSTORE
Balance Sheet
December 31, Year 4

Assets

Current Assets:	
Cash	$ 24,350
Accounts Receivable	5,800
Merchandise Inventories	5,400
Prepaid Rent	10,000
Deposit with Suppliers	8,000
Total Current Assets	$ 53,550
Equipment	$ 14,000
Less Accumulated Depreciation	(1,900)
Equipment (Net)	$ 12,100
Total Assets	$ 65,650

3.28 c. continued.

Liabilities and Shareholders' Equity

Current Liabilities:

Accounts Payable...	$ 5,600
Note Payable...	30,000
Advances from Customers	850
Interest Payable...	900
Income Tax Payable..	1,320
Total Current Liabilities	$ 38,670

Shareholders' Equity:

Common Stock...	$ 25,000
Retained Earnings..	1,980
Total Shareholders' Equity	$ 26,980
Total Liabilities and Shareholders' Equity...........	$ 65,650

3.29 (Zealock Bookstore; analysis of transactions and preparation of comparative income statements and balance sheet.) (amounts in US$)

a. T-accounts.

Cash (A)				Accounts Receivable (A)			
√	24,350			√	5,800		
(3)	75,000	1,320	(1)	(7)	327,950	320,600	(9)
(4)	8,000	31,800	(2)				
(7)	24,900	20,000	(5)				
(9)	320,600	29,400	(10)				
		281,100	(11)				
		4,000	(12)				
√	85,230			√	13,150		

Merchandise Inventory (A)				Prepaid Rent (A)			
√	5,400			√	10,000		
(6)	310,000	286,400	(7)	(5)	20,000	20,000	(13)
		22,700	(8)				
√	6,300			√	10,000		

3.29 a. continued.

Deposit with Suppliers (A)		
√	8,000	
		8,000 (4)
√	0	

Equipment (A)		
√	14,000	
√	14,000	

Accumulated Depreciation (XA)		
	1,900	√
	800	(14)
	3,000	(15)
	5,700	√

Note Payable (L)			
		30,000	√
(2)	30,000	75,000	(3)
		75,000	√

Accounts Payable (L)			
		5,600	√
(8)	22,700	310,000	(6)
(11)	281,100		
		11,800	√

Advance from Customers (L)			
		850	√
(7)	850		
		0	√

Interest Payable (L)			
		900	√
(2)	900	3,000	(16)
		3,000	√

Income Tax Payable (L)			
		1,320	√
(1)	1,320	4,080	(17)
		4,080	√

Common Stock (SE)		
	25,000	√
	25,000	√

Retained Earnings (SE)			
		1,980	√
(12)	4,000	6,120	(18)
		4,100	√

Sales Revenue (SE)			
(18)	353,700	353,700	(7)

Cost of Goods Sold (SE)			
(7)	286,400	286,400	(18)

3.29 a. continued.

Compensation Expense (SE)			
(10)	29,400	29,400	(18)

Interest Expense (SE)			
(2)	900		
(16)	3,000	3,900	(18)

Rent Expense (SE)			
(13)	20,000	20,000	(18)

Depreciation Expense (SE)			
(14)	800		
(15)	3,000	3,800	(18)

Income Tax Expense (SE)			
(17)	4,080	4,080	(18)

b.

ZEALOCK BOOKSTORE
Comparative Income Statement
For Year 5 and Year 4

	Year 5	Year 4
Sales Revenue	$ 353,700	$ 172,800
Less Expenses:		
Cost of Goods Sold	$ 286,400	$ 140,000
Compensation Expense	29,400	16,700
Interest Expense	3,900	900
Rent Expense	20,000	10,000
Depreciation Expense	3,800	1,900
Income Tax Expense	4,080	1,320
Total Expenses	$ 347,580	$ 170,820
Net Income	$ 6,120	$ 1,980

3.29 continued.

c.
ZEALOCK BOOKSTORE
Comparative Balance Sheet
December 31, Year 5 and Year 4

	Year 5	Year 4
Assets		
Current Assets:		
Cash	$ 85,230	$ 24,350
Accounts Receivable	13,150	5,800
Merchandise Inventories	6,300	5,400
Prepaid Rent	10,000	10,000
Deposit with Suppliers	—	8,000
Total Current Assets	$114,680	$ 53,550
Noncurrent Assets:		
Equipment	$ 14,000	$ 14,000
Less Accumulated Depreciation	(5,700)	(1,900)
Equipment (Net)	$ 8,300	$ 12,100
Total Assets	$122,980	$ 65,650
Liabilities and Shareholders' Equity		
Current Liabilities:		
Accounts Payable	$ 11,800	$ 5,600
Note Payable	75,000	30,000
Advances from Customers	—	850
Interest Payable	3,000	900
Income Tax Payable	4,080	1,320
Total Current Liabilities	$ 93,880	$ 38,670
Shareholders' Equity:		
Common Stock	$ 25,000	$ 25,000
Retained Earnings	4,100	1,980
Total Shareholders' Equity	$ 29,100	$ 26,980
Total Liabilities and Shareholders' Equity	$122,980	$ 65,650

3.30 (Portobello Co.; reconstructing the income statement and balance sheet.) (amounts in US$)

T-accounts to derive the amounts in the income statement and balance sheet appear below.

	Cash		
√	18,600		
(4)	10,900	4,800	(3)
(14)	210,000	115,000	(5)
		3,000	(10)
		85,000	(17)
		27,000	(19)
√	4,700		

	Accounts Receivable		
√	33,000		
(15)	228,000	210,000	(14)
√	51,000		

	Notes Receivable		
√	10,000		
		10,000	(4)
√	0		

	Interest Receivable		
√	600		
		600	(4)
√	0		

	Merchandise Inventory		
√	22,000		
(6)	95,000	88,000	(8)
(7)	11,000		
√	40,000		

	Prepaid Insurance		
√	4,500		
		3,000	(1)
√	1,500		

	Advances to Employees		
√	0		
(17)	4,000		
√	4,000		

	Prepaid Taxes		
√	0		
(19)	3,000		
√	3,000		

	Computer System (at Cost)		
√	78,000		
√	78,000		

	Accumulated Depreciation— Computer System		
		26,000	√
		13,000	(13)
		39,000	√

3.30 continued.

	Delivery Trucks			Accumulated Depreciation—Delivery Trucks	
√	0			0	√
(9)	60,000			4,500	(12)
√	60,000			4,500	√

	Accounts Payable				Notes Payable	
		36,000	√		0	√
(5)	115,000	95,000	(6)		60,000	(9)
		16,000	√		60,000	√

	Interest Payable				Dividend Payable	
		0	√		1,800	√
		2,000	(11)	(3)	4,800	6,000	(2)
		2,000	√		3,000	√

	Salaries Payable				Taxes Payable	
		6,500	√		10,000	√
(17)	6,500			(19)	10,000	4,000	(20)
		1,300	(18)			
		1,300	√		4,000	√

	Consulting Fee Payable				Advances from Customers	
		0	√		600	√
		4,800	(21)	(16)	600	1,400	(15)
		4,800	√		1,400	√

	Common Stock				Retained Earnings	
		40,000	√		45,800	√
		11,000	(7)	(2)	6,000	15,400	(22)
		51,000	√		55,200	√

3.30 continued.

Sales Revenue					Interest Revenue			
		226,600	(15)	(22)	300	300	(4)
(22)	227,200	600	(16)				

Cost of Goods Sold					Depreciation Expense			
(8)	88,000	88,000	(22)	(12)	4,500		
				(13)	13,000	17,500	(22)

Salary Expense					Tax Expense			
(17)	74,500			(19)	14,000		
(18)	1,300	75,800	(22)	(20)	4,000	18,000	(22)

Insurance Expense					Consulting Expense			
(1)	3,000	3,000	(22)	(21)	4,800	4,800	(22)

Interest Expense			
(10)	3,000		
(11)	2,000	5,000	(22)

Solutions

3.30 continued.

PORTOBELLO CO.
Income Statement
For the Year Ended December 31, Year 18

Revenues:
Sales	$ 227,200
Interest	300
Total Revenues	$ 227,500

Expenses:
Cost of Goods Sold	$ 88,000
Depreciation	17,500
Salaries	75,800
Taxes	18,000
Insurance	3,000
Consulting	4,800
Interest	5,000
Total Expenses	$ 212,100
Net Income	$ 15,400

PORTOBELLO CO.
Balance Sheet
December 31, Year 18

Assets

Current Assets:
Cash		$ 4,700
Accounts Receivable		51,000
Merchandise Inventories		40,000
Prepaid Insurance		1,500
Advances to Employees		4,000
Prepaid Property Taxes		3,000
Total Current Assets		$ 104,200

Noncurrent Assets:
Computer System—at Cost	$ 78,000	
Less Accumulated Depreciation	(39,000)	$ 39,000
Delivery Trucks	$ 60,000	
Less Accumulated Depreciation	(4,500)	55,500
Total Noncurrent Assets		$ 94,500
Total Assets		$ 198,700

3.30 continued.

Liabilities and Shareholders' Equity

Current Liabilities:

Accounts Payable..	$ 16,000
Interest Payable..	2,000
Dividend Payable..	3,000
Salaries Payable..	1,300
Taxes Payable...	4,000
Consulting Fee Payable.............................	4,800
Advances from Customers	1,400
Total Current Liabilities	$ 32,500
Note Payable..	60,000
Total Liabilities	$ 92,500

Shareholders' Equity:

Common Stock..	$ 51,000
Retained Earnings......................................	55,200
Total Shareholders' Equity	$ 106,200
Total Liabilities and Shareholders' Equity...	$ 198,700

3.31 (Computer Needs, Inc.; reconstructing the income statement and balance sheet.) (amounts in US$)

T-accounts.

	Cash				Accounts Receivable		
√	15,600			√	32,100		
(1)	37,500	164,600	(4)	(3)	159,700	151,500	(2)
(2)	151,500	21,000	(7)				
		3,388	(8)				
		4,800	(9)				
		6,000	(10)				
√	4,812			√	40,300		

	Inventory				Prepayments		
√	46,700			√	1,500		
(5)	172,100	158,100	(6)	(7)	300		
√	60,700			√	1,800		

3.31 continued.

Property, Plant, and Equipment				Accumulated Depreciation		
√	59,700				2,800	√
(10)	6,000				3,300	(11)
√	65,700				6,100	√

Accounts Payable—Merchandise				Income Tax Payable		
		37,800	√		3,388	√
(4)	164,600	172,100	(5)	(8) 3,388	3,584	(12)
		45,300	√		3,584	√

Other Current Liabilities				Mortgage Payable		
		2,900	√		50,000	√
(7)	1,700			(9) 800		
		1,200	√		49,200	√

Common Stock				Retained Earnings		
		50,000	√		8,712	√
					9,216	(13)
		50,000	√		17,928	√

Sales				Cost of Goods Sold		
		37,500	(1)	(6) 158,100	158,100	(13)
(13)	197,200	159,700	(3)			

Selling and Administrative Expense				Depreciation Expense		
(7)	19,000	19,000	(13)	(11) 3,300	3,300	(13)

3.31 continued.

	Interest Expense				Income Tax Expense	
(9)	4,000	4,000	(13)	(12)	3,584	3,584 (13)

COMPUTER NEEDS, INC.
Income Statement
For the Years Ended December 31, Year 8 and Year 7

	Year 8	Year 7
Sales	$ 197,200	$ 152,700
Cost of Goods Sold	(158,100)	(116,400)
Selling and Administrative Expense	(19,000)	(17,400)
Depreciation Expense	(3,300)	(2,800)
Interest Expense	(4,000)	(4,000)
Income Taxes	(3,584)	(3,388)
Net Income	$ 9,216	$ 8,712

COMPUTER NEEDS, INC.
Balance Sheet
For the Years Ended December 31, Year 8 and Year 7

		Year 8	Year 7
Assets			
Cash		$ 4,812	$ 15,600
Accounts Receivable		40,300	32,100
Inventories		60,700	46,700
Prepayments		1,800	1,500
Total Current Assets		$ 107,612	$ 95,900
Property, Plant, and Equipment:			
At Cost		$ 65,700	$ 59,700
Less Accumulated Depreciation		(6,100)	(2,800)
Net		$ 59,600	$ 56,900
Total Assets		$ 167,212	$ 152,800

3.31 continued.

Liabilities and Shareholders' Equity

Accounts Payable—Merchandise	$ 45,300	$ 37,800
Income Tax Payable	3,584	3,388
Other Current Liabilities	1,200	2,900
Total Current Liabilities	$ 50,084	$ 44,088
Mortgage Payable	49,200	50,000
Total Liabilities	$ 99,284	$ 94,088
Common Stock	$ 50,000	$ 50,000
Retained Earnings	17,928	8,712
Total Shareholders' Equity	$ 67,928	$ 58,712
Total Liabilities and Shareholders' Equity	$167,212	$152,800

3.32 (Embotelladora Andina S.A.; effect of errors on financial statements.) (amounts in thousands of Chilean pesos)

	Assets	Liabilities	Shareholders' Equity
a.	U/S $60,000	NO	U/S $60,000
b.	NO	U/S $82,000	O/S $82,000
c.	U/S $95,958	NO	U/S $95,958
d.	O/S $ 3,100	NO	O/S $ 3,100
e.	NO	U/S $34,500	O/S $34,500
f.	NO	O/S $17,900	U/S $17,900

3.33 (Forgetful Corporation; effect of recording errors on financial statements.) (amounts in US$)

Note: The actual and correct entries appear below to show the effect and amount of the errors, but are not required.

a. **Actual Entry:**

Cash	1,400	
Sales Revenue		1,400

Assets	=	Liabilities	+	Shareholders' Equity	(Class.)
+1,400				+1,400	IncSt → RE

3.33 a. continued.

Correct Entry:

Cash	1,400	
Advance from Customer		1,400

Assets	=	Liabilities	+	Shareholders' Equity	(Class.)
+1,400		+1,400			

Liabilities understated by $1,400 and shareholders' equity overstated by $1,400.

b. **Actual Entry:**

Cost of Goods Sold	5,000	
Cash		5,000

Assets	=	Liabilities	+	Shareholders' Equity	(Class.)
–5,000				–5,000	IncSt → RE

Correct Entries:

Machine	5,000	
Cash		5,000

Assets	=	Liabilities	+	Shareholders' Equity	(Class.)
+5,000					
–5,000					

Depreciation Expense	500	
Accumulated Depreciation		500

Assets	=	Liabilities	+	Shareholders' Equity	(Class.)
–500				–500	IncSt → RE

Assets understated by $4,500 and shareholders' equity understated by $4,500.

c. **Actual Entry:**
None for accrued interest.

3.33 c. continued.

Correct Entry:

Interest Receivable (= $2,000 X 0.12 X 60/360)   40

    Interest Revenue   40

Assets	=	Liabilities	+	Shareholders' Equity	(Class.)
+40				+40	IncSt → RE

Assets understated by $40 and shareholders' equity understated by $40.

d.   The entry is correct as recorded.

e. **Actual Entry:**

None for declared dividend.

Correct Entry:

Retained Earnings   1,500

    Dividend Payable   1,500

Assets	=	Liabilities	+	Shareholders' Equity	(Class.)
		+1,500		–1,500	Dividend

Liabilities understated by $1,500 and shareholders' equity overstated by $1,500.

f. **Actual Entries:**

Machinery   50,000

    Accounts Payable   50,000

Assets	=	Liabilities	+	Shareholders' Equity	(Class.)
+50,000		+50,000			

3.33 f. continued.

Accounts Payable.. 50,000
    Cash 49,000
    Miscellaneous Revenue 1,000

Assets	=	Liabilities	+	Shareholders' Equity	(Class.)
−49,000		−50,000		+1,000	IncSt → RE

Maintenance Expense.. 4,000
    Cash 4,000

Assets	=	Liabilities	+	Shareholders' Equity	(Class.)
−4,000				−4,000	IncSt → RE

Correct Entries:
Machinery 50,000
    Accounts Payable... 50,000

Assets	=	Liabilities	+	Shareholders' Equity	(Class.)
+50,000		+50,000			

Accounts Payable.. 50,000
    Cash 49,000
    Machinery 1,000

Assets	=	Liabilities	+	Shareholders' Equity	(Class.)
−49,000		−50,000			
−1,000					

Machinery 4,000
    Cash 4,000

Assets	=	Liabilities	+	Shareholders' Equity	(Class.)
+4,000					
−4,000					

Assets understated by $3,000 and shareholders' equity understated by $3,000.

3.34   (Prima Company; working backward to the balance sheet at the beginning of the period.) (amounts in US$)

A T-account method for deriving the solution appears below and on the following page. The end-of-year balance appears at the bottom of the T-account. The derived starting balance appears at the top. "p" indicates plug; "c" closing entry.

		Cash		
(p)	11,700			
(1)	47,000	128,000	(3)	
(2)	150,000	49,000	(4)	
		7,500	(5)	
		1,200	(6)	
		5,000	(7)	
		8,000	(8)	
Bal.	10,000			

		Marketable Securities	
(p)	12,000		
(8)	8,000		
Bal.	20,000		

		Accounts Receivable		
(p)	22,000			
(10)	153,000	150,000	(2)	
Bal.	25,000			

		Merchandise Inventory		
(p)	33,000			
(9)	127,000	130,000	(11)	
Bal.	30,000			

	Prepayments for Miscellaneous Services		
(p)	1,700		
(4)	49,000	47,700	(14)
Bal.	3,000		

	Land, Buildings, and Equipment	
(p)	40,000	
Bal.	40,000	

	Accounts Payable (for Merchandise)		
		26,000	(p)
(3)	128,000	127,000	(9)
		25,000	Bal.

		Interest Payable	
		300	(p)
(6)	1,200	1,200	(15)
		300	Bal.

3.34 continued.

Taxes Payable			
		3,500	(p)
(5)	7,500	8,000	(13)
		4,000	Bal.

Note Payable			
		20,000	(p)
		20,000	Bal.

Accumulated Depreciation			
		12,000	(p)
		4,000	(12)
		16,000	Bal.

Common Stock			
		50,000	(p)
		50,000	Bal.

Retained Earnings			
		8,600	(p)
(7)	5,000	9,100	(16c)
		12,700	Bal.

Sales			
		47,000	(1)
		153,000	(10p)
		200,000	Bal. before Closing
(16c)	200,000		
		0	

Cost of Goods Sold			
(11)	130,000	130,000	(16c)

Depreciation Expense			
(12)	4,000	4,000	(16c)

Tax Expense			
(13)	8,000	8,000	(16c)

Other Operating Expense			
(14)	47,700	47,700	(16c)

Interest Expense			
(15)	1,200	1,200	(16c)

3.34 continued.

PRIMA COMPANY
Balance Sheet
As of December 31, Year 7

Assets

Cash		$ 11,700
Marketable Securities		12,000
Accounts Receivable		22,000
Merchandise Inventory		33,000
Prepayments		1,700
Total Current Assets		$ 80,400
Land, Buildings, and Equipment	$ 40,000	
Less Accumulated Depreciation	(12,000)	28,000
Total Assets		$108,400

Liabilities and Shareholders' Equity

Accounts Payable	$ 26,000
Interest Payable	300
Taxes Payable	3,500
Total Current Liabilities	$ 29,800
Notes Payable (6%)	20,000
Total Liabilities	$ 49,800
Common Stock	$ 50,000
Retained Earnings	8,600
Total Shareholders' Equity	$ 58,600
Total Liabilities and Shareholders' Equity	$108,400

3.35 (The Secunda Company; working backward to cash receipts and disbursements.) (amounts in US$)

A T-account method for deriving the solution appears below and on the following page. After Entry (6), we have explained all revenue and expense account changes. Plugging for the unknown amounts determines the remaining, unexplained changes in balance sheet accounts. A "p" next to the entry number designates these entries. Note that the revenue and expense accounts are not yet closed to retained earnings, so dividends account for the decrease in the Retained Earnings account during the year of $10,000.

3.35 continued.

	Cash					Accounts Receivable		
Bal.	20,000				Bal.	36,000		
(7)	85,000				(1)	100,000	85,000	(7p)
		2,000	(9)					
		81,000	(10)					
		3,000	(11)					
		10,000	(12)					
Bal.	9,000				Bal.	51,000		

	Merchandise Inventory					Prepayments		
Bal.	45,000				Bal.	2,000		
(8p)	65,000	50,000	(2)				1,000	(5)
Bal.	60,000				Bal.	1,000		

	Land, Buildings, and Equipment			Cost of Goods Sold		
Bal.	40,000		Bal.	0		
			(2)	50,000		
Bal.	40,000		Bal.	50,000		

	Interest Expense				Other Operating Expenses	
Bal.	0		Bal.	0		
(3)	3,000		(4)	2,000		
			(5)	1,000		
			(6p)	26,000		
Bal.	3,000		Bal.	29,000		

	Accumulated Depreciation				Interest Payable	
	16,000	Bal.			1,000	Bal.
	2,000	(4)	(9p)	2,000	3,000	(3)
	18,000	Bal.			2,000	Bal.

3.35 continued.

	Accounts Payable					Mortgage Payable		
		30,000	Bal.				20,000	Bal.
(10p)	81,000	26,000	(6)	(11p)	3,000			
		65,000	(8)					
		40,000	Bal.				17,000	Bal.

	Common Stock				Retained Earnings		
		50,000	Bal.			26,000	Bal.
				(12p)	10,000		
		50,000	Bal.			16,000	Bal.

	Sales		
		0	Bal.
		100,000	(1)
		100,000	Bal.

SECUNDA COMPANY
Cash Receipts and Disbursements Schedule

Receipts:		
Collections from Customers...........................		$ 85,000
Disbursements:		
Suppliers of Merchandise and Other		
Services	$81,000	
Mortgage..	3,000	
Dividends	10,000	
Interest...	2,000	
Total Disbursements...............................		96,000
Change (Decrease) in Cash		$(11,000)
Cash Balance, December 31, Year 7...................		20,000
Cash Balance, December 31, Year 8...................		$ 9,000

3.36 (Tertia Company; working backward to the income statement.) (amounts in US$)

A T-account method for deriving the solution appears below and on the following two pages. Transactions (1)–(9) correspond to the numbered cash transactions information. In Transactions (10)–(25), "p" indicates that the figure was derived by a "plug" and "c" indicates a closing entry. The final check is that the debit to close Income Summary in Transaction (25) matches the plug in the Retained Earnings account.

	Cash				Accounts and Notes Receivable		
Bal.	40,000			Bal.	36,000		
(1)	144,000	114,000	(4)	(10p)	149,000	144,000	(1)
(2)	63,000	5,000	(5)				
(3)	1,000	500	(6)				
		57,500	(7)				
		1,200	(8)				
		2,000	(9)				
Bal.	67,800			Bal.	41,000		

	Merchandise Inventory				Interest Receivable		
Bal.	55,000			Bal.	1,000		
(14)	121,000	126,500	(15p)	(11p)	700	1,000	(3)
Bal.	49,500			Bal.	700		

	Prepaid Miscellaneous Services				Building, Machinery, and Equipment	
Bal.	4,000			Bal.	47,000	
(7)	57,500	56,300	(12p)			
Bal.	5,200			Bal.	47,000	

	Accounts Payable (Miscellaneous Services)				Accounts Payable (Merchandise)		
		2,000	Bal.			34,000	Bal.
		500	(13p)	(4)	114,000	121,000	(14p)
		2,500	Bal.			41,000	Bal.

3.36 continued.

Property Tax Payable				Accumulated Depreciation			
		1,000	Bal.			10,000	Bal.
(8)	1,200	1,700	(16p)			2,000	(17p)
		1,500	Bal.			12,000	Bal.

Mortgage Payable				Common Stock			
		35,000	Bal.			25,000	Bal.
(5)	5,000						
		30,000	Bal.			25,000	Bal.

Retained Earnings				Sales			
		76,000	Bal.			63,000	(2)
(9)	2,000	25,200	(18p)	(18c)	212,000	149,000	(10)
		99,200	Bal.				

Cost of Goods Sold				Interest Expense			
(15)	126,500	126,500	(18c)	(6)	500	500	(18c)

Interest Revenue				Miscellaneous Expenses			
(18c)	700	700	(11)	(12)	56,300		
				(13)	500	56,800	(18c)

Property Tax Expense				Depreciation Expense			
(16)	1,700	1,700	(18c)	(17)	2,000	2,000	(18c)

3.36 continued.

TERTIA COMPANY
Statement of Income and Retained Earnings for Year 8

Revenues:

Sales..	$ 212,000	
Interest Revenue...	700	
Total Revenues		$ 212,700
Expenses:		
Cost of Goods Sold	$ 126,500	
Property Tax Expense......................................	1,700	
Depreciation Expense	2,000	
Interest Expense	500	
Miscellaneous Expenses.................................	56,800	
Total Expenses..		187,500
Net Income...		$ 25,200
Less Dividends		(2,000)
Increase in Retained Earnings.............................		$ 23,200
Retained Earnings, Beginning of Year.................		76,000
Retained Earnings, End of Year...........................		$ 99,200

3.37 (Preparing adjusting entries.) (amounts in US$)

a. The Prepaid Rent account on the year-end balance sheet should represent eight months of prepayments. The rent per month is $2,000 (= $24,000/12), so the balance required in the Prepaid Rent account is $16,000 (= 8 X $2,000). Rent Expense for Year 6 is $8,000 (= 4 X $2,000 = $24,000 – $16,000).

Prepaid Rent..	16,000	
Rent Expense		16,000

Assets	=	Liabilities	+	Shareholders' Equity	(Class.)
+16,000				+16,000	IncSt → RE

To increase the balance in the Prepaid Rent account, reducing the amount in the Rent Expense account.

3.37 continued.

b. The Prepaid Rent account on the balance sheet for the end of Year 7 should represent eight months of prepayments. The rent per month is $2,500 (= $30,000/12), so the required balance in the Prepaid Rent account is $20,000 (= 8 X $2,500). The balance in that account is already $16,000, so the adjusting entry must increase it by $4,000 (= $20,000 – $16,000).

Prepaid Rent.. 4,000
   Rent Expense   4,000

Assets	=	Liabilities	+	Shareholders' Equity	(Class.)
+4,000				+4,000	IncSt → RE

To increase the balance in the Prepaid Rent account, reducing the amount in the Rent Expense account.

The Rent Expense account will have a balance at the end of Year 7 before closing entries of $26,000 (= $30,000 – $4,000). This amount comprises $16,000 (= $2,000 X 8) for rent from January through August and $10,000 (= $2,500 X 4) for rent from September through December.

c. The Prepaid Rent account on the balance sheet at the end of Year 8 should represent two months of prepayments. The rent per month is $3,000 (= $18,000/6), so the required balance in the Prepaid Rent account is $6,000 (= 2 X $3,000). The balance in that account is $20,000, so the adjusting entry must reduce it by $14,000 (= $20,000 – $6,000).

Rent Expense 14,000
   Prepaid Rent..   14,000

Assets	=	Liabilities	+	Shareholders' Equity	(Class.)
–14,000				–14,000	IncSt → RE

To decrease the balance in the Prepaid Rent account, increasing the amount in the Rent Expense account.

3.37 c. continued.

The Rent Expense account will have a balance at the end of Year 8 before closing entries of $32,000 (= $18,000 + $14,000). This amount comprises $20,000 (= $2,500 X 8) for rent from January through August and $12,000 (= $3,000 X 4) for rent from September through December.

d. The Wages Payable account should have a credit balance of $4,000 at the end of April, but it has a balance of $5,000 carried over from the end of March. The adjusting entry must reduce the balance by $1,000, which requires a debit to the Wages Payable account.

Wages Payable... 1,000
    Wage Expense 1,000

Assets	=	Liabilities	+	Shareholders' Equity	(Class.)
		−1,000		+1,000	IncSt → RE

To reduce the balance in the Wages Payable account, reducing the amount in the Wage Expense account.

Wage Expense is $29,000 (= $30,000 − $1,000).

e. The Prepaid Insurance account balance of $3,000 represents four months of coverage. Thus, the cost of insurance is $750 (= $3,000/4) per month. The adjusting entry for a single month is as follows:

Insurance Expense 750
    Prepaid Insurance 750

Assets	=	Liabilities	+	Shareholders' Equity	(Class.)
−750				−750	IncSt → RE

To recognize cost of one month's insurance cost as expense of the month.

f. The Advances from Tenants account has a balance of $25,000 carried over from the start of the year. At the end of Year 7, it should have a balance of $30,000. Thus, the adjusting entry must increase the balance by $5,000, which requires a credit to the liability account.

3.37 f. continued.

Rent Revenue... 5,000
    Advance from Tenants   5,000

Assets	=	Liabilities	+	Shareholders' Equity	(Class.)
		+5,000		−5,000	IncSt → RE

To increase the balance in the Advances from Tenants account, reducing the amount in the Rent Revenue account.

Rent Revenue for Year 7 is $245,000 (= $250,000 − $5,000).

g. The Depreciation Expense for the year should be $2,000 (= $10,000/5). The balance in the Accumulated Depreciation account should also be $2,000; thus, the firm must credit Retained Earnings (Depreciation Expense) by $8,000 (= $10,000 − $2,000). The adjusting entry not only reduces recorded depreciation for the period but also sets up the asset account and its accumulated depreciation contra account.

Equipment 10,000
    Accumulated Depreciation   2,000
    Depreciation Expense   8,000

Assets	=	Liabilities	+	Shareholders' Equity	(Class.)
+10,000				+8,000	IncSt → RE
−2,000					

To reduce the recorded amount in Depreciation Expense from $10,000 to $2,000, setting up the asset and its contra account.

CHAPTER 4

BALANCE SHEET: PRESENTING AND ANALYZING RESOURCES AND FINANCING

Questions, Exercises, and Problems: Answers and Solutions

4.1   See the text or the glossary at the end of the book.

4.2   Conservatism emphasizes the early recognition of losses and delayed recognition of gains. Based on conservatively reported earnings, a shareholder might sell shares of stock if he or she infers from the conservatively reported earnings that the firm is not performing well. If the economic or "true" earnings of the firm are larger, the shareholder's decision to sell his or her shares is a poor decision. Alternatively, shareholders might dismiss the management of a firm because they feel the firm is not performing well. It should be emphasized here that the principal objective of accounting reports as currently prepared is to present *fairly* the results of operations and the financial condition of the firm. Both U.S. GAAP and IFRS require reporting that results in a more conservative measurement of earnings.

4.3   One justification relates to the requirement that an asset or liability be measured with sufficient reliability. When there is an exchange between a firm and some other entity, there is market evidence of the economic effects of the transaction. The independent auditor verifies these economic effects by referring to contracts, canceled checks, and other documents underlying the transaction. If accounting recognized events without such a market exchange (for example, the increase in market value of a firm's assets), increased subjectivity would enter into the preparation of the financial statements.

4.4   The underlying principle is that acquisition cost includes all costs required to prepare an asset for its intended use. Assets provide future services. Costs that a firm must incur to obtain those expected services add value to the asset and are included in the acquisition cost measurement of the asset.

4.5   The justification relates to the uncertainty as to the ultimate economic effects of the contracts. One party or the other may pull out of the contract. The accountant may not know the benefits and costs of the contract at the time of signing. Until one party or the other begins to perform under the contract, accounting usually gives no recognition. Accountants often disclose significant contracts of this nature in the notes to the financial statements.

4.6   Accountants record assets at acquisition cost. Cash discounts reduce acquisition cost and, therefore, the amount recorded for merchandise or equipment.

4.7   a. The contract between the investors and the construction company as well as canceled checks provide evidence as to the acquisition cost.

b. Adjusted acquisition cost differs from the amount in Part *a.* by the portion of acquisition cost applicable to the services of the asset consumed during the first five years. There are several generally accepted methods of computing this amount (discussed in **Chapter 10**). A review of the accounting records for the office building should indicate how the firm calculated this amount.

c. There are at least two possibilities for ascertaining current replacement cost. One alternative is to consult a construction company to determine the cost of constructing a similar office building (that is, with respect to location, materials, and size). The accountant would then adjust the current cost of constructing a new building downward to reflect the used condition of the five-year-old office building. The current replacement cost amount could be reduced by 12.5% (= 5/40) if the asset's service potential decreases evenly with age. The actual economic decline in the value of the building during the first five years is likely to differ from 12.5% and, therefore, some other rate is probably appropriate. A second alternative for ascertaining current replacement cost is to consult a real estate dealer to determine the cost of acquiring a used office building providing services similar to the building that the investors own. The accountant might encounter difficulties in locating such a similar building.

4.7 continued.

    d.   The accountant might consult a local real estate dealer to ascertain the current market price, net of transactions cost, at which the investors might sell the building. There is always the question as to whether an interested buyer could be found at the quoted price. The accountant might also use any recent offers to purchase the building received by the investors.

    e.   The accountant might use the amount described in Part *d.* but exclude transactions cost when measuring fair value. The accountant might also measure fair value using the present value of the future net cash flows based on estimated rental receipts and operating expenses (excluding depreciation) for the building's remaining 35-year life. These cash flows are then discounted to the present using an appropriate rate of interest. The inputs to the fair value measurement are those that a market participant would use.

4.8   a.   Liability—Receivable from Supplier or Prepaid Merchandise Orders.

    b.   Liability—Investment in Bonds.

    c.   Asset—Interest Payable.

    d.   Asset—Insurance Premiums Received in Advance.

    e.   Liability—Prepaid Rent.

4.9   a.   Yes; amount of accrued interest payable.

    b.   Yes. The balance sheet reports a liability in the amount of the cash received.

    c.   No; accounting does not record executory promises.

    d.   Yes; at the expected, undiscounted value of future costs arising from sales made prior to the balance sheet date. The income statement includes warranty expense in order to recognize the expenses related to the sale in the same period as the sale. When recognizing the expense, the accountant credits a liability account for the estimated cost to provide warranty services for sales made in the current period.

4.9 continued.

e. Depends. If management determined that it was probable the firm would have to pay a reasonably estimable amount in the suit, then it would show an estimated liability.

f. No; viewed as executory.

g. Yes, at either the estimated cost to provide future flights or the fair value of the obligation to provide future flights.

4.10 a. The expected value of the liability is $90,000 (= 0.90 × $100,000 = $90,000). However, under U.S. GAAP, the liability from the lawsuit would be measured as $100,000, the most likely settlement amount. IFRS would recognize the "best" estimate as the liability, which might be $100,000 (the most likely outcome) or $90,000 (the expected value).

b. The liability for the coupons would be measured at $90,000 (= 0.09 × $1 × 1,000,000 = $90,000).

The inconsistency in the answers to Part *a*. and Part *b*. seems curious since the two situations differ only with respect to the number of possible outcomes (that is, all or nothing with respect to the lawsuit, whereas the coupon redemption rate conceivably ranges from one to one million).

4.11 a. In the definitions of assets and liabilities, *probable* is used to capture the idea that in commercial operations nothing can be entirely certain. It is used in its ordinary sense to refer to that which can be reasonably expected.

b. In the recognition criteria for liabilities with uncertain amount and/or timing, *probable* is used in U.S. GAAP to refer to a relatively high threshold of likelihood—a rule of thumb used in practice is approximately 80%. In IFRS, *probable* as recognition criterion for liabilities with uncertain amount and/or timing means "more likely than not"—approximately 51%.

4.12   (Aracel; balance sheet formats.)

a.   **U.S. GAAP Balance Sheet**. Assets and liabilities are listed on the balance sheet in order of *decreasing* liquidity, so the most liquid assets (liabilities) are shown first, under their respective categories.

ARACEL
Balance Sheet
For Fiscal Year 6
(amounts in thousands of US$)

Assets

Current Assets:	
Cash and Short-Term Investments	$ 579,643
Accounts Receivable	285,795
Inventories	202,704
Other Current Assets	132,782
Total Current Assets	$ 1,200,924
Noncurrent Assets:	
Property, Plant, and Equipment, Net	$ 2,151,212
Goodwill	192,035
Other Noncurrent Assets	451,757
Total Noncurrent Assets	$ 2,795,004
Total Assets	$ 3,995,928

Liabilities and Shareholders' Equity

Current Liabilities	$ 286,819
Noncurrent Liabilities:	
Long-Term Debt	$ 1,155,050
Other Long-Term Liabilities	350,761
Total Noncurrent Liabilities	1,505,811
Shareholders' Equity:	
Common Stock (No Par)	$ 295,501
Preferred Stock	614,496
Retained Earnings	1,293,301
Total Shareholders' Equity	$ 2,203,298
Total Liabilities and Shareholders' Equity	$ 3,995,928

4.12 continued.

b. **IFRS Balance Sheet.** Note that IFRS permits firms discretion as to how they list assets and liabilities on their balance sheet. One acceptable format is identical to that shown in Part a., the other is to list assets and liabilities in *increasing* order of liquidity, as shown here.

ARACEL
Balance Sheet
For Fiscal Year 6
(amounts in thousands of US$)

Assets

Noncurrent Assets:	
Other Noncurrent Assets	$ 451,757
Goodwill	192,035
Property, Plant, and Equipment, Net	2,151,212
Total Noncurrent Assets	$ 2,795,004
Current Assets:	
Other Current Assets	$ 132,782
Inventories	202,704
Accounts Receivable	285,795
Cash and Short-Term Investments	579,643
Total Current Assets	$ 1,200,924
Total Assets	$ 3,995,928

Liabilities and Shareholders' Equity

Shareholders' Equity:	
Common Stock (No Par)	$ 295,501
Preferred Stock	614,496
Retained Earnings	1,293,301
Total Shareholders' Equity	$ 2,203,298
Noncurrent Liabilities:	
Other Long-Term Liabilities	$ 350,761
Long-Term Debt	1,155,050
Total Noncurrent Liabilities	$ 1,505,811
Current Liabilities	$ 286,819
Total Liabilities and Shareholders' Equity	$ 3,995,928

4.13   (Delicious Foods Group; balance sheet formats.)

DELICIOUS FOODS GROUP
Balance Sheet
For Fiscal Year 7
(amounts in millions of euros)

Assets

Current Assets:		
Cash and Cash Equivalents	€	248.9
Receivables		564.6
Inventories		1,262.0
Other Current Assets		121.5
Total Current Assets	€	2,197.0
Noncurrent Assets:		
Property, Plant, and Equipment	€	3,383.1
Intangible Assets		552.1
Goodwill		2,445.7
Other Noncurrent Assets		244.0
Total Noncurrent Assets	€	6,624.9
Total Assets	€	8,821.9

Liabilities and Shareholders' Equity

Current Liabilities:		
Accounts Payable	€	1,435.8
Accrued Expenses		375.7
Income Tax Payable		58.7
Short-Term Borrowings		41.5
Long-Term Debt, Current Portion		108.9
Obligations Under Finance Lease, Current Portion		39.0
Provisions		41.8
Other Current Liabilities		119.3
Total Current Liabilities	€	2,220.7
Noncurrent Liabilities:		
Long-Term Debt	€	1,911.7
Obligations Under Finance Leases		595.9
Provisions		207.2
Other Noncurrent Liabilities		210.4
Total Noncurrent Liabilities	€	2,925.2
Total Liabilities	€	5,145.9

4.13 continued.

Shareholders' Equity:

Share Capital	€	50.1
Share Premium		2,698.9
Retained Earnings		2,355.3
Other Reserves and Adjustments		(1,428.3)
Total Shareholders' Equity	€	3,676.0
Total Liabilities and Shareholders' Equity	€	8,821.9

4.14   (Classifying financial statement accounts.)   (Unless indicated, classifications do not differ between U.S. GAAP and IFRS.)

a.   NA.

b.   NI (revenue).

c.   CC.

d.   NI (U.S. GAAP); NI and NA (IFRS).   Under U.S. GAAP, all R&D expenditures are expensed in the period incurred.   Under IFRS, the portion of R&D associated with research is expensed in the period incurred; development (D) expenditures are capitalized as a noncurrent asset on the firm's balance sheet, if the expenditures are on a product that has reached a sufficient stage (called technological feasibility).

e.   NA.

f.   CA.

g.   X.

h.   NI (expense).

i.   CA.

j.   CL.

k.   X (U.S. GAAP); X or NA (IFRS).   Under U.S. GAAP, an increase in the value of the land would not be recognized as a gain until the firm sells the land.   Under IFRS, the firm has the option to revalue the land upward prior to sale.

4.14 continued.

    l.   RE.

    m.   CL.

    n.   NL.

    o.   CL.

4.15   (Jennings Group; balance sheet relations.)

The missing items appear in boldface type (amounts in millions of ringgit [RM]).

	Year 7	Year 6	Year 5	Year 4
Current Assets	RM 10,999.2	RM **9,507.3**	RM **7,202.2**	RM 6,882.6
Noncurrent Assets	**19,179.7**	18,717.4	11,289.1	9,713.9
Total Assets	RM **30,178.9**	RM 28,224.7	RM **18,491.3**	RM **16,596.5**
Current Liabilities	RM **2,919.9**	RM 4,351.3	RM 1,494.2	RM 1,755.2
Noncurrent Liabilities	5,721.7	**7,206.5**	**7,995.1**	3,540.7
Shareholders' Equity	21,537.3	16,666.9	9,002.0	**11,300.6**
Total Liabilities and Shareholders' Equity	RM 30,178.9	RM **28,224.7**	RM 18,491.3	RM **16,596.5**

4.16   (Kyoto; balance sheet relations.)

The missing items appear in boldface type (amounts in billions of yen).

	Year 10	Year 9	Year 8	Year 7
Current Assets	¥ 1,323	¥ 1,133	¥ **1,100**	¥ 1,110
Noncurrent Assets	**784**	773	703	**760**
Total Assets	¥ **2,107**	¥ **1,906**	¥ **1,803**	¥ 1,870
Current Liabilities	¥ 1,318	¥ 1,148	¥ **1,172**	¥ 1,172
Noncurrent Liabilities	437	**460**	411	467
Total Liabilities	¥ **1,755**	¥ **1,608**	¥ 1,583	¥ **1,639**
Shareholders' Equity	**352**	298	220	**231**
Total Liabilities and Shareholders' Equity	¥ **2,107**	¥ **1,906**	¥ **1,803**	¥ **1,870**

4.17   (Finmest Corporation; balance sheet relations.)

The missing items appear in boldface type (amounts in millions of euros).

	Year 11	Year 10	Year 9	Year 8
Current Assets	€ 3,357	€ 2,995	€ 2,477	€ 2,097
Noncurrent Assets	1,897	1,973	1,427	1,473
Total Assets	€ 5,254	€ 4,968	€ 3,904	€ 3,570
Current Liabilities	€ 2,706	€ 2,610	€ 1,802	€ 1,466
Noncurrent Liabilities	957	908	810	1,109
Total Liabilities	€ 3,663	€ 3,518	€ 2,612	€ 2,575
Contributed Capital	€ 681	€ 711	€ 739	€ 634
Retained Earnings	910	739	553	361
Total Shareholders' Equity	€ 1,591	€ 1,450	€ 1,292	€ 995
Total Liabilities and Shareholders' Equity	€ 5,254	€ 4,968	€ 3,904	€ 3,570

4.18   (Ford Models; asset and liability recognition and measurement.)

Accounting does not normally recognize mutually unexecuted contracts as assets or liabilities. This contract between Danielle Evans and Ford Models is partially executed to the extent that Ford Models provides the car at the time of signing. Because the modeling agency will receive the services of Danielle Evans beginning next year, it recognizes an asset, Advances on Contracts, of $70,000 on its balance sheet at the time of signing.

4.19   (Duke University; asset recognition and measurement.)

The expenditures do not qualify as an asset because (1) Duke University cannot point to a specific future economic benefit that it controls (employees can choose to work elsewhere even though doing so sacrifices the tuition benefit), and (2) there is not a reasonably reliable measurement attribute for this benefit.

4.20   (Jennifer's Juice; asset measurement.)

The acquisition cost of the refrigeration system includes the purchase price of $1.3 million, the modification costs of $120,000, and the cost to transport and install the unit in the store of $55,000, for a total of $1,475,000. The insurance premium and the salary of the repairperson are operating expenses and are not part of the acquisition cost of the refrigeration system. Jennifer's Juice would show the amount paid for the insurance premium as a prepaid asset on its balance sheet (Prepaid Insurance). The salary of the repairperson is not recognized as an asset.

4.21   (Nordstrom; recognition of a loss contingency.)

a. Nordstrom should recognize the contingency as soon as it is probable that it has incurred a loss and it can reasonably estimate the amount of the loss. Whether the store recognizes a loss at the time of the injury on July 5, 2013, depends on the strength of the case the store feels it has against the customer's claims. If the cause of the accident was an escalator malfunction, then Nordstrom may determine that it is probable that it has incurred a liability. If, on the other hand, the customer fell while running up the clearly identified down side of the escalator, then Nordstrom may determine that it is probable that it has not incurred a liability. Attorneys, not accountants, must make these probability assessments.

    If Nordstrom does not recognize a loss at the time of the injury, the next most likely time is June 15, 2014, when the jury renders its verdict. Unless attorneys for the store conclude that it is probable that the court will reverse the verdict on appeal, Nordstrom should recognize the loss at this time.

    If management in consultation with the firm's attorneys conclude, based on the available information, that the grounds for appeal are strong, then the next most likely time to record the loss is on April 20, 2015, when the jury in the lower court reaches the same verdict as previously. This is the latest time in this case at which the store should recognize the loss. If the store had recognized a loss on June 15, 2014, in the amount of $400,000, it would recognize only the extra damage award of $100,000 on April 20, 2015.

b. Under IFRS, the threshold for recognition is also probable but the meaning differs, such that a lower probability (more than 50%) will result in liability recognition under IFRS than under U.S. GAAP (more than approximately 80%).

4.22   (Nestlé S.A.; asset recognition and measurement.)

   a.   Both U.S. GAAP and IFRS would recognize Investment in Bond (noncurrent asset), CHF800 million. Nestlé would record the bond at acquisition cost, not the amount it will receive at maturity.

   b.   Both U.S. GAAP and IFRS would recognize Prepaid Insurance (current asset); CHF240 million would be recorded initially. At Nestlé's year-end, the balance in the Prepaid Insurance account needs to be decreased to reflect the two months' usage of the insurance, reducing the balance to CHF200 [= CHF240 – (CHF240 X 2/12)] million.

   c.   Both U.S. GAAP and IFRS would recognize Option to Purchase Land (noncurrent asset), CHF6 million.

   d.   Neither U.S. GAAP nor IFRS recognizes the employment contract, a mutually unexecuted contract, as an asset.

   e.   Under U.S. GAAP, Nestlé would record only the costs of obtaining the patent as an asset on its balance sheet, Patent (noncurrent asset), CHF0.5 million. The remaining CHF80 million is an expense of the period. Under IFRS, Nestlé would recognize Research Expense of CHF48 (= 60% X CHF80) million in the period incurred and record a Development Asset (noncurrent asset) at the acquisition cost of CHF32 million (= 40% of CHF80 million) as an asset on its balance sheet, which it would depreciate over the useful life of the product. Under IFRS, Nestlé would also recognize the patent as an asset on its balance sheet, Patent (noncurrent asset), CHF0.5 million.

   f.   Under both U.S. GAAP and IFRS, Nestlé would not recognize the cocoa beans as an asset until it receives the inventory.

4.23   (Ryanair Holdings, Plc.; asset recognition and measurement.)

   a.   Under both U.S. GAAP and IFRS, a decision on the part of Ryanair's board of directors does not give rise to an asset.

   b.   Under both U.S. GAAP and IFRS, Ryanair's placing of an order does not give rise to an asset.

   c.   Under both U.S. GAAP and IFRS, Ryanair's payment gives rise to an asset on their balance sheet, Deposit on Aircraft (noncurrent asset), €60 million.

4.23 continued.

   d. Under both U.S. GAAP and IFRS, Ryanair's purchase gives rise to an asset, Landing Rights (noncurrent asset), €50 million.

   e. Under both U.S. GAAP and IFRS, Ryanair's purchase gives rise to an asset on their balance sheet, Equipment (noncurrent asset), €77 million. Ryanair would also record a liability, Mortgage Note Payable (noncurrent), €65 million.

   f. Under both U.S. GAAP and IFRS, Ryanair's purchase gives rise to an asset, Equipment (noncurrent asset), €160 million. The carrying, or book, value of the aircraft on the seller's books is not relevant to Ryanair's recording of the purchase.

4.24 (Hana Microelectronic; liability recognition and measurement.)

   a. Under both U.S. GAAP and IFRS, this arrangement is a mutually unexecuted contract; as such, it does not give rise to a liability on Hana Microelectronics's balance sheet.

   b. Under both U.S. GAAP and IFRS, Hana Microelectronics would record Advances from Customers (current liability), Bt168 million.

   c. Under both U.S. GAAP and IFRS, Hana Microelectronics would record Advances from Customers (current liability), Bt84 million, and Advances from Customers (noncurrent liability), Bt84 million.

   d. Under both U.S. GAAP and IFRS, common stock does not meet the definition of a liability because the firm need not repay the funds in a particular amount at a particular time.

   e. Under both U.S. GAAP and IFRS, Hana Microelectronic would record Notes Payable (current liability), Bt8 million, and Notes Payable (noncurrent liability), Bt16 million.

   f. Under both U.S. GAAP and IFRS, this arrangement is mutually unexecuted and, therefore, does not give rise to a liability.

   g. Under both U.S. GAAP and IFRS, this arrangement is mutually unexecuted and, therefore, does not give rise to a liability.

4.25   (Berlin Philharmonic; liability recognition and measurement.)

a.   Under both U.S. GAAP and IFRS, the Berlin Philharmonic would record Advances from Customers (current liability), €3,040,000.

b.   Under both U.S. GAAP and IFRS, the Berlin Philharmonic does not recognize a liability because it has not yet received benefits obligating it to pay.

c.   Under both U.S. GAAP and IFRS, the Berlin Philharmonic would record Accounts Payable (current liability), €185,000.

d.   Under both U.S. GAAP and IFRS, the Berlin Philharmonic would not normally recognize a liability for an unsettled lawsuit unless payment is probable and the entity can reliably estimate the loss. Because the suit has not yet come to trial, it is unclear whether any liability exists.

e.   Under both U.S. GAAP and IFRS, the Berlin Philharmonic would not recognize a liability for this mutually unexecuted contract.

f.   Under both U.S. GAAP and IFRS, accounting normally does not recognize a liability for mutually unexecuted contracts. Thus, at the time of contract signing, the Berlin Philharmonic would record no liability. In 2012, however, the firm would record a liability for the portion of the yearly compensation earned by Sir Simon Rattle each month, or Salary Payable (current liability), €0.167 million per month.

4.26   (Royal Dutch Shell; recognition and measurement of a loss contingency.)

Under both U.S. GAAP and IFRS, the recognition of a loss contingency requires that a loss be probable. Although U.S. GAAP does not define *probable*, a rule of thumb used in practice defines *probable* as greater than or equal to 80%; under IFRS, the threshold for *probable* is 51% (more likely than not). The measurement of the loss contingency depends first on whether it meets the recognition criterion; only if the loss is probable will it be measured and reported on the balance sheet. The measurement depends on which set of accounting standards is applied.

4.26 continued.

a. Refer to the preceding discussion of the recognition criteria under both U.S. GAAP and IFRS. The information given indicates that engineers view the probability of loss to be 10%. Because this probability does not meet the threshold percentages under U.S. GAAP or IFRS, no liability will be recorded under either set of accounting standards.

b. The probability of loss is now 51%. This meets the probable threshold under IFRS, but not under U.S. GAAP. Therefore, IFRS will show a liability on the balance sheet, but U.S. GAAP would not. The amount of the liability shown under IFRS would be the "best" estimate of the amount of future cash outflows. In this example, the best estimate could be either the outcome with the highest probability of occurrence, $5 million (with probability 51%), or it could be the expected loss $2.55 million (= 0.51 X $5 million + 0.49 X $0). IFRS provides enough latitude to permit either of these "best" estimates.

c. Under the environmentalists' estimates, there is a 100% probability of loss. Thus, both U.S. GAAP and IFRS would record a liability. The measurement of the amount of the liability varies under the two accounting approaches. Under U.S. GAAP, the firm would record the most likely amount of damages, or $4,000 million, because this is the estimate with the highest probability of occurrence (45% is greater than either 35% or 20%). Under IFRS, the firm would record the "best" estimate. The best estimate could be either the outcome with the highest probability of occurrence, $4,000 million (with probability 45%), or it could be the expected loss $1,910 million (= 0.45 X $4,000 million + 0.35 X $300 million + 0.20 X $25 million). IFRS provides enough latitude to permit either of these "best" estimates.

d. Under the environmentalists' estimates, the probability of loss is 85%. This exceeds the threshold for recognition of a liability under both U.S. GAAP and IFRS. Under U.S. GAAP, the amount recorded will be $5,000 million because this is the outcome with the highest probability of occurrence. The amount recorded under IFRS is the best estimate, which in this example is also likely to be $5,000 million. However, IFRS provides enough latitude that the best estimate might also be the expected value of $4,250 million (= 0.85 X $5,000 + 0.15 X $0).

4-15

4.27   (Magyar Telekom; effect of recording errors on balance sheet equation.)
        (amounts in millions of Hungarian forints [HUF])

Transaction Number	Assets	=	Liabilities	+	Shareholders' Equity
(1)	No		No		No
(2)	O/S HUF 900		O/S HUF 900		No
(3)	U/S HUF 14,500		U/S HUF 14,500		No
(4)	No[a]		No		No
(5)	U/S HUF 6,000		U/S HUF 6,000		No
(6)	U/S HUF 1,200		No		U/S HUF 1,200
(7)	No		No		No

[a]The value of total assets is correctly stated; the problem is that rather than debiting Property for the insurance payment, the firm should have debited Prepaid Insurance.

4.28   (Sivensa; effect of recording errors on balance sheet equation.) (amounts in thousands of U.S. dollars)

Transaction Number	Assets	=	Liabilities	+	Shareholders' Equity
(1)	U/S $ 8,000		U/S $ 8,000		No
(2)	O/S $ 4,000		O/S $ 4,000		No
(3)	U/S $ 800		U/S $ 800		No
(4)	O/S $ 1,000		O/S $ 1,000		No
(5)	U/S $ 2,500		No		U/S $2,500
(6)	O/S $ 4,900[a]		No		No
	U/S $ 4,900[a]				

[a]The response "No" is also acceptable here.

4.29 (Hathway Atlantic Airways Limited; balance sheet format, terminology, and accounting methods.) (amounts in millions of Hong Kong dollars [HKD])

a.

HATHWAY ATLANTIC AIRWAYS LIMITED
Balance Sheet, U.S. GAAP
(amounts in millions of HKD)

	December 31,	
	Year 11	Year 10
Assets		
Current Assets:		
Cash and Cash Equivalents[a]	HKD 21,649	HKD 15,624
Trade and Other Receivables	11,376	8,735
Inventory[b]	882	789
Assets Pledged Against Current Liabilities[c]	910	1,352
Total Current Assets	34,817	26,500
Noncurrent Assets:		
Investments in Associates	10,054	8,826
Fixed Assets	62,388	57,602
Other Long-Term Receivables and Investments	3,519	3,406
Intangible Assets	7,782	7,749
Assets Pledged Against Noncurrent Liabilities[d]	7,833	8,164
Total Noncurrent Assets	91,576	85,747
Total Assets	HKD 126,393	HKD 112,247

4.29 a. continued.

Liabilities and Shareholders' Equity

Current Liabilities:				
Trade and Other Payables	HKD	14,787	HKD	10,999
Current Portion of Long-Term				
Liabilities		4,788		7,503
Unearned Transportation Revenue ..		6,254		4,671
Income Taxes Payable[e]		2,475		2,902
Total Current Liabilities		28,304		26,075
Noncurrent Liabilities:				
Long-Term Liabilities		40,323		33,956
Retirement Benefit Obligations		268		170
Deferred Tax Liability[f]		6,771		6,508
Total Noncurrent Liabilities		47,362		40,634
Total Liabilities		75,666		66,709
Minority Interests		178		152
Shareholders' Equity:				
Share Capital		788		787
Reserves..		49,761		44,599
Total Shareholders' Equity		50,549		45,386
Total Liabilities and Share-				
holders' Equity[g]	HKD	126,393	HKD	112,247

Footnotes appear on following page.

4.29 a. continued.

Terminology

[a]Liquid Funds.

[b]Stock.

[c]Related Pledged Security Deposits (Current Portion of Long-Term Debt).

[d]Related Pledged Security Deposits (Noncurrent Portion of Long-Term Debt).

[e]Taxation.

[f]Deferred Taxation.

[g]Funds Attributable to Hathway Shareholders.

b.

HATHWAY ATLANTIC AIRWAYS LIMITED
Balance Sheet, IFRS
(amounts in millions of HKD)

	December 31, Year 11	December 31, Year 10
Assets		
Noncurrent Assets:		
Intangible Assets	HKD 7,782	HKD 7,749
Fixed Assets	62,388	57,602
Assets Pledged Against Noncurrent Liabilities[d]	7,833	8,164
Investments in Associates	10,054	8,826
Other Long-Term Receivables and Investments	3,519	3,406
Total Noncurrent Assets	91,576	85,747
Current Assets:		
Inventory[b]	882	789
Assets Pledged Against Current Liabilities[c]	910	1,352
Trade and Other Receivables	11,376	8,735
Cash and Cash Equivalents[a]	21,649	15,624
Total Current Assets	34,817	26,500
Total Assets	HKD 126,393	HKD 112,247

Solutions

4.29 b. continued.

Liabilities and Shareholders' Equity

Noncurrent Liabilities:				
Long-Term Liabilities.......................	HKD	40,323	HKD	33,956
Retirement Benefit Obligations		268		170
Deferred Tax Liability[f]		6,771		6,508
Total Noncurrent Liabilities		47,362		40,634
Current Liabilities:				
Income Taxes Payable[e]		2,475		2,902
Trade and Other Payables		14,787		10,999
Current Portion of Long-Term				
Liabilities.......................................		4,788		7,503
Unearned Transportation Revenue..		6,254		4,671
Total Current Liabilities		28,304		26,075
Total Liabilities		75,666		66,709
Shareholders' Equity:				
Minority Interests		178		152
Share Capital		788		787
Reserves..		49,761		44,599
Total Shareholders' Equity		50,727		45,538
Total Liabilities and Share-				
holders' Equity[g]........................	HKD	126,393	HKD	112,247

Terminology

[a]Liquid Funds.

[b]Stock.

[c]Related Pledged Security Deposits (Current Portion of Long-Term Debt).

[d]Related Pledged Security Deposits (Noncurrent Portion of Long-Term Debt).

[e]Taxation.

[f]Deferred Taxation.

[g]Funds Attributable to Hathway Shareholders.

4.30   (Infotech Limited; balance sheet format, terminology, and accounting method.)

a.   Infotech Limited, U.S. GAAP formatted balance sheet.

INFOTECH LIMITED
Balance Sheet
(amounts in millions of Rs. Crore)

	March 31, Year 12	March 31, Year 11
Assets		
Current Assets:		
Cash and Cash Equivalents	Rs 6,429	Rs 5,470
Accounts Receivable	3,093	2,292
Other Current Assets	2,705	1,199
Total Current Assets	Rs 12,227	Rs 8,961
Noncurrent Assets:		
Investments	Rs 964	Rs 839
Property, Plant, and Equipment	3,931	3,107
Deferred Tax Assets	99	79
Total Noncurrent Assets	Rs 4,994	Rs 4,025
Total Assets	Rs 17,221	Rs 12,986
Liabilities and Shareholders' Equity		
Current Liabilities	Rs 1,483	Rs 1,162
Provisions	2,248	662
Total Liabilities	Rs 3,731	Rs 1,824
Shareholders' Equity:		
Contributed Capital	Rs 286	Rs 286
Retained Earnings	13,204	10,876
Total Shareholders' Equity	Rs 13,490	Rs 11,162
Total Liabilities and Shareholders' Equity	Rs 17,221	Rs 12,986

4.30 continued.

   b. Infotech Limited, IFRS formatted balance sheet.

INFOTECH LIMITED
Balance Sheet
(amounts in millions of Rs. Crore)

	March 31, Year 12	Year 11
Assets		
Noncurrent Assets:		
Property, Plant, and Equipment	Rs 3,931	Rs 3,107
Deferred Tax Assets	99	79
Investments	964	839
Total Noncurrent Assets	Rs 4,994	Rs 4,025
Current Assets:		
Other Current Assets	Rs 2,705	Rs 1,199
Accounts Receivable	3,093	2,292
Cash and Cash Equivalents	6,429	5,470
Total Current Assets	Rs 12,227	Rs 8,961
Total Assets	Rs 17,221	Rs 12,986
Liabilities and Shareholders' Equity		
Provisions	Rs 2,248	Rs 662
Current Liabilities	1,483	1,162
Total Liabilities	Rs 3,731	Rs 1,824
Shareholders' Equity:		
Contributed Capital	Rs 286	Rs 286
Retained Earnings	13,204	10,876
Total Shareholders' Equity	Rs 13,490	Rs 11,162
Total Liabilities and Shareholders' Equity	Rs 17,221	Rs 12,986

4.31   (Svenson; balance sheet format, terminology, and accounting methods.)

SVENSON
U.S. GAAP Balance Sheet
For Fiscal Year 7
(amounts in millions of SEK)

Assets

Current Assets:

Cash and Cash Equivalents	SEK	28,310
Short-Term Investments		29,406
Trade Receivables		60,492
Customer Financing, Current		2,362
Other Current Receivables		15,062
Inventories		22,475
Total Current Assets	SEK	158,107

Noncurrent Assets:

Equity in Joint Ventures	SEK	10,903
Other Investments in Shares		738
Customer Financing, Noncurrent		1,012
Other Financial Assets, Noncurrent		2,918
Deferred Tax Assets		11,690
Property, Plant, and Equipment		8,404
Intellectual Property Rights, Brands		23,958
Goodwill		22,826
Total Noncurrent Assets	SEK	82,449
Total Assets	SEK	240,556

4.31 continued.

Liabilities and Shareholders' Equity

Current Liabilities:

Trade Payables	SEK	17,427
Borrowings, Current		5,896
Provisions, Current		8,858
Other Current Liabilities		44,995
Total Current Liabilities	SEK	77,176

Noncurrent Liabilities:

Provisions, Noncurrent	SEK	368
Borrowings, Noncurrent		21,320
Post-Employment Benefits		6,188
Deferred Tax Liabilities		2,799
Other Noncurrent Liabilities		1,714
Total Noncurrent Liabilities	SEK	32,389
Total Liabilities	SEK	109,565
Minority Interest		940
Shareholders' Equity		130,051
Total Liabilities and Equity	SEK	240,556

Explanation of changes to apply U.S. GAAP

1. U.S. GAAP does not permit the capitalization of development costs. Removal of these costs reduces assets by SEK3,661 million, and reduces shareholders' equity (Retained Earnings) by SEK3,661 million.

2. U.S. GAAP does not permit the upward revaluation of land. In Year 7, this upward revaluation led to land being stated at a value SEK900 million higher on Svenson's balance sheet than would have been permitted under U.S. GAAP. The upward revaluation would also have been included as an unrealized gain, in Svenson's shareholders' equity. To conform to U.S. GAAP, removal of the upward revaluation of the land would therefore reduce assets and shareholders' equity by SEK900 million for Year 7.

3. Both U.S. GAAP and IFRS require assessments for impairment of noncurrent assets. Thus, the write-down of the equipment in Year 7 from SEK2,400 to SEK1,600 would also exist under U.S. GAAP.

4.31 continued.

4. From the information provided, the probability of loss is 60% for the patent infringement lawsuit. Thus, the lawsuit meets the IFRS threshold for recognition; it does not, however, meet the probable standard under U.S. GAAP (80%). Thus, under U.S. GAAP, Svenson would not have recognized a liability for this lawsuit. Under IFRS, Svenson would have recognized the "best" estimate as the amount of the liability. This best estimate was likely SEK500, since this is the amount of expected damages with the largest probability of occurring. Another best estimate that is possible is the expected value of the range of estimates, or SEK994 million. Whatever the best estimate, the amount would need to be removed from current provisions, and added back to shareholders' equity, to derecognize this liability under U.S. GAAP. The balance sheet shown earlier displays a best estimate of SEK500.

Summary Calculations for Shareholders' Equity:

Balance per Svenson Balance Sheet, Year 7 (IFRS) ...	SEK 134,112
Removal of Capitalized Development Costs That Would Be Expensed Under U.S. GAAP	(3,661)
Removal of Upward Revaluation of Land That Would Not Have Been Made Under U.S. GAAP.....	(900)
Removal of Lawsuit Expense That Would Not Have Met the Standard for Recognition Under U.S. GAAP	500
Balance per Svenson Balance Sheet, Year 7 U.S. GAAP	SEK 130,051

Solutions

4.32   (Paul Loren Company; balance sheet format, terminology, and accounting methods.)

a.
PAUL LOREN COMPANY
U.S. GAAP Balance Sheet
For Fiscal Year 10
(amounts in millions of US$)

Assets

Current Assets:	
Cash and Cash Equivalents	$ 563.1
Short-Term Investments	584.1
Accounts Receivable, Net	381.9
Inventories	474.0
Deferred Tax Assets	103.0
Prepaid Expenses and Other	139.7
Total Current Assets	$ 2,245.8
Noncurrent Assets:	
Noncurrent Investments	$ 75.5
Property and Equipment, Net	697.2
Deferred Tax Assets	101.9
Goodwill	986.6
Intangible Assets, Net	363.2
Other Assets	148.7
Total Noncurrent Assets	$ 2,373.1
Total Assets	$ 4,618.9

Liabilities and Shareholders' Equity

Current Liabilities:	
Accounts Payable	$ 149.8
Income Tax Payable	37.8
Accrued Litigation Liability	100.0
Accrued Expenses and Other	559.7
Total Current Liabilities	$ 847.3
Noncurrent Liabilities:	
Long-Term Debt	$ 747.3
Deferred Tax Liabilities	282.1
Other Noncurrent Liabilities	126.0
Total Noncurrent Liabilities	$ 1,155.4
Total Liabilities	$ 2,002.7

4.32 a. continued.

Shareholders' Equity:

Class A Common Stock, at Par	$ 0.8
Class B Common Stock, at Par	0.4
Additional Paid-In Capital	1,243.8
Retained Earnings	2,414.9
Treasury Stock	(1,197.7)
Accumulated Other Comprehensive Income	154.0
Total Shareholders' Equity	$ 2,616.2
Total Liabilities and Equity	$ 4,618.9

Explanation of changes to apply IFRS

1. Both U.S. GAAP and IFRS require firms to impair long-lived assets if the fair value of those estimates declines below cost (adjusted for use). Thus, no changes are necessary.

2. Neither U.S. GAAP nor IFRS permits upward revaluations of inventory. Therefore, to confirm to U.S. GAAP or IFRS, Paul Loren must remove $30 million from assets (Inventory) and shareholders' equity (Retained Earnings).

3. Both U.S. GAAP and IFRS require the firm to record a liability if it is probable and reasonably estimable. From the information provided, the probability of loss is 100% for the breach of contract lawsuit. Thus, the lawsuit meets both the U.S. GAAP and IFRS threshold for recognition. Under U.S. GAAP, Paul Loren should recognize a liability of $100 million (the most likely amount) and reduce Shareholders' Equity (Retained Earnings) by the same amount. This amount is included among current liabilities under the assumption that Paul Loren expects to pay it in the coming year. Under IFRS, Paul Loren would have recognized the "best" estimate as the amount of the liability. This best estimate could be $100 million (the most likely amount) or $270 million (the expected value, equal to $0.70 \times \$100 + 0.20 \times \$500 + 0.10 \times \$1,000$). Whatever the best estimate, the amount would need to be added to current liabilities, and subtracted from Shareholders' Equity.

4.32 continued.

    b.   The only potential difference between shareholders' equity calculated under U.S. GAAP and IFRS concerns the amount recognized as the liability for the breach of contract. If IFRS records $100 million (the most likely amount), shareholders' equity under IFRS will be the same as calculated under U.S. GAAP.

CHAPTER 5

INCOME STATEMENT: REPORTING THE RESULTS
OF OPERATING ACTIVITIES

Questions, Exercises, and Problems: Answers and Solutions

5.1　See the text or the glossary at the end of the book.

5.2　Revenues measure the inflow of net assets from operating activities, and expenses measure the outflow of net assets consumed in the process of generating revenues. Thus, recognizing revenues and expenses always involves a simultaneous entry in an asset and/or liability account.

5.3　Cost is the economic sacrifice made to acquire goods or services. When the good or service acquired has reliably measurable future benefits to a firm, the cost is an asset. When the firm consumes the good or service, the cost is an expense.

5.4　Current accounting practice takes the viewpoint of shareholders by reporting the amount of net income available to shareholders after subtracting from revenues all expenses incurred in generating the revenue by claimants (for example, employees, lenders, governments) other than shareholders.

5.5　The assets and income from operations that a firm has decided to discontinue (and dispose of or abandon) will not be part of that firm's future performance. Thus, separating the two income components allows users to form better predictions of future earnings.

5.6　The revenues must be earned (the firm must have achieved substantial performance) and the amount to be received must qualify as an asset (there must be a future economic benefit and the amount must be measured with sufficient reliability). Therefore, the firm must have a reasonable expectation that it will collect the amount owed from the customer.

5.7   At the time the firm receives the cash, the firm has not yet earned the revenues because it has not done anything (i.e., it has not yet delivered the merchandise to the customer). Accounting does not permit the firm to recognize revenues until the earnings process is complete, which in this case means when the firm delivers the merchandise.

5.8   Revenues are part of the ongoing central operations of the firm, so they are relatively persistent and sustainable. In contrast, gains arise from relatively infrequent transactions, and there can be no assurance that a gain will recur in any future period. Therefore, separating the two income components allows users of financial reports to focus on the portion of income that is more likely to continue (revenues), separately from the portion that would not be expected to recur (gains), and thereby aids prediction.

5.9   It is not straightforward to compare the operating profits of two firms, even two otherwise similar firms, because authoritative guidance does not define the term "operating" or "operating profits." Although it is generally understood that this term refers to revenues less costs related to operations, there are no rules specifying what items comprise operating expenses. Further, there is no requirement that a firm even report a line in its income statement called "operating profit."

5.10   Firms do not necessarily recognize revenues when they receive cash or recognize expenses when they disburse cash. Thus, net income will not necessarily equal cash flow from operations each period. Furthermore, firms disburse cash to acquire property, plant and equipment, repay debt, and pay dividends. Thus, net income and cash flows usually differ. A profitable firm will likely borrow funds in order to remain in business, but eventually operations must generate cash to repay the borrowing.

5.11   (Neiman Marcus; revenue recognition.) (amounts in US$)

	February	March	April
a.	—	—	$ 800
b.	—	$ 2,160	—
c.	$39,200	—	—
d.	—	$ 59,400	—
e.	—	$ 9,000	$ 9,000
f.	—	$ 9,000	$ 9,000

5.12   (Fonterra Cooperative Group Limited; revenue recognition.) (amounts in New Zealand dollars [NZ$])

a. No. Fonterra has not yet delivered the milk and, therefore, has not achieved substantial performance.

b. No. Fonterra would recognize NZ$5,000 as an Advance from Customer, a current liability. When Fonterra delivered the milk, it would recognize the revenue.

c. Yes.   Fonterra would likely recognize revenues at this point of NZ$26,000, assuming the likelihood of the purchaser returning the milk is small.

d. No. Fonterra would clearly not recognize revenue on hearing that some of the milk delivered was spoiled. The question is how they record the non-sale of this milk. Typically, the firm would debit Selling, General, and Administrative Expense for NZ$6,000 to reflect the fact that spoiled milk is a normal cost of business. Fonterra would credit Accounts Receivable for NZ$6,000 to reflect the portion of the sales for which the customer will not pay. Chapter 8 discusses other treatments for such sales returns.

e. No. Accrual accounting usually recognizes revenue when a firm sells goods or services. Fonterra has only developed a technology that may or may not result in future sales.

5.12 continued.

f. No. Fonterra does not recognize revenues at the signing of the contracts. Fonterra recognizes revenues when it has performed all that it needs to do as stipulated in the contracts.

5.13 (Sun Microsystems; expense recognition.) (amounts in US$)

	June	July	August
a.	—	$ 15,000	$ 15,000
b.	$ 4,560	—	—
c.	—	$ 5,800	$ 6,300
d.	$ 600	$ 600	$ 600
e.	—	—	—
f.	—	—	$ 4,500
g.	$ 6,600	—	—

5.14 (Tesco Plc.; expense recognition.) (amounts in pounds sterling)

a. None (this is a September expense).

b. £20,000 (= £1,200,000/60) in depreciation expense.

c. £25,000 (= £300,000/12) in property tax expense.

d. £13,600 (= £3,500 + £15,500 − £5,400) in office supply expense.

e. £4,000 in maintenance and repairs expense (the repair does not extend the life beyond that originally expected).

f. None, the firm will include the deposit in the acquisition cost of the land.

g. £100,000 in rent expense; the remaining £100,000 is in prepaid rent.

5.15 (Bondier Corporation; relating net income to balance sheet changes.) (amounts in millions of US$)

a. Net Income = [($1,040 − $765) + $30 − $12] = $293 million.

b. Net Income = [($20,562 − $18,577) − ($17,444 − $15,844) − ($2,078 − $1,968) + $30 − $12] = $293 million.

5.16 (Magtelkom; relating net income to balance sheet changes.) (amounts in millions of HUF)

a. Assets = Liabilities + Shareholders' Equity.

HUF1,131,595 = HUF538,428 + (HUF128,728 + HUF67,128 + Retained Earnings).

Retained Earnings = HUF397,311.

b.

	Year 12
Retained Earnings, Beginning of Year (Part a. above)...	HUF 397,311
Plus Net Income (Plug)	60,155
Plus Adjustment...	307
Less Dividends Declared and Paid	(72,729)
Retained Earnings, End of Year	HUF 385,044

5.17 (Novo Limited; income statement relations.) (amounts in thousands of US$)

The missing items appear in boldface type below:

	Year 10	Year 9
Sales	$ 16,351,503	$ 13,978,309
Cost of Goods Sold...	(13,901,523)	(12,091,433)
Gross Profit..	$ 2,449,980	$ 1,886,876
Selling and Administrative Expense.............	(1,103,713)	(1,033,296)
Advertising Expense...	(595,902)	(488,150)
Research and Development Expense	(229,759)	(196,225)
Other Income (Expense)..................................	11,715	18,130
Profit Before Taxes..	$ 532,321	$ 187,335
Income Tax Expense	(47,613)	(26,197)
Net Income...	$ 484,708	$ 161,138

5.18   (SwissTek; income statement relations.) (amounts in millions of US$)

The missing items appear in boldface below:

	Year 13	Year 12	Year 11
Sales of Products	$ 24,816	$ **19,503**	$ 17,622
Sales of Services	4,367	3,778	3,342
Cost of Products Sold	(17,292)	(13,967)	(13,205)
Cost of Services Sold	**(2,923)**	(2,570)	(2,305)
Gross Profit..	$ 8,968	$ 6,744	$ **5,454**
Selling and Administrative Expenses ...	(4,975)	**(4,326)**	(3,780)
Other Operating Income (Expense)	**30**	139	37
Earnings Before Interest and Taxes	$ 4,023	$ 2,557	$ **1,711**
Interest and Dividend Income	273	147	**153**
Interest and Other Financial Expense...	(286)	**(307)**	(407)
Other Non-Operating Income (Expense)	**342**	(321)	(258)
Income Before Taxes................................	$ 4,352	$ 2,076	$ 1,199
Income Tax Expense	(595)	**(686)**	(464)
Net Income	$ 3,757	$ 1,390	$ 735

5.19   (James John Corporation; income and equity relations.) (amounts in millions of US$)

The missing items appear in boldface below:

JAMES JOHN CORPORATION
Comparative Balance Sheets
March 31, Years 12, 11, and 10

	March 31,		
	Year 12	Year 11	Year 10
Common Stock......................................	$ **1.1**[a]	$ **1.1**[a]	$ 1.1
Accumulated Other Comprehensive Income	**40.5**	(27.2)	0.0
Retained Earnings..............................	1,742.3	**1,379.2**[b]	1,090.3
Treasury Stock....................................	**(321.5)**[c]	(87.1)	(80.0)
Additional Paid-In Capital	872.5	783.6	**664.3**
Total Shareholders' Equity	$ 2,334.9	$ **2,049.6**	$1,675.7

5.19 continued.

Calculations:

aNo new stock issuance implies same balance in common stock for Year 12 and Year 11 as the balance in this account in Year 10.

bRetained Earnings, End of Year 11 = Retained Earnings, End of Year 10 + Net Income, Year 11 − Dividend Declared, Year 11 = $1,090.3 + $308.5 − $19.6 = $1,379.2.

cTreasury Shares, Year 12 = Treasury Shares, Year 11 + Repurchases, Year 12 = $(87.1) + $(234.4) = $(321.5).

5.20   (Palmgate Company; income and equity relations.) (amounts in millions of US$)

The missing items appear in boldface below:

PALMGATE COMPANY
Comparative Balance Sheets
December 31, Years 9, 8, and 7

	December 31,		
	Year 9	Year 8	Year 7
Income Statement Information:			
Net Income	$ 1,737.4	$ 1,353.4	$1,351.4
Other Comprehensive Income	414.4	**(276.5)**d	1.5
Balance Sheet Information:			
Common Stock	$ **732.9**a	$ **732.9**a	$ 732.9
Accumulated Other Comprehensive Income	**(1,666.8)**e	(2,081.2)	(1,804.7)
Unearned Compensation	(218.9)	(251.4)	(283.3)
Preferred Stock	197.5	222.7	253.7
Retained Earnings	10,627.5	**9,643.7**b	8,968.1
Treasury Stock	**(8,903.7)**f	**(8,073.9)**c	(7,581.0)
Additional Paid-In Capital	1,517.7	1,218.1	**1,064.4**
Total Shareholders' Equity	$ 2,286.2	$ 1,410.9	$1,350.1
Other Information:			
Dividends Declared and Paid	$ **753.6**g	$ 677.8	$ 607.2
Cost of Share Repurchases	829.8	492.9	615.6
Common Shares Issued	0	0	0

5.20 continued.

Calculations:

[a]No new shares issued, so common stock stays the same.

[b]Retained Earnings, End of Year 8 = Retained Earnings, End of Year 7 + Net Income, Year 8 – Dividend Declared, Year 8 = $8,968.1 + $1,353.4 – $677.8 = $9,643.7.

[c]Treasury Shares, Year 8 = Treasury Shares, Year 7 + Repurchases, Year 8 = $(7,581.0) + $(492.9) = $(8,073.9).

[d]Accumulated Other Comprehensive Income, End of Year 8 = Accumulated Other Comprehensive Income, End of Year 7 + Other Comprehensive Income, Year 8. $(2,081.2) = $(1,804.7) + Other Comprehensive Income, Year 8. Other Comprehensive Income, Year 8 = $(276.5).

[e]Accumulated Other Comprehensive Income, End of Year 9 = Accumulated Other Comprehensive Income, End of Year 8 + Other Comprehensive Income, Year 9. Accumulated Other Comprehensive Income, End of Year 9 = $(2,081.2) + $414.4 = $(1,666.8).

[f]Treasury Shares, Year 9 = Treasury Shares, Year 6 + Repurchases, Year 9 = $(8,073.9) + $(829.8) = $(8,903.7).

[g]Retained Earnings, End of Year 9 = Retained Earnings, End of Year 8 + Net Income, Year 9 – Dividends Declared, Year 9. $10,627.5 = $9,643.7 + $1,737.4 – Dividends Declared, Year 9. Dividends Declared, Year 9 = $753.6.

5.21   (MosTechi Corporation; accumulated other comprehensive income relations.) (amounts in millions of yen)

The missing items appear in boldface below:

MOSTECHI CORPORATION
Comparative Balance Sheets
March 31, Years 8, 7, and 6

	March 31,		
	Year 8	Year 7	Year 6
Common Stock.....................................	¥ 626,907	¥ 624,124	¥ 621,709
Accumulated Other Comprehensive Income...	**(115,493)**[b]	**(156,437)**[a]	**(385,675)**
Retained Earnings............................	**1,700,133**[c]	1,602,654	1,506,082
Treasury Stock..................................	**(3,470)**	(3,127)	(6,000)
Additional Paid-In Capital...............	1,143,423	1,136,638	1,134,222
Total Shareholders' Equity...........	¥3,351,500	¥3,203,852	¥2,870,338

Calculations:

[a]Accumulated Other Comprehensive Income, End of Year 7 = Accumulated Other Comprehensive Income, End of Year 6 + Other Comprehensive Income, Year 7 = ¥(385,675) + ¥229,238 = ¥(156,437).

[b]Accumulated Other Comprehensive Income, End of Year 8 = Accumulated Other Comprehensive Income, End of Year 7 + Other Comprehensive Income, Year 8 = ¥(156,437) + ¥40,944 = ¥(115,493).

[c]Retained Earnings, End of Year 8 = Retained Earnings, End of Year 7 + Net Income, Year 8 – Dividends Declared, Year 8 + Adjustment, Year 8 = ¥1,602,654 + ¥126,328 – ¥25,042 – ¥3,807 = ¥1,700,133.

Solutions

5.22   (Solaronx Company; accumulated other comprehensive income relations.)
(amounts in millions of US$)

The missing items appear in boldface below:

SOLARONX COMPANY
Comparative Balance Sheets
December 31, Years 12, 11, and 10

	December 31,		
	Year 12	Year 11	Year 10
Common Stock.....................................	$ 5	$ 5	$ 5
Accumulated Other Comprehensive Income...	(2,514)[e]	(1,950)[b]	(1,919)
Retained Earnings.............................	4,329[f]	3,475[c]	2,998
Treasury Stock..................................	(816)	(543)	(73)
Additional Paid-In Capital...............	10,097	9,722	9,540
Total Shareholders' Equity...........	$ 11,101[g]	$ 10,709[d]	$ 10,551[a]

Calculations:

[a]Total Shareholders' Equity, End of Year 10 = $5 – $1,919 + $2,998 – $73 + $9,540 = $10,551.

[b]Accumulated Other Comprehensive Income, End of Year 11 = Accumulated Other Comprehensive Income, End of Year 10 + Other Comprehensive Income, Year 11 = $(1,919) + $(31) = $(1,950).

[c]Comprehensive Income, Year 11 = Net Income, Year 11 + Other Comprehensive Income, Year 11. $840 = Net Income, Year 11 + $(31). Net Income, Year 11 = $871.

Retained Earnings, End of Year 11 = Retained Earnings, End of Year 10 + Net Income, Year 11 – Dividends Declared, Year 11 = $2,998 + Net Income, Year 11 – $394.

Retained Earnings, End of Year 11 = $2,998 + $871 – $394 = $3,475.

[d]Total Shareholders' Equity, End of Year 11 = $5 – $1,950 + $3,475 – $543 + $9,722 = $10,709.

5.22 continued.

[e]Accumulated Other Comprehensive Income, End of Year 12 = Accumulated Other Comprehensive Income, End of Year 11 + Other Comprehensive Income, Year 12 + Adjustment, Year 12 = $(1,950) + $774 − $1,338 = $(2,514).

[f]Comprehensive Income, Year 12 = Net Income, Year 12 + Other Comprehensive Income, Year 12. $2,057 = Net Income, Year 12 + $774. Net Income, Year 12 = $1,283.

Retained Earnings, End of Year 12 = Retained Earnings, End of Year 11 + Net Income, Year 12 − Dividends Declared, Year 12 = $3,475 + $1,283 − $429.

Therefore, Retained Earnings, End of Year 12 = $3,475 + $1,283 − $429 = $4,329.

[g]Total Shareholders' Equity, End of Year 12 = $5 − $2,514 + $4,329 − $816 + $10,097 = $11,101.

5.23   (PharmaCare; discontinued operations.) (amounts in millions of euros)

   a.   In Year 7, 51% [= €2,410/(€2,410 + €2,306)] of PharmaCare's income came from discontinued operations, compared to 10% [= €169/(€169 + €1,526)] in Year 6.

   b.   In Year 7, less than 0.2% (= €84/€51,378) of PharmaCare's total assets were associated with discontinued operations, compared to 5.2% (= €2,925/€55,891) in Year 6.

   c.   The large decline in PharmaCare's assets held for discontinued operations is due to the fact that PharmaCare disposed of the assets in Year 7. The assets are no longer owned by PharmaCare and, therefore, no longer a part of PharmaCare's balance sheet at the end of Year 7. The income those assets generated during the year prior to disposal is, however, part of PharmaCare's income for Year 7.

5.24   (Oratel S.A.E.; discontinued operations.)   (amounts in thousands of Egyptian pounds)

The missing items appear in boldface type below:

ORATEL S.A.E.
Comparative Balance Sheets
December 31, Years 13 and 12

	December 31,	
	Year 13	Year 12
Income from Continuing Operations (Before Taxes)	£ 9,293,448	£ 4,456,900
Less Taxes on Income from Continuing Operations	(2,571,426)	**(861,187**)
Income from Continuing Operations (After Tax)	£ **6,722,022**	£ 3,595,713
Income from Discontinued Operations (Net of Tax)	**5,213,066**	1,020,213
Net Income	£ 11,935,088	£ **4,615,926**
Assets Held for Discontinued Operations	£ 5,144,015	£ 7,327,709
Assets Used in Continuing Operations	34,348,838	**26,882,037**
Total Assets	£ 39,492,853	£ 34,209,746

5.25   (Cementex Corporation; income statement formats.) (amounts in millions of pesos)

The missing items appear in boldface type below:

CEMENTEX CORPORATION
IFRS Income Statements
December 31, Years 10 and 9

	December 31,	
	Year 10	**Year 9**
Net Sales	$ 236,669	$ 213,767
Cost of Sales	(157,696)	**(136,447)**
Gross Profit	$ **78,973**	$ 77,320
Administrative and Selling Expenses	(33,120)	(28,588)
Distribution Expenses	(13,405)	**(14,227)**
Other Expenses, Net	(3,281)	(580)
Operating Income	$ **29,167**	$ 33,925
Financial Expenses	(8,809)	**(5,785)**
Financial Income	862	536
Income (Expense) from Financial Instruments	2,387	(161)
Other Financial Income (Expense)	6,647	4,905
Equity in Income of Associates	1,487	1,425
Profit Before Income Tax	$ **31,741**	$ 34,845
Income Tax	(4,796)	(5,697)
Consolidated Profit	$ **26,945**	$ 29,148
Portion of Profit Attributable to Minority Interest	$ 837	$ **1,293**
Portion of Profit Attributable to Cementex Shareholders	$ **26,108**	$ 27,855

5.26 (GoodLuck Brands; income statement formats.) (amounts in millions of US$)

GOODLUCK BRANDS
Income Statements
For Years 8, 7, and 6

	Year 8	Year 7	Year 6
Net Sales	$ 8,769.0	$ 7,061.2	$ 6,145.2
Cost of Products Sold	4,618.9	3,843.0	3,342.1
Excise Taxes on Spirits and Wine	514.0	326.5	299.7
Advertising, Selling and Administrative Costs	2,070.1	1,694.4	1,433.6
Amortization of Intangibles	43.5	33.4	35.4
Restructuring Charges	21.2	—	9.8
Operating Income	$ 1,501.3	$ 1,163.9	$ 1,024.6
Interest Expense	332.4	158.9	77.3
Other Financial Expense (Income)	(40.2)	78.9	(47.0)
Net Financial Expense (Income)	$ 292.2	$ 237.8	$ 40.3
Profit Before Taxes	$ 1,209.1	$ 926.1	$ 994.3
Less Income Taxes	311.1	324.5	261.1
Income from Continuing Operations	$ 898.0	$ 601.6	$ 733.2
Income from Discontinued Operations, Net of Tax	—	39.5	67.8
Net Profit	$ 898.0	$ 641.1	$ 801.0
Portion of Profit Owned by Minority Interests	$ 67.9	$ 20.0	$ 17.2
Portion of Profit Owned by Shareholders	$ 830.1	$ 621.1	$ 783.8

5.27 (Broyo Corporation; correcting errors in income statement transactions.) (amounts in millions of euros)

a. Broyo should not have recognized revenue on this transaction because it has yet to perform on the contract. Revenues are overstated by €200 and Cost of Goods Sold is overstated by €160, so income is overstated by €40.

b. Broyo should not have recorded the advance from customer as revenues. It is a liability (Advance from Customer). Revenues are, therefore, overstated by €20.

5.27 continued.

    c.   Broyo should have recorded Revenues of €45, and Cost of Goods Sold of €36, for a gross profit of €9.

    d.   Because the expenditures do not qualify as capitalized development costs, they should have been expensed not capitalized. Broyo's income in Year 13 is, therefore, overstated by €11.

    e.   Broyo had performed all of its obligations with the customer, so on December 1, Year 13, it should have recognized Revenues of €266, and Cost of Goods Sold of €250. Because they did not, Revenues are understated by €266, Cost of Goods Sold is understated by €250, and Gross Profit is understated by €16.

    f.   The sale of a plant is not a recurring part of Broyo's business. Therefore, it should not be included as part of Revenues and Cost of Goods Sold, which pertain to recurring transactions. Revenues are, therefore, overstated by €100, and Cost of Goods Sold is overstated by €80. The sale of the plant generated a gain of €20, which should have been included in Other Operating Income.

5.28   (Dragonfly Limited; correcting errors in income statement transactions.) (amounts in Singapore dollars)

    a.   In Year 7, Dragonfly's revenues are overstated by $1,000. These revenues should have been recognized in Year 6.

    b.   Dragonfly had not performed its obligations under the agreement as of February 2. Thus, it should not have recognized revenues at that time. Dragonfly did perform those obligations by the end of the fiscal year (in September). As a result, its revenues and expenses are correctly stated for Year 7 for this transaction.

    c.   Dragonfly correctly recorded the results of this transaction as a separate line item, below Gross Profit on its income statement.

    d.   Because the firm should have capitalized the development costs, expenses for Year 7 are overstated by $1,232.

5.28 continued.

e. Interest income on investments is not part of Dragonfly's normal recurring operations. It should not have been recorded as revenues, but as a component of Financial Costs. Net Revenues are, therefore, overstated by $230, and financial income is understated by $230.

f. Dragonfly should have expensed the advertising costs in Year 7. Because it did not, Selling and Marketing Costs are understated by $15,000.

5.29 (SeaBreeze, Inc.; classification and interpretation of income statements.) (amounts in millions of yuan)

a. The ¥10,000 in Gains on Sales of Assets should not have been included in Sales Revenues because the gains do not reflect a transaction that the firm is regularly engaged in as part of its business model. The gain should have been recorded below the gross margin line and identified as a non-recurring item. Gross Profit would decline by ¥10,000.

b. Net Financial Income of ¥13,800 should have been reported below the gross profit line, because it is not part of the normal, core part of the firm's operations. Removing Net Financial Income will reduce Gross Profit by ¥13,800.

c. The firm included a ¥6,000 write-down of inventory in Selling, General, and Administrative Expenses. Normally in this industry, such a write-down is included in Cost of Sales. Adding the write-down to Cost of Sales would cause Gross Profit to decrease by ¥6,000.

d. The firm included research and development expenditures of ¥34,000 in Cost of Sales. None of the expenditures related to proven technologies (and so were correctly not capitalized). So, even though the expenditures should be expensed on the income statement, R&D is typically not part of Cost of Sales. Removing the R&D from Cost of Sales would cause Gross Profit to increase by ¥34,000.

e. The results of discontinued operations should be shown separately on the income statement, below the margin line. Removing discontinued operations will cause Gross Profit to decline by ¥22,000.

5.29 continued.

Each of the above transactions belongs in the income statement (implying that net income is calculated correctly) but is not correctly displayed in the income statement (implying that gross profit may be calculated incorrectly).

A summary of the effects of reclassifying the items on gross profit and net income is provided below:

	Gross Profit	Net Income
Original Amount	¥ 154,039	¥ 31,921
Effect of (a)	(10,000)	No effect on Net Income
Effect of (b)	(13,800)	No effect on Net Income
Effect of (c)	(6,000)	No effect on Net Income
Effect of (d)	34,000	No effect on Net Income
Effect of (e)	(22,000)	No effect on Net Income
Revised Amount	¥ 136,239	¥ 31,921

5.30 (Dyreng Plc.; classification and interpretation of income statements.) (amounts in thousands of euros)

a. Dyreng should not have recognized any revenues (nor any costs) of this project in Year 11 because it had performed no work. Year 11 Revenues are overstated by €240, causing both Gross Profit and Profit Before Taxes and Discontinued Operations to be overstated by this amount.

b. Year 11 Revenues are overstated by €700 and expenses are overstated by €660. The revenues and associated costs should have been recorded in Year 10 when the work was performed. The receipt of cash is irrelevant to the timing of the revenue recognition. Year 11 Gross Profits and Profit Before Taxes and Discontinued Operations are overstated by €40 (= €700 – €660).

c. The sale of the office building was not a normal part of Dyreng's operations. It should not, therefore, have been included in Revenues or Cost of Sales. The net effect of the sale, a loss of €40, should have been included in Other Operating Income. Gross Profit is understated by €40, but Profit Before Taxes and Discontinued Operations are correctly stated.

d. Other Operating Income is overstated by €45. Gross Profit is correctly stated, but Pre-tax Profit from Continuing Operations is overstated by €45.

5.30 continued.

e. Dyreng performed all work in Year 11, and so should have recognized Revenues of €450 and Cost of Sales of €230. Year 11 Gross Profits and Profit Before Taxes and Discontinued Operations are both understated by €220 (= €450 – €230).

f. The sale of the advertising space is not a normal part of Dyreng's business model. It should, therefore, have been included as a source of Other Operating Income, not as a reduction to Cost of Sales. In addition, only half of the amount should have been recognized because Dyreng has not performed completely on this obligation. Gross Profit is, therefore, overstated by €960, whereas Profit Before Taxes and Discontinued Operations are overstated by €480.

A summary of the effects of reclassifying the items on gross profit and net income is provided below:

	Gross Profit	Profit Before Taxes and Discounted Operations
Original Amount	€ 4,795.3	€ 604.5
Effect of (a)	(240.0)	(240.0)
Effect of (b)	(700.0)	(700.0)
Effect of (c)	40.0	No effect
Effect of (d)	No effect	(45.0)
Effect of (e)	220.0	220.0
Effect of (f)	(960.0)	(480.0)
Revised Amount	€ 3,155.3	€ (640.5)

5.31 (Calculation of tax rates.) (amounts in millions of US$)

a. Year 9: $7,712/$87,548 = 8.8%; Year 10: $8,093/$88,396 = 9.2%.

b. Year 9: $11,757/$87,548 = 13.4%; Year 10: $11,534/$88,396 = 13.0%.

c. Year 9: $4,045/$11,757 = 34.4%; Year 10: $3,441/$11,534 = 29.8%.

d. The improved profitability clearly relates to an improved income tax position. The ratio of income before income taxes to revenues computed in Part b. indicates that profitability before taxes decreased between Year 9 and Year 10.

CHAPTER 6

STATEMENT OF CASH FLOWS

Questions, Exercises, and Problems: Answers and Solutions

6.1   See the text or the glossary at the end of the book.

6.2   One can criticize a single income statement using a cash basis of accounting from two standpoints: (1) it provides a poor measure of operating performance each period because of the inaccurate matching of revenues and expenses (see discussion in Chapter 4), and (2) it excludes important investing (acquisitions and sales of long-lived assets) activities and financing (issuance or redemption of bonds or capital stock) activities of a firm that affect cash flow.

6.3   Accrual accounting provides a measure of operating performance that relates inputs to outputs without regard to when a firm receives or disburses cash. Accrual accounting portrays the resources of a firm and the claims on those resources without regard to whether the firm holds the resource in the form of cash. Although accrual accounting may satisfy user's needs for information about operating performance and financial position, it does not provide sufficient information about the cash flow effects of a firm's operating, investing, and financing activities. The latter is the purpose of the statement of cash flows.

6.4   The statement of cash flows reports changes in the investing and financing activities of a firm. Significant changes in property, plant, and equipment affect the structure of assets on the balance sheet, for example, the age of the assets. Significant changes in long-term debt or capital stock affect the maturity structure of debt and the mix of debt versus shareholder financing.

6.5   The indirect method reconciles net income, the primary measure of a firm's profitability, with cash flow from operations. Some argue that the relation between net income and cash flow from operations is less evident when a firm reports using the direct method. More likely, the frequent use of the indirect method prior to the issuance of FASB *Statement No. 95* probably explains its continuing popularity. Why might accountants have preferred the indirect method before FASB *Statement No. 95*? We have heard the following: The direct method's format resembles the income statement. Where the income statement has a line for revenues, the direct method has a line for cash collections from customers. Where the income statement has a line for cost of goods sold, the direct method might have a line for payments to suppliers of income. Where the income statement has a line for income tax expense, the direct method has a line for income tax payments. The resemblance of the two statements, the income statement and the direct method presentation in the statement of cash flows, might cause confusion. Some argue that preparing the direct method costs more. But you can see how easy preparing the direct method's version is; you learn how in this chapter.

6.6   The classification in the statement of cash flows under U.S. GAAP parallels that in the income statement, where interest on debt is an expense but payments on the principal amount of the debt are a reduction in a liability, not an expense. This is, in our opinion, a weak explanation. The overarching rule seems to be that "if it's in the income statement, it's operating." We think that repayment of principal on borrowings and interest on borrowings are both financing transactions. IFRS permits firms to classify cash interest payments as a financing activity.

6.7   The classification in the statement of cash flows parallels that in the income statement, where interest on debt is an expense but dividends are a distribution of earnings, not an expense. This is, in our opinion, a weak explanation. The overarching rule seems to be that "if it's in the income statement, it's operating." We think that dividends on shares and interest on borrowings are both financing transactions. IFRS permits firms to classify cash interest payments as a financing activity.

6.8   Firms generally use accounts payable directly in financing purchases of inventory and other operating costs. Firms might use short-term bank financing indirectly in financing accounts receivable, inventories, or operating costs or use it to finance acquisitions of noncurrent assets or reductions in long-term financing. Thus, the link between short-term bank financing and operations is less direct and may not even relate to operating activities. To achieve consistency in classification, U.S. GAAP specifies that changes in short-term bank loans are financing activities.

6.9   This is an investing and financing transaction whose disclosure helps the statement user understand why property, plant, and equipment and long-term debt changed during the period. Because the transaction does not affect cash directly, firms must distinguish it from investing and financing transactions that do affect cash flow.

6.10   Both are correct, but the writer's point is not expressed clearly. Depreciation expense is a charge to operations that does not require cash. If revenues precisely equal total expenses, there will be a retention of net funds in the business equal to the amount of the depreciation. As long as replacement of the depreciating assets is not necessary, it is possible to finance expansion without resorting to borrowing or the issuance of additional stock.

        The "reader" is correct in saying that depreciation in itself is not a source of cash and that the total cash available would not have increased by adding larger amounts to the depreciation accounts. The source of cash is sales to customers.

        When one considers income tax effects, however, depreciation expenses do save cash because taxable income and, hence, income tax expense using cash are lower than they would be in the absence of depreciation charges.

6.11   The firm must have increased substantially its investment in accounts receivable or inventories or decreased substantially its current liabilities.

6.12   The firm might be capital intensive and, therefore, subtracted substantial amounts of depreciation expense in computing net income. This depreciation expense is added back to net income in computing cash flow from operations. In addition, the firm might have decreased significantly its investment in accounts receivable or inventories or increased its current liabilities.

6.13 Direct Method: The accountant classifies the entire cash proceeds from the equipment sale as an investing activity. Indirect Method: As above, the entire cash proceeds appear as an investing activity. Because the calculation of cash flow from operations starts with net income (which includes the gain on sale of equipment), the accountant must subtract the gain to avoid counting cash flow equal to the gain twice, once as an operating activity and once as an investing activity.

6.14 (Microchem Corporation; derive sales revenue from data in the statement of cash flows and balance sheet.) (amounts in millions of euros)

Cash Collections for the Year		€ 33,551
Accounts Receivable, End of Year	€ 5,334	
Accounts Receivable, Beginning of Year	5,196	
Add: Increase in Receivables		138
Sales for the Year		€ 33,689

6.15 (Electropin Company; derive cost of goods sold from data in the statement of cash flows.) (amounts in millions of US$)

Cash Payments for Inventories for the Year	$ 64,713
Subtract: Increase in Inventories for the Year	(1,753)
Cost of Goods Sold for the Year	$ 62,960

6.16 (Taylor Stores; derive cost of goods sold from data in the statement of cash flows.) (amounts in millions of US$)

Cash Payments for Inventories for the Year	$ 646.9
Add: Increase in Accounts Payable for Inventories	5.9
Subtract: Increase in Inventories for the Year	(5.7)
Cost of Goods Sold for the Year	$ 647.1

6.17 (Yoshi Group; derive wages and salaries expense from data in the statement of cash flows.) (amounts in millions of yen)

Cash Payments for Wages and Salaries for the Year	¥ 8,853
Subtract: Decrease in Wages and Salaries Payable During the Year	(21)
Wages and Salaries Expense for the Year	¥ 8,832

6.18   (JAJ Incorporated; derive cash disbursements for dividends.) (amounts in millions of US$)

Net Income for the Year	$ 5,030
Retained Earnings, End of Year .... $ 28,132	
Retained Earnings, Beginning of Year .... (26,571)	
Subtract: Increase in Retained Earnings	(1,561)
Dividends Declared for the Year......................................	$ 3,469
Subtract: Increase in Dividends Payable During the Year	(233)
Cash Paid for Dividends During the Year (Financing Activity)...	$ 3,236

Refer to Exhibit 6.12. Line (10) increases and Line (11) decreases by $3,236.

6.19   (Gillette Limited; effect of borrowing and interest on statement of cash flows.) (amounts in millions of pounds sterling)

Cash... 250	
Bonds Payable	250

Change in Cash	=	Change in Liabilities	+	Change in Shareholders' Equity	−	Change in Non-cash Assets
+250 Finan		+250				

October 1 bond issue. Refer to Exhibit 6.12. Line (11) increases by £250. Line (8) increases by £250.

Interest Expense... 3.75	
Interest Payable [(0.06/12) × £250 × 3 Months].........	3.75

Change in Cash	=	Change in Liabilities	+	Change in Shareholders' Equity	−	Change in Non-cash Assets
		+3.75		−3.75		

Refer to Exhibit 6.12. Line (3) decreases by £3.75. Line (4) increases by £3.75.

6.20   (Radion Corporation; effect of income taxes on statement of cash flows.) (amounts in millions of US$)

Income Tax Expense.. 161.5
Income Taxes Payable... 18.0
    Cash 179.5

Change in Cash	=	Change in Liabilities	+	Change in Shareholders' Equity	−	Change in Non-cash Assets
−179.5 Opns		−18.0		−161.5		

18.0 = 78.1 − 60.1.   Refer to Exhibit 6.12.   Line (2) increases by $179.5.   Line (3) decreases by $161.5.   Line (5) increases by $18.0.   Line (11) decreases by $179.5.

6.21   (Jennings Company; effect of rent transactions on statement of cash flows.) (amounts in US$)

Rent Expense.. 1,200
    Prepaid Rent 1,200

Change in Cash	=	Change in Liabilities	+	Change in Shareholders' Equity	−	Change in Non-cash Assets
				−1,200		−1,200

January rent expense.

Prepaid Rent 18,000
    Cash 18,000

Change in Cash	=	Change in Liabilities	+	Change in Shareholders' Equity	−	Change in Non-cash Assets
−18,000 Opns						+18,000

Payment on February 1.

6.21 continued.

Rent Expense... 16,500

   Prepaid Rent   16,500

Change in Cash	=	Change in Liabilities	+	Change in Shareholders' Equity	–	Change in Non-cash Assets
				–16,500		–16,500

Rent expense for February through December; $18,000/12 per month = $1,500. 11 × $1,500 = $16,500.

All of these combine in a single journal entry as follows:

Rent Expense... 17,700

Prepaid Rent   300

   Cash   18,000

Change in Cash	=	Change in Liabilities	+	Change in Shareholders' Equity	–	Change in Non-cash Assets
–18,000 Opns				–17,700		+300

All transactions of the year. Refer to Exhibit 6.12. Line (2) increases by $18,000. Line (3) decreases by $17,700. Line (5) increases by $300. Line (11) decreases by $18,000.

6.22   (Infotech Corporation; calculating components of cash inflow from operations.) (amounts in thousands of US$)

Sales for the Year... $ 14,508

Add: Decrease in Receivables   782

Cash Collections from Customers for the Year .... $ 15,290

6.23   (Infotech Corporation; calculating components of cash outflow from operations.) (amounts in thousands of US$)

a.   Cost of Goods Sold for the Year .... $ 11,596

     Subtract: Increase in Accounts Payable for Inventories...... (90)

     Subtract: Decrease in Inventories for the Year...................   (66)

     Cash Payments for Inventories for the Year .... $ 11,440

6.23 continued.

    b. Other Expenses, Total.. $ 2,276
        Subtract: Decrease in Prepayments for Other Costs.............. (102)
        Add: Decrease in Wages and Salaries Payable During the
          Year.. 240
        Cash Payments to Employees and Suppliers of Other
          Services for the Year.. $ 2,414

6.24   (Spreadsheet for understanding the relation between changes in income statement items and changes in items in the statement of cash flows.) (amounts in US$)

    a. S1 changes from $10 to $12.

    b. Lines [1], [2], and [4] of the statement of cash flows do not change.
       Line [3] changes from $7 to $11.
       Line [5] changes from ($1) to ($5).
       S1 does not change.

    c. Lines [1], [3], and [5] do not change.
       Line [2] changes from ($15) to ($17).
       Line [4] changes from $4 to $2.
       S1 changes from $10 to $8.

6.25   (Dearing Incorporated; working backward from changes in Buildings and Equipment account.) (amounts in millions of US$)

Buildings and Equipment (Original Cost)		Accumulated Depreciation	
Balance, 1/1.........................	$16,825	Balance, 1/1.......................	$ 4,914
Outlays During Year..........	1,314	Depreciation During Year.	1,253
	$18,139		$ 6,167
Balance, 12/31....................	17,369	Balance, 12/31...................	5,465
Retirements During Year...	$ 770	Retirements During Year .	$ 702

Proceeds = Book Value at Retirement
         = $770 – $702
         = $68.

6.26   (Incloud Airlines; preparing a statement of cash flows from changes in balance sheet accounts.) (amounts in thousands of US$)

a.   **INCLOUD AIRLINES**
                                        Statement of Cash Flows
                                        For the Year
                                        (amounts in thousands of US$)

Operations:

Net Income	$ 474,378
Additions:	
Depreciation Expense...	264,088
Decrease in Accounts Receivable...........................	15,351
Increase in Other Current Liabilities......................	114,596
Subtractions:	
Increase in Inventories	(15,117)
Increase in Prepayments...	(16,776)
Decrease in Accounts Payable	(660)
Cash Flow from Operations...	$ 835,860
Investing:	
Acquisition of Property, Plant, and Equipment.........	$ (1,134,644)
Increase in Other Non-operating Assets...................	(8,711)
Cash Flow from Investing...	$ (1,143,355)
Financing:	
Increase in Long-Term Debt	$ 244,285
Increase in Common Stock	96,991
Payment of Dividends[a]...	(133,499)
Increase in Non-operating Liabilities	140,026
Cash Flow from Financing..	$ 347,803
Net Change in Cash..	$ 40,308
Cash, Beginning of Year..	378,511
Cash, End of Year	$ 418,819

[a]Net Income of $474,378 less Increase in Retained Earnings of $340,879 = Dividends of $133,499.

b.   Cash flow from operations exceeds net income primarily because of the addback for depreciation expense and increases in other current liabilities. Incloud invested in substantial capital investments during the year. The amount of such purchases exceeded the amount of cash flows generated from operations. Incloud Airlines relied on long-term debt and common stock to make up the needed amount.

6.27 (Bamberger Enterprises; calculating and interpreting cash flow from operations.) (amounts in thousands of US$)

a. Net Income .... $ 290
   Additions:
   Depreciation Expense 210
   Decrease in Accounts Receivable 780
   Decrease in Inventories 80
   Decrease in Prepayments 100
   Increase in Accounts Payable 90
   Subtraction:
   Decrease in Other Current Liabilities .... (240)
   Cash Flow from Operations .... $ 1,310

b. Bamberger Enterprises decreased its non-cash current assets, particularly accounts receivable, generating positive cash flows. Although it repaid other current liabilities, the reduction in accounts receivable dominated and caused cash flow from operations to exceed net income.

6.28 (Finanka; calculating and interpreting cash flow from operations.) (amounts in millions of euros)

a.

	2013	2012	2011	2010
Net Income	€ 3,847	€ 2,542	€ 1,689	€ 1,032
Depreciation Expense	1,009	665	509	465
(Inc.) Dec. in Accounts Receivable	(2,304)	(982)	(1,573)	(272)
(Inc.) Dec. in Inventories	(422)	(362)	(103)	(121)
(Inc.) Dec. in Prepayments	49	(33)	(17)	77
Inc. (Dec.) in Accounts Payable	458	312	140	90
Inc. (Dec.) in Other Current Liabilities	923	867	1,049	450
Cash Flow from Operations	€ 3,560	€ 3,009	€1,694	€ 1,721

6.28 continued.

b. The addback for depreciation, a non-cash expense, causes cash flow from operations to exceed net income each year, except 2013. Inventories increased in line with increases in net income. The company increases its accounts payable to finance the increased inventories. The firm also increased other current liabilities to finance growing operations. Variations in the relation between net income and cash flow from operations result from variations in accounts receivable. Unusually large increases in accounts receivable in 2011 and 2013 cause cash flow from operations to approximately equal net income in 2011 and to be less than net income in 2013. The variations in accounts receivable might result from a conscious effort by Finanka to vary credit terms to stimulate sales. It may also reflect conditions in the economy that cause its customers to delay payments in some years.

6.29   (Market Star; calculating and interpreting cash flows.) (amounts in millions of US$)

a.
MARKET STAR
Comparative Statement of Cash Flows
(amounts in millions of US$)

	2013	2012	2011
Operations			
Net Income	$ 499	$ 363	$ 279
Depreciation and Amortization......	226	196	164
(Inc.) Dec. in Accounts Receivable...	(514)	(648)	(238)
(Inc.) Dec. in Inventories.................	(98)	(13)	(35)
(Inc.) Dec. in Prepayments	(125)	10	(64)
Inc. (Dec.) in Accounts Payable	277	786	330
Inc. (Dec.) in Other Current Liabilities.....................................	420	278	70
Cash Flow from Operations........	$ 685	$ 972	$ 506
Investing			
Acquisition of Property, Plant, and Equipment............................	$ (150)	$ (130)	$ (115)
Acquisition of Investments in Securities	(885)	(643)	(469)
Cash Flow from Investing...........	$ (1,035)	$ (773)	$ (584)

6.29 a. continued.

Financing			
Long-Term Debt Issued	\$ 599	\$ 83	\$ 208
Common Stock Issued			
(Reacquired)................................	(187)	(252)	42
Dividends Paid................................	(122)	(104)	(88)
Cash Flow from Financing..........	\$ 290	\$ (273)	\$ 162
Change in Cash..................................	\$ (60)	\$ (74)	\$ 84

b.   Interpreting cash flow from operations for a marketing services firm requires a comparison of the change in accounts receivable from clients and accounts payable to various media. Marketing services firms act as agents between these two constituents. In Year 2011 and Year 2012, the increase in accounts payable slightly exceeded the increase in accounts receivable, indicating that Market Star used the media to finance its accounts receivable. In Year 2013, however, accounts payable did not increase nearly as much as accounts receivable. It is unclear whether the media demanded earlier payment, whether the media offered incentives to pay more quickly, or some other reason. As a consequence, cash flow from operations decreased in Year 2013. Cash flow from operations continually exceeds expenditures on property, plant, and equipment. This relation is not surprising, given that marketing services firms are not capital intensive. Market Star invested significantly in other entities during the three years. The classification of these investments as noncurrent suggests that they were not made with temporarily excess cash but as a more permanent investment. Cash flow from operations was not sufficient to finance both capital expenditures and these investments, except in Year 2012. The firm relied on long-term debt to finance the difference. Given that marketing services firms are labor intensive, one might question the use of debt instead of equity financing for these investments. In fact, Market Star repurchased shares of its common stock in Year 2012 and Year 2013. Thus, the capital structure of the firm became more risky during the three years.

6.30 (Largay Corporation; effects of gains and losses from sales of equipment on cash flows.) (amounts in thousands of US$)

	a.	b.	c.
Operations:			
Net Income	$ 100	$ 102	$ 98
Depreciation Expense	15	15	15
Gain on Sale of Equipment	—	(2)	—
Loss on Sale of Equipment	—	—	2
Changes in Working Capital Accounts	(40)	(40)	(40)
Cash Flow from Operations	$ 75	$ 75	$ 75
Investing:			
Sale of Equipment	$ 10	$ 12	$ 8
Acquisition of Buildings and Equipment	(30)	(30)	(30)
Cash Flow from Investing	$ (20)	$ (18)	$ (22)
Financing:			
Repayment of Long-Term Debt	$ (40)	$ (40)	$ (40)
Change in Cash	$ 15	$ 17	$ 13
Cash, Beginning of Year	27	27	27
Cash, End of Year	$ 42	$ 44	$ 40

The instructor should note for the students that Cash Flow from Operations remains constant. Income changes, but the gain or loss on sale of equipment is not an operating source or use of cash.

6.31 (Effect of various transactions on statement of cash flows.) (amounts in US$)

Note to instructors: We use this question for in-class discussion. We seldom assign it for actual homework. A favorite form of question for examinations is to present a schematic statement of cash flows and to ask which lines certain transactions affect and how much. When we use this problem in class, we tell students that it makes a good examination question; this serves to strengthen their interest in the discussion.

a. Amortization Expense 600
    Patent 600

Change in Cash	=	Change in Liabilities	+	Change in Shareholders' Equity	–	Change in Non-cash Assets
				–600		–600

6.31 a. continued.

(3) Decreases by $600; reduces net income through amortization expense.

(4) Increases by $600; amount of expense is added back to net income in deriving cash flow from operations.

No effect on net cash flow from operations or cash.

b. Factory Site 50,000

    Common Stock 50,000

Change in Cash	=	Change in Liabilities	+	Change in Shareholders' Equity	–	Change in Non-cash Assets
				+50,000		+50,000

The transaction does not appear in the statement of cash flows because it does not affect cash. The firm must disclose information about the transaction in a supplemental schedule or note.

c. Inventory 7,500

    Accounts Payable 7,500

Change in Cash	=	Change in Liabilities	+	Change in Shareholders' Equity	–	Change in Non-cash Assets
		+7,500				+7,500

(4) Increases by $7,500; operating increase in cash from increase in Accounts Payable.

(5) Increases by $7,500; operating decrease in cash for increase in inventory.

The net effect of these two transactions is to leave cash from operations unchanged because the amounts added and subtracted change in such a way as to cancel out each other.

6.31 continued.

d. Inventory.. 6,000
     Cash.. 6,000

Change in Cash	=	Change in Liabilities	+	Change in Shareholders' Equity	–	Change in Non-cash Assets
–6,000 Opns						+6,000

(2) Increases by $6,000; use of cash in operations.

(5) Increase the subtraction by $6,000; increase in Inventory account, subtracted.

(11) Decreases by $6,000.

The net effect is to reduce cash from operations and cash by $6,000 the cash expenditure for an operating asset, inventory.

e. Fire Loss.. 1,500
    Inventory... 1,500

Change in Cash	=	Change in Liabilities	+	Change in Shareholders' Equity	–	Change in Non-cash Assets
				–1,500		–1,500

(3) Decreases by $1,500; net income goes down.

(4) Increases by $1,500; additions go up because inventory, not cash, was destroyed. OK to show as a reduction to a subtraction for Line (5).

No net effect on cash flow including cash flow from operations or cash.

6.31 continued.

f.　Cash 1,450
　　　Accounts Receivable 1,450

Change in Cash	=	Change in Liabilities	+	Change in Shareholders' Equity	−	Change in Non-cash Assets
+1,450 Opns						−1,450

(1)　Increases by $1,450 for collection of cash from customers.

(4)　Increases by $1,450; operating increase in cash reflected by decrease in the amount of Accounts Receivable. OK to show as a reduction in the subtraction on Line (5).

(11)　Increases by $1,450.

Cash flow from operations increases by $1,450, which causes cash to increase by $1,450.

g.　Cash 10,000
　　　Bonds Payable 10,000

Change in Cash	=	Change in Liabilities	+	Change in Shareholders' Equity	−	Change in Non-cash Assets
+10,000 Finan		+10,000				

(8)　Increases by $10,000; increase in cash from security issue.

(11)　Increases by $10,000.

6.31 continued.

h. Cash.. 4,500

     Equipment (Net).. 4,500

Change in Cash	=	Change in Liabilities	+	Change in Shareholders' Equity	−	Change in Non-cash Assets
+4,500 Invst						−4,500

    (6) Increases by $4,500; increase in cash from sale of noncurrent asset.

    (11) Increases by $4,500.

6.32   (Heidi's Hide-Out; inferring cash flows from financial statement data.) (amounts in US$)

a.   Sales Revenue from Retail Customers .... $ 120,000

    Less Increase in Accounts Receivable from Retail Customers ($8,900 – $8,000)................................ (900)

    Plus Increase in Advances from Retail Customers ($10,000 – $9,000)................................ 1,000

    Cash Collected from Retail Customers .... $ 120,100

b.   Rent Expense.. $ (33,000)

    Less Increase in Advances to Landlords ($5,600 – $5,000).. (600)

    Less Decrease in Rent Payable to Landlords ($5,300 – $6,000).. (700)

    Cash Paid to Landlords .... $ (34,300)

c.   Wage Expense.. $ (20,000)

    Less Increase in Advances to Employees ($1,500 – $1,000) .... (500)

    Less Decrease in Wages Payable to Employees ($1,800 – $2,000) .... (200)

    Cash Paid to Employees .... $ (20,700)

6.32 continued.

d. Cost of Retail Merchandise Sold .... $ (90,000)
Plus Decrease in Inventory of Retail Merchandise
($10,000 – $11,000) 1,000
Less Increase in Advances to Suppliers of Retail
Merchandise ($10,500 – $10,000) .... (500)
Less Decrease in Accounts Payable to Suppliers of Retail
Merchandise ($7,700 – $8,000) .... (300)
Cash Paid to Suppliers of Retail Merchandise .... $ (89,800)

6.33 (Digit Retail Enterprises, Inc.; inferring cash flows from balance sheet and income statement data.) (amounts in US$)

a. Sales Revenue .... $ 270,000
Less Increase in Accounts Receivable ($38,000 –
$23,000) .... (15,000)
Less Decrease in Advances from Customers ($6,100 –
$8,500) .... (2,400)
Cash Received from Customers During 2013 .... $ 252,600

b. Cost of Goods Sold .... $ (145,000)
Less Increase in Merchandise Inventory ($65,000 –
$48,000) .... (17,000)
Acquisition Cost of Merchandise Purchased During 2013 .. $ (162,000)

c. Acquisition Cost of Merchandise Purchased During 2013
(from Part b.) .... $ (162,000)
Plus Increase in Accounts Payable—Merchandise
Suppliers ($20,000 – $18,000) 2,000
Cash Paid for Acquisitions of Merchandise During 2013.... $ (160,000)

d. Salaries Expense .... $ (68,000)
Plus Increase in Salaries Payable ($2,800 – $2,100) 700
Cash Paid to Salaried Employees During 2013 .... $ (67,300)

e. Insurance Expense .... $ (5,000)
Less Increase in Prepaid Insurance ($12,000 – $9,000) ...... (3,000)
Cash Paid to Insurance Companies During 2013 .... $ (8,000)

6.33 continued.

f.

Rent Expense		$ (12,000)
Plus Decrease in Prepaid Rent ($0 – $2,000)		2,000
Plus Increase in Rent Payable ($3,000 – $0)		3,000
Cash Paid to Landlords for Rental of Space During 2013		$ (7,000)

g.

Increase in Retained Earnings ($11,800 – $11,500)		$ 300
Less Net Income		(9,600)
Dividend Declared		$ (9,300)
Less Decrease in Dividend Payable ($2,600 – $4,200)		(1,600)
Cash Paid for Dividends During 2013		$ (10,900)

h.

Depreciation Expense		$ (20,000)
Plus Increase in Accumulated Depreciation ($35,000 – $20,000)		15,000
Accumulated Depreciation of Property, Plant, and Equipment Sold		$ (5,000)
Cost of Property, Plant, and Equipment Sold ($100,000 – $90,000)		10,000
Book Value of Property, Plant, and Equipment Sold		$ 5,000
Plus Gain on Sale of Property, Plant, and Equipment		3,200
Cash Received from Sale of Property, Plant, and Equipment		$ 8,200

6.34 (Hale Company; preparing and interpreting a statement of cash flows using a T-account work sheet.) (amounts in US$)

a.

HALE COMPANY
Statement of Cash Flows
For the Year

Operations:

Net Income	$ 44,000	
Additions:		
Depreciation Expense	54,000	
Increase in Accounts Payable	5,000	
Subtractions:		
Increase in Accounts Receivable......................	(13,000)	
Increase in Inventory...	(11,000)	
Decrease in Interest Payable............................	(2,000)	
Cash Flow from Operations......................................		$77,000
Investing:		
Sale of Equipment	$ 5,000	
Acquisition of Equipment....................................	(55,000)	
Cash Flow from Investing...		(50,000)
Financing:		
Dividends	$(10,000)	
Retirement of Portion of Mortgage Payable	(11,000)	
Cash Flow from Financing..		(21,000)
Net Change in Cash..		$ 6,000
Cash, January 1		52,000
Cash, December 31		$58,000

6.34 a. continued.

The amounts in the T-account work sheet below are in thousands of U.S. dollars.

Cash

√	52				

Operations

Net Income	(1)	44	13	(5)	Increase in
Depreciation	(3)	54			Accounts
Increase in Accounts					Receivable
Payable	(8)	5	11	(6)	Increase in
					Inventory
			2	(9)	Decrease in
					Interest Payable

Investing

Sale of Equipment	(4)	5	55	(7)	Acquisition of
					Equipment

Financing

			10	(2)	Dividends
			11	(10)	Decrease in
					Mortgage
					Payable
√	58				

Accounts Receivable		Inventory		Land	
√	93	√	151	√	30
(5)	13	(6)	11		
√	106	√	162	√	30

Buildings and Equipment (Cost)			Accumulated Depreciation			Accounts Payable		
√	790				460	√		136	√
(7)	55	15 (4)	(4)	10	54 (3)		5 (8)
√	830				504	√		141	√

6.34 a. continued.

Interest Payable				Mortgage Payable				Common Stock		
		10	√			120	√		250	√
(9)	2			(10)	11					
		8	√			109	√		250	√

Retained Earnings			
		140	√
(2)	10	44	(1)
		174	√

6.34 continued.

b. Deriving Direct Method Cash Flow from Operations Using Data from T-Account Work Sheet (all dollar amounts in thousands of US$)

1. Copy income statement and cash flow from operations; see column (a) in the display below.

2. Copy Information from T-Account work sheet next to related income statement item; see columns (b) and (c) in the display below.

3. Sum across rows to derive direct receipts and expenditures; see column (d) in the display below.

Operations	Indirect Method	Changes in Related Balance Sheet Accounts from T-Account Work Sheet	Direct Method	From Operations: Receipts Less Expenditures
	(a)	(b)	(c)	(d)	
Revenues..... $1,200	$ (13)	= Accounts Receivable Increase	$1,187	Receipts from Customers
Cost of Goods Sold...... (788)	5 / (11)	= Accounts Payable Increase / = Merchandise Inventory Increase	(794)	Payments for Merchandise
Wages and Salaries..... (280)	—	= Other Current Liabilities Increase	(280)	Payments for Wages and Salaries
Depreciation Expense.... (54)	54	(Expense Not Using Cash)	—	
Interest Expense.......... (12)	(2)	= Interest Payable Decrease	(14)	Payments for Interest
Income Tax Expense...... (22)	—	= Income Taxes Payable Increase	(22)	Payments for Income Taxes
Net Income........... $ 44	Totals $ 44		$ 77	= Cash Flow from Operations Derived via Direct Method
	$ 77 = Cash Flow from Operations Derived via Indirect Method			

6.34 continued.

c. Statement of Cash Flows presenting the direct method and a reconciliation of income to cash flows from operations.

HALE COMPANY
Statement of Cash Flows
For the Year

Operating Activities:
  Sources of Cash:
    Cash Received from Customers $1,187,000
  Uses of Cash:
    Payments to Suppliers .... (794,000)
    Payments to Employees.................................... (280,000)
    Interest Payments .... (14,000)
    Tax Payments .... (22,000)
Cash Flow from Operations...................................... $77,000

Reconciliation of Net Income to Cash from Operations:		
Net Income	$	44,000
Depreciation..		54,000
Changes in Operating Accounts:		
Accounts Receivable		(13,000)
Inventory...		(11,000)
Accounts Payable		5,000
Interest Payable...		(2,000)
Cash from Operations......................................	$	77,000

Investing Activities:
  Cash Used for New Acquisition of Equipment.... $ (55,000)
  Cash Received from Disposition of Equipment ... 5,000
Net Cash Provided by (Used for) Investing.............. (50,000)
Financing Activities:
  Cash Used for Dividends .... $ (10,000)
  Cash Used to Pay Portion of Mortgage .... (11,000)
Net Cash Provided by (Used for) Financing............. (21,000)
Net Change in Cash for Year................................... $ 6,000
Cash, January 1 52,000
Cash, December 31 .... $58,000

6.34 continued.

    d. Cash flow from operations was sufficient to finance acquisitions of equipment during the year. The firm used the excess cash flow to pay dividends and retire long-term debt.

6.35   (Dickerson Manufacturing Company; preparing and interpreting a statement of cash flows using a T-account work sheet.) (amounts in US$)

    a.

DICKERSON MANUFACTURING COMPANY
Statement of Cash Flows
For the Year

Operations:		
Net Income	$ 568,000	
Additions:		
Depreciation	510,000	
Loss on Sale of Machinery	5,000	
Increase in Accounts Payable	146,000	
Increase in Taxes Payable	16,000	
Increase in Short-Term Payables	138,000	
Subtractions:		
Increase in Accounts Receivable	(106,000)	
Increase in Inventory	(204,000)	
Cash Flow from Operations		$1,073,000
Investing:		
Sale of Machinery	$ 25,000	
Acquisition of Land	(36,000)	
Acquisition of Buildings and Machinery	(1,018,000)	
Cash Flow from Investing		(1,029,000)
Financing:		
Issue of Common Stock	$ 32,000	
Dividends Paid	(60,000)	
Bonds Retired	(50,000)	
Cash Flow from Financing		(78,000)
Net Change in Cash		$ (34,000)
Cash, January 1		358,000
Cash, December 31		$ 324,000

6.35 a. continued.

The amounts in the T-account work sheet below are in thousands of U.S. dollars.

Cash

√		358				

Operations

Net Income	(1)	568	106	(5)	Increase in
Depreciation Expense	(3)	510			Accounts
Loss on Sale of					Receivable
Equipment	(4)	5	204	(6)	Increase in
Increase in Accounts					Inventory
Payable	(9)	146			
Increase in Taxes					
Payable	(10)	16			
Increase in Other					
Short-Term Payables	(11)	138			

Investing

Sale of Machinery	(4)	25	1,018	(7)	Acquisition of
					Buildings and
					Machinery
			36	(8)	Acquisition of
					Land

Financing

Issue of Common Stock	(13)	32	60	(2)	Dividends
			50	(12)	Retirement of
					Bonds
√		324				

Accounts Receivable			Inventory		
√	946		√	1,004	
(5)	106		(6)	204	
√	1,052		√	1,208	

6.35 a. continued.

Buildings and Machinery			
√	8,678		
(7)	1,018	150	(4)
√	9,546		

Accumulated Depreciation— Buildings and Machinery			
		3,974	√
(4)	120	510	(3)
		4,364	√

Land			
√	594		
(8)	36		
√	630		

Accounts Payable		
	412	√
	146	(9)
	558	√

Taxes Payable		
	274	√
	16	(10)
	290	√

Other Short-Term Payables		
	588	√
	138	(11)
	726	√

Bonds Payable			
		1,984	√
(12)	50		
		1,934	√

Common Stock		
	1,672	√
	32	(13)
	1,704	√

Retained Earnings			
		2,676	√
(2)	60	568	(1)
		3,184	√

b. Dickerson Manufacturing Company is capital intensive. Its cash flow from operations exceeds net income because of the depreciation expense addback. Cash flow from operations appears substantial, but so are its expenditures for building and equipment. The firm's relatively low dividend payout rate suggests that it expects large capital expenditures to continue.

6.36   (GTI, Inc.; preparing direct method of deriving cash flow from operations from data in published report.) (amounts in thousands of US$)

a.   **T-Account Work Sheet for 2012**

		Cash			
	√	430			

Operations

Net Income	(1)	417	168	(3)	Increase in Accounts Receivable
Depreciation Expense	(6)	641			
Amortization Expense	(8)	25			
			632	(4)	Increase in Inventories
			154	(5)	Increase in Prepayments
			769	(10)	Decrease in Accounts Payable
			299	(12)	Decrease in Other Current Liabilities
			37	(14)	Decrease in Other Noncurrent Liabilities

Investing

			1,433	(7)	Acquisition of Property, Plant, and Equipment
			391	(9)	Acquisition of Patent

Financing

Issue of Notes Payable	(11)	220	12	(2)	Dividends Paid
Increase in Long-Term Debt	(13)		2,339		
Increase in Preferred Stock	(15)	289			
Increase in Common Stock	(16)	9			

	√	475			

6.36 a. continued.

Accounts Receivable		
√	3,768	
(3)	168	
√	3,936	

Inventories		
√	2,334	
(4)	632	
√	2,966	

Prepayments		
√	116	
(5)	154	
√	270	

Property, Plant, and Equipment (Net)			
√	3,806		
(7)	1,433	641	(6)
√	4,598		

Other Noncurrent Assets			
√	193		
(9)	391	25	(8)
√	559		

Accounts Payable		
	1,578	√
(10)	769	
	809	√

Notes Payable to Banks		
	11	√
	220	(11)
	231	√

Other Current Liabilities		
	1,076	√
(12)	299	
	777	√

Long-Term Debt		
	2,353	√
	2,339	(13)
	4,692	√

Other Noncurrent Liabilities		
	126	√
(14)	37	
	89	√

Preferred Stock		
	0	√
	289	(15)
	289	√

Common Stock		
	83	√
	2	(16)
	85	√

6.36 a. continued.

Additional Paid-In Capital				Retained Earnings		
	4,385	√			1,035	√
	7	(16)	(2)	12	417	(1)
	4,392	√			1,440	√

T-Account Work Sheet for 2013

Cash

√	475	

Operations

			2,691	(1)	Net Loss
Decrease in Accounts Receivable	(3)	1,391	13	(10)	Decrease in Accounts Payable (Inventory)
Decrease in Inventories	(4)	872			
Decrease in Prepayments	(5)	148	82	(12)	Decrease in Other Current Liabilities
Depreciation Expense	(6)	625			
Amortization Expense	(8)	40			
Increase in Other Noncurrent Liabilities	(14)	24			

Investing

Sale of Patents	(9)	63	54	(7)	Acquisition of Property, Plant, and Equipment

Financing

Issue of Notes Payable to Banks	(11)	2,182	8	(2)	Dividends Paid
Increase in Common Stock	(15)	3	2,608	(13)	Decrease in Long-Term Debt
	√	367			

6.36 a. continued.

Accounts Receivable		
√ 3,936		
	1,391	(3)
√ 2,545		

Inventories		
√ 2,966		
	872	(4)
√ 2,094		

Prepayments		
√ 270		
	148	(5)
√ 122		

Property, Plant, and Equipment (Net)			
√ 4,598			
(7) 54	625	(6)	
√ 4,027			

Other Noncurrent Assets		
√ 559		
	40	(8)
	63	(9)
√ 456		

Accounts Payable		
	809	√
(10) 13		
	796	√

Notes Payable to Banks		
	231	√
	2,182	(11)
	2,413	√

Other Current Liabilities		
	777	√
(12) 82		
	695	√

Long-Term Debt		
	4,692	√
(13) 2,608		
	2,084	√

Other Noncurrent Liabilities		
	89	√
	24	(14)
	113	√

Preferred Stock		
	289	√
	289	√

Common Stock		
	85	√
	1	(15)
	86	√

6.36 a. continued.

Additional Paid-In Capital			Retained Earnings		
4,392		√		1,440	√
	2	(15)	(1)	2,691	
			(2)	8	
4,394		√	√	1,259	

b.

GTI, INC.
Statement of Cash Flows
For 2012 and 2013

	2013	2012
Operations:		
Net Income (Loss)	$ (2,691)	$ 417
Depreciation Expense	625	641
Amortization Expense	40	25
Inc. (Dec.) in Other Noncurrent Liabilities.....	24	(37)
(Inc.) Dec. in Accounts Receivable...................	1,391	(168)
(Inc.) Dec. in Inventories.................................	872	(632)
(Inc.) Dec. in Prepayments	148	(154)
Inc. (Dec.) in Accounts Payable to Suppliers		
of Inventory...	(13)	(769)
Inc. (Dec.) in Other Current Liabilities	(82)	(299)
Cash Flow from Operations...............................	$ 314	$ (976)
Investing:		
Sale of Patents..	$ 63	$ —
Acquisition of Property, Plant, and		
Equipment..	(54)	(1,433)
Acquisition of Patents	—	(391)
Cash Flow from Investing.................................	$ 9	$ (1,824)
Financing:		
Inc. (Dec.) in Notes Payable to Banks	$ 2,182	$ 220
Inc. (Dec.) in Long-Term Debt	(2,608)	2,339
Increase in Preferred Stock............................	—	289
Increase in Common Stock	3	9
Dividends Paid..	(8)	(12)
Cash Flow from Financing.................................	$ (431)	$ 2,845
Net Change in Cash..	$ (108)	$ 45
Cash, Beginning of Year...................................	475	430
Cash, End of Year...	$ 367	$ 475

6.36 continued.

c. Deriving Direct Method Cash Flow from Operations Using Data from T-Account Work Sheet (all dollar amounts in thousands of US$)

2012
1. Copy income statement and cash flow from operations; see column (a) in the display below.
2. Copy information from T-account work sheet next to related income statement item; see columns (b) and (c) in the display below.
3. Sum across rows to derive direct receipts and expenditures; see column (d) in the display below.

Operations, 2012	(a)	Indirect Method (b)	Changes in Related Balance Sheet Accounts from T-Account Work Sheet (c)	Direct Method (d)	From Operations: Receipts Less Expenditures 2012
Revenues	$ 22,833	$ (168)	= Accounts Receivable Increase	$ 22,665	Receipts from Customers
Cost of Goods Sold	(16,518)	(769)	= Accounts Payable for Inventories Decrease	(17,919)	Payments for Inventories
		(632)	= Inventory Increase		
Selling and Administrative Expenses	(4,849)	641	= (Expense Not Using Cash)	(4,673)	Payments for Selling and Administrative Services
		25	= (Expense Not Using Cash)		
		(154)	= Increase in Prepayments		
		(299)	= Decrease in Other Current Liabilities		
		(37)	= Decrease in Other Noncurrent Liabilities		
Interest Expense	(459)	—	= Interest Payable (no change in balance sheet)	(459)	Payments for Interest
Income Tax Expense	(590)	—	= Income Taxes Payable Increase	(590)	Payments for Income Taxes
Net Income	$ 417	$ 417 Totals			
		$ (976)	= Cash Flow from Operations Derived via Indirect Method	$ (976) =	Cash Flow from Operations Derived via Direct Method

Solutions

6.36 continued.

    d.   Cash flow from operations was negative during 2012, despite positive net income, primarily because GTI reduced accounts payable and other current liabilities. The increases in receivables, inventories, and prepayments suggest that GTI grew during 2012 relative to 2011. One usually finds in these cases that current operating liabilities increase as well. The reduction in these current liabilities occurred either because GTI chose to use cash to liquidate these obligations or because creditors forced the firm to repay. GTI obtained the cash needed to finance the operating cash flow shortfall and capital expenditures by increasing short- and long-term debt and issuing preferred stock.

        GTI experienced a net loss in 2013, but its cash flow from operations turned positive. The firm reduced receivables, inventories and prepayments with only minor reductions in current operating liabilities. The small reductions in current operating liabilities relative to the declines in current operating assets reflect either a stretching of short-term creditors or a return to a normal level of current operating liabilities after the repayment made in 2012. GTI dramatically decreased capital expenditures in 2013 and replaced long-term debt with short-term borrowing.

6.37   (Carter Corporation; interpreting a statement of cash flows based on the direct method for presenting cash flow from operations.) (amounts in millions of US$)

	2013
a.	
Net Revenues	$ 76,329.5
Less Cash Receipts from Revenues	(61,986.3)
Increase in Accounts Receivable	$ 14,343.2
b. Cash Paid for Inventory	$ 45,772.6
Increase in Accounts Payable for Inventory	181.4
Purchases for Inventory	$ 45,954.0
Less Cost of Revenues	(60,221.8)
Change (Decrease) in Inventories for the Year	$ (14,267.8)

Beginning Inventory + Purchases − COGS = Ending Inventory
Purchases − COGS = Ending Inventory − Beginning Inventory
Change in Inventory = Purchases − COGS

6.37 continued.

    c.   Amount Paid for Interest .... $ 468.2
           Interest Expense..   (434.6)
           Payment Exceeded Expenses by .... $ 33.6

    d.   The company acquired another large company.

6.38   (Carter Corporation; interpreting a statement of cash flows based on the direct method for presenting cash flow from operations.) (amounts in millions of US$)

    a.   **2012**

	2012
Net Revenues...	$ 43,821.4
Less Cash Receipts from Revenues...................................	(43,273.7)
Increase in Accounts Receivable	$ 547.7

    b.

Cost of Revenues	$ 32,079.2
Increase in Inventories for the Year..................................	624.1
Purchases for Inventory...	$ 32,703.3
Less Cash Paid for Inventory...	(31,422.1)
Increase in Accounts Payable for Inventory......................	$ 1,281.2

Beginning Inventory + Purchases − COGS = Ending Inventory
Purchases − COGS = Ending Inventory − Beginning Inventory
Purchases = Ending Inventory − Beginning Inventory + COGS

Purchases − Cash Paid = Increase in Accounts Payable

    c.   Amount Paid for Interest .... $ 228.1
           Interest Expense..   (215.8)
           Payment Exceeded Expenses by .... $ 12.3

6.39   (Quintana Company; working backward through the statement of cash flows.) (amounts in thousands of US$)

QUINTANA COMPANY
Condensed Balance Sheet
January 1, 2013
(amounts in thousands of US$)

Assets

Current Assets:

Cash	$ 20	
Accounts Receivable	190	
Merchandise Inventories	280	
Total Current Assets		$ 490
Land		50
Buildings and Equipment	$ 405	
Less Accumulated Depreciation	(160)	245
Investments		140
Total Assets		$ 925

Liabilities and Shareholders' Equity

Current Liabilities:

Accounts Payable	$ 255	
Other Current Liabilities	130	
Total Current Liabilities		$ 385
Bonds Payable		60
Common Stock		140
Retained Earnings		340
Total Liabilities and Shareholders' Equity		$ 925

Following are T-accounts for deriving the solution. Entries (1)–(13) are reconstructed from the statement of cash flows. Changes for the year are appropriately debited or credited to end-of-year balances to get beginning-of-year balances. T-account amounts are shown in thousands.

6.39 continued.

Cash				Accounts Receivable				Merchandise Inventories		
	20				190				280	
(1)	200	30	(4)	(4)	30			(5)	40	
(2)	60	40	(5)							
(3)	25	45	(6)							
(7)	40	130	(10)							
(8)	15	200	(13)							
(9)	10									
(11)	60									
(12)	40									
√	25			√	220			√	320	

Land				Buildings and Equipment				Accumulated Depreciation		
	50				405					160
		10	(9)	(10)	130	35	(8)	(8)	20	60	(2)
√	40			√	500					200	√

Investments				Accounts Payable				Other Current Liabilities		
	140					255				130
		40	(7)			25	(3)	(6)	45	
√	100					280	√			85	√

Bonds Payable			Common Stock			Retained Earnings		
		60			140			340
		40	(12)		60	(11)	(13)	200	200	(1)
		100	√		200	√			340	√

6.40   (Swoosh Shoes, Inc.; interpreting the statement of cash flows.)

a. Swoosh Shoes' growth in sales and net income led to increases of account receivable and inventories. Swoosh Shoes, however, did not increase its accounts payable and other current operating liabilities to help finance the buildup in current assets. Thus, its cash flow from operations decreased.

b. Swoosh Shoes increased its acquisitions of property, plant, and equipment to provide the firm with operating capacity to sustain its rapid growth. Swoosh Shoes also acquired investments in securities of other firms. It is not clear from the statement of cash flows whether the investments represented short-term investments of temporarily excess cash (a current asset) or long-term investments made to develop an operating relation with another firm (noncurrent asset).

c. Swoosh Shoes used cash flow from operations during 2011 and 2012 to finance its investing activities. The excess cash flow after investing activities served to repay short- and long-term debt and pay dividends. Cash flow from operations during 2013 was insufficient to finance investing activities. Swoosh Shoes engaged in short-term borrowing to make up the shortfall and finance the payment of dividends.

d. Operating cash flows should generally finance the payment of dividends. Either operating cash flows or long-term sources of capital should generally finance acquisitions of property, plant, and equipment. Thus, Swoosh Shoes' use of short-term borrowing seems inappropriate. One might justify such an action if Swoosh Shoes (1) expected cash flow from operations during 2014 to return to its historical levels, (2) expected cash outflows for property, plant, and equipment to decrease during 2014, or (3) took advantage of comparatively low short-term borrowing rates during 2013 and planned to refinance this debt with long-term borrowing during 2014.

6.41   (Spokane Paper Group; interpreting the statement of cash flows.)

a. Forest products companies are capital intensive. Depreciation is therefore a substantial non-cash expense each year. The addback for depreciation converts a net loss each year into positive cash flow from operations. Note that cash flow from operations increased each year as the net loss decreased.

6.41 continued.

b. Spokane Paper Group had substantial changes in its property, plant, and equipment during the three years. It likely built new, more efficient production facilities and sold off older, less efficient facilities.

c. For the three years combined, Spokane Paper Group reduced its long-term debt and replaced it with preferred stock. The sales of forest products are cyclical. When the economy is in a recession, as apparently occurred during the three years, the high fixed cost of capital-intensive manufacturing facilities can result in net losses. If Spokane Paper Group is unable to repay debt on schedule during such years, it causes expensive financial distress or even bankruptcy. Firms have more latitude with respect to dividends on preferred stock than interest on debt. Thus, a shift toward preferred stock and away from long-term debt reduces the bankruptcy risk of Spokane Paper Group. Note that Spokane Paper Group continued to pay, and even increase, dividends despite operating at a net loss. Most shareholders prefer less rather than more fluctuation in their dividends over the business cycle.

6.42 (Interpreting statement of cash flow relations.)

a. **American Airlines**—Property, plant, and equipment comprises a large proportion of the total assets of American Airlines. Depreciation expense is a major expense for the airline. The firm operated at a net loss for the year, but the addback for depreciation resulted in a positive cash flow from operations. Cash flow from operations was not sufficient to fund capital expenditures on new property, plant, and equipment. American Airlines is apparently growing since its capital expenditures exceed depreciation expense for the year. The firm financed its capital expenditures in part with cash flow from operations and in part with the issuance of additional long-term debt and capital stock. The net effect of the cash flow from financing is a reduction in liabilities and an increase in capital stock (actually preferred stock). Operating at a net loss increases the risk of bankruptcy. Perhaps American Airlines reduced the amount of debt in its capital structure to reduce fixed payment claims and substituted preferred stock that generally requires dividend payments only when declared by the board of directors.

6.42 continued.

b. **American Home Products**—Because of patent protection, pharmaceutical companies tend to generate relatively high profit margins and significant cash flows from operations. Although the manufacturing process for pharmaceutical products is capital intensive, cash flow from operations is usually sufficient to fund capital expenditures. American Home Products used the excess cash flow to pay dividends and repurchase capital stock. The firm also borrowed short-term funds and invested the proceeds in the acquisition of another business. Borrowing short term to finance investments in long-term assets is usually undesirable because the firm must repay the debt before the long-term assets generate sufficient cash flow. Perhaps American Home Products needed to borrow short term to consummate the acquisition, with the expectation of refinancing the short-term debt with long-term borrowing soon after the acquisition. Alternatively, American Home Products might have anticipated a decline in long-term rates in the near future and borrowed short term until long-term rates actually declined.

c. **Interpublic Group**—An advertising agency serves as a link between clients desiring advertising time and space and various media with advertising time and space to sell. Thus, the principal asset of an advertising agency is accounts receivable from clients, and the principal liability is accounts payable to various media. Interpublic Group reports an increase in accounts receivable of $66 million and an increase in accounts payable of $59 million. Thus, the firm appeared to manage its receivables/payables position well. Advertising agencies lease most of the physical facilities used in their operations. They purchase equipment for use in designing and producing advertising copy. Thus, they must make some capital expenditures. Cash flow from operations, however, is more than sufficient to finance acquisitions of equipment. Interpublic Group used the excess cash flow plus the proceeds of additional short- and long-term borrowing to pay dividends, repurchase capital stock, and increase cash on the balance sheet.

6.42 continued.

  d. **Procter & Gamble**—Procter & Gamble's brand names create high profit margins and cash flows from operations. Cash flow from operations is more than adequate to finance capital expenditures. Note that capital expenditures significantly exceed depreciation, suggesting that the firm is still in a growth mode. The firm used the excess cash flow to repay short- and long-term debt and to pay dividends.

  e. **Reebok**—Cash flow from operations for Reebok is less than net income plus depreciation, a somewhat unusual relationship for a seasoned firm. Reebok increased its accounts receivable and inventories during the year but did not stretch its accounts payable commensurably. The financing section of the statement of cash flows suggests that Reebok might have used short-term debt to finance some of its working capital needs. Cash flow from operations was still more than sufficient to fund capital expenditures. One explanation for the sufficiency of cash flow from operations to cover capital expenditures is that Reebok is not very capital intensive. The relation between depreciation expense and net income supports this explanation. Reebok outsources virtually all of its manufacturing. Reebok used the excess cash flows from operating and investing activities to pay dividends and repurchase its capital stock.

  f. **Texas Instruments**—Like American Home Products and Upjohn (discussed later), Texas Instruments invests heavily in technology to create a competitive advantage. Patents and copyrights on computer hardware, software, and other products serve as a barrier to entry by competitors and provide Texas Instruments with an attractive profit margin. Texas Instruments differs from the two pharmaceutical companies with respect to the amount of depreciation relative to net income. Despite generating less than one-half of the net income of American Home Products, Texas Instruments has more than twice the amount of depreciation expense and capital expenditures. Thus, Texas Instruments is likely more capital intensive than the other two technology-based companies. Note that the changes in individual working capital accounts are relatively large, compared to the amount of net income. These relations suggest, although do not prove, that the

6.42 f. continued.

operations of Texas Instruments grew significantly during the year. Cash flow from operations was sufficient to fund capital expenditures and increase the balance of cash on the balance sheet. Note that Texas Instruments issued capital stock during the year and repaid long-term debt. The amounts involved, however, are small.

g. **Limited Brands**—Current assets and current liabilities dominate the balance sheets of retailers. Thus, working capital management is of particular importance. Limited Brands increased its current liabilities in line with increases in accounts receivable and inventories. Thus, cash flow from operations approximately equals net income plus depreciation. Limited Brands invested most of the cash flow from operations in additional property, plant, and equipment, the acquisition of other businesses, the repayment of short-term debt, and the payment of dividends.

h. **Upjohn**—This problem includes Upjohn primarily to compare and contrast it with American Home Products, also a pharmaceutical company. Both companies generated sufficient cash flow from operations to fund capital expenditures and pay dividends. Upjohn sold a portion of its business during the year and invested the proceeds in marketable securities.

6.43 (Fierce Fighters Corporation; interpreting direct and indirect methods.)

a. We think this is hopeless. We cannot write a coherent explanation of the decline from these data alone, at least not without further analysis.

b. Some academics think that even the question is nonsense—that is, trying to explain changes in the data which themselves explain changes in cash. The statement of cash flows explains the change in the cash account from year to year. Consider that the statement of income and retained earnings explains the change in Retained Earnings from year to year. Most analysts think it sensible comparing income statements from one year to the next, to understand the causes of the change in income (which itself explains the causes of part of the changes in Retained Earnings). We think it sensible comparing statements of cash flows from one year to the next to explain the causes of the changes in cash flow from operations (which itself explains the causes of part of the changes in Cash).

6.43 b. continued.

> In this case, the decline in cash flow from operations appears to result from a decreased margin of collections from customers for sales. The focus must be on what is going on with long-term and other sales contracts. From 2012 to 2013, we see increased payments to suppliers and employees that the analysis should investigate. We cannot be sure what is happening, but we can see where to inquire. Focus on those contracts, not on the changes in balance sheet operating accounts.

c. A reader can more easily interpret the direct method. The fundamental problem with the indirect method is that not a single number is itself a cash flow. So, changes in those numbers from year to year do not illuminate.

6.44 (Issues in manipulating cash flows from operations.)

a. This will increase cash flow from operations, assuming that had the maintenance been done this period, the firm would have paid for it this period. This may be an unsound management practice, as improper maintenance will increase long-run costs.

b. This will not increase cash flow from operations. It will conserve cash, but when the firm spends the cash, it appears as an investing use, not an operating use. This can be an unsound management practice.

c. Most simple transactions of this sort will not increase cash flow from operations, but they will generate investing or financing cash flows.

d. Not paying on time for items related to employment activities will, in the short run, increase cash flow from operations. Suppliers will catch on and will likely demand different payment terms, or higher prices, to compensate them for the slower payments.

e. Same issues as in Part *d*. above.

6.44 continued.

f. This will increase cash flow from operations in the period of sale but will reduce it in the next period if the customers request cash refunds. If both the buyer and the seller agree that the customer has no real use for the goods, and both sides of the sale agree that it will be unwound in the next period, this practice is fraud and will result in overstated revenue and income, as well as increased cash flow from operations. Such side agreements, often written by sales staff into so-called *side letters*, are illegal.

CHAPTER 7

INTRODUCTION TO FINANCIAL STATEMENT ANALYSIS

Questions, Exercises, and Problems: Answers and Solutions

7.1 See the text or the glossary at the end of the book.

7.2 The increase in the cost of goods sold to sales percentage could result from increases in the purchase prices of inventory items or increases in the cost of theft or product obsolescence which the firm could not pass on to the customers by way of higher prices. The increase in the cost of goods sold to sales percentage could result from increased competition or weak economic conditions which forced the firm to lower prices. The increase in the cost of goods sold to sales percentage could result from a combination of factors affecting both the numerator and denominator. Thus, interpreting a change in this expense percentage requires careful analysis.

7.3 The numerator in the ROA formula should reflect the income generated by all assets, irrespective of how those assets are financed. Because net income deducts interest charges on borrowings in arriving at net income, we must add back to net income the interest expense that has been deducted. The adjustment also considers the tax effects of deducting interest expense. The correct adjustment is, therefore, to add back to net income the aftertax cost of interest expense, equal to interest expense times one minus the tax rate.

7.4 Assets other than accounts receivable, inventory, or fixed assets must have increased at a faster rate than the increase in sales. Perhaps the firm issued debt or common stock, thereby increasing cash or marketable securities. Perhaps the firm made a corporate acquisition using its common stock as consideration and recognized intangible assets.

7.5   For two otherwise identical firms, the firm with preferred stock in its capital structure will have a higher ROE because ROE measures the return to the firm's *common* shareholders. Preferred stock is not included in measuring the common shareholders' equity, the denominator of the ROE ratio. Thus, holding all other factors constant, the firm with preferred stock in its capital structure will have a smaller amount of common equity (a smaller denominator in the ROE ratio), which will cause ROE to be higher.

7.6   The first company apparently has a relatively small profit margin and must rely on asset turnover (probably inventory turnover in particular) to generate a satisfactory rate of return. A discount department store is an example. The second company, on the other hand, has a larger profit margin and does not need as much asset turnover as the first company to generate a satisfactory rate of return. A chemical company is an example of the latter.

7.7   Management strives to keep its inventories at a level that is neither too low so that it loses sales nor too high so that it incurs high storage costs. Thus, there is an optimal level of inventory for a particular firm in a particular period and an optimal inventory turnover ratio.

7.8   The rate of return on equity exceeds (is less than) the rate of return on assets when the financial leverage of the firm is greater (less) than 1.0.

7.9   It would be unusual to have a firm generate superior performance on both the profit margin and asset turnover dimension. The reason is that these two ratios typically reflect tradeoffs that are either imposed on the firm by industry forces (such as barriers to entry) or by the business models that work well in the industry. For example, the oil-refining industry requires a relatively high level of fixed assets. The high fixed assets lead to low asset turnover ratios, but high profit margins. The high profit margins come about because oil-refining firms face less price competition because the high level of fixed assets acts as a barrier to entry to new firms. Grocery stores are the opposite: they require relatively low levels of assets to operate. As a result, (i) barriers to entry are small, leading to price competitiveness and low profit margins, but (ii) asset turnover ratios are high because the asset levels are low. A new firm could conceivably generate both superior profit margin and superior asset turnover performance. However, one would expect that such superior results would immediately attract competition, forcing profit margins to decrease, and possibly volumes to erode as well.

7.10   A firm cannot continually increase the amount of debt in the capital structure without limit. Increasing the debt level increases the risk to the common shareholders. These shareholders will not tolerate risk levels that they consider too high. Also, the cost of borrowing increases as a firm assumes larger proportions of debt. At some point, the financial leverage effects start working to the disadvantage of the common shareholders.

7.11   (Calem and Garter; calculating and disaggregating rate of return on assets.) (amounts in millions of US$)

a. **Calem:** $\dfrac{\$76}{\$1,473} = 5.16\%$.

Garter: $\dfrac{\$2,335}{\$29,183} = 8.00\%$.

b.

Return on Assets	=	Profit Margin	X	Total Assets Turnover Ratio
Calem:				
$\dfrac{\$76}{\$1,473}$	=	$\dfrac{\$76}{\$2,352}$	X	$\dfrac{\$2,352}{\$1,473}$
5.16%	=	3.23%	X	1.6
Garter:				
$\dfrac{\$2,335}{\$29,183}$	=	$\dfrac{\$2,335}{\$22,787}$	X	$\dfrac{\$22,787}{\$29,183}$
8.00%	=	10.24%	X	0.8

c. Garter has a higher ROA, the result of a higher profit offset by a lower total assets turnover. Garter's higher profit margin might result from its larger size, permitting it to benefit from spreading fixed costs over a larger sales base. Garter also generates revenues from franchise fees, which increase net income but not sales revenue. Garter's lower total assets turnover might result from having the land and buildings of some of its franchisees on its balance sheet but not including the sales of these franchisees in its sales.

7.12   (Profitability analysis for two types of retailers.) (amounts in millions of US$)

Company A is the specialty retailer because of its higher profit margin and lower total assets turnover, relative to Company B (the discount store chain). The specialized, branded products permit Company A to price its products for a higher profit margin. Company B's prices are lower, and thereby it generates a faster turnover of merchandise.

	Return on Assets	=	Profit Margin	X	Total Assets Turnover Ratio
Company A:	$\dfrac{\$476}{\$2,458}$	=	$\dfrac{\$476}{\$3,750}$	X	$\dfrac{\$3,750}{\$2,458}$
	19.4%	=	12.7%	X	1.5
Company B:	$\dfrac{\$243}{\$2,574}$	=	$\dfrac{\$243}{\$6,834}$	X	$\dfrac{\$6,834}{\$2,574}$
	9.4%	=	3.6%	X	2.7

7.13   (Mobilex; calculating and disaggregating rate of return on common shareholders' equity.) (amounts in millions of US$)

a.

Year	Numerator	Denominator	Return on Equity
2011	$ 36,130	$ 106,471	33.9%
2012	39,500	112,515	35.1%
2013	40,610	117,803	34.5%

b. **Profit Margin**

Year	Numerator	Denominator	Profit Margin
2011	$ 36,130	$ 370,680	9.75%
2012	39,500	377,635	10.46%
2013	40,610	404,552	10.04%

7.13 b. continued.

Total Assets Turnover

Year	Numerator	Denominator	Total Assets Turnover
2011	$ 370,680	$ 201,796	1.84
2012	377,635	213,675	1.77
2013	404,552	230,549	1.75

Financial Leverage Ratio

Year	Numerator	Denominator	Financial Leverage Ratio
2011	$ 201,796	$ 106,471	1.90
2012	213,675	112,515	1.90
2013	230,549	117,803	1.96

c. The rate of return on equity was relatively steady during the three years. Between 2011 and 2012, the profit margin and the financial leverage ratio increased but the total assets turnover decreased. Sales increased at a higher rate in 2013 than in 2012 but the profit margin declined. Mobilex might have increased expenditures on exploration or development of petroleum resources in 2013, which lowered net income and thus reduced the profit margin. The higher sales level should have provided Mobilex with benefits of economies of scale, but any such benefits were offset by higher other expenses.

7.14 (Profitability analysis for two companies.) (amounts in millions of US$)

a.

	Return on Assets	=	Profit Margin	X	Total Assets Turnover
Company A:	$\dfrac{\$476}{\$2,458}$	=	$\dfrac{\$476}{\$3,750}$	X	$\dfrac{\$3,750}{\$2,458}$
	19.4%	=	12.7%	X	1.5
Company B:	$\dfrac{\$934}{\$5,594}$	=	$\dfrac{\$934}{\$6,143}$	X	$\dfrac{\$6,143}{\$5,594}$
	16.7%	=	15.2%	X	1.1

7.14 continued.

b.

	Return on Equity	=	Profit Margin	X	Total Assets Turnover	X	Financial Leverage Ratio
Company A:	$\dfrac{\$476}{\$2,256}$	=	$\dfrac{\$476}{\$3,750}$	X	$\dfrac{\$3,750}{\$2,458}$	X	$\dfrac{\$2,458}{\$2,256}$
	21.1%	=	12.7%	X	1.5	X	1.1
Company B:	$\dfrac{\$934}{\$2,566}$	=	$\dfrac{\$934}{\$6,143}$	X	$\dfrac{\$6,143}{\$5,594}$	X	$\dfrac{\$5,594}{\$2,566}$
	36.4%	=	15.2%	X	1.1	X	2.2

c. Company A is the operator of coffee shops, and Company B is the brand-name motorcycle manufacturer. Company A typically leases the space for its restaurants and, therefore, has few fixed assets. It sells for cash and, therefore, has few accounts receivable. It will maintain some inventory, but the need for freshness of its foods suggests a rapid turnover. Thus, we would expect Company A to have the faster total assets turnover. Company B needs fixed assets to manufacture its motorcycles. The smaller profit margins for Company A are somewhat of a surprise. Competition from other coffee shops and supermarkets with fresh ground coffees probably dampens its profit margins. Company A's low financial leverage ratio reflects its lack of assets to use as collateral for borrowing. The manufacturing of motorcycles is essentially an assembly operation, but Company B needs facilities for the assembly operation. These assets serve as collateral for borrowing.

7.15 (Profitability analysis for two companies.) (amounts in millions of US$)

a.

	Return on Assets	=	Profit Margin	X	Total Assets Turnover
Company A:	$\dfrac{\$6,986}{\$52,010}$	=	$\dfrac{\$6,986}{\$38,334}$	X	$\dfrac{\$38,334}{\$52,010}$
	13.4%	=	18.2%	X	0.74
Company B:	$\dfrac{\$6,999}{\$187,882}$	=	$\dfrac{\$6,999}{\$93,469}$	X	$\dfrac{\$93,469}{\$187,882}$
	3.7%	=	7.5%	X	0.50

7-6

7.15 continued.

b.

	Return on Equity	=	Profit Margin	X	Total Assets Turnover	X	Financial Leverage Ratio
Company A:	$\dfrac{\$6,986}{\$39,757}$	=	$\dfrac{\$6,986}{\$38,334}$	X	$\dfrac{\$38,334}{\$52,010}$	X	$\dfrac{\$52,010}{\$39,757}$
	17.5%	=	18.2%	X	0.74	X	1.3
Company B:	$\dfrac{\$6,999}{\$49,558}$	=	$\dfrac{\$6,999}{\$93,469}$	X	$\dfrac{\$93,469}{\$187,882}$	X	$\dfrac{\$187,882}{\$49,558}$
	14.1%	=	7.5%	X	0.50	X	3.8

c.   Company A is the semiconductor manufacturer and Company B is the telecommunications provider. Both of these firms are fixed-asset intensive, so their total assets turnovers are small. Their ROAs and ROEs differ with respect to profit margin and financial leverage. Semiconductors are technology-intensive products and can command high profit margins if the products are on the technology edge. Telecommunication services, on the other hand, are commodity products and are difficult to differentiate from competitors. The technological intensity of semiconductors leads to short product life cycles. Firms in this industry tend not to take on substantial debt because of the short product life cycles. Telecommunication services are somewhat less technology intensive, at least with respect to the need to create the technologies. Firms in the telecommunications industry have capital-intensive fixed assets that can serve as collateral for borrowing and a somewhat more stable revenue stream, relative to semiconductors.

7.16   (Delta, Inc., and SunnyDay Company; analyzing accounts receivable for two companies.) (amounts in millions of US$)

a.   **Delta, Inc.**   **SunnyDay**

$$\frac{\$61,133}{0.5(\$6,152 + \$7,693)}$$ $$\frac{\$13,873}{0.5(\$2,702 + \$2,964)}$$

= 8.8 times per year.   = 4.9 times per year.

b. $\dfrac{365}{8.8}$ = 41.5 days. $\dfrac{365}{4.9}$ = 74.5 days.

c.   Delta sells primarily to individuals who pay with credit cards. Delta collects these accounts receivable quickly. SunnyDay sells to businesses. Customers may require SunnyDay to finance their purchases. Customers may also delay paying SunnyDay until their computers are set up and working properly. SunnyDay may also offer liberal credit terms as an inducement to businesses to purchase its computers.

7.17   (Funtime, Inc.; analyzing inventories over three years.) (amounts in millions of euros)

a.

Year	Numerator	Denominator	Inventory Turnover
2011	€ 2,806	€ 415	6.76
2012	3,038	380	7.99
2013	3,193	406	7.86

7.17 continued.

b.

Year	Numerator	Denominator	Days Inventory Held
2011	365	6.76	54.0
2012	365	7.99	45.7
2013	365	7.86	46.4

c.

Year	Numerator	Denominator	Cost of Goods Sold Percentage
2011	€ 2,806	€ 5,179	54.2%
2012	3,038	5,650	53.8%
2013	3,193	5,970	53.5%

d. Funtime experienced an increasing inventory turnover and a decreasing cost of goods sold to sales percentage between 2011 and 2012. Toys are trendy products. Funtime's products might have received rapid market acceptance, so that it was able both to move products more quickly and to achieve a higher gross margin on products sold. The faster turnover for trendy products means that Funtime would not need to mark down products in order to sell them or to incur additional storage costs. Funtime's cost of goods sold to sales percentage declined further in 2013 but its inventory turnover declined. Sales increased 9.1% [= (€5,650/€5,179) − 1] between 2011 and 2012 but only 5.7% [= (€5,970/€5,650) − 1] between 2012 and 2013. Perhaps Funtime increased inventory levels in 2013 expecting a larger sales increase than actually occurred. The unsold inventory resulted in a decrease in the inventory turnover rate.

7.18 (Mickey Group; analyzing fixed-asset turnover over three years.) (amounts in millions of pounds sterling)

a.

Year	Numerator	Denominator	Fixed Asset Turnover
2011	£31,374	£15,362	2.04
2012	33,747	16,174	2.09
2013	35,510	16,270	2.18

7.18 continued.

b. The fixed-asset turnover increased during the three-year period. Mickey Group reduced its capital expenditures in 2012 and its capital expenditures in 2013 were not as large as in 2011. Its capital expenditures each year do not differ significantly from its depreciation expense. Thus, Mickey Group seems to be approximately maintaining its level of investment in fixed assets, while its sales grow. Thus, the fixed-asset turnover increases.

7.19 (FleetSneak; calculating and interpreting short-term liquidity ratios.) (amounts in millions of US$)

a. **Current Ratio**

Year	Numerator	Denominator	Current Ratio
2010	$ 5,528	$ 2,031	2.72
2011	6,351	1,999	3.18
2012	7,346	2,613	2.81
2013	8,077	2,584	3.13

Quick Ratio

Year	Numerator	Denominator	Quick Ratio
2010	$ 3,349	$ 2,031	1.65
2011	4,087	1,999	2.04
2012	4,686	2,613	1.79
2013	5,342	2,584	2.07

7.19 continued.

b. Cash Flow from Operations to Current Liabilities Ratio

Year	Numerator	Denominator	Cash Flow from Operations to Current Liabilities Ratio
2011	$ 1,571	$ 2,015.0[a]	78.0%
2012	1,668	2,306.0[b]	72.3%
2013	1,879	2,598.5[c]	72.3%

[a]0.5($2,031 + $1,999) = $2,015.0.

[b]0.5($1,999 + $2,613) = $2,306.0.

[c]0.5($2,613 + $2,584) = $2,598.5.

Accounts Receivable Turnover Ratio

Year	Numerator	Denominator	Accounts Receivable Turnover Ratio
2011	$13,740	$ 2,191.0[a]	6.27
2012	14,955	2,322.5[b]	6.44
2013	16,326	2,439.0[c]	6.69

[a]0.5($2,120 + $2,262) = $2,191.0.

[b]0.5($2,262 + $2,383) = $2,322.5.

[c]0.5($2,383 + $2,495) = $2,439.0.

Inventory Turnover Ratio

Year	Numerator	Denominator	Inventory Turnover Ratio
2011	$ 7,624	$ 1,730.5[a]	4.41
2012	8,368	1,944.0[b]	4.30
2013	9,165	2,099.5[c]	4.37

[a]0.5($1,650 + $1,811) = $1,730.5.

[b]0.5($1,811 + $2,077) = $1,944.0.

[c]0.5($2,077 + $2,122) = $2,099.5.

7.19 b. continued.

Accounts Payable Turnover Ratio

Year	Numerator	Denominator	Accounts Payable Turnover Ratio
2011	$ 7,785[a]	$ 777.5[d]	10.01
2012	8,634[b]	863.5[e]	10.00
2013	9,210[c]	996.0[f]	9.25

[a]$7,624 + $1,811 − $1,650 = $7,785.   [d]0.5($780 + $775) = $777.5.

[b]$8,368 + $2,077 − $1,811 = $8,634.   [e]0.5($775 + $952) = $863.5.

[c]$9,165 + $2,122 − $2,077 = $9,210.   [f]0.5($952 + $1,040) = $996.0.

c.   The short-term liquidity risk of FleetSneak did not change significantly during the three-year period. The current and quick ratios fluctuated but are well above 1.0. Its cash flow from operations to current liabilities ratio declined slightly but is well above the 40% benchmark for a healthy company. FleetSneak increased its accounts receivable turnover each year, providing operating cash flows. Its inventory turnover was relatively stable. Although the accounts payable turnover decreased between 2012 and 2013, providing operating cash flows, it does not appear that the slower rate of paying suppliers is due to a shortage of liquid assets. Another factor affecting the assessment of short-term liquidity risk is the increased profit margin, net income divided by revenues, between 2011 and 2012. The increasing profit margin ultimately provides more cash than if the profit margin had remained stable.

7.20   (Geneva, S.A.; calculating and interpreting short-term liquidity ratios.) (amounts in millions of euros)

a.   **Current Ratio**

Year	Numerator	Denominator	Current Ratio
2010	€ 22,828	€ 18,811	1.21
2011	26,865	23,063	1.16
2012	21,933	20,178	1.09
2013	21,610	26,175	0.83

7.20 a. continued.

Quick Ratio

Year	Numerator	Denominator	Quick Ratio
2010	€ 17,527	€ 18,811	0.93
2011	20,381	23,063	0.88
2012	16,185	20,178	0.80
2013	15,053	26,175	0.58

b. **Cash Flow from Operations to Current Liabilities Ratio**

Year	Numerator	Denominator	Cash Flow from Operations to Current Liabilities Ratio
2011	€ 8,461	€20,937.0[a]	40.4%
2012	9,197	21,620.5[b]	42.5%
2013	11,030	23,176.5[c]	47.6%

[a]0.5(€18,811 + €23,063) = €20,937.0.

[b]0.5(€23,063 + €20,178) = €21,620.5.

[c]0.5(€20,178 + €26,175) = €23,176.5.

Accounts Receivable Turnover Ratio

Year	Numerator	Denominator	Accounts Receivable Turnover Ratio
2011	€ 73,135	€ 8,416.5[a]	8.69
2012	78,533	9,124.5[b]	8.61
2013	89,625	9,186.0[c]	9.76

[a]0.5(€7,640 + €9,193) = €8,416.5.

[b]0.5(€9,193 + €9,056) = €9,124.5.

[c]0.5(€9,056 + €9,316) = €9,186.0.

7.20 b. continued.

Inventory Turnover Ratio

Year	Numerator	Denominator	Inventory Turnover Ratio
2011	€ 30,435	€ 4,897.5[a]	6.21
2012	32,474	5,119.0[b]	6.34
2013	37,530	5,295.0[c]	7.09

[a]$0.5(€4,545 + €5,250) = €4,897.5.$
[b]$0.5(€5,250 + €4,988) = €5,119.0.$
[c]$0.5(€4,988 + €5,602) = €5,295.0.$

Accounts Payable Turnover Ratio

Year	Numerator	Denominator	Accounts Payable Turnover Ratio
2011	€ 31,140[a]	€ 6,511.0[d]	4.78
2012	32,212[b]	7,480.5[e]	4.31
2013	38,144[c]	8,188.0[f]	4.66

[a]$€30,435 + €5,250 – €4,545 = €31,140.$
[b]$€32,474 + €4,988 – €5,250 = €32,212.$
[c]$€37,530 + €5,602 – €4,988 = €38,144.$
[d]$0.5(€5,871 + €7,151) = €6,511.0.$
[e]$0.5(€7,151 + €7,810) = €7,480.5.$
[f]$0.5(€7,810 + €8,566) = €8,188.0.$

7.20 continued.

c. The current and quick ratios both declined during the last four years, with a significant decline in 2013. The gradual decline over time occurs in part because of the increase in the accounts receivable and inventory turnovers. The significant decline in 2013 occurs because of the increase in bank loans. Offsetting these signals of increased risk, however, is an increase in the cash flow from operations to current liabilities ratio, related in part to the increased rate of accounts receivable and inventory turnovers. This ratio also increased because of increased profitability. The ratio of net income to revenues was 8.9% (= €6,498/€73,135) in 2011 and 9.9% (= €8,874/€89,625) in 2013. The cash flow from operations to current liabilities ratio exceeded the 40% threshold for healthy companies in all three years. The levels of the current and quick ratios were marginal prior to the end of 2013 and at an undesirable level at the end of 2013. Thus, the short-term liquidity ratios provide mixed signals of risk. The increased profitability coupled with improved accounts receivable and inventory turnover ratios suggest the overall short-term liquidity risk of Geneva is low.

7.21 (Kyoto Electric; calculating and interpreting long-term liquidity ratios.) (amounts in billions of Japanese yen)

a. **Long-Term Debt Ratio**

Year	Numerator	Denominator	Long-Term Debt Ratio
2010	¥7,391	¥11,540 + ¥2,360	53.2%
2011	7,150	11,247 + 2,502	52.0%
2012	6,278	10,814 + 2,780	46.2%
2013	5,871	10,488 + 3,034	43.4%

Debt-Equity Ratio

Year	Numerator	Denominator	Debt-Equity Ratio
2010	¥7,391	¥2,360	313.2%
2011	7,150	2,502	285.8%
2012	6,278	2,780	225.8%
2013	5,871	3,034	193.5%

7.21 continued.

b. **Cash Flow from Operations to Total Liabilities Ratio**

Year	Numerator	Denominator	Cash Flow from Operations to Total Liabilities Ratio
2011	¥1,411	0.5(¥11,540 + ¥ 11,247)	12.4%
2012	936	0.5(¥11,247 + ¥ 10,814)	8.5%
2013	1,074	0.5(¥10,814 + ¥ 10,488)	10.1%

Interest Coverage Ratio

Year	Numerator	Denominator	Interest Coverage Ratio Earned
2011	¥538	¥165	3.3
2012	635	161	3.9
2013	651	155	4.2

c. The proportion of long-term debt in the capital structure declined during the three-year period, but still appears to be at a high level. The cash flow from operations to average total liabilities ratio is low, relative to the 20% level commonly found for healthy firms. The interest coverage ratio was low in 2011 but improved by 2013. If this firm were a manufacturer, we would probably conclude that its long-term liquidity risk level is high. However, Kyoto Electric has a monopoly position in its service area. Regulators would not likely allow the firm to experience bankruptcy. Its protected status allows it to carry heavier levels of debt than a nonregulated manufacturing firm.

7.22   (Arctagon; calculating and interpreting long-term liquidity ratios.) (amounts in millions of euros)

a. **Long-Term Debt Ratio**

Year	Numerator	Denominator	Long-Term Debt Ratio
2010	€ 1,206	€ 7,760 + € 4,301	10.0%
2011	6,760	17,448 + 11,264	23.5%
2012	16,416	53,114 + 31,947	19.3%
2013	15,106	52,749 + 38,662	16.5%

Debt-Equity Ratio

Year	Numerator	Denominator	Debt-Equity Ratio
2010	€ 1,206	€ 4,301	28.0%
2011	6,760	11,264	60.0%
2012	16,416	31,947	51.4%
2013	15,106	38,662	39.1%

b. **Cash Flow from Operations to Total Liabilities Ratio**

Year	Numerator	Denominator	Cash Flow from Operations to Total Liabilities Ratio
2011	€ 6,034	0.5(€ 7,760 + € 17,448)	47.9%
2012	6,828	0.5(€ 17,448 + € 53,114)	19.4%
2013	8,539	0.5(€ 53,114 + € 52,749)	16.1%

Interest Coverage Ratio

Year	Numerator	Denominator	Interest Coverage Ratio
2011	€ 4,160	€ 404	10.3
2012	6,624	895	7.4
2013	11,538	676	17.1

7.22 continued.

    c.   The long-term debt levels increased significantly during 2011 but steadily declined during 2012 and 2013. Despite the decline in the debt ratios, the cash flow from operations to total liabilities ratio declined during the three-year period and was less than the 20% benchmark for a healthy company at the end of 2013. The interest coverage ratio is at a healthy level in all three years. This problem illustrates the difficulties encountered interpreting financial ratios based on average amounts for a year when a significant increase occurs in the numerator or denominator. This problem also shows the importance of assessing profitability in concert with assessing risk. Although the long-term debt ratios appear low for a capital-intensive company, steel companies experience variations in sales with changes in economic activity. Because of their high levels of fixed costs, net income will vary with changes in sales and decrease the level of long-term debt considered desirable.

7.23   (Effect of various transactions on financial statement ratios.)

Transaction	Return on Equity	Current Ratio	Liabilities to Assets Ratio
a.	No Effect	(1)	Increase
b.	Increase	Increase	Decrease
c.	No Effect	No Effect	No Effect
d.	No Effect	(2)	Decrease
e.	No Effect	Increase	No Effect
f.	Increase	Decrease	Increase
g.	Decrease	Increase	Decrease
h.	No Effect	Decrease	Increase

(1) The current ratio remains the same if it was one to one prior to the transaction, decreases if it was greater than one, and increases if it was less than one.

(2) The current ratio remains the same if it was equal to one prior to the transaction, increases if it was greater than one, and decreases if it was less than one.

7.24   (Effect of various transactions on financial statement ratios.)

Transaction	Working Capital	Quick Ratio
a.	Increase	Increase
b.	Decrease	Decrease
c.	No Effect	Decrease
d.	Increase	Increase
e.	No Effect	Increase
f.	Increase	Decrease*

*Assumption that quick ratio of acquired business is 0.75 or greater; otherwise the ratio increases.

7.25   (Bullseye Corporation; calculating and interpreting profitability and risk ratios in a time series setting.) (amounts in millions of US$)

a. 1.   Return on Assets $= \dfrac{\$2,849}{0.5(\$38,599 + \$46,373)} = 6.7\%.$

2.   Profit Margin $= \dfrac{\$2,849}{\$61,471} = 4.6\%.$

3.   Total Assets Turnover $= \dfrac{\$61,471}{0.5(\$38,599 + \$46,373)} = 1.4 \text{ times.}$

4.   Other Revenues/ Sales $= \dfrac{\$1,918}{\$61,471} = 3.1\%.$

5.   Cost of Goods Sold/Sales $= \dfrac{\$41,895}{\$61,471} = 68.2\%.$

6.   Selling and Administrative Expense/Sales $= \dfrac{\$16,200}{\$61,471} = 26.4\%.$

7.   Interest Expense/Sales $= \dfrac{\$669}{\$61,471} = 1.1\%.$

7.25 a. continued.

8. Income Tax Expense/Sales $= \dfrac{\$1,776}{\$61,471} = 2.9\%.$

9. Accounts Receivable Turnover Ratio $= \dfrac{\$61,471}{0.5(\$6,194 + \$8,054)} = 8.6$ times.

10. Inventory Turnover Ratio $= \dfrac{\$41,895}{0.5(\$6,254 + \$6,780)} = 6.4$ times.

11. Fixed Asset Turnover $= \dfrac{\$61,471}{0.5(\$22,681 + \$25,908)} = 2.5$ times.

12. Return on Equity $= \dfrac{\$2,849}{0.5(\$15,633 + \$15,307)} = 18.4\%.$

13. Financial Leverage Ratio $= \dfrac{0.5(\$38,599 + \$46,373)}{0.5(\$15,633 + \$15,307)} = 2.7.$

14. Current Ratio $= \dfrac{\$18,906}{\$11,782} = 1.6.$

15. Quick Ratio $= \dfrac{\$2,450 + \$8,054}{\$11,782} = 0.9.$

16. Accounts Payable Turnover Ratio $= \dfrac{(\$41,895 + \$6,780 - \$6,254)}{0.5(\$6,575 + \$6,721)} = 6.4$ times.

17. Cash Flow from Operations to Current Liabilities Ratio $= \dfrac{\$4,125}{0.5(\$11,117 + \$11,782)} = 36.0\%.$

18. Liabilities to Assets Ratio $= \dfrac{\$31,066}{\$46,373} = 67.0\%.$

7.25 a. continued.

19.   Long-Term Debt Ratio $= \dfrac{\$16,939}{\$46,373} = 36.5\%.$

20.   Debt-Equity Ratio $= \dfrac{\$16,939}{\$15,307} = 110.7\%.$

21.   Cash Flow from Operations to Total Liabilities Ratio $= \dfrac{\$4,125}{0.5(\$22,966 + \$31,066)} = 15.3\%.$

22.   Interest Coverage Ratio $= \dfrac{(\$2,849 + \$1,776 + \$669)}{\$669} = 7.9 \text{ times.}$

b. **Rate on Assets (ROA)**

Bullseye's ROA increased between the fiscal years ended January 31, 2011 and 2012 and then decreased between fiscal years ended January 31, 2012 and 2013. The improved ROA between 2011 and 2012 results from an increased profit margin. The decreased ROA between 2012 and 2013 results from both a decreased profit margin and a decreased total assets turnover.

Profit Margin The changes in the profit margin result primarily from changes in the selling and administrative expense to sales percentage. Sales increased 12.9% between 2011 and 2012 but only 6.2% between 2012 and 2013. Most administrative expenses and some selling expenses are relatively fixed in amount. Variations in sales growth cause this expense percentage to vary as well.

Total Assets Turnover The total assets turnover declined between 2012 and 2013. Bullseye experienced declines in all three individual asset turnovers. These declines are also likely due to the significant decline in the growth rate in sales in 2013. Customers perhaps purchased more on credit and did not pay as quickly. Bullseye geared its inventory levels expecting a higher growth rate in sales than actually occurred, slowing the inventory turnover. The firm opened new stores expecting a larger growth in sales than occurred, slowing the fixed asset turnover.

7.25 continued.

c. **Return on Equity**

ROE follows the same path as ROA, increasing between 2011 and 2012 and then decreasing between 2012 and 2013. The total assets turnover declined between 2012 and 2013 for the reasons discussed in Part *b*. above. The financial leverage ratio declined between 2011 and 2012 and increased between 2012 and 2013. The decreased financial leverage ratio between 2011 and 2012 resulted primarily from the retention of earnings. Total liabilities changed only slightly between the end of 2011 and 2012, but shareholders' equity increased because of the retention of earnings. The financial leverage ratio increased between 2012 and 2013 for two principal reasons: an increase in long-term debt and the repurchase of common stock. The increased financial leverage ratio in 2013 moderated the decline in ROA and resulted in a smaller decline in ROE than would have otherwise been the case.

d. **Short-Term Liquidity Risk**

The current and quick ratios of Bullseye vary inversely with changes in the accounts receivable and inventory turnovers. Increased turnovers for these assets between 2011 and 2012 resulted in declines in the current and quick ratios, whereas decreased turnovers for these assets between 2012 and 2013 resulted in increases in the current and quick ratios. When turnovers increase, the firm turns accounts receivable and inventories into cash more quickly, which the firm can use to pay current liabilities, invest in new stores, or pay dividends. When turnovers decrease, the opposite occurs. The levels of the current and quick ratios are not at troublesome levels in any year. The cash flow from operations to current liabilities ratio declined between 2012 and 2013 and was less than the 40% benchmark in 2013. The decline below 40% in 2013 occurred because of decreases in the accounts receivable and inventory turnovers and an increase in the accounts payable turnover. Either the sales growth rate will return to more normal levels in 2014 or Bullseye will adjust its accounts receivable and inventory policies for a lower level of sales growth. Thus, Bullseye does not exhibit high short-term liquidity risk.

7.25 continued.

    e. **Long-Term Solvency Risk**
        The debt ratios declined between 2011 and 2012 and increased between 2012 and 2013, as Part *b*. discusses. The cash flow from operations to total liabilities declined between 2012 and 2013 for the reasons discussed in Part *d*. Although this ratio is below the 20% benchmark in 2013, it is likely the result of the slower rate of sales growth experienced in that year. The interest coverage ratio declined in all three years but is not at a level in any year that would suggest high long-term liquidity risk. Thus, Bullseye does not exhibit high long-term liquidity risk.

7.26   (Cartoo, Taggle, and Wilmet; profitability and risk analysis in a cross-section setting.)

    a.   Wilmet's advantage over Taggle Corporation on ROA is a higher total assets turnover that more than offsets a lower profit margin.

       Profit Margin: Taggle Corporation's advantage on the profit margin results from a higher other revenues to sales percentage and a lower cost of goods sold to sales percentage, offset by a higher selling and administrative expense to sales percentage, a higher advertising expense to sales percentage, and a larger tax burden. Possible explanations for these differences in the revenue and expenses percentage are as follows:

        • Higher Other Revenues to Sales Percentage for Taggle Corporation: Taggle Corporation offers its own credit card, which generates interest revenues. Wilmet sells for cash or permits customers to use third-party credit cards. Wilmet collects cash within three days of sales, whereas Taggle Corporation collects cash in approximately 40 days of sale. This longer period of outstanding accounts receivable for Taggle Corporation provides interest on customers' unpaid balances.

7.26 a. continued.

- Lower Cost of Goods Sold to Sales Percentage for Taggle Corporation: Taggle sells a higher proportion of brand name and trend merchandise than Wilmet, enabling higher markups on cost when setting selling prices. Wilmet's size likely permits it to purchase merchandise for a lower per unit cost than Taggle Corporation but Wilmet passes this cost savings to customers through lower prices. Taggle Corporation also provides for a more pleasant shopping experience (wider aisles, less inventory per square foot, more employees to provide customer service), permitting it to mark up selling prices and thereby lower the cost of goods sold to sales percentage relative to Wilmet.

- Higher selling and administrative expenses to sales percentage for Taggle Corporation: Several factors might explain this higher percentage. First, Taggle Corporation is significantly smaller than Wilmet, so Taggle Corporation must spread relatively fixed administrative costs over a smaller sales base. Note that the fixed assets per square foot for Taggle Corporation and Wilmet are similar but Taggle Corporation does not generate the sales per square foot that Wilmet achieves. Second, Taggle Corporation has lower sales per employee, suggesting that it hires more sales personnel to offer customers a more pleasant shopping experience. Third, Taggle Corporation incurs costs in administrating its credit card operation (credit granting and collection, uncollectible accounts).

- Higher advertising expense to sales percentage for Taggle Corporation: Taggle Corporation likely advertises its brand name and trend merchandise, whereas everyday lower prices attract customers to Wilmet.

7.26 a. continued.

- Higher tax burden for Taggle Corporation: We measure tax burden by relating income tax expense to income before income taxes.

Taggle:
2011:   3.2%/(5.3% + 3.2%) = 37.6%
2012:   3.3%/(5.5% + 3.3%) = 37.5%
2013:   3.3%/(5.3% + 3.3%) = 38.4%

Wilmet:
2011:   2.0%/(4.0% + 2.0%) = 33.3%
2012:   2.0%/(3.9% + 2.0%) = 33.9%
2013:   2.0%/(3.8% + 2.0%) = 34.5%

Taggle Corporation derives all of its income from within the United States, whereas Wilmet might derive some of its income in lower tax rate countries abroad.

Total Assets Turnover: Wilmet's advantage on total assets turnover results from faster accounts receivable, inventory, and fixed assets turnovers. Explanations for the faster asset turnovers are as follows:

- Faster accounts receivable turnover for Wilmet: Wilmet does not have its own credit card and collects from third-party credit card companies within three days of sale.

- Faster inventory turnover for Wilmet: Wilmet has an everyday low price strategy, which emphasizes turnover over profit margin. Wilmet derives a higher percentage of its sales from superstores than does Taggle Corporation. These superstores carry perishable grocery products, which turn over more quickly than household products.

- Faster fixed asset turnover for Wilmet: Wilmet has approximately the same cost of fixed assets per square foot as Taggle Corporation but generates much higher sales per square foot. The latter results from its aggressive pricing policies and higher inventory per square foot.

7.26 continued.

b. Wilmet's advantage over Cartoo on ROA is a higher profit margin for ROA and a higher total assets turnover.

Profit Margin: Wilmet's advantage on profit margin results from a lower cost of goods sold to sales percentage and a lower advertising expense to sales percentage offset by a lower other revenues to sales percentage, a higher selling and administrative expense to sales percentage, and a higher income tax burden. Possible explanations for differences in these revenue and expense percentages are as follows:

- Lower cost of goods sold to sales percentage for Wilmet: One possible explanation is that Wilmet has a higher proportion of non-grocery products in its sales mix that have a higher markup on cost than do grocery products. The differences in the inventory turnovers of Wilmet and Cartoo provide some support for this explanation. Another possibility is that the retailing market in the United States, Wilmet's emphasis, is less competitive than in Europe, Cartoo's emphasis.

- Lower advertising expense to sales percentage for Wilmet: Less competition in Wilmet's principal markets and an established reputation for everyday low prices might permit Wilmet to advertise less. A more competitive European market might require Cartoo to advertise more. Also, Cartoo has a larger number of store brands than Wilmet. Cartoo must conduct advertising for each store brand, in contrast to Wilmet's fewer store brands.

- Lower other revenues to sales percentage for Wilmet: The problem data indicate that Cartoo derives license fees from firms using the Cartoo name, which might account for its higher other revenues to sales percentage.

- Higher selling and administrative expenses to sales percentage for Wilmet: One would expect the larger size of Wilmet to provide it with economies of scale in spreading fixed administrative costs over a larger sales base and result in a lower selling and administrative expense to sales percentage. Also, the larger number of different store concepts for Cartoo should increase its administrative cost relative to Wilmet. Thus, the explanation for the higher selling and administrative expense for Wilmet must lie elsewhere. One possibility is that compensation levels for Cartoo

7.26 b. continued.

are higher than those for Wilmet. Cartoo, however, has higher sales per employee, offsetting any compensation cost disadvantage. Another possibility is that these firms include different cost items in cost of goods sold and in selling and administrative expenses. Note that the combined amounts for these two expense percentages are approximately the same for these two firms, supportive of this explanation.

- Higher tax burden for Wilmet. The calculation of the tax burdens is as follows:

Cartoo:
2011:   1.3%/(3.1% + 1.3%) = 29.5%
2012:   1.3%/(3.1% + 1.3%) = 29.5%
2013:   1.2%/(2.9% + 1.2%) = 29.3%

Wilmet:
2011:   2.0%/(4.0% + 2.0%) = 33.3%
2012:   2.0%/(3.9% + 2.0%) = 33.9%
2013:   2.0%/(3.8% + 2.0%) = 34.5%

The problem does not provide sufficient information to explain these differences in average tax burdens. These firms operate with a different geographical sales mix, which could account for the differences.

Total Assets Turnover We examine each of the companies' individual asset turnovers to understand Wilmet's advantage on total assets turnover.

- Larger accounts receivable turnover for Wilmet: Cartoo likely has accounts receivable for fees from licensees, which slows its accounts receivable turnover. Wilmet's advantage on the accounts receivable turnover will not likely explain its larger total asset turnover because accounts receivable comprise only 2% of its assets.

7.26 b. continued.

- Smaller inventory turnover for Wilmet: Wilmet may have a smaller percentage of grocery products in its sales mix than Cartoo. Also, Wilmet has much larger stores than Cartoo but derives much smaller sales per square foot. Cartoo seems to emphasize turnover of inventory. The slower inventory turnover will not explain the larger total asset turnover for Wilmet.

- Similar fixed asset turnovers for Wilmet and Cartoo. The cost per square foot of store space is significantly larger for Cartoo than for Wilmet, due perhaps to more costly land or higher building costs of smaller stores. Yet, Cartoo derives larger sales per square foot than Wilmet, largely offsetting any cost disadvantage on the cost of land and buildings.

- Other assets comprise a lower percentage of total assets for Wilmet. Both firms have grown by acquiring established retail chains. Such acquisitions result in the recognition of intangibles and goodwill. Cartoo apparently has grown more by acquisition than Wilmet, as both the higher proportion of other assets and the larger number of store brands indicate. These other assets lower the total assets turnover of Cartoo.

c. Cartoo is the most risky, with Taggle Corporation and Wilmet showing low levels of risk.

Short-term Liquidity Risk: Cartoo has the lowest current ratios, and those ratios are significantly less than 1.0. Its cash flow from operations to current liabilities ratios are smaller than the desired 40% level. It stretches its creditors longer than Taggle Corporation or Wilmet. The longer days accounts payable for Cartoo might result from different credit terms provided by suppliers or from less of an ability to pay suppliers. Wilmet's short-term liquidity ratios are at healthy levels in general. One might question its low quick ratio; however, Wilmet essentially sells for cash, so has few accounts receivable.

7.26 c. continued.

> **Long-Term Liquidity Risk:** Cartoo's ratios are not at healthy levels. Its debt levels are the highest of the three firms. Although Cartoo reduced its debt levels during the three-year period, they are still extremely high. Its cash flow from operations to total liabilities ratios are less than the 20% benchmark in all three years. Its interest coverage ratio is at a satisfactory level.

7.27 (Gappo Group and Limito Brands; calculating and interpreting profitability and risk ratios.)

The financial statement ratios on pages 7-31, 7-32, and 7-33 form the basis for the responses to the questions raised.

a. Limito has a higher ROA in the fiscal year ended August 31, 2013, the result of a higher profit margin, offset by a lower total assets turnover. The higher profit margin results from a higher other revenues to sales percentage and a lower selling and administrative expenses to sales percentage. The higher other revenues results primarily from gains on the divestment of stores. The analyst would need to examine previous years to see if Limito regularly sells stores or if the gains in fiscal year 2013 are unusual. The lower selling and administrative expense to sales percentage for Limito is unexpected, given its smaller size and need to emphasize its more fashion-oriented product line. The lower cost of goods sold to sales percentage for Gappo occurs because its clothes are more standardized than those of Limito, perhaps permitting lower manufacturing costs (for example, from quantity discounts on materials, fewer machine setups, less training of employees). Gappo probably also incurs fewer inventory writedowns from obsolescence because its clothing line is less fashion oriented.

7.27 a. continued.

The slower total asset turnover of Limito is not due to either inventories or fixed assets, because Limito has faster turnover ratios for these assets. Accounts receivable comprises such a small proportion of the total assets of Limito that the differences in the accounts receivable turnover ratios exert very little influence on the total assets turnover. The difference in total assets turnover relates to the proportion of Other Noncurrent Assets on the balance sheet of each company. Other Noncurrent Assets averages 4.9% of total assets for Gappo for the two years, whereas it averages 35.2% of total assets for Limito. Other Noncurrent Assets likely relates to goodwill and other intangibles from corporate acquisitions. These items increase total assets and reduce the total assets turnover.

The larger rate of return on assets of Limito carries over to the rate of return on common shareholders' equity. In addition to larger operating profitability, Limito carries substantially more financial leverage, enhancing its profitability advantage over Gappo.

b. The current and quick ratios vary considerably between fiscal 2012 and fiscal 2013, but neither company appears risky by these measures. Limito pays its suppliers more quickly than Gappo. The cash flow from operations to average current liabilities ratios for Gappo and Limito both exceed the 40% benchmark, particularly for Gappo. Although neither company appears to have much short-term liquidity risk, the ratios for Limito are not as strong as those of Gappo.

c. Limito has higher levels of debt than Gappo. Its cash flow from operations to total liabilities ratio is less than the 20% benchmark. Its interest coverage ratio is less than that of Gappo but not at a troublesome level. Thus, Limito has higher long-term liquidity risk.

7.27 continued.

		Gappo Group	Limito Brands
1.	Return on Assets	$= \dfrac{\$867}{0.5(\$7,838 + \$8,544)} = 10.6\%.$	$= \dfrac{\$718}{0.5(\$7,437 + \$7,093)} = 9.9\%.$
2.	Profit Margin	$= \dfrac{\$867}{\$15,763} = 5.5\%.$	$= \dfrac{\$718}{\$10,134} = 7.1\%.$
3.	Total Assets Turnover	$= \dfrac{\$15,763}{0.5(\$7,838 + \$8,544)} = 1.9$ times per year.	$= \dfrac{\$10,134}{0.5(\$7,437 + \$7,093)} = 1.4$ times per year.
4.	Other Revenues/Sales	$= \dfrac{\$117}{\$15,763} = 0.7\%.$	$= \dfrac{(\$146 + 230)}{\$10,134} = 3.7\%.$
5.	Cost of Goods Sold to Sales	$= \dfrac{\$10,071}{\$15,763} = 63.9\%.$	$= \dfrac{\$6,592}{\$10,134} = 65.0\%.$
6.	Selling and Administration Expenses to Sales	$= \dfrac{\$4,377}{\$15,763} = 27.8\%.$	$= \dfrac{\$2,640}{\$10,134} = 26.1\%.$
7.	Interest Expenses to Sales	$= \dfrac{\$26}{\$15,763} = 0.2\%.$	$= \dfrac{\$149}{\$10,134} = 1.5\%.$
8.	Income Tax Expenses to Sales	$= \dfrac{\$539}{\$15,763} = 3.4\%.$	$= \dfrac{\$411}{\$10,134} = 4.1\%.$
9.	Accounts Receivable Turnover	$= \dfrac{\$15,763}{0.5(\$0 + \$0)} = $ N/A.	$= \dfrac{\$10,134}{0.5(\$355 + \$176)} = 38.2$ times per year.
10.	Inventory Turnover	$= \dfrac{\$10,071}{0.5(\$1,575 + \$1,796)} = 6.0$ times per year.	$= \dfrac{\$6,592}{0.5(\$1,251 + \$1,770)} = 4.4$ times per year.

7.27 continued.

11. Fixed Asset Turnover

$$= \frac{\$15{,}763}{0.5(\$3{,}267 + \$3{,}197)} = 4.9 \text{ times per year.}$$

$$\frac{\$10{,}134}{0.5(\$1{,}862 + \$1{,}862)} = 5.4 \text{ times per year.}$$

12. Return on Equity

$$= \frac{\$867}{0.5(\$4{,}274 + \$5{,}174)} = 18.4\%.$$

$$\frac{\$718}{0.5(\$2{,}219 + \$2{,}955)} = 27.8\%.$$

13. Financial Leverage Ratio

$$= \frac{0.5(\$7{,}838 + \$8{,}544)}{0.5(\$4{,}274 + \$5{,}174)} = 1.7.$$

$$\frac{0.5(\$7{,}437 + \$7{,}093)}{0.5(\$2{,}219 + \$2{,}955)} = 2.8.$$

14. Current Ratio:
August 31, 2012

$$= \frac{\$5{,}029}{\$2{,}272} = 2.2.$$

$$\frac{\$2{,}771}{\$1{,}709} = 1.6.$$

August 31, 2013

$$= \frac{\$4{,}086}{\$2{,}433} = 1.7.$$

$$\frac{\$2{,}919}{\$1{,}374} = 2.1.$$

15. Quick Ratio:
August 31, 2012

$$= \frac{\$2{,}644}{\$2{,}272} = 1.2.$$

$$\frac{(\$500 + \$176)}{\$1{,}709} = 0.4.$$

August 31, 2013

$$= \frac{\$1{,}939}{\$2{,}433} = 0.8.$$

$$\frac{(\$1{,}018 + \$355)}{\$1{,}374} = 1.0.$$

16. Days Accounts Receivable

$$= \frac{365}{0} = \text{N/A.}$$

$$\frac{365}{38.2} = 9.6.$$

17. Days Inventory

$$= \frac{365}{6.0} = 60.8.$$

$$\frac{365}{4.4} = 83.0.$$

18. Accounts Payable Turnover

$$= \frac{(\$10{,}071 + \$1{,}575 - \$1{,}796)}{0.5(\$1{,}006 + \$772)} = 11.1.$$

$$\frac{(\$6{,}592 + \$1{,}251 - \$1{,}770)}{0.5(\$517 + \$593)} = 10.9.$$

7.27 continued.

19. Days Accounts Payable $= \dfrac{365}{11.1} = 32.9.$ $\qquad \dfrac{365}{10.9} = 33.5.$

20. Cash Flow from Operations to Current Liabilities $= \dfrac{\$2,081}{0.5(\$2,433 + \$2,272)} = 88.5\%.$ $\qquad \dfrac{\$765}{0.5(\$1,374 + \$1,709)} = 49.6\%.$

21. Liabilities to Assets Ratio:

August 31, 2012 $= \dfrac{\$3,370}{\$8,544} = 39.4\%.$ $\qquad \dfrac{\$4,138}{\$7,093} = 58.3\%.$

August 31, 2013 $= \dfrac{\$3,564}{\$7,838} = 45.5\%.$ $\qquad \dfrac{\$5,218}{\$7,437} = 70.2\%.$

22. Long-Term Debt Ratio:

August 31, 2012 $= \dfrac{\$188}{\$8,544} = 2.2\%.$ $\qquad \dfrac{\$1,665}{\$7,093} = 23.5\%.$

August 31, 2013 $= \dfrac{\$50}{\$7,838} = 0.6\%.$ $\qquad \dfrac{\$2,905}{\$7,437} = 39.1\%.$

23. Debt-Equity Ratio:

August 31, 2012 $= \dfrac{\$188}{\$5,174} = 3.6\%.$ $\qquad \dfrac{\$1,665}{\$2,955} = 56.3\%.$

August 31, 2013 $= \dfrac{\$50}{\$4,274} = 1.2\%.$ $\qquad \dfrac{\$2,905}{\$2,219} = 130.9\%.$

24. Cash Flow from Operations to Total Liabilities $= \dfrac{\$2,081}{0.5(\$3,564 + \$3,370)} = 60.0\%.$ $\qquad \dfrac{\$765}{0.5(\$5,218 + \$4,138)} = 16.4\%.$

25. Interest Coverage Ratio $= \dfrac{(\$867 + \$539 + \$26)}{\$26} = 55.1 \text{ times.}$ $\qquad \dfrac{(\$718 + \$411 + \$149)}{\$149} = 8.6 \text{ times.}$

Solutions

7.28   (Depkline plc; interpreting profitability and risk ratios.)

a. The increasing profit margin results from an increase in the investment income to sales percentage and to a decrease in the selling and administrative expense to sales percentage. The problem does not provide sufficient information to interpret the increasing investment income percentage. Growth in sales perhaps permits the firm to spread relatively fixed administrative expenses over a larger sales base and, thereby, reduce the selling and administrative expense to sales percentage.

b. The decreased total assets turnover in 2013 results from declines in the accounts receivable, inventory, and fixed asset turnovers. Sales grew at only 6.3% in 2013, after growing 7.6% in 2011 and 8.5% in 2012. Perhaps the firm expected faster growth in sales in 2013 than occurred and geared its plant capacity, inventory levels, and credit policies to such a faster growth.

c. The slower accounts receivable and inventory turnovers should have led to an increase in these current assets. A decline in the current ratio likely therefore occurs because of increased current liabilities. The days accounts payable declined between 2012 and 2013 and, therefore, is not the cause of an increase in current liabilities. Observe that the liabilities to assets ratio increased 5.8 percentage points (= 68.0% − 62.2%), whereas the long-term debt ratio increased 4.1 percentage points (= 22.8% − 18.7%). The remaining increase in the liabilities to assets ratio likely relates to increases in current liabilities.

d. The two cash flow ratios declined between 2011 and 2012 and increased between 2012 and 2013. The debt ratios indicate that both total debt and long-term debt decreased between 2011 and 2012 and increased between 2012 and 2013. These changes in debt levels should have had the opposite effects on the cash flow ratios than those observed. Thus, the decline in the cash flow ratio between 2011 and 2012 likely resulted from a decline in cash flow from operations and the increase between 2012 and 2013 likely resulted from an increase in cash flow from operations. The problem does not provide sufficient information to examine cash flow from operations further.

7.29   (Scantania; interpreting profitability and risk ratios.)

a. The increase in the profit margin results from decreases in the cost of goods sold to sales percentage and the selling and administrative expense to sales percentage. Both of these expenses include depreciation and other fixed costs. Scantania experienced rapid sales growth in all three years and likely benefited from economies of scale as it spread these fixed costs over a larger sales base. Investment and net financing income as a percentage of revenues both declined and would not account for the increased profit margin.

b. Economies of scale (see the discussion in Part *a.* above) explains the decreased cost of goods sold to sales percentage but not the increasing inventory turnover. Any benefits from economies of scale affect both the numerator and denominator of the inventory turnover ratio. One possibility is that the firm instituted just-in-time manufacturing, which reduced raw materials and finished goods inventories and lowered inventory-carrying costs. Another possibility is that the sales mix shifted to higher margin, made-to-order vehicles. The high growth rates in sales also suggest that Scantania enjoyed pricing advantages for its products and experienced little difficulty in selling its products quickly.

c. The growth rate in sales in 2013 was higher than in 2011 and 2012. Perhaps Scantania had geared its productive capacity for 2013 for sales growth of approximately 12%. With a 19.4% sales growth in 2013, Scantania had to utilize its plant capacity more intensely, driving up the fixed-asset turnover. Another possibility is that Scantania enjoyed pricing advantages in its markets and was able to increase sales revenue without having to raise production levels.

d. Scantania must have experienced increases in cash, investments, or other assets besides accounts receivable, inventories, or fixed assets. The firm's annual report indicates that other noncurrent assets increased during these years.

e. Cash flow from operations likely increased as a result of the increase in the accounts receivable and inventory turnovers and the decrease in the days accounts payable. The explanation does not appear to be in the denominator of these cash flow ratios because total liabilities to assets did not change significantly and the long-term debt ratio declined.

7.29 continued.

    f.   The increase in the accounts receivable and inventory turnovers moderated the increase in current assets for these two items, thereby affecting the numerator of these ratios. The firm might have sold marketable securities and used the cash proceeds to acquire property, plant and equipment, to pay dividends, or other purposes. Current liabilities likely increased as a percentage of total assets, given that the liabilities to assets ratio increased 2.6 percentage points (= 72.9% – 70.3%), whereas the long-term debt ratio increased only 1.4 percentage points (= 21.7% – 20.3%).

7.30   (Detective analysis—identify company.)

There are various approaches to this exercise. One approach begins with a particular company, identifies unique financial characteristics (for example, steel companies have a high proportion of property, plant, and equipment among their assets), and then searches the common-size financial data to identify the company with that unique characteristic. Another approach begins with the common-size data, identifies unusual financial statement relationships (for example, Firm (12) has a high proportion of cash, marketable securities, and receivables among its assets), and then looks over the list of companies to identify the one most likely to have that unusual financial statement relationship. This teaching note employs both approaches.

Firm (12)—The high proportions of cash, marketable securities, and receivables for Firm (12) suggest that it is Fortis, the Dutch insurance and banking company. Insurance companies receive cash from premiums each year and invest the funds in various investment vehicles until needed to pay insurance claims. They recognize premium revenue from the cash received and investment income from investments each year. They must match against this revenue an appropriate portion of the expected cost of insurance claims from policies in force during the year. Fortis includes this amount on the line labeled Operating Expenses in Exhibit 7.28. Operating revenues also includes interest revenue on loans made. One might ask: Why does Fortis have such a high proportion of financing in the form of current liabilities? This balance sheet category includes the estimated cost of claims not yet paid from insurance in force. It also includes deposits by customers to its banks. One might also ask: What types of quality of earnings issues arise for a company like Fortis? One issue relates to the measurement of insurance claims expense each period.

7.30 continued.

The ultimate cost of claims will not be known with certainty until customers make claims and the firm makes settlements. Prior to that time, Fortis must estimate what that cost will be. The need to make such estimates creates the opportunity to manage earnings and lowers the quality of earnings. Another issue relates to estimated uncollectible loans. Fortis recognizes interest revenue from loans each year and must match against this revenue the cost of any loans that will not be repaid. The need to make such estimates also provides management with an opportunity to manage earnings and therefore lowers the quality of earnings.

Firms (2), (3), (5), and (9)—There are four firms with research and development (R&D) expenses, (2), (3), (5) and (9). These are likely to be Nestlé, Roche Holding, Sun Microsystems, and Toyota Motor in some combination.

Roche Holding and Sun Microsystems are more technology oriented and therefore likely to have a higher percentage of R&D to sales. This suggests that they are Firms (2) and (9) in some combination. The inventories of Firm (9) turn over more slowly at 1.4 times per year (= 27.2/20) than those of Firm (2) at 16.1 times per year (= 45.2/2.8). Firm (9) is also more capital intensive than firm (2). This suggests that Firm (2) is Sun Microsystems and Firm (9) is Roche Holdings. Sun uses only 11.8 cents in fixed assets for each dollar of sales generated. These ratios are consistent with Sun's strategy of outsourcing most of its manufacturing operations. The inventory turnover of Roche is consistent with the making of fewer production runs for each pharmaceutical product to gain production efficiencies. The manufacture of pharmaceuticals is highly automated, consistent with the slower fixed asset turnover of Roche. These two firms have the highest profit margins of the twelve firms studied. Sun is a technology leader in engineering workstations and servers. Roche sells products protected by patents. These advantages permit the firms to achieve high profit margins. Roche has a very high proportion of its assets in cash and marketable securities. It generates interest revenue from these investments, which it includes in other revenues. It is interesting to observe the relatively small cost of goods sold to sales percentage for Roche. The manufacturing cost of pharmaceutical products primarily includes the cost of the chemical raw materials, which machines combine into various drugs. Pharmaceutical firms must price their products significantly above manufacturing costs to recoup their investments in R&D. Note also that Sun has very little long-term debt in

Solutions

7.30 continued.

its capital structure. Computer products have short product life cycles. Lenders are reluctant to lend for a long period because of the concern for technological obsolescence. Computer companies that outsource their production also have few assets that can serve as collateral for long-term borrowing.

This leaves Firms (3) and (5) as Nestlé and Toyota Motor in some combination. Firm (5) has a larger amount of receivables relative to sales than Firm (3), consistent with Toyota Motor providing financing for its customers' purchases of automobiles. Nestlé will have receivables from wholesalers and distributors of its food products as well, but not to the extent of the multi-year financing of automobiles. The inventory turnover of Firm (3) is 4.5 times a year (= 44.5%/9.9%), whereas the inventory turnover of Firm (5) is 10.6 times a year (= 68%/6.4%). One might at first expect a food processor to have a much higher inventory turnover than an automobile manufacturer, suggesting that Firm (3) is Toyota Motor and Firm (5) is Nestlé. Toyota Motor, however, has implemented just-in-time inventory systems, which speed its inventory turnover. Nestlé tends to manufacture chocolates to meet seasonal demands, and therefore carries inventory somewhat longer than one might expect. Firm (3) has a much higher percentage of selling and administrative expense to sales than Firm (5). Both of these firms advertise their products heavily. It is difficult to know why one would have a substantially different percentage than the other. The profit margin of Firm (3) is substantially higher than that of Firm (5). The auto industry is more competitive than at least the chocolate side of the food industry. However, other food products encounter extensive competition. Firm (5) has a high proportion of intercorporate investments. Japanese companies tend to operate within groups, called *kieretsu*. The members of the group make investments in the securities of other firms within the group. This would suggest that Firm (5) is Toyota Motor. Another characteristic of Japanese companies is their heavier use of debt in their capital structures. One of the members of these Japanese corporate groups is typically a bank, which lends to group members as needed. With this more-or-less assured source of funds, Japanese firms tend to take on more debt. Although the ratios give somewhat confusing signals, Firm (3) is Nestlé and Firm (5) is Toyota Motor.

7.30 continued.

Firms (10) and (11)—Firms (10) and (11) are unique in that they are both very fixed-asset intensive. Electric utilities and telecommunication firms both utilize fixed assets in the delivery of their services. Firm (11) is the most fixed-asset intensive of the two firms and carries a higher proportion of long-term debt. Electric-generating plants are more fixed-asset intensive than the infrastructure needed for distribution of telecommunication services. This would suggest that Firm (10) is Deutsche Telekon and Firm (11) is Tokyo Electric Power. The telecommunication industry is going through deregulation whereas Tokyo Electric Power still has a monopoly position in Japan. Thus, the selling and administrative expense to operating revenues percentage for Deutsche Telekon is substantially higher than for Tokyo Electric Power.

Firms (6) and (8)—Two of the remaining industries are also capital intensive, but not to the extent of Deutsche Telekon and Tokyo Electric Power. These firms are Accor, a hotel group, and Arbed-Acier, a steel manufacturer. Firms (6) and (8) require the next highest fixed assets per dollar of sales after Firms (10 and (11). Thus, Firms (6) and (8) are Accor and Arbed-Acier in some combination. Firm (8) has virtually no inventories, whereas Firm (6) has substantial inventories. This suggests that Firm (6) is Arbed-Acier, the steel company, and Firm (8) is Accor, the hotel group. Accor has grown in recent years by acquiring established hotel chains. Accor allocates a portion of the purchase price to goodwill in its acquisitions, which accounts for its higher percentage for Other Assets. Steel products are commodities, whereas hotels have some brand recognition appeal. These factors may explain the higher profit margin for Firm (6) than for Firm (8).

Firm (7)—Firm (7) has an unusually high proportion of its assets in receivables and in current liabilities. Although this pattern would be typical for a commercial bank, we identified Firm (12) earlier as the financial institution. The pattern is also typical for an advertising agency, which creates and sells advertising copy for clients (for which it has a current receivable) and purchasing time and space on various media to display it (for which it has a current liability). Additional evidence that Firm (7) is Interpublic Group is the high percentage for Other Assets, representing goodwill from acquisitions. Firm (7) also has a relatively high profit margin percentage, reflective of its ability to differentiate its creative services.

7.30 continued.

Firm (1)—Firm (1) is distinguished by its high cost of goods sold to sales and small profit margin percentages. This pattern suggests commodity products with low value added. Of the remaining firms, this characterizes a grocery business. Firm (1) is Carrefour. Its combination of a rapid receivables turnover of 11.8 times per year (= 100/8.5) and rapid inventory turnover of 8.9 times per year (= 87.8/9.9) are also consistent with a grocery business. Current liabilities comprise more than half of its financing. Current assets make up a similarly high proportion of its current assets.

Firm (4)—The remaining firm is Firm (4), which is Marks & Spencer the department store chain. Firm (4) has substantial receivables, consistent with having a credit card.

7.31 (Bullseye Corporation; preparing pro forma financial statements.)

a. See attached pro forma financial statements and related financial ratios (pages 7-41 to 7-46).

b. Bullseye Corporation needs to increase borrowing. Cash flow from operations is positive in each year. Thus, the financing need does not appear to be short term. Although Bullseye Corporation increases long-term debt at the growth rate in property, plant, and equipment, the amount invested in property, plant, and equipment at the end of fiscal 2013 of $25,908 million is larger than long-term debt at the end of fiscal 2013 of $16,939. Growing long-term debt at the same growth rate as property, plant, and equipment does not adequately finance the fixed assets. If we assume that long-term debt increases at 2 times the growth rate in property, plant, and equipment, long-term debt (after reclassifications to current liabilities), grows 20% (= 2 times 10%) annually and provides adequate cash.

c. The pro forma financial statement ratios indicate a decreasing ROE. The projected profit margin and total assets turnover ratios are stable. The declining ROE results from a declining capital structure leverage ratio. Even if we grow long-term debt at 2 times the growth rate in property, plant, and equipment (see Part *b.* above), the financial leverage ratio and ROE decline. The reason for the declining

7.31 c. continued.

financial leverage ratio is that retained earnings grows faster than borrowing. Still further increases in borrowing to stabilize the financial leverage ratio results in too much cash on the balance sheet. Bullseye Corporation would then need to increase its dividends or repurchase common stock with the excess cash. To stabilize the capital structure leverage ratio, Bullseye Corporation needs to increase borrowing, increase the growth rate in dividends, or repurchase common stock.

We used a spreadsheet program that rounds to many decimal places to generate the following pro forma financial statements. Rounding causes some of the subtotals and totals to differ from the sum of the amounts that comprise them.

BULLSEYE CORPORATION
PRO FORMA INCOME STATEMENT
YEAR ENDED DECEMBER 31
(amounts in millions of US$)

	2013	2014	2015	2016	2017	2018
Sales Revenue........	$ 61,471	$ 67,003	$ 73,034	$ 79,607	$ 86,771	$ 94,581
Other Revenues	1,918	2,010	2,191	2,388	2,603	2,837
Total Revenues ..	$ 63,389	$ 69,013	$ 75,225	$ 81,995	$ 89,374	$ 97,418
Expenses:						
Cost of Goods Sold..............	$ 41,895	$ 45,629	$ 49,736	$ 54,212	$ 59,091	$ 64,409
Selling and Administration.	16,200	17,421	18,989	20,698	22,561	24,591
Interest..............	669	934	911	906	894	913
Income Taxes	1,776	1,911	2,124	2,348	2,595	2,852
Total Expenses	$ 60,540	$ 65,895	$ 71,760	$ 78,164	$ 85,141	$ 92,766
Net Income............	$ 2,849	$ 3,118	$ 3,465	$ 3,831	$ 4,233	$ 4,652
Less Dividends	442	513	595	690	800	928
Increase in Retained Earnings .	$ 2,407	$ 2,606	$ 2,870	$ 3,141	$ 3,433	$ 3,724

(See Following Page for Assumptions)

7.31 c. continued.

Assumptions:

Growth Rate of Sales ...	9.0%	
Other Revenues	3.0%	of sales
Cost of Goods Sold	68.1%	of sales
Selling and Administration Expense	26.0%	of sales
Interest Expense	5.0%	on average amount of interest-bearing debt
Income Tax Rate	38.0%	of income before income taxes
Dividends	16.0%	growth rate

7-42

7.31 c. continued.

BULLSEYE CORPORATION
PRO FORMA BALANCE SHEET
DECEMBER 31
(amounts in millions of US$)

	2013	2014	2015	2016	2017	2018
Cash	$ 2,450	$ 1,778	$ 768	$ 680	$ (668)	$ 292
Accounts Receivable	8,054	8,779	9,569	10,430	11,369	12,392
Inventories	6,780	7,390	8,055	8,780	9,571	10,432
Prepayments	1,622	1,768	1,927	2,101	2,290	2,496
Total Current Assets	$ 18,906	$ 19,715	$ 20,319	$ 21,991	$ 22,561	$ 25,612
Property, Plant, and Equipment	25,908	28,499	31,349	34,484	37,932	41,725
Other Assets	1,559	1,559	1,559	1,559	1,559	1,559
Total Assets	$ 46,373	$ 49,773	$ 53,227	$ 58,033	$ 62,052	$ 68,896
Accounts Payable	$ 6,721	$ 7,507	$ 8,001	$ 8,902	$ 9,523	$ 10,561
Notes Payable	0	0	0	0	0	0
Current Portion—Long-Term Debt	1,964	1,951	1,251	2,236	107	2,251
Other Current Liabilities	3,097	3,376	3,680	4,011	4,372	4,765
Total Current Liabilities	$ 11,782	$ 12,833	$ 12,932	$ 15,149	$ 14,001	$ 17,577
Long-Term Debt	16,939	16,487	16,759	15,976	17,456	16,725
Other Noncurrent Liabilities	2,345	2,556	2,786	3,037	3,310	3,608
Total Liabilities	$ 31,066	$ 31,876	$ 32,477	$ 34,162	$ 34,767	$ 37,910
Common Stock	$ 68	$ 68	$ 68	$ 68	$ 68	$ 68
Additional Paid-in Capital	2,656	2,656	2,656	2,656	2,656	2,656
Retained Earnings	12,761	15,367	18,237	21,378	24,812	28,536
Accumulated Other Comprehensive Income	(178)	(194)	(211)	(231)	(251)	(274)
Total Shareholders' Equity	$ 15,307	$ 17,897	$ 20,750	$ 23,872	$ 27,284	$ 30,986
Total Liabilities and Shareholders' Equity	$ 46,373	$ 49,773	$ 53,227	$ 58,033	$ 62,052	$ 68,896

(See Following Page for Assumptions)

7.31 c. continued.

(Assumptions for Pro Forma Balance Sheet)

Assumptions:

Cash	PLUG					
Accounts Receivable	Sales Growth Rate					
Inventory......................	Sales Growth Rate					
Prepayments	Sales Growth Rate					
Property, Plant, and Equipment................	10.0% Growth Rate					
Other Assets	0.0% Growth Rate					
Accounts Payable Turnover	6.4	6.5	6.5	6.5	6.5	6.5
Merchandise Purchases		46,240	50,401	54,937	59,882	65,271
Average Payables........		7,114	7,754	8,452	9,213	10,042
Notes Payable	No change					
Other Current Liabilities	Sales Growth Rate					
Long-Term Debt	Property, Plant, and Equipment Growth Rate					
Other Noncurrent Liabilities	Sales Growth Rate					
Common Stock, APIC	0.0% Growth Rate					
Accumulated Other Comprehensive Income	Sales Growth Rate					

7.31 c. continued.

BULLSEYE CORPORATION
PRO FORMA STATEMENT OF CASH FLOWS
FOR THE YEAR ENDED DECEMBER 31
(amounts in millions of US$)

Cash Flow Statement	2013	2014	2015	2016	2017	2018
Operations:						
Net Income	$ 2,849	$ 3,118	$ 3,465	$ 3,831	$ 4,233	$ 4,653
Depreciation	1,659	1,825	2,007	2,208	2,429	2,672
Other	485	195	213	232	253	275
(Inc.)/Dec. in Accounts Receivable	(602)	(725)	(790)	(861)	(939)	(1,023)
(Inc.)/Dec. in Inventory	(525)	(610)	(665)	(725)	(790)	(861)
(Inc.)/Dec. in Prepayments	(38)	(146)	(159)	(173)	(189)	(206)
Inc./(Dec.) in Accounts Payable	111	786	495	901	621	1,038
Inc./(Dec.) in Other Current Liabilities	186	279	304	331	361	393
Cash Flow from Operations	$ 4,125	$ 4,722	$ 4,869	$ 5,743	$ 5,979	$ 6,940
Investing:						
Acquisition of Property, Plant, and Equipment	$ (4,369)	$ (4,416)	$ (4,857)	$ (5,343)	$ (5,877)	$ (6,465)
Other Investing	0	0	0	0	0	0
Cash Flow from Investing	$ (4,369)	$ (4,416)	$ (4,857)	$ (5,343)	$ (5,877)	$ (6,465)
Financing:						
Inc./(Dec.) in Short-Term Borrowing	$ 500	$ 0	$ 0	$ 0	$ 0	$ 0
Inc./(Dec.) in Long-Term Borrowing	6,291	(465)	(427)	201	(649)	1,413
Inc./(Dec.) in Common Stock	(2,598)	0	0	0	0	0
Dividends	(442)	(513)	(595)	(690)	(800)	(928)
Other Financing	(44)	0	0	0	0	0
Cash Flow from Financing	$ 3,707	$ (978)	$ (1,022)	$ (489)	$ (1,449)	$ 485
Change in Cash	$ 1,637	$ (672)	$ (1,010)	$ (88)	$ (1,348)	$ 960
Cash, Beginning of Year	813	2,450	1,778	768	680	(668)
Cash, End of Year	$ 2,450	$ 1,778	$ 768	$ 680	$ (668)	$ 292
Cash Balance from Balance Sheet	2,450	1,778	768	680	(668)	292
Difference	$ 0	$ 0	$ 0	$ 0	$ 0	$ 0

7.31 c. continued.

(Assumptions for Pro Forma Statement of Cash Flows)

Assumptions:

Depreciation Growth Rate	Same as Property, Plant, and Equipment
Other Operating Add-backs........................	Change in Other Noncurrent Liabilities and Change in Accumulated Other Comprehensive Income
Other Investing Cash Flows	Change in Other Noncurrent Assets
Other Financing Cash Flows	Zero

BULLSEYE CORPORATION
PRO FORMA FINANCIAL RATIOS

	2013	2014	2015	2016	2017	2018
Return on Assets.....................	6.7%	6.5%	6.7%	6.9%	7.0%	7.1%
Profit Margin	4.6%	4.7%	4.7%	4.8%	4.9%	4.9%
Total Assets Turnover.............	1.4	1.4	1.4	1.4	1.4	1.4
Cost of Goods Sold/Sales..........	68.2%	68.1%	68.1%	68.1%	68.1%	68.1%
Selling and Administrative Expenses/Sales	26.4	26.0%	26.0%	26.0%	26.0%	26.0%
Interest Expense/Sales	1.1%	1.4%	1.2%	1.1%	1.0%	1.0%
Income Tax Expense/Sales	2.9%	2.9%	2.9%	2.9%	3.0%	3.0%
Accounts Receivable Turn-over Ratio	8.6	8.0	8.0	8.0	8.0	8.0
Inventory Turnover Ratio	6.4	6.4	6.4	6.4	6.4	6.4
Fixed-Assets Turnover Ratio.................................	2.5	2.5	2.4	2.4	2.4	2.4
Return on Equity	18.4%	18.8%	17.9%	17.2%	16.6%	16.0%
Financial Leverage Ratio	2.7	2.9	2.7	2.5	2.3	2.2
Current Ratio	1.60	1.54	1.57	1.45	1.61	1.46
Quick Ratio.............................	0.89	0.82	0.80	0.73	0.76	0.72
Cash Flow from Operations/Current Liabilities	36.0%	38.4%	37.8%	40.9%	41.0%	44.0%
Accounts Payable Turnover Ratio.....................................	6.4	6.5	6.5	6.5	6.5	6.5
Liabilities to Assets Ratio	67.0%	64.0%	61.0%	58.9%	56.0%	55.0%
Long-Term Debt Ratio	36.5%	33.1%	31.5%	27.5%	28.1%	24.3%
Debt-Equity Ratio....................	110.7%	92.1%	80.8%	66.9%	64.0%	54.0%
Cash Flow from Operations/Total Liabilities	15.3%	15.0%	15.1%	17.2%	17.3%	19.1%
Interest Coverage Ratio...........	7.9	6.4	7.1	7.8	8.6	9.2

CHAPTER 8

REVENUE RECOGNITION, RECEIVABLES, AND ADVANCES FROM CUSTOMERS

Questions, Exercises, and Problems: Answers and Solutions

8.1   See the text or the glossary at the end of the book.

8.2   The cost recovery method defers revenue recognition past the point where the seller has delivered goods to the customer. It is used when there is considerable uncertainty about the amount of cash to be collected. There is typically no uncertainty about the cost to the seller because the customer typically has possession of the goods. The completed contract method is applied to long-term contracts in which the outcome (either the cost to be incurred by the seller or the amount to be collected or both) is uncertain. The cost recovery method recognizes revenues equal to cash received and sets expenses equal to revenues until all costs are recovered, whereas the completed contract recognizes neither revenue nor expense until the entire contract is completed. The completed contract recognizes revenue at the point where the seller delivers the promised item to the customer.

8.3   Both approaches apply accounting criteria to determine the amount and timing of revenue recognition when an arrangement with a customer (a contract) is not yet complete. The percentage-of-completion method uses the cost of work performed to date as the criterion. The accounting for a multiple-element arrangement first determines the number of separable components (or deliverables) in the contract; the criterion for revenue recognition timing is the performance of a deliverable and the amount is based on the relative selling price of the deliverable, as a portion of the total contract price.

8.4   The gross amount of accounts receivable is the amount owed by customers. The allowance account provides a rough estimate of the credit quality of those customers; changes in the allowance shed light on changes in the credit quality of customers.

8.5   a. Most businesses ought not to set credit policies so stringent that they have no uncollectible accounts. To do so would require extremely careful screening of customers, which is costly, and the probable loss of many customers who will take their business elsewhere. So long as the total revenues collected from credit sales, including finance charges and other fees, exceed the sum of both selling costs (including the costs of uncollectible accounts) and the cost of goods sold on credit, the firm should not be concerned if some percentage of its accounts receivable are uncollectible.

       b. When the larger uncollectible accounts result from a credit-granting policy that increases income overall. A business might liberalize its credit policy by extending credit to a new group of customers with the intent of generating net revenues from the new credit customers that exceed the cost of goods sold to them and the selling expenses of executing the sales, including the expenses of uncollectible accounts. The extension of credit to new customers can increase net income even though it results in more uncollectible accounts.

       c. A higher percentage of uncollectible accounts is better when the overall value to the firm of the receipts from selling goods and services to customers exceeds the total costs of those sales, including the costs of uncollectible accounts.

8.6   If a firm computes the Bad Debt Expense amount at the end of the accounting period but writes off specific accounts receivable during the period as information about uncollectible accounts becomes available, then the Allowance for Uncollectibles will have a debit balance whenever the amount of accounts written off during the period exceeds the opening credit balance in the Allowance account. Firms prepare balance sheets only after making adjusting entries. Both the Bad Debt Expense and the Allowance for Uncollectibles accounts must be brought up to date with appropriate adjusting entries before preparing the balance sheet. Because the Allowance for Uncollectibles account is an asset contra, it will always show a credit (or perhaps a zero) balance after making adjusting entries.

8.7   Manufacturing firms typically do not identify a customer or establish a firm selling price until they sell products. Thus, these firms do not satisfy the criteria for revenue recognition while production is taking place. In contrast, construction companies might identify a customer and establish a contract price before construction begins. In addition, the production process for a manufacturing firm is usually shorter than for a construction firm. The recognition of revenue at the time of production or at the time of sale does not result in a significantly different pattern of income for a manufacturing firm. For a construction company, the pattern of income could differ significantly.

8.8   Under the installment method, accountants recognize proportionate parts of the costs incurred as expenses each period as they recognize proportionate parts of the selling price as revenues. Under the cost-recovery-first method, costs match dollar for dollar with revenues until revenues equal total costs. Thus, the income patterns differ because of the *expense*-recognition pattern, not the revenue-recognition pattern.

8.9   Application of the installment method requires a reasonably accurate estimate of the total amount of cash the firm expects to receive from customers, but a firm cannot use this method unless cash collections are uncertain. The cost-recovery-first method does not require such an estimate.

8.10   First, the obligation to customers in the event the firm does not publish the magazines is $45,000. Second, recognition of a liability of $32,000 requires a remaining credit of $13,000 to some other account. Recognizing the $13,000 as income is inappropriate because the publisher has not yet provided the required services. Including the $13,000 in some type of deferred income account (a liability) has the same effect on total liabilities as reporting the Advances from Customers at $45,000.

8.11   Both customer returns and bad debts ultimately affect the net cash collected from customers. In accounting for estimated sales returns, the firm debits a contra revenue account (thus reducing net revenues), and in accounting for bad debt expense, the firm typically debits an expense account, which does not affect net revenues. The accounting is similar in that income is reduced in the period in which sales occur, not in the period in which the customer returns an item or when a customer's account is determined to be uncollectible.

8.12   Deferred Gross Margin is the difference between the Account Receivable from the customer (the amount of cash that the firm will collect if the customer pays all that is owed) and the seller's cost (the amount that will be recognized as cost of goods sold). Thus, the amount recognized as Deferred Gross Margin will be recognized as the margin on the sale if the customer pays in full. Conceptually, Deferred Gross Margin is not a liability because the seller has no further obligations to the customer. As a practical matter, many firms classify this account as a liability.

8.13   (Revenue recognition for various businesses.)

We have found this question to be an excellent one for class discussion because it forces the student to think about both revenue *and* expense timing and measurement questions. It also generates active student interest. Some of the items are relatively obvious, whereas others require more discussion.

a.   Time of sale; there may be an allowance for sales returns.

b.   Probably as work progresses using the percentage-of-completion method. Students might discuss whether the identity of the customer matters, for example, the U.S. government versus a relatively weak government with lower credit quality. This question gets at the issue of whether the amount of cash the firm will receive is subject to reasonably accurate estimation.

c.   Probably as the firm collects cash using the installment method. U.S. GAAP (**Codification Topic 976-605**) provides special guidance for retail land sales that is beyond the scope of this textbook.

d.   At the time of sale.

e.   At the time the firm picks citrus products and delivers them to customers. We ask students if their response would change if the citrus firm had a five-year contract at a set price to supply a particular quantity of citrus products to a citrus processor. The issue here is whether, given uncertainties about future weather conditions, the citrus grower will be able to make delivery on the contract. Citrus fruit is an example of a biological asset; IFRS but not U.S. GAAP provides special guidance for biological assets that is beyond the scope of this textbook (IAS 41, *Agriculture*, revised 2003).

8.13 continued.

   f.   U.S. GAAP (**Codification Topic 926**) but not IFRS provides special guidance for film and similar arrangements. The firm should not recognize revenue until it meets all of the following conditions:

1. The firm knows the sales price.

2. The firm knows the cost of the film or can reasonably estimate the loss.

3. The firm is reasonably assured as to the collectibility of the selling price.

4. A licensee has accepted the film in accordance with the license agreement.

5. The film is available (that is, the licensee can exercise the right to use the film and all conflicting licenses have expired).

Revenue recognition from the sale of rights to the television network is appropriate as soon as the firm meets these conditions even though the license period is three years. The firm cannot recognize revenues from the sale of subsequent rights to others until the three-year licensing period has expired. An important question in this example is when to recognize the production costs as an expense. Should the firm recognize all of the costs as an expense on the initial sale to the television network? Or, should it treat some portion of the costs as an asset, matched against future sales of license rights? Most accountants would probably match all of the costs against revenue from the television network license agreement, unless the firm has signed other license agreements for periods beginning after the initial three-year period at the same time as the television license agreement.

   g.   At the time of sale of each house to a specific buyer.

8.13 continued.

h. At the time of sale to a specific buyer at a set price. This will vary, depending on who owns the whiskey during the aging process. We pose the following situation: Suppose a particular whiskey producer has an on-going supplier relationship with a whiskey distributor. The quantity purchased by the distributor and the price set depend on supply and demand conditions at the time aged whiskey is brought to the market. The supplier always purchases some minimum quantity. When should the firm recognize revenue? This question gets at the issue of measuring revenue in a reasonably reliable manner.

i. After a loan is made, with the passage of time.

j. The alternatives here are (1) as customers make reservations, (2) as customers incur a liability or pay cash, or (3) as the agency receives cash from commissions. The second alternative is probably best. However, past experience may provide sufficient evidence as to the proportion of reservations that customers ultimately confirm to justify earlier recognition.

k. At the completion of the printing activity and delivery of the product to the customer.

l. The issue here is whether to recognize revenue when the firm sells coupons to food stores or when customers turn in the coupons for redemption. One might argue for revenue recognition at the time of sale of the coupons, since the seller must have some estimate of the redemption rate in setting the price for the sale of the coupons.

m. At the time the wholesaler delivers food products to stores.

n. The issue here is whether to recognize revenue while the livestock is growing. A grower of timber faces a similar issue. This question is similar to Part *h.* above.

o. One alternative is to apply the percentage-of-completion method. In practice firms use several methods.

8.14   (Income recognition for various business arrangements.)

a. Company A is selling software and access to data and other software. At the time of initial delivery of the software, Company A has been paid, so the price is fixed and collectibility is not a problem. Company A has a two-year obligation remaining, to provide both an active Web site and updates. If the firm can reasonably disaggregate the initial selling price into the portion applicable to the software and the portion applicable to the later services, then it could recognize the software sales as revenues at the time of delivery and then recognize the remaining selling price over the two-year period as customers use the Web-accessed services. If not, then recognizing the revenue ratably over the two-year period seems more appropriate. In addition, IFRS would require that Company A be able to reliably measure its costs to be incurred.

b. The issue for Company B is the ability of the newly formed SAPs to pay for the software. Their ability to pay depends on the number of customers they sign up and the collection of cash from these customers. Although Company B has performed and has transferred the risks and rewards of ownership to the customer, there is uncertainty about the amount of cash that will be collected. Therefore, Company B may apply a revenue recognition method that is based on cash collections.

c. The issue for Company C is whether it satisfies the criterion that revenues must be "earned" at the beginning of the two-year period (collectibility of cash is not an issue). That is, Company C may have to recognize revenue as it performs its obligation to provide access over two years.

d. Assuming that collectibility is not an issue, Company D will earn the fee over the period during which it performs its obligation to provide the customer with access to the auction site. If this period is short (less than one accounting period) then Company D should be able to recognize the fee at the time of initial listing. The timing of its recognition of the transaction fee depends on the predictability of buyers backing out on the purchase because this affects the amount of

8.14 d. continued.

cash that Company D will ultimately collect. If the probability of buyers backing out is either low or highly predictable or both, then recognizing the transaction fee at the time of the transaction is appropriate. If Company D cannot reliably measure the amount of revenue that it will ultimately earn on the transaction fee, it should delay the recognition of the transaction fee until the transaction is completed.

e. Company E should recognize the fee paid by the supplier as revenue, not the selling price of the product as revenue and the cost of the good as cost of goods sold. Company E bears none of the risk of purchasing and holding the product in this case. The timing of revenue recognition is determined by the point at which Company E has performed all of its obligations.

f. Company F assumes more product risk in this case than in Part e. and has many of the characteristics of a retailer. It assumes the risk of not selling the specified minimum number of units and pays to store and ensure those units. It could probably justify recognizing revenue for the specified minimum number of units each month and cost of goods sold expense for the cost of those units.

g. Company G has performed its obligation to the customer at the time it delivers the computer. However, the amount of cash that Company G will collect is uncertain. The issue for Company G is its ability to estimate at the time of the initial sale of the computer the cost of rebates that will have to be paid to the internet service provider after the time of the sale. If this amount is highly predictable, then Company G can justify recognizing the full selling price as revenue at the time of sale and the initial 10% cost of the rebate and any additional later cost of reallocated rebates as an expense. However, if linked computer/internet sales are a new arrangement, Company G may have difficulty estimating the cost of reallocated rebates. The $400 rebate appears to be a substantial amount relative to the selling price of the personal computer. The arrangement seems to be more to stimulate sales of the Internet service provider than those of Company G, given the 0.90/0.10 cost-sharing percentages. If predictability of the reallocated rebate cost is highly uncertain, than recognizing the selling

8.14 g. continued.

> price minus $360 (= 0.9 × $400) as revenue at the time of sale of the computer and the remaining $360 ratably over the three-year period seems appropriate. Actual costs of any reallocated rebates would be recognized as incurred each year.

h. Collectibility of the revenue is not an issue. However, Company H has not performed its obligations at the inception of the contract. Company H performs its obligations to the customer during the one-year contract period. It should recognize one-twelfth of the annual fee each month, as time passes and the contract provisions are satisfied.

i. Assuming that Company I has performed its obligations, the issue for Company I is the ability to measure the cash-equivalent value of the common stock. Company I has clearly received an asset from the customer; the issue is determining a reliable measurement for that asset.

j. This is a barter transaction. To justify recognizing revenue from advertising space sold and expense for advertising space purchased, these companies would need to demonstrate evidence of a price that they would charge for a cash sale of the advertising space to other customers, with some reasonable expectation of being able to collect this price. The best evidence to support such an expectation would be actual cash transactions at this price. This transaction has zero effect on earnings, because the amount of expense for space purchased equals the amount of revenue for space sold, but it does clearly affect both the revenue line and the expense line for each firm.

8.15 (Meaning of allowance for uncollectible accounts.)

a. This characterization of the allowance account is incorrect. The allowance account normally has a credit balance, and assets have debit balances. Firms do not set aside assets in an amount equal to the credit balance in the allowance account.

b. This characterization of the allowance account is incorrect for the same reasons as in Part *a*. above. Firms do not set aside cash in an amount equal to the balance in the allowance account.

8.15 continued.

c. This characterization of the allowance account is incorrect. The balance in the allowance accounts is an estimate of the amount from sales on account in all periods, not just the current period, that firms have not yet collected nor expect to collect.

d. This characterization of the allowance account is incorrect. It is a more nearly correct characterization of the allowance for sale returns.

e. This characterization of the allowance account is correct.

f. This characterization of the allowance account is incorrect. The issue with uncollectible accounts is nonpayment of amounts owed, not an obligation to pay cash or transfer assets.

g. This characterization is incorrect for the same reasons the characterization in Part *f*. is incorrect.

h. This characterization is incorrect because the Allowance for Uncollectible Accounts accumulates amounts recognized as Bad Debt Expense. A portion of the balance in the allowance account does likely result from recognizing bad debt expense during the current period. However, the balance also includes portions of bad debt expense of earlier periods as well. There is no way to know how much of the balance in the allowance account relates to provisions made during the current period versus earlier periods.

i. Deferred revenues, advances from customers, have credit balances and are liabilities. The firm owes cash to those making advances if the firm does not deliver the goods and services as promised. The firm does not receive cash when it credits the allowance for uncollectibles account, nor does it owe cash to customers.

j. This characterization is incorrect. When firms credit the allowance account, they debit bad debt expense, a part of the retained earnings account. Thus, the allowance account indirectly links with retained earnings but is not an accurate characterization of its nature.

8.16   (Pret a Manger; revenue recognition at time of sale and advances from customers.) (amounts in pounds sterling)

a.   Journal entry to record original transaction; customer pays in cash:

Cash.. 8.40
    Sales Revenue 8.40

Assets	=	Liabilities	+	Shareholders' Equity	(Class.)
+8.40				+8.40	IncSt → RE

b.   Journal entry to record transaction that includes card; customer pays in cash:

Cash.. 48.40
    Advances from Customer (Card) 40.00
    Sales Revenue 8.40

Assets	=	Liabilities	+	Shareholders' Equity	(Class.)
+48.40		+40.00		+8.40	IncSt → RE

c.   Journal entry to record transaction; customer pays with card:

Advances from Customer (Card) 8.40
    Sales Revenue 8.40

Assets	=	Liabilities	+	Shareholders' Equity	(Class.)
		−8.40		+8.40	IncSt → RE

8.17   (Bed, Bath & Beyond; revenue recognition at time of sale and advances from customers.)

Cash.. 556.5
    Sales Revenue 280.0
    Advances from Customer (Gift Certificate)...........   250.0
    Sales Taxes Payable..   26.5

Assets	=	Liabilities	+	Shareholders' Equity	(Class.)
		+250.0			
+556.5		+26.5		+280.0	IncSt → RE

8.18   (Marks and Spencer Group; revenue recognition at time of sale.) (amounts in millions of pounds sterling)

a.   Journal entry to recognize revenues and expenses:

Accounts Receivable, Gross...................................... 9,022.0
Cost of Goods Sold.. 5,535.2
   Sales Revenue 9,022.0
   Merchandise Inventory...................................... 5,535.2

Assets	=	Liabilities	+	Shareholders' Equity	(Class.)
+9,022.0				+9,022.0	IncSt → RE
−5,535.2				−5,535.2	IncSt → RE

b.   Journal entry to recognize sales returns and bad debts expense (combined):

Sales Returns... 90.22
Bad Debt Expense 135.33
   Allowance for Doubtful Accounts and Sales
     Returns.. 225.55

Assets	=	Liabilities	+	Shareholders' Equity	(Class.)
				−90.22	IncSt → RE
−225.55				−135.33	IncSt → RE

c.   Beginning Balance, Allowance... £   1.10
Sales Returns 90.22
Bad Debt Expense 135.33
Less Ending Balance, Allowance... (3.30)
   Total Returns and Write-offs... £ 223.35

8.19   (Lentiva Group Limited; revenue recognition at time of sale.) (amounts in US$)

Separate Selling Price of Laptop Component (= $1,500 X
   50,000 Laptops) .... $ 75,000,000
Separate Selling Price of Training Component (= $100 X
   50,000 Laptops) 5,000,000
   Total .... $ 80,000,000

8.19 continued.

Journal Entries on January 1, 2013

Cash...15,000,000
Accounts Receivable..60,000,000
   Sales Revenue..70,312,500
   Advances from Customer...4,687,500

Assets	=	Liabilities	+	Shareholders' Equity	(Class.)
+15,000,000		+4,687,500		+70,312,500	IncSt → RE
+60,000,000					

To record the sale of the laptops and training services.

The laptop sales meet the criteria for recognizing revenue equaling $70,312,500 [= ($75,000,000/$80,000,000) × $75,000,000]. The training revenue equaling $4,687,500 [= ($5,000,000/$80,000,000) × $75,000,000] is deferred and will be earned as training services are delivered.

Cost of Goods Sold 60,000,000
   Inventory 60,000,000

Assets	=	Liabilities	+	Shareholders' Equity	(Class.)
−60,000,000				−60,000,000	IncSt → RE

To record the cost of the laptop sales.

Journal Entries on December 31, 2013

Advances from Customer... 2,343,750
Cost of Training Services... 1,250,000
   Sales Revenue...2,343,750
   Salaries Payable..1,250,000

Assets	=	Liabilities	+	Shareholders' Equity	(Class.)
		−2,343,750		+2,343,750	IncSt → RE
		+1,250,000		−1,250,000	IncSt → RE

To record the revenues and expenses for training services provided during 2013. Revenues equal $2,343,750 (= $4,687,500/2 years); Expenses equal $1,250,000 [= ($50 per laptop × 50,000 laptops)/2 years].

8.19 continued.

Journal Entries on December 31, 2014

Advances from Customer...	2,343,750	
Cost of Training Services..	1,250,000	
Sales Revenue...		2,343,750
Salaries Payable...		1,250,000

Assets	=	Liabilities	+	Shareholders' Equity	(Class.)
		−2,343,750		+2,343,750	IncSt → RE
		+1,250,000		−1,250,000	IncSt → RE

To record the revenues and expenses for training
services provided during 2014. Revenues equal
$2,343,750 (= $4,687,500/2 years); Expenses equal
$1,250,000 [= ($50 per laptop × 50,000 laptops)/2 years].

8.20   (Morrison's Cafeteria; journal entries for coupons.) (amounts in US$)

a. **January**

Cash...	50,100	
Sales Revenue		48,000
Coupon Liability		2,100

Assets	=	Liabilities	+	Shareholders' Equity	(Class.)
+50,100		+2,100		−48,000	IncSt → RE

Coupon Liability	1,600	
Sales Revenue		1,600

Assets	=	Liabilities	+	Shareholders' Equity	(Class.)
		−1,600		+1,600	IncSt → RE

February

Cash...	50,700	
Sales Revenue		48,500
Coupon Liability		2,200

Assets	=	Liabilities	+	Shareholders' Equity	(Class.)
+50,700		+2,200		−48,500	IncSt → RE

8.20 a. continued.

Coupon Liability 2,300
    Sales Revenue 2,300

Assets	=	Liabilities	+	Shareholders' Equity	(Class.)
		−2,300		+2,300	IncSt → RE

March
Cash.. 52,400
    Sales Revenue 50,000
    Coupon Liability 2,400

Assets	=	Liabilities	+	Shareholders' Equity	(Class.)
+52,400		+2,400		+50,000	IncSt → RE

Coupon Liability 2,100
    Sales Revenue 2,100

Assets	=	Liabilities	+	Shareholders' Equity	(Class.)
		−2,100		+2,100	IncSt → RE

b. The Coupon Liability account has a balance of $4,700 (= $4,000 + $2,100 − $1,600 + $2,200 − $2,300 + $2,400 − $2,100) on March 31.

8.21 (Abson Corporation; journal entries for service contracts.) (amounts in US$)

a. **1/31/13–3/31/13**
Cash... 180,000
    Service Contract Fees Received in Advance........ 180,000

Assets	=	Liabilities	+	Shareholders' Equity	(Class.)
+180,000		−180,000			

To record sale of 300 annual contracts.

3/31/13
Service Contract Fees Received in Advance............ 22,500
    Contract Revenues 22,500

8.21 a. continued.

Assets	=	Liabilities	+	Shareholders' Equity	(Class.)
		−22,500		+22,500	IncSt → RE

To recognize revenue on 200 contracts sold during the first quarter; 1.5/12 × $180,000.

1/01/13–3/31/13
Service Expenses 32,000
    Cash (and Other Assets and Liabilities)   32,000

Assets	=	Liabilities	+	Shareholders' Equity	(Class.)
−32,000				−32,000	IncSt → RE

4/01/13–6/30/13
Cash 300,000
    Service Contract Fees Received in Advance   300,000

Assets	=	Liabilities	+	Shareholders' Equity	(Class.)
+300,000		−300,000			

To record the sale of 500 annual contracts.

6/30/13
Service Contract Fees Received in Advance 82,500
    Contract Revenues   82,500

Assets	=	Liabilities	+	Shareholders' Equity	(Class.)
		−82,500		+82,500	IncSt → RE

To recognize revenue on 500 contracts sold during the second quarter and 300 contracts outstanding from the first quarter:
    First Quarter:
        3/12   × $180,000   = $ 45,000
    Second Quarter:
        1.5/12 × $300,000   =   37,500
                                $ 82,500

8.21 a. continued.

4/01/13–6/30/13

Service Expenses 71,000

    Cash (and Other Assets and Liabilities)   71,000

Assets	=	Liabilities	+	Shareholders' Equity	(Class.)
–71,000				–71,000	IncSt → RE

7/01/13–9/30/13

Cash.. 240,000

    Service Contract Fees Received in Advance   240,000

Assets	=	Liabilities	+	Shareholders' Equity	(Class.)
+240,000		–240,000			

To record the sale of 400 annual contracts.

9/30/13

Service Contract Fees Received in Advance 150,000

    Contract Revenues   150,000

Assets	=	Liabilities	+	Shareholders' Equity	(Class.)
		–150,000		+150,000	IncSt → RE

To recognize revenue on 400 contracts sold during the
third quarter and 800 contracts outstanding from sales
in prior quarters:

    First Quarter Sales:

        3/12   x $180,000 = $ 45,000

    Second Quarter Sales:

        3/12   x $300,000 =   75,000

    Third Quarter Sales:

        1.5/12 x $240,000 =   30,000

                          = $ 150,000

8.21 a. continued.

7/01/13–9/30/13

Service Expenses 105,000

Cash (and Other Assets and Liabilities)   105,000

Assets	=	Liabilities	+	Shareholders' Equity	(Class.)
−105,000				−105,000	IncSt → RE

b. Balances in Service Contract Fees Received in Advance Account:

January 1, 2013...	—
Less First Quarter Expirations	$ (22,500)
Plus First Quarter Sales..	180,000
March 31, 2013..	$ 157,500
Less Second Quarter Expirations	(82,500)
Plus Second Quarter Sales	300,000
June 30, 2013	$ 375,000
Less Third Quarter Expirations	(150,000)
Plus Third Quarter Sales..	240,000
September 30, 2013	$ 465,000
Less Fourth Quarter Expirations	(195,000)
Plus Fourth Quarter Sales..	120,000
December 31, 2013...	$ 390,000

OR

Contracts	x	Balance Remaining	x	$600	=	Amount
300	x	1.5/12	x	$600	=	$ 22,500
500	x	4.5/12	x	$600	=	112,500
400	x	7.5/12	x	$600	=	150,000
200	x	10.5/12	x	$600	=	105,000
						$ 390,000

8.22 (Diversified Technologies; allowance method for uncollectible accounts.) (amounts in US$)

a. $5,076 (= 0.04 x $126,900).

8.22 continued.

    b. Accounts Receivable Gross ($126,900 – $94,300 – $2,200) .... $ 30,400
       Less Allowance for Uncollectible Accounts ($5,076 – $2,200) .... (2,876)
       Accounts Receivable Net .... $ 27,524

8.23   (York Company; aging of accounts receivable.) (amounts in US$)

Bad Debt Expense.. 9,050
   Allowance for Uncollectible Accounts   9,050

Assets	=	Liabilities	+	Shareholders' Equity	(Class.)
–9,050				–9,050	IncSt → RE

The Allowance account requires a balance of $25,050 [= (0.005 × $1,200,000) + (0.01 × $255,000) + (0.10 × $75,000) + (0.30 × $30,000)]. The adjusting entry *increases* the Allowance account by $9,050 (= $25,050 – $16,000) and recognizes Bad Debt Expense for the period by the same amount.

8.24   (Dove Company; aging of accounts receivable.) (amounts in US$)

Bad Debt Expense.. 3,700
   Allowance for Uncollectible Accounts   3,700

Assets	=	Liabilities	+	Shareholders' Equity	(Class.)
–3,700				–3,700	IncSt → RE

The Allowance account requires a balance of $20,900 [= (0.005 × $400,000) + (0.01 × $90,000) + (0.10 × $40,000) + (0.70 × $20,000)]. The required charge for Bad Debt Expense is, therefore, $3,700 (= $20,900 – $17,200).

8.25   (Hamilia S.A.; aging of accounts receivable.) (amounts in euros)

Allowance for Uncollectible Accounts 21,500
   Bad Debt Expense   21,500

Assets	=	Liabilities	+	Shareholders' Equity	(Class.)
+21,500				+21,500	IncSt → RE

8.25 continued.

The Allowance account requires a balance of €75,100 [= (0.005 X €980,000) + (0.03 X €130,000) + (0.15 X €102,000) + (0.75 X €68,000)]. The adjusting entry *decreases* the allowance account by €21,500 (= €96,600 − €75,100) and recognizes a credit to Bad Debt Expense by the same amount.

8.26   (Seward Corporation; reconstructing events when using the allowance method.) (amounts in US$)

a.   Accounts Receivable... 240,000

      Sales Revenue 240,000

Assets	=	Liabilities	+	Shareholders' Equity	(Class.)
+240,000				+240,000	IncSt → RE

b.   Bad Debt Expense 4,800

      Allowance for Uncollectible Accounts.................. 4,800

Assets	=	Liabilities	+	Shareholders' Equity	(Class.)
−4,800				−4,800	IncSt → RE

c.   Allowance for Uncollectible Accounts ($8,700 + $4,800 − $9,100)... 4,400

      Accounts Receivable....................................... 4,400

Assets	=	Liabilities	+	Shareholders' Equity	(Class.)
+4,400					
−4,400					

d.   Cash ($82,900 + $240,000 − $4,400 − $87,300)....... 231,200

      Accounts Receivable.. 231,200

Assets	=	Liabilities	+	Shareholders' Equity	(Class.)
+231,200					
−231,200					

8.27   (Pandora Company; allowance method: reconstructing journal entry from events.) (amounts in US$)

Bad Debt Expense.. 3,700
   Allowance for Uncollectible Accounts   3,700

Assets	=	Liabilities	+	Shareholders' Equity	(Class.)
−3,700				−3,700	IncSt → RE

Write-off of $2,200 + Ending Balance of Allowance of $5,000 − Beginning Balance of $3,500 = $3,700.

8.28   (Milton Corporation; allowance method: reconstructing journal entries from events.) (amounts in US$)

Accounts Receivable.. 75,000,000
   Sales Revenue..   75,000,000

Assets	=	Liabilities	+	Shareholders' Equity	(Class.)
+75,000,000				+75,000,000	IncSt → RE

$750,000 is 1% of Sales Revenue; Sales Revenue = $750,000/0.01.

Assets	=	Liabilities	+	Shareholders' Equity	(Class.)
+21,500				+21,500	IncSt → RE

Bad Debt Expense.. 750,000
   Allowance for Uncollectible Accounts   750,000

Assets	=	Liabilities	+	Shareholders' Equity	(Class.)
−750,000				−750,000	IncSt → RE

Allowance for Uncollectible Accounts ($1,400,000 +
   $750,000 − $1,550,000)... 600,000
      Accounts Receivable   600,000

Assets	=	Liabilities	+	Shareholders' Equity	(Class.)
+600,000					
−600,000					

8.28 continued.

Cash ($15,200,000 + $75,000,000 − $600,000 −
   $17,600,000) 72,000,000
      Accounts Receivable   72,000,000

Assets	=	Liabilities	+	Shareholders' Equity	(Class.)
+72,000,000					
−72,000,000					

8.29   (Reconstructing events from journal entries.) (amounts in US$)

a.   Bad debt expense for the period is $2,300 using the allowance method.

b.   A firm writes off specific customers' accounts totaling $450 as uncollectible under the allowance method.

c.   A firm realizes that its expected uncollectibles in the future are less than the amount already reserved in the allowance for uncollectibles. It records a credit to Bad Debt Expense for $200 to reduce the balance in the Allowance for Uncollectibles to the necessary (lower) amount.

8.30   (Heath Company; journal entries for the allowance method.) (amounts in US$)

a.   **2011**
   Bad Debt Expense (0.03 × $340,000) 10,200
      Allowance for Uncollectible Accounts   10,200

Assets	=	Liabilities	+	Shareholders' Equity	(Class.)
−10,200				−10,200	IncSt → RE

   Allowance for Uncollectible Accounts 1,800
      Accounts Receivable   1,800

Assets	=	Liabilities	+	Shareholders' Equity	(Class.)
+1,800					
−1,800					

8.30 a. continued.

2012

Bad Debt Expense (0.03 × $450,000)...................... 13,500
   Allowance for Uncollectible Accounts.................   13,500

Assets	=	Liabilities	+	Shareholders' Equity	(Class.)
−13,500				−13,500	IncSt → RE

Allowance for Uncollectible Accounts...................... 8,300
   Accounts Receivable...   8,300

Assets	=	Liabilities	+	Shareholders' Equity	(Class.)
+8,300					
−8,300					

2013

Bad Debt Expense (0.03 × $580,000)...................... 17,400
   Allowance for Uncollectible Accounts.................   17,400

Assets	=	Liabilities	+	Shareholders' Equity	(Class.)
−17,400				−17,400	IncSt → RE

Allowance for Uncollectible Accounts...................... 14,100
   Accounts Receivable...   14,100

Assets	=	Liabilities	+	Shareholders' Equity	(Class.)
+14,100					
−14,100					

b.   Yes. Uncollectible accounts arising from sales in 2011, 2012, and 2013 total $42,600, which equals 3.1% (= $42,600/$1,370,000) of total sales on account during the three-year period.

8.31   (Schneider Corporation; journal entries for the allowance method.)
        (amounts in US$)

a. **2011**
    Bad Debt Expense (0.02 X $750,000)...................... 15,000
        Allowance for Uncollectible Accounts.................   15,000

Assets	=	Liabilities	+	Shareholders' Equity	(Class.)
−15,000				−15,000	IncSt → RE

Allowance for Uncollectible Accounts...................... 1,300
    Accounts Receivable...   1,300

Assets	=	Liabilities	+	Shareholders' Equity	(Class.)
+1,300					
−1,300					

2012
Bad Debt Expense (0.02 X $1,200,000).................... 24,000
    Allowance for Uncollectible Accounts.................   24,000

Assets	=	Liabilities	+	Shareholders' Equity	(Class.)
−24,000				−24,000	IncSt → RE

Allowance for Uncollectible Accounts...................... 11,200
    Accounts Receivable...   11,200

Assets	=	Liabilities	+	Shareholders' Equity	(Class.)
+11,200					
−11,200					

2013
Bad Debt Expense (0.02 X $2,400,000).................... 48,000
    Allowance for Uncollectible Accounts.................   48,000

Assets	=	Liabilities	+	Shareholders' Equity	(Class.)
−48,000				−48,000	IncSt → RE

8.31 a. continued.

Allowance for Uncollectible Accounts...................... 23,600
    Accounts Receivable... 23,600

Assets	=	Liabilities	+	Shareholders' Equity	(Class.)
+23,600					
−23,600					

b. Yes. The actual loss experience is 1.9% (= $82,500/$4,350,000) of sales on account for sales during 2011 through 2013.

8.32 (Fujitsu Limited; reconstructing events when using the allowance method.) (amounts in millions of Japanese yen)

a. Accounts Receivable... 5,100,163
    Sales Revenue 5,100,163

Assets	=	Liabilities	+	Shareholders' Equity	(Class.)
+5,100,163				+5,100,163	IncSt → RE

b. Bad Debt Expense (0.01 X ¥5,100,163) 51,002
    Allowance for Uncollectible Accounts................. 51,002

Assets	=	Liabilities	+	Shareholders' Equity	(Class.)
−51,002				−51,002	IncSt → RE

c. Allowance for Uncollectible Accounts...................... 50,877
    Accounts Receivable... 50,877

Assets	=	Liabilities	+	Shareholders' Equity	(Class.)
+50,877					
−50,877					

¥50,877 = ¥6,781 + ¥51,002 − ¥6,906.

8.32 continued.

    d. Cash... 4,880,538

          Accounts Receivable...   4,880,538

Assets	=	Liabilities	+	Shareholders' Equity	(Class.)
+4,880,538					
−4,880,538					

¥4,880,538 = ¥885,300 + ¥5,100,163 − ¥50,877 − ¥1,054,048.

8.33   (WollyMartin Limited; effects of transactions involving suppliers and customers on cash flows.) (amounts in euros)

    a. 127,450 = 130,000 − (8,600 − 8,000) + (750 − 700) − 2,000
                     = 130,000 − 600 + 50 − 2,000.

    b. 84,700   = 85,000 − (7,500 − 7,000) + (11,200 − 11,000)
                     = 85,000 − 500 + 200.

8.34   (Shannon Construction Company; percentage-of-completion and completed contract methods of income recognition.) (amounts in US$)

Percentage-of-Completion Method

Year	Degree of Completion	Revenue	Expense	Income
2012	$1,200,000/$4,800,000 = 25.0%	$1,500,000	$1,200,000	$ 300,000
2013	$3,000,000/$4,800,000 = 62.5%	3,750,000	3,000,000	750,000
2014	$ 600,000/$4,800,000 = 12.5%	750,000	600,000	150,000
		$6,000,000	$4,800,000	$1,200,000

Completed Contract Method

Year	Revenue	Expense	Income
2012	—	—	—
2013	—	—	—
2014	$6,000,000	$4,800,000	$1,200,000
	$6,000,000	$4,800,000	$1,200,000

8.35   (Raytheon; percentage-of-completion and completed contract methods of income recognition.) (amounts in millions of US$)

Percentage-of-Completion Method

Year	Degree of Completion	Revenue	Expense	Income
2011	$200/$700 = 28.6%	$ 257.4	$ 200	$ 57.4
2012	$200/$700 = 28.6%	257.4	200	57.4
2013	$300/$700 = 42.8%	385.2	300	85.2
		$ 900.0	$ 700	$ 200.0

Completed Contract Method

Year	Revenue	Expense	Income
2011	—	—	—
2012	—	—	—
2013	$ 900	$ 700	$ 200
	$ 900	$ 700	$ 200

8.36   (Cunningham Realty Partners; installment and cost recovery methods of income recognition.) (amounts in US$)

Installment Method

Year	Revenue	(PLUG) Expense[b]	Income[a]
2013	$ 30,000	$ 20,000	$ 10,000
2014	30,000	20,000	10,000
2015	30,000	20,000	10,000
2016	30,000	20,000	10,000
	$ 120,000	$ 80,000	$ 40,000

[a]Income = Gross Margin Percentage × Cash Received, or ($40,000/ $120,000) × $30,000 = $10,000.

[b]Expense = Revenue – Income = $30,000 – $10,000 = $20,000.

Cost-Recovery-First Method

Year	Revenue	Expense	Income
2013	$ 30,000	$ 30,000	$ -0-
2014	30,000	30,000	-0-
2015	30,000	20,000	10,000
2016	30,000	-0-	30,000
	$ 120,000	$ 80,000	$ 40,000

8.37   (Installment and cost recovery methods of income recognition.) (amounts in millions of US$)

Installment Method

| | | (PLUG) | |
Year	Revenue	Expense[b]	Income[a]
2012	$ 24	$ 19	$ 5
2013	24	19	5
2014	24	19	5
	$ 72	$ 57	$ 15

[a] Income = Gross Margin Percentage × Cash Received, or ($15/$72) × $24 = $5 million.

[b] Expense = Revenue – Income = $24 – $5 = $19 million.

Cost-Recovery-First Method

Year	Revenue	Expense	Income
2012	$ 24	$ 24	$ -0-
2013	24	24	-0-
2014	24	9	15
	$ 72	$ 57	$ 15

8.38   (Nordstrom; revenue recognition at and after time of sale.) (amounts in US$)

a. **December 2013**

Cash.. 8,000,000
Accounts Receivable...24,000,000
    Advances from Customers (Gift Cards)   12,000,000
    Sales Revenue   20,000,000

Assets	=	Liabilities	+	Shareholders' Equity	(Class.)
+8,000,000					
+24,000,000		+12,000,000		+20,000,000	IncSt → RE

8.38 a. continued.

Cost of Goods Sold.. 7,200,000
    Merchandise Inventory..   7,200,000

Assets	=	Liabilities	+	Shareholders' Equity	(Class.)
−7,200,000				−7,200,000	IncSt → RE

b. **Adjusting Entries for December 2013**

Bad Debt Expense 240,000
Sales Returns 400,000
    Allowance for Uncollectibles and Returns   640,000

Assets	=	Liabilities	+	Shareholders' Equity	(Class.)
−640,000				−240,000	IncSt → RE
				−400,000	IncSt → RE

c. **Nordstrom Earned Income Before Taxes**

Sales Revenue	$ 20,000,000
Less Sales Returns	(400,000)
Net Sales Revenue	$ 19,600,000
Cost of Goods Sold..	(7,200,000)
Bad Debt Expense	(240,000)
Income Before Taxes..	$ 12,160,000

d. **January 2014**

Advances from Customers (Gift Cards) 6,000,000
Cost of Goods Sold.. 3,600,000
    Sales Revenue   6,000,000
    Merchandise Inventory...   3,600,000

Assets	=	Liabilities	+	Shareholders' Equity	(Class.)
−3,600,000		−6,000,000		−3,600,000	IncSt → RE
				+6,000,000	IncSt → RE

8.38 d. continued.

Sales Returns.. 120,000
    Allowance for Uncollectibles and Sales
      Returns... 120,000

Assets	=	Liabilities	+	Shareholders' Equity	(Class.)
−120,000				−120,000	IncSt → RE

To record estimated sales returns of $120,000 [= 0.02 × ($6,000,000)] on merchandise purchased with gift cards during January 2014.

8.39 (Hilton Garden Inn; revenue recognition at and after time of sale.) (amounts in US$)

a. **February 2, 2013:** Journal entry to record internet special reservation for four nights at $150 per night.

Cash.. 600
    Advances from Customer...................................... 600

Assets	=	Liabilities	+	Shareholders' Equity	(Class.)
+600		+600			

February 20, 2013: Journal entry to record revenue after services supplied.

Advances from Customer....................................... 600
    Sales Revenue 600

Assets	=	Liabilities	+	Shareholders' Equity	(Class.)
		−600		+600	IncSt → RE

8.39 continued.

b. **February 2, 2013:** Journal entry to record internet special reservation for four nights at $150 per night.

Cash.. 600
    Advances from Customer.................................... 600

Assets	=	Liabilities	+	Shareholders' Equity	(Class.)
+600		+600			

February 14, 2013: Journal entry to record revenue after customer cancels the reservation.

Advances from Customers..................................... 600
    Sales Revenue 600

Assets	=	Liabilities	+	Shareholders' Equity	(Class.)
		−600		+600	IncSt → RE

c. **February 2, 2013:** Journal entry to record refundable room reservation for four nights at $220 per night.

Cash.. 880
    Advances from Customer.................................... 880

Assets	=	Liabilities	+	Shareholders' Equity	(Class.)
+880		+880			

February 20, 2013: Journal entry to record revenue after services supplied.

Advances from Customer.. 880
    Sales Revenue 880

Assets	=	Liabilities	+	Shareholders' Equity	(Class.)
		−880		+880	IncSt → RE

8.39 continued.

d. **February 2, 2013:** Journal entry to record refundable room reservation for four nights at $220 per night.

Cash... 880
    Advances from Customer...................................... 880

Assets	=	Liabilities	+	Shareholders' Equity	(Class.)
+880		+880			

February 14, 2013: Journal entry to record cancellation of refundable room reservation.

Advances from Customer.. 880
    Cash.. 880

Assets	=	Liabilities	+	Shareholders' Equity	(Class.)
−880		−880			

e. **February 2, 2013:** Journal entry to record refundable room reservation for four nights at $220 per night.

Cash... 880
    Advances from Customer...................................... 880

Assets	=	Liabilities	+	Shareholders' Equity	(Class.)
+880		+880			

February 16, 2013: Journal entry to record revenue (for one night) after customer cancels the reservation after 3 p.m., and to refund the remaining three nights.

Advances from Customer.. 880
    Sales Revenue 220
    Cash.. 660

Assets	=	Liabilities	+	Shareholders' Equity	(Class.)
−660		−880		+220	IncSt → RE

8.40 (Stone Pest Control; revenue recognition at and after time of sale.) (amounts in US$)

    a. **January 4, 2013:** Journal entry to record revenue for pest control services rendered.

Cash	80	
Sales Revenue		80

Assets	=	Liabilities	+	Shareholders' Equity	(Class.)
+80				+80	IncSt → RE

    b. **January 4, 2013:** Journal entry to record pest control services rendered for cash.

Cash	180	
Sales Revenue		180

Assets	=	Liabilities	+	Shareholders' Equity	(Class.)
+180				+180	IncSt → RE

    c. The contract has three elements: quarterly service (selling price of $320 = $80 per service X 4 service calls per year), termite inspection (selling price of $100), and interim service calls at request of customer (selling price = expected value if sold separately = $80 given one visit expected). The total value of the contract is $500 (= $320 + $100 + $80). The portion of the contract associated with the service calls is 64% (= $320/$500), or 16% for each service call (= $80/$500); the portion associated with the interim service requests is 16% (= $80/$500); the portion associated with the termite inspection is 20% (= $100/$500).

January 4, 2013: Journal entry to record contract for pest control services.

Cash	300	
Advances from Customer		300

Assets	=	Liabilities	+	Shareholders' Equity	(Class.)
+300		+300			

8.40 c. continued.

Advances from Customers 108
    Sales Revenue   108

Assets	=	Liabilities	+	Shareholders' Equity	(Class.)
		−108		+108	IncSt → RE

To record sales for first quarterly service call and termite inspection of $108 [= (16% × $300) + (20% × $300)].

d. and e.

Stone should recognize the portion of the contract price associated with the interim service calls, $48 (= 16% × $300) pro rata over the life of the contract. Specifically, Stone should record the following journal entry at the end of each month, January–December.

Advances from Customer 4
    Sales Revenue   4

Assets	=	Liabilities	+	Shareholders' Equity	(Class.)
		−4		+4	IncSt → RE

To recognize sales for interim service calls of $4 (= $48/12 months).

Stone would not recognize incremental revenue on April 30, 2013, when it sprays for ants.

8.41 (Kajima Corporation; analyzing changes in accounts receivable.) (amounts in millions of Japanese yen)

a. **(1) Sales on Account**

	2012	2011	2010
Accounts Receivable ...	1,891,466	1,775,274	1,687,380
Sales Revenue.........	1,891,466	1,775,274	1,687,380

Assets	=	Liabilities	+	Shareholders' Equity	(Class.)
+1,891,466				+1,891,466	IncSt → RE
+1,775,274				+1,775,274	IncSt → RE
+1,687,380				+1,687,380	IncSt → RE

(2) Provision for Estimated Uncollectible Accounts

	2012	2011	2010
Bad Debt Expense	1,084	3,152	2,999
Allowance for Uncollectible Accounts..............	1,084	3,152	2,999

Assets	=	Liabilities	+	Shareholders' Equity	(Class.)
−1,084				−1,084	IncSt → RE
−3,152				−3,152	IncSt → RE
−2,999				−2,999	IncSt → RE

(3) Write-Off of Actual Bad Debts

	2012	2011	2010
Allowance for Uncollectible Accounts	6,471[a]	820[b]	8,099[c]
Accounts Receivable.....................	6,471	820	8,099

[a]¥10,673 + ¥1,084 − ¥5,286 = ¥6,471.

[b]¥8,341 + ¥3,152 − ¥10,673 = ¥820.

[c]¥13,441 + ¥2,999 − ¥8,341 = ¥8,099.

8.41 a. continued.

Assets	=	Liabilities	+	Shareholders' Equity	(Class.)
+6,471/–6,471					
+820/–820					
+8,099/–8,099					

(4) Collection of Cash from Customers

	2012	2011	2010
Cash	1,723,338[d]	1,761,584[e]	1,606,456[f]
Accounts Receivable	1,723,338	1,761,584	1,606,456

[d]¥468,387 + ¥1,891,466 − ¥6,471 − ¥630,044 = ¥1,723,338.

[e]¥455,517 + ¥1,775,274 − ¥820 − ¥468,387 = ¥1,761,584.

[f]¥382,692 + ¥1,687,380 − ¥8,099 − ¥455,517 = ¥1,606,456.

Assets	=	Liabilities	+	Shareholders' Equity	(Class.)
+1,723,338/ −1,723,338					
+1,761,584 −1,761,584					
+1,606,456/ −1,606,456					

8.41 continued.

b.

	2012	2011	2010

(1) Accounts Receivable Turnover
2012: ¥1,891,466/0.5(¥624,758 + ¥457,714) . 3.49
2011: ¥1,775,274/0.5(¥457,714 + ¥447,176) .   3.92
2010: ¥1,687,380/0.5(¥447,176 + ¥369,251) .   4.13

(2) Bad Debt Expense/Revenues
2012: ¥1,084/¥1,891,466 .... 0.06%
2011: ¥3,152/¥1,775,274 ....   0.18%
2010: ¥2,999/¥1,687,380 ....   0.18%

(3) Allowance for Uncollectible Accounts/
    Gross Accounts Receivable at End of
    Year
2012: ¥5,286/¥630,044 .... 0.84%
2011: ¥10,673/¥468,387 ....   2.28%
2010: ¥8,341/¥455,517 ....   1.83%

(4) Accounts Written Off/Average Gross
    Accounts Receivable
2012: ¥6,471/0.5(¥630,044 + ¥468,387) 1.18%
2011: ¥820/0.5(¥468,387 + ¥455,517) 0.18%
2010: ¥8,099/0.5(¥455,517 + ¥382,692) 1.93%

c. The accounts receivable turnover ratio decreased during the three-year period from 4.13 (in 2010) to 3.92 (in 2011) to 3.49 (in 2012). The firm decreased the amount of accounts written off between 2010 and 2011, from 1.93% to 0.18%, leading to a decrease in the allowance account relative to the gross accounts receivable. The firm decreased its provision for estimated uncollectible accounts in 2012 (the percentage of bad debt expense to sales declined from 0.18% in 2010 and 2011 to 0.06% in 2012), consistent with the buildup in the allowance account. The accounts written off as a percentage of gross accounts receivable increased in 2012, from 0.18% in 2011 to 1.18% in 2012, perhaps because credit conditions worsened in that year. The latter is consistent with the decrease in the accounts receivable turnover ratio, from 3.92 in 2011 to 3.49 in 2012.

8.42   (Polaris Corporation; analyzing changes in accounts receivable.) (amounts in millions of US$)

a.

	2013	2012	2011	2010
Allowance for Uncollectible Accounts, Beginning of Year.......	$ 138.1	$ 115.1	$ 111.0	$ 97.8
Plus Bad Debt Expense..................	36.8	40.1	20.1	20.1
Less Accounts Written Off (Plug) ..	(2.9)	(17.1)	(16.0)	(6.9)
Allowance for Uncollectible Accounts, End of Year.................	$ 172.0	$ 138.1	$ 115.1	$ 111.0

b.

	2013	2012	2011	2010
Accounts Receivable, Gross at Beginning of Year	$ 605.6	$ 599.2	$ 566.7	$ 539.5
Plus Sales on Account[a]	3,660.1	3,221.6	2,809.7	2,479.1
Less Accounts Written Off.............	(2.9)	(17.1)	(16.0)	(6.9)
Less Cash Collections from Credit Customers (Plug).......................	(3,582.4)	(3,198.1)	(2,761.2)	(2,445.0)
Accounts Receivable, Gross at End of Year..	$ 680.4	$ 605.6	$ 599.2	$ 566.7

[a]Total Sales X 0.75.

c.

	2013	2012	2011	2010
Cash Collections from Cash Sales[a]	$ 1,220.0	$1,073.9	$ 936.6	$ 826.4
Cash Collections from Credit Customers (from Part *b*.)...........	3,582.4	3,198.1	2,761.2	2,445.0
Total Cash Collected from Customers	$ 4,802.4	$4,272.0	$3,697.8	$3,271.4

[a]Total Sales X 0.25.

d.

Total Sales/Average Accounts Receivable, Net:	2013	2012	2011	2010
$4,880.1/0.5($508.4+ $467.5)	10.00			
$4,295.4/0.5($467.5 + $484.1) ...		9.03		
$3,746.3/0.5($484.1 + $455.7) ...			7.97	
$3,305.4/0.5($455.7 + $441.7) ...				7.37

8.43   (Aracruz Celulose; analyzing disclosures of accounts receivable.) (amounts in thousands of US$)

a. Carrying Value = Accounts Receivable, Net.
    For 2012: $361,603 (= $365,921 – $4,318).
    For 2011: $285,795 (= $290,429 – $4,634).

b. Total Amount Customers Owe = Accounts Receivable, Gross.
    For 2012: $365,921.
    For 2011: $290,429.

c. Journal Entries for Bad Debt Expense:

    2012
    Bad Debt Expense 117
        Allowance for Uncollectible Accounts 117

Assets	=	Liabilities	+	Shareholders' Equity	(Class.)
–117				–117	IncSt → RE

    Bad Debt Expense equals $117 (= $4,318 + $433 – $4,634).

    2011
    Bad Debt Expense 592
        Allowance for Uncollectible Accounts 592

Assets	=	Liabilities	+	Shareholders' Equity	(Class.)
–592				–592	IncSt → RE

    Bad Debt Expense equals $592 (= $4,634 + $25 – $4,067).

8.44   (Metso Corporation; analyzing disclosures of accounts receivable.) (amounts in millions of euros)

a. Carrying Value = Accounts Receivable, Net.
    For 2012: €1,274.
    For 2011: €1,218.

8.44 continued.

    b. Total Amount Customers Owe = Accounts Receivable, Gross.
        For 2012: €1,310 = €1,274 + €36.
        For 2011: €1,253 = €1,218 + €35.

    c. Journal Entries for Write-Offs:

2012

Allowance for Doubtful Accounts   5
    Accounts Receivable, Gross   5

Assets	=	Liabilities	+	Shareholders' Equity	(Class.)
–5					
+5					

Write-off equals €5 (= €35 + €13 – €7 – €36).

2011

Allowance for Doubtful Accounts   6
    Accounts Receivable, Gross   6

Assets	=	Liabilities	+	Shareholders' Equity	(Class.)
–6					
+6					

Write-off equals €6 (= €35 + €10 – €4 – €35).

8.45   (Pins Company; reconstructing transactions affecting accounts receivable and uncollectible accounts.) (amounts in US$)

    a. $192,000 Dr. = $700,000 – $500,000 – $8,000.

    b. $6,000 Cr. = (0.02 X $700,000) – $8,000.

    c. $21,000 = $10,000 + $11,000.

    d. $16,000 = $6,000 + $10,000.

    e. $676,000 = $192,000 + $800,000 – $16,000 – $300,000.

    f. $289,000 = $300,000 – $11,000.

8.46 (Effect of errors involving accounts receivable on financial statement ratios.)

		Rate of Return on Assets	Accounts Receivable Turnover Ratio	Liabilities to Assets Ratio
a. Bad Debt Expense .... Allowance for Uncollectible Accounts	X X	$\dfrac{O/S}{O/S} = O/S$	$\dfrac{NO}{O/S} = U/S$	$\dfrac{NO}{O/S} = U/S$

Assets	=	Liabilities	+	Shareholders' Equity	(Class)
−Amount				−Amount	IncSt → RE

		Rate of Return on Assets	Accounts Receivable Turnover Ratio	Liabilities to Assets Ratio
b. Allowance for Uncollectible Accounts .... Accounts Receivable	X X	$\dfrac{NO}{NO} = NO$	$\dfrac{NO}{NO} = NO$	$\dfrac{NO}{NO} = NO$

Assets	=	Liabilities	+	Shareholders' Equity	(Class)
+Amount					
−Amount					

		Rate of Return on Assets	Accounts Receivable Turnover Ratio	Liabilities to Assets Ratio
c. Advances from Customers .... Accounts Receivable	X X	$\dfrac{NO}{O/S} = U/S$	$\dfrac{NO}{O/S} = U/S$	$\dfrac{O/S}{O/S} = O/S$

Assets	=	Liabilities	+	Shareholders' Equity	(Class)
−Amount		−Amount			

8-41

Solutions

8.46 continued.

d. Sales Revenue... X
       Accounts Receivable.. X

Assets	=	Liabilities	+	Shareholders' Equity	(Class)
−Amount				−Amount	

$\dfrac{O/S}{O/S} = O/S$ $\dfrac{O/S}{O/S} = O/S$ $\dfrac{NO}{O/S} = U/S$

Inventory... X
   Cost of Goods Sold

Assets	=	Liabilities	+	Shareholders' Equity	(Class)
+Amount				+Amount	

e. Sales Return.. X
       Accounts Receivable.. X

Assets	=	Liabilities	+	Shareholders' Equity	(Class)
−Amount				−Amount	

$\dfrac{O/S}{O/S} = O/S$ $\dfrac{O/S}{O/S} = O/S$ $\dfrac{NO}{O/S} = U/S$

Inventory... X
   Cost of Goods Sold

Assets	=	Liabilities	+	Shareholders' Equity	(Class)
+Amount				+Amount	

Note: This problem asks only for the net effect of each error on the three financial ratios. The journal entries and the numerator and denominator effects show the reason for the net effect.

8.47 (Areva Group: income recognition for a nuclear generator manufacturer.) (amounts in millions of US$)

a.1. Percentage-of-Completion Method

Year	Incremental Percentage Complete	Revenue Recognized	Expenses Recognized	Income
2013	340/1,700 (0.20)	$ 400	$ 340	$ 60
2014	238/1,700 (0.14)	280	238	42
2015	238/1,700 (0.14)	280	238	42
2016	238/1,700 (0.14)	280	238	42
2017	238/1,700 (0.14)	280	238	42
2018	238/1,700 (0.14)	280	238	42
2019	170/1,700 (0.10)	200	170	30
Total.....	120/120 (1.00)	$ 2,000	$ 1,700	$ 300

2. Completed Contract Method

Year	Revenue Recognized	Expenses Recognized	Income
2013	-0-	-0-	-0-
2014	-0-	-0-	-0-
2015	-0-	-0-	-0-
2016	-0-	-0-	-0-
2017	-0-	-0-	-0-
2018	-0-	-0-	-0-
2019	$ 2,000	$ 1,700	$ 300
Total....	$ 2,000	$ 1,700	$ 300

b. Journal Entries:

1. Percentage-of-Completion Method

2012
December 20, 2012: At time of contract signing.
Cash... 20
   Advances from Customer.....................................   20

Assets	=	Liabilities	+	Shareholders' Equity	(Class.)
+20		+20			

8.47 b. continued.

2013

Construction in Process 340

    Cash.. 340

Assets	=	Liabilities	+	Shareholders' Equity	(Class.)
+340					
−340					

Cash.. 100

Advances from Customer..................................... 20

Receivable from Customer.................................... 280

    Sales Revenue 400

Assets	=	Liabilities	+	Shareholders' Equity	(Class.)
+100		−20		+400	IncSt → RE
+280					

Cost of Sales.. 340

    Construction in Process 340

Assets	=	Liabilities	+	Shareholders' Equity	(Class.)
−340				−340	IncSt → RE

2014–2018

Construction in Process 238

    Cash.. 238

Assets	=	Liabilities	+	Shareholders' Equity	(Class.)
+238					
−238					

Cash.. 100

Receivable from Customer.................................... 180

    Sales Revenue 280

Assets	=	Liabilities	+	Shareholders' Equity	(Class.)
+100				+280	IncSt → RE
+180					

8.47 b. continued.

Cost of Sales.. 238
   Construction in Process 238

Assets	=	Liabilities	+	Shareholders' Equity	(Class.)
−238				−238	IncSt → RE

2019

Construction in Process 170
   Cash.. 170

Assets	=	Liabilities	+	Shareholders' Equity	(Class.)
+170					
−170					

Cash.. 1,380
   Receivable from Customer.................................. 1,180
   Sales Revenue 200

Assets	=	Liabilities	+	Shareholders' Equity	(Class.)
+1,380				+200	IncSt → RE
−1,180					

Cost of Sales.. 170
   Construction in Process 170

Assets	=	Liabilities	+	Shareholders' Equity	(Class.)
−170				−170	IncSt → RE

2. Completed Contract Method

2012

December 20, 2012: At time of contract signing.
Cash.. 20
   Advances from Customer.................................... 20

Assets	=	Liabilities	+	Shareholders' Equity	(Class.)
+20		+20			

8.47 b. continued.

2013

Construction in Process 340

    Cash.. 340

Assets	=	Liabilities	+	Shareholders' Equity	(Class.)
+340					
−340					

Cash.. 100

    Advances from Customer.................................... 100

Assets	=	Liabilities	+	Shareholders' Equity	(Class.)
+100		+100			

2014–2018

Construction in Process 238

    Cash.. 238

Assets	=	Liabilities	+	Shareholders' Equity	(Class.)
+238					
−238					

Cash.. 100

    Advances from Customer.................................... 100

Assets	=	Liabilities	+	Shareholders' Equity	(Class.)
+100		+100			

2019

Construction in Process 170

    Cash.. 170

Assets	=	Liabilities	+	Shareholders' Equity	(Class.)
+170					
−170					

8.47 b. continued.

Cash 1,380
Advances from Customer 620
 Sales Revenue 2,000

Assets	=	Liabilities	+	Shareholders' Equity	(Class.)
+1,380		−620		+2,000	IncSt → RE

Cost of Sales 1,700
 Construction in Process 1,700

Assets	=	Liabilities	+	Shareholders' Equity	(Class.)
−1,700				−1,700	IncSt → RE

8.48 (Flanikin Construction Company; income recognition for a contractor.) (amounts in US$)

a. **Calculation of Revenues, Expenses, and Income**

  1. **Percentage-of-Completion Method**

Year	Incremental Percentage Complete	Revenue Recognized	Expenses Recognized	Income
2010	12/120 (0.10)	$ 18,000,000	$ 12,000,000	$ 6,000,000
2011	36/120 (0.30)	54,000,000	36,000,000	18,000,000
2012	48/120 (0.40)	72,000,000	48,000,000	24,000,000
2013	24/120 (0.20)	36,000,000	24,000,000	12,000,000
Total.......	120/120 (1.00)	$180,000,000	$120,000,000	$ 60,000,000

  2. **Completed Contract Method**

Year	Revenue Recognized	Expenses Recognized	Income
2010	-0-	-0-	-0-
2011	-0-	-0-	-0-
2012	-0-	-0-	-0-
2013	$180,000,000	$120,000,000	$60,000,000
Total....	$180,000,000	$120,000,000	$60,000,000

8.48 continued.

b. **Journal Entries**

1. **Percentage-of-Completion Method**

2010

Construction in Process 12

    Accounts Payable 12

Assets	=	Liabilities	+	Shareholders' Equity	(Class.)
+12		+12			

Cash.. 36

    Advances from Customer..................................... 18

    Sales Revenue 18

Assets	=	Liabilities	+	Shareholders' Equity	(Class.)
+36		+18		+18	IncSt → RE

Cost of Sales.. 12

    Construction in Process 12

Assets	=	Liabilities	+	Shareholders' Equity	(Class.)
−12				−12	IncSt → RE

2011

Construction in Process 36

    Accounts Payable 36

Assets	=	Liabilities	+	Shareholders' Equity	(Class.)
+36		+36			

Cash.. 45

Advances from Customer... 9

    Sales Revenue 54

Assets	=	Liabilities	+	Shareholders' Equity	(Class.)
+45		−9		+54	IncSt → RE

8.48 b. continued.

Cost of Sales... 36
    Construction in Process 36

Assets	=	Liabilities	+	Shareholders' Equity	(Class.)
−36				−36	IncSt → RE

2012

Construction in Process 48
    Accounts Payable 48

Assets	=	Liabilities	+	Shareholders' Equity	(Class.)
+48		+48			

Cash... 45
Advances from Customer....................................... 9
Receivable from Customer..................................... 18
    Sales Revenue.. 72

Assets	=	Liabilities	+	Shareholders' Equity	(Class.)
+45		−9		+72	IncSt → RE
+18					

Cost of Sales... 48
    Construction in Process 48

Assets	=	Liabilities	+	Shareholders' Equity	(Class.)
−48				−48	IncSt → RE

2013

Construction in Process 24
    Accounts Payable 24

Assets	=	Liabilities	+	Shareholders' Equity	(Class.)
+24		+24			

8.48 b. continued.

Cash.. 54
    Receivable from Customer................................. 18
    Sales Revenue 36

Assets	=	Liabilities	+	Shareholders' Equity	(Class.)
+54				+36	IncSt → RE
−18					

Cost of Sales... 24
    Construction in Process 24

Assets	=	Liabilities	+	Shareholders' Equity	(Class.)
−24				−24	IncSt → RE

2. Completed Contract Method

2010
Construction in Process 12
    Accounts Payable 12

Assets	=	Liabilities	+	Shareholders' Equity	(Class.)
+12		+12			

Cash.. 36
    Advances from Customer................................. 36

Assets	=	Liabilities	+	Shareholders' Equity	(Class.)
+36		+36			

2011
Construction in Process 36
    Accounts Payable 36

Assets	=	Liabilities	+	Shareholders' Equity	(Class.)
+36		+36			

8.48 b. continued.

Cash 45
    Advances from Customer   45

Assets	=	Liabilities	+	Shareholders' Equity	(Class.)
+45		+45			

2012
Construction in Process 48
    Accounts Payable   48

Assets	=	Liabilities	+	Shareholders' Equity	(Class.)
+48		+48			

Cash 45
    Advances from Customer   45

Assets	=	Liabilities	+	Shareholders' Equity	(Class.)
+45		+45			

2013
Construction in Process 24
    Accounts Payable   24

Assets	=	Liabilities	+	Shareholders' Equity	(Class.)
+24		+24			

Cash 54
Advances from Customer 126
    Sales Revenue   180

Assets	=	Liabilities	+	Shareholders' Equity	(Class.)
+54		−126		+180	IncSt → RE

8.48 b. continued.

Cost of Sales.. 120

    Construction in Process ,.................................... 120

Assets	=	Liabilities	+	Shareholders' Equity	(Class.)
−120				−120	IncSt → RE

c. The percentage-of-completion method probably gives the best measure of Flanikin's performance each year under the contract. The original estimates of costs on the contract turned out to be correct. Also, the periodic cash collections suggest that the firm will probably collect cash in the amount of the contract price.

8.49 (Furniture Retailers; income recognition when collection from the customer is uncertain.) (amounts in US$)

a. **Installment Method**

(1) **January 2013**

Accounts Receivable.. 8,400

    Inventory.. 6,800

    Deferred Gross Margin...................................... 1,600

Assets	=	Liabilities	+	Shareholders' Equity	(Class.)
+8,400					
−6,800		+1,600			

(2) **When Furniture Retailer Receives Each Payment**

The customer will make 21 payments of $400 each. The gross margin percentage is 19% (= $1,600/$8,400). When each monthly payment is received, Furniture Retailers will recognize $400 of revenues and $76 (= 0.19 × $400) of Deferred Gross Margin.

Cash.. 400

Deferred Gross Margin... 76

Cost of Goods Sold (Plug)....................................... 324

    Sales Revenue 400

    Accounts Receivable.. 400

8.49 a. continued.

Assets	=	Liabilities	+	Shareholders' Equity	(Class.)
+400		−76		−324	IncSt → RE
−400				+400	IncSt → RE

b. **Cost Recovery Method**

(1) **January 2013**

Accounts Receivable... 8,400
   Inventory... 6,800
   Deferred Gross Margin.. 1,600

Assets	=	Liabilities	+	Shareholders' Equity	(Class.)
+8,400		+1,600			
−6,800					

(2) **When Each Payment Is Received**

The customer will make 21 payments of $400 each. Furniture Retailers will recover the $6,800 cost of furniture after the customer has made seventeen payments (= $6,800/$400). To record the first seventeen payments, Furniture Retailers makes the following journal entry:

Cash.. 400
Cost of Goods Sold... 400
   Sales Revenue 400
   Accounts Receivable.. 400

Assets	=	Liabilities	+	Shareholders' Equity	(Class.)
+400				+400	IncSt → RE
−400				−400	IncSt → RE

8.49 b. continued.

To record the last four payments, Furniture Retailers makes the following journal entry:

Cash.. 400
Deferred Gross Margin... 400
    Sales Revenue 400
    Accounts Receivable.. 400

Assets	=	Liabilities	+	Shareholders' Equity	(Class.)
+400		−400		+400	IncSt → RE
−400					

8.50   (Appliance Sales and Service; revenue recognition when collection is uncertain.) (amounts in US$)

a.   Customer makes all 10 payments.

(1) **Installment Method**

July 2013
The customer will make 10 payments of $244 each, so the total amount owed is $2,440. The gross margin percentage of 9% on this sale means that the deferred gross margin is $220 (= 9% × $2,440). The difference between the amount of cash the customer has promised to pay ($2,440) and the deferred gross margin ($220) is credited to inventory.

Accounts Receivable... 2,440
    Inventory... 2,220
    Deferred Gross Margin.. 220

Assets	=	Liabilities	+	Shareholders' Equity	(Class.)
+2,440		+220			
−2,220					

8.50 a. continued.

When Each Payment Is Received. When each monthly payment is received, Appliance Sales and Service will recognize $244 revenue and $22 (= 9% × $244) of Deferred Gross Margin.

Cash...	244
Deferred Gross Margin...	22
Cost of Goods Sold (Plug)...	222
Sales Revenue	244
Accounts Receivable...	244

Assets	=	Liabilities	+	Shareholders' Equity	(Class.)
+244		−22		+244	IncSt → RE
−244				−222	IncSt → RE

(2) **Cost Recovery Method**

July 2013
The customer will make 10 payments of $244 each. Appliance Sales and Service will not recover the entire $2,220 cost of appliances until after the customer has made all payments. The journal entry at the time of sale is:

Accounts Receivable...	2,440
Inventory..	2,220
Deferred Gross Margin...	220

Assets	=	Liabilities	+	Shareholders' Equity	(Class.)
+2,440		+220			
−2,220					

Solutions

8.50 a. continued.

To Record the First Nine Payments of $244:

Cash...	244
Cost of Goods Sold...	244
Sales Revenue	244
Accounts Receivable...	244

Assets	=	Liabilities	+	Shareholders' Equity	(Class.)
+244				+244	IncSt → RE
−244				−244	IncSt → RE

To Record the Last Payment of $244.

After the ninth payment, Appliance Sales and Service has recognized $2,196 (= 9 × $244) of the total cost of goods sold of $2,220. The remainder, $24, is recognized on receipt of the last payment.

Cash...	244
Cost of Goods Sold...	24
Deferred Gross Margin...	220
Sales Revenue	244
Accounts Receivable...	244

Assets	=	Liabilities	+	Shareholders' Equity	(Class.)
+244		−220		+244	IncSt → RE
−244				−24	IncSt → RE

b. Customer stops making payments after November 2013.

(1) Installment Method

The customer has made the first five payments (July–November 2013) so the amount owed is $1,220 [= $2,440 − (5 × $244)].

Deferred Gross Margin.............................	110
Loss on Repossessed Appliances.............................	130
Inventory—Repossessed Appliances.......................	980
Accounts Receivable...	1,220

8.50 b. continued.

Assets	=	Liabilities	+	Shareholders' Equity	(Class.)
+980		−110		−130	IncSt → RE
−1,220					

(2) Cost Recovery Method

The customer has made the first five payments (July–November 2013) so the amount owed is $1,220 [= $2,440 − (5 × $244)].

Deferred Gross Margin..	220	
Loss on Repossession..	20	
Inventory—Repossessed Appliances........................	980	
Accounts Receivable...		1,220

Assets	=	Liabilities	+	Shareholders' Equity	(Class.)
+980		−220		−20	IncSt → RE
−1,220					

8.51 (J. C. Spangle; point-of-sale versus installment method of income recognition.) (amounts in US$)

a.	2013	2012
Sales	$ 300,000	$ 200,000
Expenses:		
Cost of Goods Sold*.................................	$ 186,000	$ 120,000
All Other Expenses....................................	44,000	32,000
Total Expenses	$ 230,000	$ 152,000
Net Income...	$ 70,000	$ 48,000

*Calculation	2013	2012
Beginning Inventory	$ 60,000	$ 0
Purchases	240,000	180,000
Goods Available	$ 300,000	$ 180,000
Ending Inventory	(114,000)	(60,000)
Cost of Goods Sold	$ 186,000	$ 120,000

Cost of Goods Sold/Sales:
2012—$120,000/$200,000 = 60%.
2013—$186,000/$300,000 = 62%.

8.51 continued.

b.

	2013	2012
Collections from Customers	$ 230,000	$ 90,000
Expenses:		
Merchandise Cost of Collections*	$ 140,400	$ 54,000
All Other Expenses....................................	44,000	32,000
Total Expenses	$ 184,400	$ 86,000
Net Income..	$ 45,600	$ 4,000

*Calculation	2013	2012
Merchandise Cost of Collections:		
Of Goods Sold:		
In 2012, 60% of $90,000.....................		$ 54,000
In 2013, 60% of $110,000..................	$ 66,000	
Of Goods Sold in 2013:		
62% of $120,000	74,400	
	$ 140,400	$ 54,000

An Alternative Presentation Would Be:	2013	2012
Realized Gross Margin	$ 89,600	$ 36,000
All Other Expenses..............................	44,000	32,000
Net Income..	$ 45,600	$ 4,000

8.52   (Pickin Chicken, Inc., and Country Delight, Inc.; revenue recognition for a franchise.) (amounts in US$)

a.

Year	Pickin Chicken, Inc.	Country Delight, Inc.
2011	$ 400,000 (= $50,000 × 8)	$ 160,000 (= $20,000 × 8)
2012	250,000 (= $50,000 × 5)	148,000 (= $20,000 × 5 + $6,000 × 8)
2013	0	78,000 (= $6,000 × 13)
2014	0	78,000 (= $6,000 × 13)
2015	0	78,000 (= $6,000 × 13)
2016	0	78,000 (= $6,000 × 13)
2017	0	30,000 (= $6,000 × 5)
Total..	$ 650,000	$ 650,000

b. The issue here is whether sufficient uncertainty exists regarding the amount the firm will ultimately collect to justify postponing revenue recognition until the time of collection. The business failure rate among franchisees is high, suggesting substantial uncertainty about collectibility of amounts owed.

8.53 (Income recognition for various types of businesses.)

a. **Amgen**—The principal income recognition issue for Amgen is the significant lag between the incurrence of research and development expenditures and the realization of sales from any resulting products. Research and development expenditures represent a significant percentage of revenues. Established pharmaceutical firms have established products as well as products in the pipeline and, therefore, research and development expenditures represent both a smaller and a more stable percentage of revenues. U.S. GAAP requires firms to expense research and development expenditures in the year incurred; as discussed in later chapters, IFRS specifies a different treatment for development expenditures.

Brown-Forman—The principal revenue recognition issue for Brown-Forman is whether it should recognize the increase in value of hard liquors while they are aging (that is, revalue the liquors to market value each year) or wait until the liquors are sold at the end of the aging process. Most accountants would argue that the market values of aging liquors are too uncertain prior to sale to justify periodic revaluations and revenue recognition. Brown-Forman should include in the cost of the liquor inventory not only the initial production costs but also the cost incurred during the aging process. In this way, the firm can match total incurred costs with revenues generated at the time of sale.

Deere—Deere faces issues of revenue recognition with respect to both the sale of farm equipment to dealers and the provision of financing services. The concern with respect to the sale of farm equipment to dealers is the right of dealers to return any unsold equipment. If dealers have no right of return, then recognition of revenue at the time of sale is appropriate. If dealers can return any equipment discovered to be faulty prior to sale and the amount of such returns is reasonably

8.53 a. continued.

predictable, then Deere can reduce the amount of revenue recognized each year for estimated returns. If dealers can return any unsold equipment, then delaying recognition of revenue until the dealer sells the equipment is appropriate. Deere should match the cost of manufacturing the equipment against the sales revenue. Deere reports research and development expense in its income statement; it is not clear what proportions of these expenditures Deere makes to enhance existing products versus to develop new products. U.S. GAAP does not permit firms to capitalize and amortize research and development costs.

Deere should accrue revenue from financing (interest) and insurance (premiums) services over time. To achieve matching, Deere should capitalize and amortize any initial administrative costs to check customer credit quality and prepare legal documents.

Fluor—The appropriate timing of revenue recognition for Fluor depends on the basis for pricing its services. If the fee is fixed for a particular construction project, then Fluor should recognize the fee in relation to the degree of completion of the construction project. If the fee is a percentage of total construction costs incurred on the project, then Fluor should recognize revenue in relation to costs incurred. If the fee is a percentage of the costs incurred by Fluor (for example, salaries of their employees working on the project), then it should recognize revenue in relation to the incurrence of these costs. It seems clear that the percentage-of-completion method of revenue recognition is more appropriate than the completed contract method.

Golden West—Golden West should recognize interest revenue from home mortgage loans as time passes. It should provide for estimated uncollectible accounts each year. The uncollectible amount should reflect the resale value of homes repossessed. The more difficult question relates to recognition of revenue from points. One possibility is to recognize the full amount in the initial year of the loan, based on the reasoning that the points cover the cost of originating the loan. Both the points and the administrative costs would be recognized in full in the initial year of the loan. An alternative view is that the points effectively reduce the amount lent by the savings and loan company and increase its yield beyond the stated interest rate. This view suggests that Golden West should amortize the points over the term of the loan and match against this revenue amortization of the initial administrative costs to set up the loan. Golden West should recognize interest expense on deposits as time passes. There is no direct relation between interest expense on deposits and interest revenue from loans so Golden West matches interest expense to the period it is incurred.

Merrill Lynch—The principal income recognition issue for Merrill Lynch is whether it should report financial instruments held as assets and liabilities at their acquisition cost or their fair value. These assets and liabilities generally have easily measured fair values and may be held for short periods (days or weeks). Thus, one can argue that use of current fair values is appropriate. However, we are still left with the question as to whether the unrealized gain or loss should flow through to the income statement immediately or wait until realization at the time of sale. The argument for immediate recognition is that Merrill Lynch takes short-term financing and investing positions for short-term returns. Its income statement should reflect its operating performance during this period. The case for not recognizing the unrealized gains and losses is that they could reverse prior to realization and, in any case, will be realized very soon. Merrill Lynch should recognize revenue from fee-based services as it provides the services.

Rockwell Collins—The absence of research and development expense from the income statement suggests that Rockwell Collins charges all such costs to specific contracts. These costs become expenses as Rockwell Collins recognizes revenue from the contracts. The multi-year nature of its contracts and the credit quality of the U.S. government suggest use of the percentage-of-completion method of income recognition. One difficulty encountered in applying the percentage-of-completion method is that Rockwell Collins's contracts for some projects are continually renewed. This procedure makes it difficult to identify a single contract price and accumulate costs for a single contract, which the percentage-of-completion method envisions.

8.53 continued.

b. **Amgen**—Amgen realized the highest profit margin of the seven companies. Its biotechnology products are protected by patents. It therefore maintains a monopoly position. Note that the cost of manufacturing its products is a small percent of revenues. Amgen's major cost is for research and development. Sales of its existing products are not only sufficient to cover its high, on-going research work but to provide a substantial profit margin as well. Its relatively low revenue to assets percentage is somewhat unexpected, given that its major "assets" are patents and research scientists. The reason for this low percentage (reason not provided in the case) is that cash and marketable securities comprise approximately 25% of its assets. These assets generated a return of approximately 3% during the year. This rate of return decreased the overall ratio of revenues to assets for Amgen.

Brown-Forman—Brown-Forman realized the third highest profit margin among the seven companies. If one views the excise taxes as a reduction in revenues rather than as an expense, its profit margin is 10.4% [= 8.8%/(100.0% − 15.4%)]. Concerns about excess alcoholic drinking in recent years have resulted in some exodus of companies from the industry, leaving the remaining companies with a larger share of a smaller market. The products of Brown-Forman carry brand name recognition, permitting the firm to obtain attractive prices.

Deere—Deere's relatively low profit margin reflects (1) weaknesses in the farming industry in recent years, which puts downward pressure on margins, and (2) decreased interest rates, which lowers profit margins. The revenue-to-assets percentage of Deere reflects its capital-intensive manufacturing operations and the low interest rate on outstanding loans to dealers and customers.

Fluor—The low profit margin of Fluor reflects the relatively low value added of construction services. It may also reflect recessionary conditions when construction activity is weak and profit margins are thin.

8.53 b. continued.

Golden West—The 12% profit margin (ignoring an addback for interest expense, which is common for financial services firms) seems high, relative to interest rates in recent years. Recall though that Golden West pays short-term interest rates on its deposits but obtains long-term interest rates on its loans. An upward-sloping yield curve provides a positive differential. Also, the existence of shareholders' equity funds in the capital structure means that Golden West has assets earning returns for which it recognizes no expense in its income statement (that is, firms do not recognize an expense for the implicit cost of shareholders' funds). Note also that the ratio of revenue to assets is only 0.1. Thus, the assets of Golden West earned a return of only 1.2% (= 12.0% × 0.1) during the year.

Merrill Lynch—The lower profit margin for Merrill Lynch relative to Golden West reflects in part the fact that both the investments and financing of Merrill Lynch are short term. Merrill Lynch, however, realizes revenue from fee-based services. Firms like Merrill Lynch can differentiate these services somewhat and realize attractive profit margins. However, such services have been quickly copied by competitors in recent years, reducing the profit margins accordingly.

Rockwell Collins—This profit margin is in the middle of the seven companies. Factors arguing for a high profit margin include Rockwell-Collins's technological know-how and its role in long-term contracts with the U.S. government. Factors arguing for a lower profit margin include cutbacks in defense expenditures and excess capacity in the aerospace industry.

8.54   (Understanding the purpose of the Allowance for Uncollectible Accounts account.)

This case has the following history. Over the last several years, we have lectured to audit committee, and other board members, about the meaning of the requirement that audit committee members be financially literate, as specified by the New York Stock Exchange and the NASDAQ in its listing requirements. Many experienced members suggest our criteria for literacy are too stringent because, they say, I do not need to know all that accounting stuff, as I know how to ask the tough questions. We believe that being able to ask tough questions is not enough, if the questioner cannot evaluate the answers, recognizing incorrect answers and being able

Solutions

8.54 continued.

to ask follow-up questions for correct, but only partial, answers. We devised a Tough Questions Quiz virtually identical to this case. Of the audit committee members who have taken the quiz [as you might imagine, its hard to get them to do so], the median number of correct responses is just under half. Former SEC Commissioner Arthur Levitt contributed to the malaise of the financially illiterate audit committee by saying in a speech that he wanted board members to be able to ask the tough questions, without adding and they should be able to evaluate the answers.

a. This response does not address the question. Judging the adequacy of the allowance account focuses on estimating the portion of accounts receivable that a firm does not expect to collect. Thus, the question concerns the valuation of accounts receivable net of estimated uncollectibles. The CFO in essence is saying that even if the firm has more uncollectibles than the amount in the allowance account the firm will survive. The CFO's response does not demonstrate an understanding of the purpose of the allowance account.

b. This response demonstrates an understanding of the need to evaluate bad debt expense every accounting period. The amount of bad debt expense this period is intended to result in a balance in the Allowance for Uncollectibles account that reflects the amount of accounts receivable that a firm does not expect to collect. This amount pertains to sales made both this period and in previous periods, not just sales made this period.

c. This response demonstrates an understanding that the allowance account should reflect the estimated amounts of accounts receivable that the firm does not expect to collect. It also shows that the CFO knows to use an aging of accounts receivable to judge the adequacy of the balance in the account. The misunderstanding is that the allowance account reflects the estimated amounts from sales of all periods, not just the current period, that the firm does not expect to collect.

d. This response demonstrates an accurate understanding of the purpose of the allowance account and the approach a firm should follow to judge the adequacy of the amount in the allowance account.

8.54 continued.

    e.   This response does not address the question. The CFO addresses the appropriateness of writing off accounts that were written off. It does not address the adequacy of the balance in the allowance account to cover accounts not yet written off.

    f.   This confirmation of receivables simply evidences that a valid receivable exists. It does not provide evidence about what portion of these receivables the firm does and does not expect to collect, which is the question asked.

    g.   This response demonstrates an understanding that the allowance account should carry a sufficient balance to equal amounts from the current and prior periods' sales that the firm does not expect to collect. It also shows a need to assess the adequacy of the balance in the allowance account each period. Finally, it shows the use of external benchmarks to assess the adequacy of the amount of bad debt expense. The one remaining response that would have demonstrated even more understanding about the adequacy of the balance in the allowance account was for the CFO to state that the benchmark percentages from the credit reporting agencies have historically matched the firm's credit loss experience.

This page is intentionally left blank

CHAPTER 9

WORKING CAPITAL

Questions, Exercises, and Problems: Answers and Solutions

9.1 See the text or the glossary at the end of the book.

9.2 Prepayments are future economic benefits that a firm will receive because it has exchanged cash for the right to receive services in the future. Firms charge the asset to expense over the period during which it receives services. All assets promise future economic benefits, so all assets are prepayments.

9.3 The underlying principle is that acquisition cost includes all costs required to prepare an asset for its intended use. Assets provide future services. Costs that a firm must incur to obtain those expected services are, therefore, included in the acquisition cost valuation of the asset. In the case of merchandise inventory, this includes the costs associated with obtaining the goods (purchase price, transportation costs, insurance costs). For manufactured inventory, acquisition costs include direct labor, direct materials, and manufacturing overhead.

9.4 Depreciation on manufacturing equipment is a product cost and remains in inventory accounts until the firm sells the manufactured goods. Depreciation on selling and administrative equipment is a period expense, because the use of such equipment does not create an asset with future service potential.

9.5 Both the Merchandise Inventory and Finished Goods Inventory accounts include the cost of completed units ready for sale. A merchandising firm acquires the units in finished form and debits Merchandise Inventory for their acquisition cost. A manufacturing firm incurs direct material, direct labor, and manufacturing overhead costs in transforming the units to a finished, salable condition. The Raw Materials Inventory and Work-in-Process Inventory accounts include such costs until the completion of manufacturing operations. Thus, the accountant debits the Finished Goods Inventory account for the cost of producing completed units. The accountant

9.5 continued.

credits both the Merchandise Inventory and Finished Goods Inventory accounts for the cost of units sold and reports the inventory accounts as current assets on the balance sheet.

9.6   Accounting reports cost flows, not flows of physical quantities. Cost-flow assumptions trace costs, not physical flows of goods. With specific identification, management can manipulate cost flows by controlling physical flow of goods.

9.7   Rising Purchase Prices
Higher Inventory Amount: FIFO
Lower Inventory Amount: LIFO
Higher Cost of Goods
    Sold Amount: LIFO
Lower Cost of Goods
    Sold Amount: FIFO

9.8   Suppliers often grant a discount if customers pay within a certain number of days after the invoice date, in which case this source of funds has an explicit interest cost. Suppliers who do not offer discounts for prompt payment often include an implicit interest change in the selling price of the product. Customers in this second category should delay payment as long as possible because they are paying for the use of the funds. Firms should not delay payment to such an extent that it hurts their credit rating and raises their cost of financing.

9.9   The Parker School should accrue the salary in ten monthly installments of $360,000 each at the end of each month, September through June. It will have paid $300,000 at the end of each of these months, so that by the end of the reporting year, it reports a current liability of $600,000 [= $3,600,000 − (10 × $300,000)].

9.10   It is cheaper (and, therefore, more profitable) to repair a few sets than to have such stringent quality control that the manufacturing process produces zero defectives. An allowance is justified when firms expect to have warranty costs. Manufacturers of TV sets for use on space ships or heart pacemakers should strive for zero defects.

9.11   **Similarities:** The accountant makes estimates of future events in both cases. The accountant charges the cost of estimated uncollectibles or warranties to income in the period of sale, not in the later period when specific items become uncollectible or break down. The income statement reports the charge against income as an expense in both cases, although some accountants report the charge for estimated uncollectibles as a revenue contra.

Differences: The balance sheet account showing the expected costs of future uncollectibles reduces an asset account, whereas that for estimated warranties appears as a liability.

9.12   A reversal implies that the previously accrued charge turned out to be too high, in light of the new information (including realized expenditures). Because the reversal lowers the amount of expense reported in the current period, it increases income.

9.13   (Accounting for prepayments.) (amounts in millions of euros)

a. Journal entry to record insurance premium payments in 2012, 2011, and 2010:

Prepayments	50.0	
Cash		50.0

b. Adjusting journal entries required each year.

2011:

Insurance Expense	66.3	
Prepayments		66.3

To adjust Prepayments for the amount consumed during 2011, of €66.3 million (= €42.1 + €50.0 – €25.8).

2012:

Insurance Expense	45.1	
Prepayments		45.1

To adjust Prepayments for the amount consumed during 2012, of €45.1 million (= €25.8 + €50.0 – €30.7).

9.14   (Liquid Crystal Display Corporation; accounting for prepayments.) (amounts in millions of Korean won [KRW])

    a. Adjusting journal entry to record portion of prepaid rent consumed during each month, January–March:

Rent Expense	86,775	
Prepaid Rent...		86,775

        Rent expense is KRW86,774.6667 million (= KRW260,324 million/ 3 months). To correct rounding errors, use 86,774 for every third month.

    b. March 31, 2012: To record prepayment of rent for next 12 months.

Prepaid Rent...	1,382,436	
Cash		1,382,436

        To record cash prepayments for 12 months of rent of KRW1,382,436 (= 345,609 X 4 quarters) million. The 2012 ending balance of Prepayments of KRW345,609 million consists of 3 months of prepaid rent. The total amount prepaid as of March 31, 2012 is, therefore, KRW345,609 X €4 = KRW1,382,436.

    c. Adjusting journal entry to record portion of prepaid rent consumed during each month, April–December.

Rent Expense	115,203	
Prepaid Rent...		115,203

        Rent expense is KRW115,203 million (= KRW1,382,436 million/12 months); alternatively, note that the balance of Prepayments at December 31, 2012 consists of 3 months of prepaid rent (KRW115,203 = KRW345,609/3 months).

9.15   (Ringgold Winery; identifying inventory cost inclusions.) (amounts in US$)

Ringgold should include the costs to acquire the grapes, process them into wine, and mature the wine, but not the expenditures on advertising or research and development. Thus, the cost of the wine inventory (prior to its sale) is $3,673,000 (= $2,200,000 + $50,000 + $145,000 + $100,000 + $250,000 + $600,000 + $120,000 + $180,000 + $28,000).

9.16 (Trembly Department Store; identifying inventory cost inclusions.)
(amounts in US$)

a.	Purchase Price	$ 300,000
b.	Freight Cost	13,800
c.	Salary of Purchasing Manager	3,000
d.	Depreciation, Taxes, Insurance, and Utilities on Warehouse	27,300
e.	Salary of Warehouse Manager	2,200
f.	Merchandise Returns	(18,500)
g.	Cash Discounts Taken	(4,900)
	Acquisition Cost	$ 322,900

The underlying principle is that inventories should include all costs required
to get the inventory ready for sale. The purchase of the inventory items
(items *a.*, *c.*, *f.*, and *g.*) provides the physical goods to be sold, the freight cost
(item *b.*) puts the inventory items in the place most convenient for sale, and
the storage costs (items *d.* and *e.*) keep the inventory items until the time of
sale. Economists characterize these costs as providing form, place, and time
utility, or benefits. Although accounting theory suggests the inclusion of
each of these items in the valuation of inventory, some firms might exclude
items *c.*, *d.*, *e.*, and *g.* on the basis of lack of materiality.

9.17 (ResellFast; effect of inventory valuation on the balance sheet and net
income.) (amounts in millions of US$)

	Carrying Value	Effect on Income
Q1	$ 20.0	$ 0.0
Q2	16.5	(3.5)
Q3	16.5	0.0
Q4	0.0	11.0

9.18 (Target Corporation; inventory and accounts payable journal entries.)
(amounts in millions of US$)

a. Beginning Balance in Merchandise Inventory + Purchases of Inventory =
Amount Sold (Cost of Goods Sold) + Ending Balance in Merchandise
Inventory.

$6,254 + Purchases = $41,895 + $6,780; solve for Purchases.
Purchases = $42,421.

9.18 continued.

b. Merchandise Inventory.. 42,421
     Accounts Payable...   42,421

c. Beginning Balance in Accounts Payable + Purchases of Merchandise Inventory = Payments to Vendors + Ending Balance in Accounts Payable.

$6,575 + $42,421 = Payments to Vendors + $6,721.
Payments to Vendors = $42,275.

Accounts Payable... 42,275
     Cash   42,275

9.19 (Tesco Plc.; inventory and accounts payable journal entries.) (amounts in millions of pounds sterling)

a. Trade Payables 43,558
     Cash   43,558

b. Beginning Balance in Trade Payables + Purchases of Merchandise Inventory = Payments to Venders + Ending Balance in Trade Payables.

£3,317 + Purchases of Merchandise Inventory = £43,558 (from Part a.) + £3,936.

Purchases of Merchandise Inventory = £44,177.

Merchandise Inventory.. 44,177
     Accounts Payable...   44,177

c. Beginning Balance in Merchandise Inventory + Purchases of Inventory = Amount Sold (Cost of Goods Sold) + Ending Balance in Merchandise Inventory.

£1,911 + £44,177 (from Part b.) = Cost of Goods Sold + £2,420.
Cost of Goods Sold = £43,668.

Cost of Goods Sold 43,668
     Merchandise Inventory   43,668

9.20 (Fun-in-the-Sun Tanning Lotion Company; income computation for a manufacturing firm.) (amounts in US$)

Manufacturing Costs Incurred During the Year:

Raw Materials	$ 56,300
Direct Labor	36,100
Manufacturing Overhead	26,800
Total Manufacturing Costs Incurred	$ 119,200
Less Manufacturing Costs Assigned to Work-in-Process Inventory	(12,700)
Cost of Units Completed During the Year	$ 106,500
Less Cost of Ending Inventory of Finished Goods	(28,500)
Cost of Goods Sold	$ 78,000

9.21 (GenMet; income computation for a manufacturing firm.) (amounts in millions of US$)

Sales	$ 6,700.2
Less Cost of Goods Sold	(2,697.6)
Less Selling and Administrative Expenses	(2,903.7)
Less Interest Expense	(151.9)
Income Before Income Taxes	$ 947.0
Income Tax Expense at 35%	(331.5)
Net Income	$ 615.5

Work-in-Process Inventory, October 31, 2012	$ 100.8
Plus Manufacturing Costs Incurred During Fiscal Year 2013	2,752.0
Less Work-in-Process Inventory, October 31, 2013	(119.1)
Cost of Goods Completed During Fiscal Year 2013	$ 2,733.7
Plus Finished Goods Inventory, October 31, 2012	286.2
Less Finished Goods Inventory, October 31, 2013	(322.3)
Cost of Goods Sold	$ 2,697.6

9.22 (Crystal Chemical Corporation; income computation for a manufacturing firm.) (amounts in millions of euros)

Sales	€ 32,632
Less Cost of Goods Sold	(28,177)
Less Marketing and Administrative Expenses	(2,436)
Less Interest Expense	(828)
Income Before Income Taxes	€ 1,191
Income Tax Expense at 35%	(417)
Net Income	€ 774

9.22 continued.

Work-in-Process Inventory, December 31, 2012		€ 843
Plus Manufacturing Costs Incurred During 2013		28,044
Less Work-in-Process Inventory, December 31, 2013		(837)
Cost of Goods Completed During 2013		€ 28,050
Plus Finished Goods Inventory, December 31, 2012		2,523
Less Finished Goods Inventory, December 31, 2013		(2,396)
Cost of Goods Sold		€ 28,177

9.23   (Warren Company; effect of inventory errors.)

a. NO/None.   f. US/Understatement by $1,000.
b. NO/None.   g. US/Understatement by $1,000.
c. US/Understatement by $1,000.   h. NO/None.
d. OS/Overstatement by $1,000.   i. NO/None.
e. OS/Overstatement by $1,000.

9.24   (Cemex S.A.; lower of cost or market for inventory.) (amounts in millions of Mexican pesos)

a. $20,187 million (= $19,631 + $556).

b. Journal entry to record impairment charge for inventory at the end of the year:

Impairment Loss on Inventory	131	
Allowance for Impairment		131

9.25   (Ericsson; lower of cost or market for inventory.) (amounts in millions of Swedish kronor [SEK])

a. SEK22,475 million (= SEK25,227 – SEK2,752).

b. Journal entry to record impairment charge for inventory during the year:

Impairment Loss on Inventory	1,276	
Allowance for Impairment		1,276

The carrying value of the inventory is now
SEK2,224 (= SEK3,500 – SEK1,276).

9.25 continued.

   c.   January: Journal entry to record a reversal of a portion of the impairment charge for inventory taken in the preceding year:

Allowance for Impairment....................................... 576
   Reversal of Impairment Loss on Inventory......... 576
To reverse a portion of the impairment loss;
SEK576 = SEK2,800 − SEK2,224.

   d.   U.S. GAAP would not permit Ericsson to reverse a previous impairment of inventory.

9.26   (Sun Health Foods; computations involving different cost-flow assumptions.) (amounts in US$)

		a.	b. Weighted	c.
	Units	FIFO	Average	LIFO
Goods Available for Sale............	2,500	$10,439	$10,439	$ 10,439
Less Ending Inventory................	(420)	(1,722)[a]	(1,754)[c]	(1,806)[e]
Goods Sold	2,080	$ 8,717[b]	$ 8,685[d]	$ 8,633[f]

[a]$(420 \times \$4.10) = \$1,722$.
[b]$(460 \times \$4.30) + (670 \times \$4.20) + (500 \times \$4.16) + (450 \times \$4.10) = \$8,717$.
[c]$(\$10,439/2,500) \times 420 = \$1,754$.
[d]$(\$10,439/2,500) \times 2,080 = \$8,685$.
[e]$(420 \times \$4.30) = \$1,806$.
[f]$(870 \times \$4.10) + (500 \times \$4.16) + (670 \times \$4.20) + (40 \times \$4.30) = \$8,633$.

9.27   (Arnold Company; computations involving different cost-flow assumptions.)
(amounts in US$)

		a.	**b.** Weighted	**c.**
	Pounds	**FIFO**	**Average**	**LIFO**
Raw Materials Available for Use	10,700	$24,384	$24,384	$ 24,384
Less Ending Inventory	(3,500)	(8,110)[a]	(7,976)[c]	(7,818)[e]
Raw Materials Issued to Production	7,200	$16,274[b]	$16,408[d]	$ 16,566[f]

[a](3,000 × $2.32) + (500 × $2.30) = $8,110.

[b](1,200 × $2.20) + (2,200 × $2.25) + (2,800 × $2.28) + (1,000 × $2.30) = $16,274.

[c]($24,384/10,700) × 3,500 = $7,976.

[d]($24,384/10,700) × 7,200 = $16,408.

[e](1,200 × $2.20) + (2,200 × $2.25) + (100 × $2.28) = $7,818.

[f](3,000 × $2.32) + (1,500 × $2.30) + (2,700 × $2.28) = $16,566.

9.28   (Harmon Corporation; effect of LIFO on financial statements over several
periods.) (amounts in US$)

a.
Year	Ending Inventory	
2011	19,000 × $20	$ 380,000
2012	10,000 × $20	$ 200,000
2013	(10,000 × $20) + (10,000 × $30)	$ 500,000

b.
Year	Cost of Goods Sold	
2011	64,000 × $20	$ 1,280,000
2012	(92,000 × $25) + (9,000 × $20)	$ 2,480,000
2013	110,000 × $30	$ 3,300,000

9.28 b. continued.

Year	Income	
2011	$2,048,000 – $1,280,000	$ 768,000
2012	$4,040,000 – $2,480,000	$ 1,560,000
2013	$5,280,000 – $3,300,000	$ 1,980,000

9.29 (EKG Company; LIFO provides opportunity for income manipulation.) (amounts in US$)

a. Largest cost of goods sold results from producing 70,000 (or more) additional units at a cost of $22 each, giving cost of goods sold of $1,540,000.

b. Smallest cost of goods sold results from producing no additional units, giving cost of goods sold of $980,000 [= ($8 x 10,000) + ($15 x 60,000)].

c.

	Income Reported	
	Minimum	Maximum
Revenues ($30 x 70,000)	$2,100,000	$2,100,000
Less Cost of Goods Sold	(1,540,000)	(980,000)
Gross Margin	$ 560,000	$1,120,000

9.30 (Cat Incorporated; conversion from LIFO to FIFO.) (amounts in millions of US$)

	LIFO	Difference	FIFO
Beginning Inventory	$ 6,351	$ 2,403	$ 8,754
Production Costs (Plug)	33,479	—	33,479
Goods Available for Sale (Plug)	$ 39,830	$ 2,403	$ 42,233
Less Ending Inventory	(7,204)	(2,617)	(9,821)
Cost of Goods Sold	$ 32,626	$ (214)	$ 32,412

9.31 (Falcon Motor Company; analysis of LIFO and FIFO disclosures.) (amounts in millions of US$)

a. Falcon Motor Company uses LIFO, so the carrying value of its inventories would be $10,121 million as of December 31, 2013, and $10,017 as of December 31, 2012.

9.31 continued.

b.

	LIFO	Difference	FIFO
Beginning Inventory..............	$ 10,017	$ 1,015	$ 11,032
Production Costs (Plug)........	142,691	—	142,691
Goods Available for Sale (Plug)..................................	$ 152,708	$ 1,015	$ 153,723
Less Ending Inventory..........	(10,121)	(1,100)	(11,221)
Cost of Goods Sold...............	$ 142,587	$ (85)	$ 142,502

9.32 (McGee Associates; journal entries for payroll.) (amounts in US$)

a.

Wage and Salary Expense.......................................	700,000	
Withholding and FICA Taxes Payable		210,000
Wages and Salaries Payable.............................		490,000

Amounts payable to and for employees.

Wage and Salary Expense.......................................	114,800	
Taxes Payable..		70,000
Payable to Profit Sharing Fund		28,000
Vacation Liability		16,800

Employer's additional wage expense; estimated vacation liability is $16,800 (= 1.20 × $14,000).

b. $814,800 = $700,000 + $114,800.

9.33 (Hurley Corporation; accounting for uncollectible accounts and warranties.) (amounts in US$)

a. **Allowance for Uncollectible Accounts**

Balance, December 31, 2011...	$ 355
Plus Bad Debt Expense for 2012: 0.02 × $18,000	360
Less Accounts Written Off (Plug).....................................	(310)
Balance, December 31, 2012...	$ 405
Plus Bad Debt Expense for 2013: 0.02 × $16,000	320
Less Accounts Written Off (Plug).....................................	(480)
Balance, December 31, 2013...	$ 245

9.33 continued.

    b. **Estimated Warranty Liability**

Balance, December 31, 2011	$ 1,325
Plus Warranty Expense for 2012: 0.06 × $18,000	1,080
Less Actual Warranty Costs (Plug)	(870)
Balance, December 31, 2012	$ 1,535
Plus Warranty Expense for 2013: 0.06 × $16,000	960
Less Actual Warranty Costs (Plug)	(775)
Balance, December 31, 2013	$ 1,720

9.34   (Miele Company; journal entries for warranty liabilities and subsequent expenditures.) (amounts in euros)

    a. **Last Year**

Accounts Receivable	1,200,000	
Sales Revenue		1,200,000
Warranty Liability	12,000	
Cash		12,000
Expenditures actually made.		
Warranty Expense	48,000	
Warranty Liability		48,000
0.04 × €1,200,000.		

    Current Year

Accounts Receivable	1,500,000	
Sales Revenue		1,500,000
Warranty Liability	50,000	
Cash		50,000
Expenditures actually made.		
Warranty Expense	60,000	
Warranty Liability		60,000
0.04 × €1,500,000.		

    b. €76,000 = €30,000 + €48,000 − €12,000 + €60,000 − €50,000.

9.35   (Kingspeed Bikes; journal entries for warranty liabilities and subsequent expenditures.) (amounts in US$)

a. **2011**

Cash	800,000	
Sales Revenue		800,000

Warranty Liability	22,000	
Cash		13,200
Parts Inventory		8,800

Warranty Expense	48,000	
Warranty Liability		48,000

0.06 X $800,000 = $48,000.

2012

Cash	1,200,000	
Sales Revenue		1,200,000

Warranty Liability	55,000	
Cash		33,000
Parts Inventory		22,000

Warranty Expense	72,000	
Warranty Liability		72,000

0.06 X $1,200,000 = $72,000.

2013

Cash	900,000	
Sales Revenue		900,000

Warranty Liability	52,000	
Cash		31,200
Parts Inventory		20,800

Warranty Expense	54,000	
Warranty Liability		54,000

0.06 X $900,000 = $54,000.

b. $48,000 − $22,000 + $72,000 − $55,000 + $54,000 − $52,000 = $45,000.

9.36   (Sappi Paper Limited; journal entries for restructuring liabilities and subsequent expenditures.) (amounts in millions of South African rand [ZAR])

Restructuring Provision	32	
Cash		32

To record cash expenditures on previously accrued restructuring costs.

Restructuring Expense	7	
Restructuring Provision		7

During the year, Sappi recognized restructuring charges of ZAR7 million [= ZAR41 – (ZAR32 + ZAR16)].

9.37   (Delchamps Group; journal entries for restructuring liabilities and subsequent expenditures.) (amounts in millions of euros)

a. **Journal entries for 2012**

Restructuring Expense	14.2	
Restructuring Provision		14.2

To record new restructuring charges made during 2012.

Restructuring Provision	7.3	
Restructuring Expense		7.3

To record the reversal of prior period restructuring charges.

Restructuring Provision	40.0	
Cash		40.0

To record cash expenditures to settle restructuring Provisions; 40.0 = [(84.0 + 14.2) – (7.3 + 50.9)].

b. Delchamps will report a total restructuring provision of €50.9, classified as follows on its balance sheet:

Current Portion of Restructuring Provision	€ 12.5 million
Noncurrent Portion of Restructuring Provision	€ 38.4 million

9.37 continued.

    c.   Delchamps's income in 2012 is lower by €6.9 million (= €14.2 million – €7.3 million). The net change in income of €6.9 million is added to income as a noncash expense to calculate cash flow from operations in the statement of cash flows:

9.38   (Katherine's Outdoor Furniture; preparation of journal entries and income statement for a manufacturing firm.) (amounts in US$)

    a.   (1) Raw Materials Inventory.................................. 667,200
                   Accounts Payable 667,200

         (2) Work-in-Process Inventory............................... 689,100
                   Raw Materials Inventory............................ 689,100

         (3) Work-in-Process Inventory............................... 432,800
                   Selling Expenses 89,700
                   Administrative Expenses 22,300
                   Cash.. 544,800

         (4) Work-in-Process Inventory............................... 182,900
                   Selling Expenses 87,400
                   Administrative Expenses 12,200
                   Accumulated Depreciation........................... 282,500

         (5) Work-in-Process Inventory............................... 218,500
                   Selling Expenses 55,100
                   Administrative Expenses 34,700
                   Cash.. 308,300

         (6) Finished Goods Inventory 1,564,500
                   Work-in-Process Inventory........................... 1,564,500

         (7) Accounts Receivable... 2,400,000
                   Sales Revenue 2,400,000

         (8) Cost of Goods Sold 1,536,600
                   Finished Goods Inventory 1,536,600
        $182,700 + $1,564,500 – $210,600 = $1,536,600.

9.38 continued.

b.

KATHERINE'S OUTDOOR FURNITURE
Income Statement
For the Month of January

Sales		$2,400,000
Less Expenses:		
Cost of Goods Sold......................................	$1,536,600	
Selling...	232,200	
Administrative..	69,200	(1,838,000)
Net Income...		$ 562,000

Note: Instead of using a functional classification of expenses (that is, selling, administrative), classification by their nature (salary, depreciation, other operating) is acceptable.

9.39 (Lord Cromptom Plc.; flow of manufacturing costs through the accounts.) (amounts in pounds sterling)

a.	Beginning Raw Materials Inventory......................................	£ 46,900
	Raw Materials Purchased..	429,000
	Raw Materials Available for Use	£ 475,900
	Subtract Ending Raw Materials Inventory...........................	(43,600)
	Cost of Raw Materials Used...	£ 432,300
	Beginning Factory Supplies Inventory.................................	£ 7,600
	Factory Supplies Purchased...	22,300
	Factory Supplies Available for Use	£ 29,900
	Subtract Ending Factory Supplies Inventory........................	(7,700)
	Cost of Factory Supplies Used...	£ 22,200

9.39 continued.

b.

Beginning Work-in-Process Inventory	£110,900
Cost of Raw Materials Used (from Part *a.*)	432,300
Cost of Factory Supplies Used (from Part *a.*)	22,200
Direct Labor Costs Incurred	362,100
Heat, Light, and Power Costs	10,300
Insurance	4,200
Depreciation of Factory Equipment	36,900
Prepaid Rent Expired	3,600
Total Beginning Work-in-Process and Manufacturing Costs Incurred	£982,500
Subtract Ending Work-in-Process Inventory	(115,200)
Cost of Units Completed and Transferred to Finished Goods Storeroom	£867,300

c.

Beginning Finished Goods Inventory	£ 76,700
Cost of Units Completed and Transferred to Finished Goods Storeroom (from Part *b.*)	867,300
Subtract Ending Finished Goods Inventory	(71,400)
Cost of Goods Sold	£872,600

d. Net Income is £110,040 [= (1 – 0.40)(£1,350,000 – £872,600 – £246,900 – £47,100)].

9.40 (Sedan Corporation; flow of manufacturing costs.) (amounts in millions of yen)

a. Ending Balance of Total Inventory = Ending Balance of Raw Materials and Supplies Inventory + Ending Balance of Work-in-Process Inventory + Ending Balance of Finished Goods Inventory.

Ending Balance of Total Inventory = ¥374,210 + ¥239,937 + ¥1,211,569 = ¥1,825,716 million.

b. Beginning Finished Goods Inventory + Cost of Units Completed = Cost of Products Sold + Write-downs + Ending Finished Goods Inventory.

¥1,204,521 + Cost of Units Completed = ¥20,452,338 + 0 + ¥1,211,569. Cost of Units Completed = ¥20,459,386 million.

9.40 continued.

   c.   Beginning Balance in Work-in-Process Inventory + Direct Materials + Direct Labor + Overhead = Cost of Units Completed + Ending Balance in Work-in-Process Inventory.

¥236,749 + Raw Material and Supplies Costs + ¥12,000,000 = ¥20,459,386 (from Part *b*.) + ¥236,937.

Raw Material and Supplies Costs = ¥8,462,574 million.

Work-in-Process Inventory..	8,462,574	
Raw Materials and Supplies Inventory..............		8,462,574

   d.   Beginning Balance in Raw Materials Inventory + Raw Materials Purchases = Raw Materials Used in Production + Ending Balance of Raw Materials Inventory.

¥362,686 + Raw Materials and Supplies Purchases = ¥8,462,574 + ¥374,210.

Raw Materials and Supplies Purchases = ¥8,474,098 million.

Raw Materials and Supplies Inventory..................	8,474,098	
Accounts Payable..		8,474,098

9.41   (Minevik Group; flow of manufacturing costs.) (amounts in millions of Swedish kronor [SEK])

   a.   Ending Balance of Total Inventory = Ending Balance of Raw Materials Inventory + Ending Balance of Work-in-Process Inventory + Ending Balance of Finished Goods Inventory.

Ending Balance of Total Inventory = SEK6,964 + SEK5,157 + SEK13,180 = SEK25,301 million.

   b.

Loss on Impairment of Inventory	281	
Finished Goods Inventory....................................		281

9.41 continued.

    c.   Cost of Sales, after Write-down = Cost of Sales, before Write-down + Write-down.

         SEK57,222 = (Cost of Sales, before Write-down) + SEK281.
         Cost of Sales, before Write-down = SEK56,941 million.

    d.   Beginning Finished Goods Inventory + Cost of Units Completed = Cost of Sales + Write-downs + Ending Finished Goods Inventory.

         SEK8,955 + Cost of Units Completed = SEK56,941 + SEK281 + SEK13,180.

         Cost of Units Completed = SEK61,447 million.

    e.   Beginning Balance in Work-in-Process Inventory + Direct Materials + Direct Labor + Overhead = Cost of Units Completed + Ending Balance in Work-in-Process Inventory.

         SEK4,093 + Direct Material Costs + 3 × Direct Material Costs = SEK61,447 (from Part d.) + SEK5,157.

         Direct Material Costs = SEK62,511/4 = SEK15,628 million.

Work-in-Process Inventory......................................	15,628	
Raw Materials Inventory......................................		15,628

    f.   Beginning Balance in Raw Materials Inventory + Raw Materials Purchases = Raw Materials Used in Production + Ending Balance of Raw Materials Inventory.

         SEK5,690 + Raw Material Purchases = SEK15,628 (from Part e.) + SEK6,964.

         Raw Materials Purchases = SEK16,902 million.

9.42   (Good Luck Brands; lower-of-cost-or-market valuation; U.S. GAAP versus IFRS.) (amounts in millions of US$)

a. No journal entry will be recorded because U.S. GAAP does not permit firms to write-up the value of their inventory above its acquisition cost.

b. **Journal Entry:**

Impairment Loss on Inventory   167
    Merchandise Inventory   167
$167 = $2,047.6 − $1,880.6.

c. No journal entry will be recorded because U.S. GAAP does not permit firms to reverse previous write-downs of inventory.

d. **If IFRS Were Used:**

For Part *a*.: No (same answer), because IFRS does not permit firms to write-up the value of their inventory above its acquisition cost.

For Part *b*.: No (same answer), because IFRS also requires firms to report inventory at the lower of cost or market value.

For Part *c*.: Yes (different answer), because IFRS permits firms to reverse previous write-downs up to the original acquisition cost of the inventory. Had it applied IFRS, Good Luck Brands would have recorded the following reversal journal entry:

Merchandise Inventory 81.7
    Reversal of Impairment Loss 81.7
$81.7 = $1,962.3 − $1,880.6.

9.43   (Burton Corporation; detailed comparison of various choices for inventory accounting.) (amounts in US$)

	FIFO	LIFO	Weighted Average
Inventory, 1/1/2011	$ 0	$ 0	$ 0
Purchases During 2011	14,400	14,400	14,400
Goods Available for Sale During 2011	$14,400	$14,400	$ 14,400
Less Inventory, 12/31/2011	(3,000)[1]	(2,000)[2]	(2,400)[3]
Cost of Goods Sold for 2011	$11,400	$12,400	$ 12,000
Inventory, 1/1/2012	$ 3,000 [1]	$ 2,000 [2]	$ 2,400 [3]
Purchases During 2012	21,000	21,000	21,000
Goods Available for Sale During 2012	$24,000	$23,000	$ 23,400
Less Inventory, 12/31/2012	(5,000)[4]	(6,200)[5]	(5,850)[6]
Cost of Goods Sold for 2012	$19,000	$16,800	$ 17,550

[1] $200 \times \$15 = \$3,000$.

[2] $200 \times \$10 = \$2,000$.

[3] $(\$14,400/1,200) \times 200 = \$2,400$.

[4] $500 \times \$10 = \$5,000$.

[5] $(200 \times \$10) + (300 \times \$14) = \$6,200$.

[6] $(\$23,400/2,000) \times 500 = \$5,850$.

a. $11,400.   d. $19,000.
b. $12,400.   e. $16,800.
c. $12,000.   f. $17,550.

g. FIFO results in higher net income for 2011. Purchase prices for inventory items increased during 2011. FIFO uses older, lower purchase prices to measure cost of goods sold, whereas LIFO uses more recent, higher prices.

h. LIFO results in higher net income for 2012. Purchase prices for inventory items decreased during 2012. LIFO uses more recent, lower prices to measure cost of goods sold, whereas FIFO uses older, higher prices.

9.44 (Hanover Oil Products; effect of FIFO and LIFO on income statement and balance sheet.) (amounts in US$)

a.

	FIFO	LIFO
Beginning Inventory	$ 0	$ 0
Purchases:		
1/1: 4,000 @ $1.40	$ 5,600	$ 5,600
1/13: 6,000 @ $1.46	8,760	8,760
1/28: 5,000 @ $1.50	7,500	7,500
Total Purchases	$ 21,860	$ 21,860
Available for Sale	$ 21,860	$ 21,860
Less Ending Inventory:		
FIFO: 2,000 X $1.50	(3,000)	
LIFO: 2,000 X $1.40		(2,800)
Cost of Goods Sold	$ 18,860	$ 19,060

b.

	FIFO	LIFO
Beginning Inventory	$ 3,000	$ 2,800
Purchases:		
2/5: 7,000 @ $1.53	$ 10,710	$ 10,710
2/14: 6,000 @ $1.47	8,820	8,820
2/21: 10,000 @ $1.42	14,200	14,200
Total Purchases	$ 33,730	$ 33,730
Available for Sale	$ 36,730	$ 36,530
Less Ending Inventory:		
FIFO: 3,000 X $1.42	(4,260)	
LIFO: (2,000 X $1.40) + (1,000 X $1.53)		(4,330)
Cost of Goods Sold	$ 32,470	$ 32,200

c.

	FIFO	LIFO
Beginning Inventory	$ 4,260	$ 4,330
Purchases:		
3/2: 6,000 @ $1.48	$ 8,880	$ 8,880
3/15: 5,000 @ $1.54	7,700	7,700
3/26: 4,000 @ $1.60	6,400	6,400
Total Purchases	$ 22,980	$ 22,980
Available for Sale	$ 27,240	$ 27,310
Less Ending Inventory:		
FIFO: 1,000 X $1.60	(1,600)	
LIFO: 1,000 X $1.40		(1,400)
Cost of Goods Sold	$ 25,640	$ 25,910

9.44 continued.

d. Acquisition costs increased during January. During such periods, LIFO generally provides larger cost of goods sold amounts than FIFO because LIFO uses the most recent higher cost. Acquisition costs decreased during February. Under these circumstances, FIFO generally results in higher cost of goods sold because it uses the higher older cost. During March, acquisition costs increased. There was a liquidation of LIFO layers, however, which makes it more difficult to generalize about which cost-flow assumption results in the higher cost of goods sold. LIFO results in the higher cost of goods sold in this case because the effect of increasing purchase costs dominated the effect of the LIFO liquidation.

e.

	January		February		March	
	FIFO	**LIFO**	**FIFO**	**LIFO**	**FIFO**	**LIFO**
(1) Sales.........	$20,840	$20,840	$35,490	$35,490	$28,648	$28,648
(2) Cost of Goods Sold ..	18,860	19,060	32,470	32,200	25,640	25,910
(2)/(1)..............	90.5%	91.5%	91.5%	90.7%	89.5%	90.4%

f. LIFO provides the most stable cost of goods sold to sales percentage because LIFO cost of goods sold amounts reflect current replacement cost more fully than FIFO. The firm prices its gasoline at a 10% markup on current replacement cost, so the cost of goods sold to sales percentage under LIFO will be closer to 90.9% (= 1/1.1) than FIFO.

g.

Available for Sale (from Part c.)....................	$ 27,240	$ 27,310
Plus Additional Purchases: 2,000 × $1.60 ..	3,200	3,200
Less Ending Inventory:		
FIFO: 3,000 × $1.60...................................	(4,800)	
LIFO: (2,000 × $1.40) + (1,000 × $1.53)		(4,330)
Cost of Goods Sold	$ 25,640	$ 26,180

Costs of goods sold will not change under FIFO because the additional purchases simply increase both the quantity and valuation of the ending inventory. Cost of goods sold increases under LIFO because the additional purchases increase the quantity of ending inventory but the purchase price paid substitutes for the LIFO layers liquidated in measuring cost of goods sold.

9.45   (Burch Corporation; reconstructing underlying events from ending inventory amounts [adapted from CPA examination].) (amounts in US$)

  a. Down. Notice that lower of cost or market is lower than acquisition cost (FIFO); current market price is less than cost.

  b. Up. FIFO means last-in, still-here. The last purchases (FIFO = LISH) cost $44,000 and the earlier purchases (LIFO = FISH) cost $41,800. Also, lower-of-cost-or-market basis shows acquisition costs, which are greater than or equal to current cost.

  c. LIFO Cost. Other things being equal, the largest income results from the method that shows the largest *increase* in inventory during the year.

    Margin = Revenues – Cost of Goods Sold
        = Revenues – Beginning Inventory – Purchases + Ending Inventory
        = Revenues – Purchases + Increase in Inventory.

  Because the beginning inventory in 2010 is zero, the method with the largest closing inventory amount implies the largest increase and hence the largest income.

  d. Lower of Cost or Market. The method with the "largest increase in inventory" during the year in this case is the method with the smallest decrease, because all methods show declines in inventory during 2011. Lower of cost or market shows a decrease in inventory of only $3,000 during 2011—the other methods show larger decreases ($3,800; $4,000).

  e. Lower of Cost or Market. The method with the largest increase in inventory: $10,000. LIFO shows a $5,400 increase, whereas FIFO shows $8,000.

  f. LIFO Cost. The lower income for all three years results from the method that shows the smallest increase in inventory over the three years. Because all beginning inventories were zero under all methods, we need merely find the method with the smallest ending inventory at 2012 year-end.

9.45 continued.

g. FIFO lower by $2,000. Under FIFO, inventories increased $8,000 during 2012. Under lower of cost or market, inventories increased $10,000 during 2012. Lower of cost or market has a bigger increase—$2,000—and therefore lower of cost or market shows a $2,000 larger income than FIFO for 2012.

9.46 (Wilson Company; LIFO layers influence purchasing behavior and provide opportunity for income manipulation.) (amounts in US$)

Cost per Pound	Layer	Beginning Inventory Cost ($000)	+ Purchases Cost ($000)	− Ending Inventory Pounds	Cost ($000)	= Cost of Goods Sold ($000)
a. (Controller)	2003	$ 60.0	—	2,000	$ 60.0	—
	2008	9.2	—	200	9.2	—
	2009	19.2	—	400	19.2	—
	2012	72.8	—	1,400	72.8	—
7,000 @ $62/lb	2013	—	$ 434.0	—	—	434.0
		$ 161.2	$ 434.0	4,000	$ 161.2	$ 434.0

Cost per Pound	Layer	Beginning Inventory Cost ($000)	+ Purchases Cost ($000)	− Ending Inventory Pounds	Cost ($000)	= Cost of Goods Sold ($000)
b. (Purchasing	2003	$ 60.0	—	600	$ 18.0	$ 42.0
Agent)	2008	9.2	—	—	—	9.2
	2009	19.2	—	—	—	19.2
	2012	72.8	—	—	—	72.8
3,600 @ $62/lb	2013	—	$ 223.2	—	—	223.2
		$ 161.2	$ 223.2	600	$ 18.0	$ 366.4

c. Controller's Policy COGS $62/lb .... $ 434.00
Less Purchasing Agent's COGS .... (366.40)
Controller's Extra Deductions .... $ 67.60
Tax Rate: 40% .... X 0.40
Controller's Tax Savings .... $ 27.04
Controller's Extra Cash Costs for Inventory: 3,400 @
  $10/lb .... $ 34.00

9.46 continued.

d.   The economically sound action is to follow the purchasing agent's advice. The controller's policy does save taxes but not as much in taxes as the extra inventory costs. This response presumes that allowing inventory quantities to decrease to 600 pounds does not negatively affect operations prior to replenishing the inventory. A quality of earnings issue arises because the increase in net income that results from the LIFO liquidations is nonrecurring. Except for the older costs in the base layer of 600 units, new LIFO layers will use higher current costs. Liquidating those new layers in later years will not likely increase earnings as much as the current year's liquidations produced. One might argue that following the purchasing agent's advice does not raise an ethical issue because it is the economically sound action. However, management does have some discretion (see Part e.) as to whether to deplete inventories to 600 units or to stop short of that amount of depletion. To the extent that management has an earning target in mind and can choose the amount of inventory depletion to achieve that level of earnings, some would argue that ethical issues arise.

e.   To maximize income for 2013, liquidate all our LIFO inventory layers, 4,000 lb with total cost $161,200, and purchase only 3,000 lb at $62 each during 2013. To minimize income, acquire 7,000 lb at $62 each.

Policy	Cost of Goods Sold for 2013
Minimum Income:	
7,000 lb X $62	$ 434,000
Maximum Income:	
4,000 lb of Old Layers	(161,200)
3,000 lb at $62	(186,000)
Income Spread Before Taxes	$ 86,800
Taxes at 40%	(34,720)
Income Spread After Taxes	$ 52,080

By manipulating purchases of expensium, Wilson Company reports after-tax income anywhere in the range from $50,000 (by following the controller's policy) up to $102,080 (= $50,000 + $52,080) by acquiring only 3,000 lb and liquidating all LIFO layers.

9.47   (Sedan Corporation; interpreting inventory disclosures.)   (amounts in millions of Japanese yen)

a. **March 31, 2013:**

If Sedan had used FIFO, inventory values would have been ¥13,780 less than LIFO amounts.

Ending Balance of Total Inventory (FIFO) = (¥374,210 + ¥239,937 + ¥1,211,569) − ¥13,780 = ¥1,825,716 − ¥13,780 = ¥1,811,936 million.

March 31, 2012:

If Sedan had used FIFO, inventory values would have been ¥30,360 less than LIFO amounts.

Ending Balance of Total Inventory (FIFO) = (¥362,686 + ¥236,749 + ¥1,204,521) − ¥30,360 = ¥1,803,956 − ¥30,360 = ¥1,773,596 million.

b. Beginning Balance in Finished Goods (FIFO) + Cost of Units Completed = Cost of Products Sold (FIFO) + Ending Balance in Finished Goods (FIFO).

Beginning Balance of Finished Goods Inventory (FIFO) = ¥1,204,521 − ¥30,360 = ¥1,174,161 million.

Ending Balance of Finished Goods Inventory (FIFO) = ¥1,211,569 − ¥13,780 = ¥1,197,789 million.

¥1,174,161 + ¥20,459,386 (from Problem 9.40, Part *b.*) = Cost of Products Sold (FIFO) + ¥1,197,789.

Cost of Goods Sold (FIFO) = ¥20,435,758 million.

Also, could calculate as follows:

Cost of Goods Sold (LIFO)	¥ 20,452,338
Change in LIFO reserve (¥30,360 − ¥13,780)	(16,580)
Cost of Goods Sold (FIFO)	¥ 20,435,758

9.48   (Central Appliance; allowance method for warranties; reconstructing transactions.) (amounts in US$)

    a. $720,000 = $820,000 (Goods Available for Sale) − $100,000 (Beginning Inventory).

    b. $700,000 = $820,000 (Goods Available for Sale) − $120,000 (Ending Inventory).

    c. $21,000 = $6,000 (Cr. Balance) + $15,000 (Dr. Balance).

    d. $20,000 = $5,000 (Required Cr. Balance) + $15,000 (Existing Dr. Balance).

    e.

Warranty Liability	21,000	
Various Assets Used for Repairs		21,000
Repairs made during 2013.		

Warranty Expense	20,000	
Warranty Liability		20,000
Expense recognition for 2013.		

Cost of Goods Sold	700,000	
Merchandise Inventory		700,000
Cost of goods sold is goods available for sale less ending inventory.		

9.49   (Bayer Group; interpreting restructuring disclosures.) (amounts in millions of euros)

    a.

Restructuring Provision	134	
Cash		134
To record utilizations.		

Restructuring Provision	31	
Reversal of Restructuring Expense		31
To record reversal.		

9.49 continued.

b. Journal entry to record additions to Restructuring Provision during the year:

Restructuring Expense 128
    Restructuring Provision 128
To record €128 million of restructuring charges
made during the year.

Beginning Balance of Restructuring Provision + Additions = Utilizations + Net Other Effects + Reversals + Ending Balance of Restructuring Provision €196 + Additions = €134 + €5 + €31 + €154.

Additions = €128 million.

CHAPTER 10

LONG-LIVED TANGIBLE AND INTANGIBLE ASSETS

Questions, Exercises, and Problems: Answers and Solutions

10.1   See the text or the glossary at the end of the book.

10.2   The central concept underlying GAAP for these three items is the ability to identify and reliably measure expected future benefits. The self-constructed building has physical substance and the accountant can observe the effect of an expenditure on the physical structure of the building. The building provides evidence of future benefits. Research and development (R&D) expenditures may give rise to an intangible, such as a patent on a new technology. The accountant cannot, however, observe the physical creation of an asset with future benefits when a firm makes R&D expenditures. Thus, reliably identifying and measuring future benefits is problematic. U.S. GAAP does not permit recognition of an asset for research and development expenditures. Expenditures on software development present an in-between case. The programming underlying the software is embedded in a computer but the accountant can observe how well the software works. When the software has not yet reached the stage of technological feasibility, future benefits are uncertain. Thus, U.S. GAAP treats expenditures up to this point as expenses of the period when incurred. When software reaches the point of technological feasibility, future benefits become more certain. U.S. GAAP, therefore, permits firms to capitalize software development expenditures after this point.

10.3   The central concept underlying U.S. GAAP for these three items is the ability to identify and reliably measure expected future benefits. Expenditures to research new drugs may give rise to future benefits, but identifying the existence of those future benefits while research progresses is problematic. Thus, U.S. GAAP requires immediate expensing of research and development expenditures. The external market transaction for a patent on a new drug validates both the existence and fair value of the patent. U.S. GAAP, therefore, recognizes the patent as an asset. In-process R&D has characteristics of the previous two cases. Whether the in-process project will yield future benefits is uncertain, suggesting that firms

10.3 continued.

should expense such expenditures at the time of acquisition. An external market transaction between independent parties suggests the existence of future benefits, supporting recognition of an asset until such time as the status of the research project becomes more certain. FASB *Statement No. 141 (Revised)* requires firms to recognize as an asset the fair value of in-process R&D acquired in a corporate acquisition, placing greater weight on the evidence provided by the external market transaction than on the uncertainty of future benefits.

10.4   Over the life of the project, income is the same regardless of whether the firm capitalizes interest or expenses it. Capitalizing and then amortizing interest versus expensing it affects the timing but not the total amount of income. Capitalizing interest defers expense from the construction period to the periods of use. This increases income in the years of construction and decreases it in the periods of use. In periods of use, depreciation charges are larger.

10.5   A long-lived asset with a finite life is expected to provide benefits for a limited amount of time. Benefits will eventually decline to zero, either because of physical use, obsolescence, or disposal. Firms depreciate or amortize assets with finite lives. Note that firms must estimate the finite life in most cases. U.S. GAAP and IFRS treat assets that have an extended life, but for which the length of that life is highly uncertain, as having an indefinite life. U.S. GAAP and IFRS do not require firms to depreciate or amortize assets with an indefinite life. U.S. GAAP and IFRS require that these assets—in fact, all long-lived assets—be tested annually for possible asset impairment.

10.6   Thames must demonstrate that the brand names amortized have a finite life and those not amortized have an indefinite life. Thames would examine the age of particular brand names, the pace at which brand names come in and out of favor in a particular industry, and similar factors in deciding the classification of a particular brand name acquired. This process likely involves considerable subjectivity, but it is subject to audit by the Thames independent accountant.

10.7　The treatment of this change in depreciable life would depend on the reason for and the materiality of the change. The change in this case appears prompted by new governmental regulations imposed on the airline industry. If the change in expected life is material, the firm can make a case for recognizing an asset impairment loss and revising its depreciation going forward. If the impact is not material, the airline might treat the change in depreciable life as a change in an estimate and spread the effect of the change over the current and future years. The purpose of this question is to demonstrate that judgments are often required in applying authoritative guidance.

10.8　The relevant question to apply authoritative guidance is whether the expenditure maintained the originally expected useful life or extended that useful life. Firms should expense, as maintenance or repairs, expenditures that maintain the originally expected five-year life. In this case, the expenditure both maintains and extends the useful life. A portion of the expenditure should appear as an expense immediately (perhaps two-thirds) and a portion (perhaps one-third) should increase the depreciable base for the asset. The portion of the expenditure treated as an asset would be based on the extent to which the expenditure increased the useful life.

10.9　U.S. GAAP compares the undiscounted cash flows from an asset to its carrying value to determine if an impairment loss has occurred. The rationale is that an impairment loss has not occurred if a firm will receive cash flows in the future at least equal to the carrying value of the asset. Receiving such cash flows will permit the firm to recover the carrying value. This criterion ignores the time value of money. Cash received earlier has more economic value than cash received later, but this criterion ignores such differences.

10.10　The cash recoverability criterion requires firms to estimate the expected undiscounted cash flows. This estimate requires projection of cash flows for a specified number of periods. Non-amortized intangibles have an indefinite life. For indefinite lived assets, it is not possible to project the total undiscounted cash flows because it is not possible to discern when the forecasted cash flows stop.

10.11   An asset impairment loss that arises during a period results from a decline in fair value due to some external event. Fair values are based on discounted cash flows, not undiscounted cash flows. Therefore, using undiscounted cash flows to signal an impairment loss ignores the actual decline in fair value that occurred. Firms will not recognize the asset impairment loss as long as the undiscounted cash flows exceed the carrying value of the asset.

10.12   The excess purchase price will affect net income if and when the firm recognizes a goodwill impairment loss. A goodwill impairment loss results when the acquirer will not recover the carrying amount of the purchased goodwill. Firms must test goodwill annually for possible impairment. Management might, however, operate the acquired entity in such a way that its value increases over time, thereby offsetting the effect of any initial overpayment.

10.13   (Outback Steakhouse; calculating acquisition costs of long-lived assets.) (amounts in US$)

The relative market values of the land and building are 20% (= $52,000/$260,000) for the land and 80% (= $208,000/$260,000) for the building. We use these percentages to allocate the combined $260,000 cost of the land and building.

	Land	Building
Purchase Price of Land and Building.......	$ 52,000	$ 208,000
Legal Costs Split 20% and 80%...............	2,520	10,080
Renovation Costs.......................................	—	35,900
Property and Liability Insurance Costs During Renovation Split 20% and 80%...	800	3,200
Property Taxes During Renovation Split 20% and 80%.......................................	1,000	4,000
Total..	$ 56,320	$ 261,180

Note: One might argue that the split of the insurance and property taxes should recognize the increase in market value of the building as a result of the renovation and use some other percentages besides 20% and 80%. Note also that the insurance and property taxes for the period after opening are expenses of the first year of operation.

10.14 (Classifying expenditure as asset or expense. These solutions apply U.S. GAAP.)

    a.   (3) Expense.

    b.   (3) Expense.

    c.   (3) Expense.

    d.   (1) Noncurrent asset (machine).

    e.   (3) Expense.

    f.   (3) Expense.

    g.   (2) Current asset (inventory).

    h.   (1) Noncurrent asset (equipment).

    i.   (3) Expense.

    j.   (1) Noncurrent asset (ore deposit).

    k.   (1) Current asset (prepayment).

    l.   (1) Current asset (marketable securities).

    m.   (2) Current asset product cost (inventories).

    n.   (1) Noncurrent asset (trademark).

    o.   (1) Noncurrent asset (copyright).

    p.   (1) Noncurrent asset (computer software).

    q.   (3) Expense. Acquired in-process research and development (IPR&D) is recognized as an asset when the item is acquired as part of a business combination.

10-5

10.15   (Bolton Company; cost of self-constructed assets.) (amounts in US$)

Land: $70,000 + $2,000 (14) = $72,000.

Factory Building: $200,000 (1) + $12,000 (2) + $140,000 (3) + $6,000 (5) −
$7,000 (7) + $10,000 (8) + $8,000 (9) + $3,000[a] (10) + $8,000 (11) + $4,000
(13) + $1,000[a] (15) = $385,000.

Office Building: $20,000 + $13,000 (4) = $33,000.

Site Improvements: $5,000 (12).

> [a]The firm might expense these items. It depends on the rationality of the firm's "self-insurance" policy.

Item (6) is omitted because firms may not recognize opportunity costs in financial reports.

Item (16) is omitted because no arm's length transaction occurred in which the firm earned a profit.

10.16   (Duck Vehicle Manufacturing Company; cost of self-developed product.)

The first four items qualify as research and development costs which, under U.S. GAAP, the firm must expense in the year incurred. It might appear that the firm should capitalize the cost of the prototype because it acquires the prototype from an external contractor. Completion of a prototype does not, however, signify a viable product. Purchasing the prototype externally versus constructing it internally does not change the accounting.

The firm should capitalize the legal fees to register and establish the patent as part of the cost of the patent. The firm might consider this cost as sufficiently immaterial to warrant treatment as an asset and expense it immediately.

The firm should capitalize the cost of the castings and amortize them over the expected useful life of the vehicle. The cost of the manufacturing permits and the cost of manufacturing the first vehicle are product costs that increase work-in-process inventory.

10.17   (Bulls Eye Stores; calculating interest capitalized during construction.) (amounts in US$)

Capitalized Interest on Borrowing Directly Related to
  Construction: 0.06 X $2,000,000 .... $ 120,000
Capitalized Interest of Other Borrowing: 0.07 X $1,400,000   98,000
  Total Interest Capitalized .... $ 218,000

10.18   (Nexor; amount of interest capitalized during construction.) (amounts in US$)

a.   Average Construction = ($30,000,000 + $60,000,000)/2 = $45,000,000.

	Interest Anticipated
Relevant Loans	
$ 25,000,000 at 8%	$2,000,000
20,000,000 at 6%	1,200,000
$ 45,000,000	$3,200,000

b.   Interest Expense 8,000,000
       Interest Payable   8,000,000
     ($25,000,000 X 0.08) + ($100,000,000 X 0.06).

     Construction-in-Process 3,200,000
       Interest Expense   3,200,000

c.   Interest Expense 8,000,000
       Interest Payable   8,000,000
     ($25,000,000 X 0.08) + ($100,000,000 X 0.06).

     Construction-in-Process 7,100,000
       Interest Expense   7,100,000
     ($25,000,000 X 0.08) + ($85,000,000 X 0.06).

10.19   (Carlton, Inc.; calculations for various depreciation methods.) (amounts in US$)

	2013	2014	2015
a. Straight-Line (Time) Method	$14,000	$14,000	$14,000
($88,800 − $4,800)/6 = $14,000.			
b. Straight-Line (Use) Method	$12,600	$14,000	$15,400
$84,000/30,000 = $2.80 per hour.			

Solutions

10.20   (Luck Delivery Company; calculations for various depreciation methods.)
(amounts in US$)

a.   **Depreciation Charge (Straight-Line)**
2013 .... $ 6,000   ($30,000/5)
2014 6,000
2015 6,000
2016 6,000
2017 6,000
$30,000

b.   **Depreciation Charge (Double-Declining-Balance)**
2013 .... $12,000   ($30,000 X 0.40)
2014 7,200   ($18,000 X 0.40)
2015 4,320   ($10,800 X 0.40)
2016 3,240   ($6,480/2)
2017 3,240   (balance)
$30,000

c.   **Depreciation Charge (Sum-of-the-Years'-Digits)**
2013 .... $10,000   ($30,000 X 5/15)
2014 8,000   ($30,000 X 4/15)
2015 6,000   ($30,000 X 3/15)
2016 4,000   ($30,000 X 2/15)
2017 2,000   ($30,000 X 1/15)
$30,000

d.   **Tax Depreciation**
2013 .... $ 6,000   (= $30,000 X 0.20)
2014 9,600   (= $30,000 X 0.32)
2015 5,760   (= $30,000 X 0.192)
2016 3,450   (= $30,000 X 0.115)
2017 3,450   (= $30,000 X 0.115)
2018 1,740   (= $30,000 X 0.058)
$30,000

10.21   (Thom Corporation; change in depreciable life and salvage value.)
(amounts in US$)

Carrying Value on January 1, 2013: $10,000,000 − {2 X [($10,000,000 −
$1,000,000)/6]} = $7,000,000. Depreciation expense for 2013 based on the
new depreciable life and salvage value is $3,200,000 [= ($7,000,000 −
$600,000)/2].

10.22   (Florida Manufacturing Corporation; journal entries for revising estimate of service life.) (amounts in US$)

a.   Work-in-Process Inventory...................................... 2,400
      Accumulated Depreciation..................................   2,400
      ($180,000 − $7,200)/144 = $1,200 per month.

b.   Work-in-Process Inventory...................................... 14,400
      Accumulated Depreciation..................................   14,400
      12 × $1,200 = $14,400.

c.   Depreciation to 1/1/2019 = 62 months × $1,200 = $74,400.
      Remaining depreciation = $180,000 − $74,400 − $3,840 = $101,760.
      Remaining life = 168 months − 62 months = 106 months as of
         8/30/2019.
      Depreciation charge per month = $101,760/106 = $960.

      Work-in-Process Inventory...................................... 13,440
      Accumulated Depreciation..................................   13,440
      (8 × $1,200) + (4 × $960) = $13,440.

d.   By March 31, 2024, the machine has been on the new depreciation schedule for September 2019 through March 2024 (55 months total). Accumulated depreciation is $84,000 + (55 × $960) = $84,000 + $52,800 = $136,800.

      Carrying value is $180,000 − $136,800 = $43,200; sale at $40,000 results in a loss of $3,200 (= $40,000 − $43,200).

      Journal entries are as follows:

      Work-in-Process Inventory...................................... 2,880
      Accumulated Depreciation..................................   2,880
      3 × $960 = $2,880; to bring depreciation up to
      date as of 3/31/2024.

      Cash.. 40,000
      Accumulated Depreciation....................................... 136,800
      Loss on Disposal of Machinery............................... 3,200
      Machinery...   180,000

10.23 (Disney World; distinguishing repairs versus improvements.) (amounts in US$)

Repair: (1.00/1.20 × $30,200) + $86,100 + (1.00/1.25 × $26,900) + $12,600 = $145,387.

Improvement: (0.20/1.20 × $30,200) + (0.25/1.25 × $26,900) = $10,413.

10.24 (Wildwood Properties; computing the amount of an impairment loss on tangible long-lived assets.) (amounts in US$)

The undiscounted cash flows total $12,400,000 [= ($1,400,000 × 6) + $4,000,000]. The carrying value of the building of $15,000,000 exceeds the undiscounted estimated cash flows, so an impairment loss has occurred. The present value of the expected cash flows when discounted at 10% is $8,355,244 [= ($1,400,000 × 4.35526) + ($4,000,000 × 0.56447) = $6,097,364 + $2,257,880]. The impairment loss is, therefore, $6,644,756 (= $15,000,000 − $8,355,244) under both U.S. GAAP and IFRS.

10.25 (Kieran Corporation; computing the amount of impairment loss.) (amounts in US$)

	Carrying Value	Undis- counted Cash Flows	Impair- ment Loss Recog- nized	Fair Value	Amount of Loss
Land....................	$ 550,000	$ 575,000	No	$ 550,000	$ 0
Buildings............	580,000	600,000	No	580,000	0
Equipment..........	1,200,000	950,000	Yes	800,000	400,000
Goodwill..............	500,000[a]	—	Yes	270,000	230,000
Total	$ 2,830,000			$2,200,000	$ 630,000

[a]$500,000 = $2,400,000 − $400,000 − $600,000 − $900,000.

After recognizing the impairment losses on the property, plant, and equipment, the carrying value of Kieran Corporation is $2,430,000 (= $550,000 for land + $580,000 for buildings + $800,000 for equipment + $500,000 for goodwill). The carrying value of $2,430,000 exceeds the fair value of the entity of $2,200,000, so a goodwill impairment loss may have occurred. The fair value column above shows the allocation of the $2,200,000 fair value to identifiable assets, with the residual of $270,000 attributed to goodwill. The carrying value of the goodwill of $500,000 exceeds its implied fair value of $270,000, so Kieran Corporation recognizes an impairment loss on the goodwill of $230,000.

10.26 (Fedup Express; computing the gain or loss on sale of equipment.) (amounts in US$)

Annual depreciation is $7,000 [= ($48,000 – $6,000)/6]. Depreciation expense for the first six months of 2013 is $3,500.

Depreciation Expense	3,500	
Accumulated Depreciation		3,500

The carrying value of the delivery truck after the entry above is $16,500 [= $48,000 – (4.5 X $7,000)]. The accumulated depreciation totals $31,500 (= 4.5 X $7,000). The entry to record the sale is:

Cash..	14,000	
Accumulated Depreciation	31,500	
Loss on Sale of Delivery Truck	2,500	
Delivery Truck...		48,000

10.27 (Wilcox Corporation; working backward to derive proceeds from disposition of plant assets.) (amounts in US$)

Cost of Equipment Sold:	$400,000 + $230,000 – $550,000 = $80,000.
Accumulated Depreciation on Equipment Sold:	$180,000 + $50,000 – $160,000 = $70,000.
Carrying Value of Equipment Sold:	$80,000 – $70,000 = $10,000.
Proceeds of Sale:	$10,000 + $4,000 = $14,000.

10.28 (Journal entries to correct accounting errors.) (amounts in US$)

a.
Depreciation Expense...	375	
Accumulated Depreciation..................................		375

$3,000 X 0.25 X 6/12 = $375.

Accumulated Depreciation.......................................	1,875	
Loss on Disposal of Equipment	325	
Equipment		2,200

$3,000 X 0.25 X 2.5 = $1,875. $3,200 + $3,000 – $4,000 = $2,200. $800 selling price – $1,125 carrying value = $325 loss.

b.
Accumulated Depreciation.......................................	5,000	
Truck...		5,000

10.28 continued.

   c.   Depreciation Expense.. 60

           Accumulated Depreciation................................... 60

        $1,200 x 0.10 x 6/12 = $60.

        Accumulated Depreciation....................................... 270

           Theft Loss.. 270

        $1,200 x 0.10 x 27/12 = $270.

10.29   (Moon Macrosystems; recording transactions involving tangible and intangible assets.) (amounts in US$)

   a.   Office Equipment... 400,000

        Computer Software... 40,000

           Cash... 440,000

   b.   Office Equipment... 20,000

        Computer Software... 10,000

           Cash... 30,000

   c.   **2011 and 2012**

        Depreciation Expense [($400,000 + $20,000 –

        $40,000)/10]... 38,000

        Amortization Expense [($40,000 + $10,000)/4] 12,500

           Accumulated Depreciation................................... 38,000

           Computer Software... 12,500

   d.   Impairment Loss of Computer Software

        ($40,000 + $10,000 – $12,500 – $12,500)........... 25,000

           Computer Software... 25,000

   e.   Depreciation Expense [($400,000 + $20,000 –

        $38,000 – $38,000 – $56,000)/12] 24,000

           Accumulated Depreciation............................... 24,000

10.29 continued.

 f. Depreciation Expense.. 24,000
   Accumulated Depreciation....................................   24,000

  Cash.. 260,000
  Accumulated Depreciation ($38,000 + $38,000 +
   $24,000 + $24,000)... 124,000
  Loss on Sale of Office Equipment 36,000
   Office Equipment..   420,000

10.30 (Cloud Airlines; effect on net income of changes in estimates for depreciable assets.) (amounts in US$)

Income has been about $180 million (= 0.06 X $3 billion) per year.

Reconciliation of Plant Data:

Airplanes' Cost...	$ 2,500,000,000
Less Salvage Value (10%)	250,000,000
Depreciable Basis	$ 2,250,000,000
Divided by 10-Year Life Equals Yearly Depreciation Charges...	$ 225,000,000
Times 4 Years Equals Accumulated Depreciation............	$ 900,000,000
Plus Net Carrying Value..	1,600,000,000
Airplanes' Cost...	$ 2,500,000,000

New Depreciation Charge:

Net Carrying Value	$ 1,600,000,000
Less Salvage Value (12% of Cost)...............................	300,000,000
Depreciation Basis..	$ 1,300,000,000
Divided by 10 (= 14 – 4) Years Equals Revised Yearly Depreciation Charge..	$ 130,000,000

Increase in Pretax Income:

Old Depreciation Charges...	$	225,000,000
New Depreciation Charges		130,000,000
	$	95,000,000
Multiplied by (1 – tax rate) = 1 – 0.35 = 0.65		X .65
Increase in After-Tax Income.......................................	$	61,750,000

Income will rise by about 34.3% (= $61.75/$180.0).

Note that a modest change in depreciation parameters can significantly affect net income.

10.31   (Recognizing and measuring impairment losses.) (amounts in US$)

a. The loss occurs because of an adverse action by a governmental entity. The undiscounted cash flows of $50 million are less than the carrying value of the building of $60 million. An impairment loss has therefore occurred. The fair value of the building of $32 million is less than the carrying value of $60 million. Thus, the amount of the impairment loss is $28 million (= $60 million – $32 million). The journal entry to record the impairment loss is (in millions):

Loss from Impairment	28	
Accumulated Depreciation	20	
Building		48

This entry records the impairment loss, eliminates the accumulated depreciation, and writes down the building to its fair value of $32 million (= $80 – $48).

b. The undiscounted cash flows of $70 million exceed the carrying value of the building of $60 million. Thus, no impairment loss occurs according to the definition in U.S. GAAP. An *economic* loss occurred but U.S. GAAP does not recognize it.

c. The loss arises because the accumulated costs significantly exceed the amount originally anticipated. The carrying value of the building of $25 million exceeds the undiscounted future cash flows of $22 million. Thus, an impairment loss has occurred.   The impairment loss recognized equals $9 million (= $25 million – $16 million). The journal entry is (in millions):

Loss from Impairment	9	
Construction in Process		9

d. The loss occurs because of a significant decline in the fair value of the patent. U.S. GAAP requires calculation of the impairment loss on the patent before computing the impairment loss on goodwill.   The undiscounted future cash flows of $18 million are less than the carrying value of the patent of $20 million. Thus, an impairment loss occurred. The amount of the loss is $8 million (= $20 million – $12 million). The journal entry to record the loss is (in millions):

Loss from Impairment	8	
Patent		8

10.31 d. continued.

The second step is to determine if an impairment loss on the goodwill occurred. The fair value of the entity is $25 million. The carrying value after writing down the patent is $27 million (= $12 million for patent and $15 million for goodwill). Thus, a goodwill impairment loss occurred. If the fair value of the patent is $12 million, the market value of the goodwill is $13 million. The impairment loss on goodwill is therefore $2 million (= $15 million – $13 million). The journal entry is (in millions):

Loss from Impairment 2
    Goodwill..   2

e. The loss occurs because of a significant change in the business climate for Chicken Franchisees. One might question whether this loss is temporary or permanent. U.S. GAAP discusses but rejects the use of a permanency criterion in identifying impairment losses. Thus, an impairment loss occurs in this case because the future undiscounted cash flows of $6 million from the franchise rights are less than the carrying value of the franchise rights of $10 million. The amount of the impairment loss is $7 million (= $10 million – $3 million). The journal entry is (in millions):

Impairment Loss 7
    Franchise Rights   7

This entry assumes that Chicken Franchisees does not use an Accumulated Amortization account.

10.32 (Pfizer; expensing versus capitalizing research and development costs.) (amounts in millions of US$)

		Year 1	Year 2	Year 3	Year 4
a.	**Expense Costs as Incurred**				
	Other Income	$ 30	$ 30	$ 30	$ 30
	Additional Income from R&D:				
	First Year's R&D.......	36	36	36	
	Second Year's R&D....		36	36	36
	Third Year's R&D......			36	36
	Fourth Year's R&D....				36
	R&D Expense......................	(90)	(90)	(90)	(90)
	Income (Loss) Before Taxes.............................	$ (24)	$ 12	$ 48	$ 48

		Year 1	Year 2	Year 3	Year 4
b.	**Capitalize and Amortize over 3 Years (Including Year of Occurrence)**				
	Other Income	$ 30	$ 30	$ 30	$ 30
	Additional Income from R&D:				
	First Year's R&D.......	36	36	36	
	Second Year's R&D....		36	36	36
	Third Year's R&D......			36	36
	Fourth Year's R&D....				36
	R&D Amortization Expense:				
	First Year's R&D.......	(30)	(30)	(30)	
	Second Year's R&D....		(30)	(30)	(30)
	Third Year's R&D......			(30)	(30)
	Fourth Year's R&D....				(30)
	Income Before Taxes..........	$ 36	$ 42	$ 48	$ 48
	Deferred R&D Asset on Balance Sheet:				
	First Year's R&D.......	$ 60	$ 30		
	Second Year's R&D....		60	$ 30	
	Third Year's R&D......			60	$ 30
	Fourth Year's R&D....				60
	Total.................................	$ 60	$ 90	$ 90	$ 90

10.32 continued.

    c.   The expensing policy leads to higher expenses and lower income before income taxes, in the first two years. After that, the two policies are the same. When the firm ceases to spend on R&D, the policy of expensing will show higher income in the two years when the benefits of prior R&D continue, but there are no matching expenses. There are no expenses under policy **(1)**, but policy **(2)** continues to show amortization expense. Thus, policy **(1)** is more conservative in the sense that it results in smaller cumulative income before taxes until the firm ceases to spend on R&D. Policy **(1)** also results in smaller assets on the balance sheet because, unlike policy **(2)**, it shows no asset for Deferred R&D Costs.

    d.   The pre-tax income under the two policies will continue to be the same if there is no growth or change in policy. Policy **(2)** will show a lower rate of return on total assets and a lower rate of return on stockholders' equity than will policy **(1)** because the asset and equity totals are larger under policy **(2)** under policy **(1)**.

10.33   (Comerica Mills; interpreting disclosures regarding long-lived assets.) (amounts in millions of US$)

    a.   Comerica Mills purchased software for its internal use from a software developer. Comerica Mills expects to receive future benefits from using the software and the acquisition cost provides evidence of the amount of expected future benefits.

    b.   Yes. The computer software has a finite life because of technological obsolescence and would be depreciated.

    c.   Average Total Life: $0.5(\$5,806 - \$54 - \$252 + \$6,096 - \$61 - \$276)/\$421 = 13.4$ years.

        Average Age: $0.5(\$2,809 + \$3,082)/\$421 = 7.0$ years.

    d.   Yes. The accumulated depreciation account increased by $273 (= $3,082 − $2,809). Depreciation expense increased accumulated depreciation by $421. Thus, the accumulated depreciation on assets sold or abandoned was $148 (= $273 − $421).

10.33 continued.

e. Comerica Mills has grown heavily by corporate acquisitions. Intangibles comprise 57.9% (= $10,529/$18,184) of total assets. Because GAAP does not require firms to recognize internally developed intangibles, these intangibles arise from corporate acquisitions.

f. Yes. The amount for brands and goodwill increased. Because firms cannot write up assets for increases in fair value, the increased amounts suggest a small acquisition during the year.

g. Patents have a specified legal life. Trademarks are subject to renewal at the end of their legal life as long as a firm continues to use them. Comerica Mills must intend not to renew these trademarks.

h. Comerica Mills must expect the brand names to have an indefinite life. The firm would need to provide evidence based on past experience for its brand names and from industry experience to convince its independent accountants that the timing of any cessation of benefits is highly uncertain.

i. Comerica Mills shows amounts in its Construction in Progress account. Thus, Comerica Mills must capitalize a portion of interest expense. The reported amount is the net of total interest cost minus the amount capitalized in Construction in Progress.

10.34 (Hargon, Inc.; interpreting disclosures regarding long-lived assets.) (amounts in millions of US$)

a. No. Firms do not commence recognizing depreciation until they put an asset into service. The assets under construction have not yet reached that stage.

b. Average Total Life: 0.5($7,321 − $294 − $958 + $8,688 − $398 − $1,271)/$593 = 11.0 years.

Average Age: 0.5($2,283 + $2,767)/$593 = 4.3 years.

c. Yes. Accumulated depreciation experienced a net increase of $484 (= $2,767 − $2,283) during the year. Depreciation increased the Accumulated Depreciation account by $593. Thus, accumulated depreciation on assets sold or abandoned was $109 (= $484 − $593).

10.34 continued.

d. Hargon is in an industry subject to technological change. Thus, any technology-based intangible likely has a finite life and is, therefore, subject to amortization. The Developed Product Technology likely relates to specific biotechnology products it currently sells. Either Hargon or another company will likely develop new products that will lead to obsolescence in the near future. The Core Technology intangible relates to basic findings and principles that affect the development and sale of biotechnology products in general. One might expect this item to have a longer useful life than Developed Product Technology. Given the relatively young age of the biotechnology industry, however, the extent to which core technologies will last is uncertain. Hargon could probably make a stronger case for treating Core Technologies as an intangible with an indefinite life than is the case for Developed Product Technology. It apparently chose to treat it as having a finite life. The Trade Name likely attaches to a particular product and, like Developed Product Technology, is subject to replacement by a more technologically advanced product. The Acquired Technology Rights arise from contractual arrangements that have prescribed time limits during which Hargon can enjoy the benefits.

e. Average Total Life: 0.5($4,950 + $5,219)/$370 = 13.7 years.

Average Age: 0.5($1,208 + $1,472)/$370 = 3.6 years.

f. It appears that Hargon made no corporate acquisition during 2013 because the acquisition cost of Core Technology and Trade Name remained the same. The decrease in the acquisition cost of Developed Product Technology might have occurred because of the discontinuance of a particular product or because of the recognition of an asset impairment loss on that intangible.

g. Goodwill likely includes technologies that are not separately identifiable, the value of research scientists, and perhaps some overpayment for acquired companies.

h. Hargon shows amounts in its Construction in Progress account. Thus, Hargon must capitalize a portion of interest expense. The reported amount is the net of total interest cost minus the amount capitalized in Construction in Progress.

10.35   (HP3; interpreting disclosures regarding long-lived assets.) (amounts in millions of US$)

a. Average Total Life: 0.5($15,024 – $534 + $16,411 – $464)/$1,922 = 7.9 years.

Average Age: 0.5($8,161 + $8,613)/$1,922 = 4.4 years.

b. Yes. The Accumulated Depreciation account increased $452 (= $8,613 – $8,161). Depreciation increased the Accumulated Depreciation account by $1,922. Thus, the accumulated depreciation on assets sold or abandoned was $1,470 (= $452 – $1,922).

c. Customer Contracts have a specific term and, therefore, have a finite life. Core Technology likely involves technologies related to the design of computer hardware and software in general and is not product specific. Given the pace of change in the computer industry, even core technologies change over time. HP3 would likely encounter difficulties in convincing its independent accountants that core technologies do not have a finite, albeit uncertain, life. Patents have a 20-year life, although the technological life in the computer industry is much shorter. Trademarks are renewable as long as a firm continues to use them. HP3 must expect to discontinue using the trademarks.

d. Average Remaining Total Life: 0.5($4,612 + $6,122)/$783 = 6.9 years.

Average Age: 0.5($2,682 + $3,465)/$783 = 3.9 years.

e. At the time of the acquisition, the Casio name was highly recognizable. HP3 likely had no difficulty convincing its independent accountants that the brand name had an indefinite life. Given the elapsed time since the acquisition and the merging of Casio products into HP3's line of offerings, one wonders whether HP3 will write off the brand name at some point.

f. Yes. The amount of each intangible, except the Casio brand name, increased during 2013. HP3 allocated a portion of the purchase price to these intangibles, with most of the increase involving goodwill.

CHAPTER 11

NOTES, BONDS, AND LEASES

Questions, Exercises, and Problems: Answers and Solutions

11.1 See the text or the glossary at the end of the book.

11.2 Generally, accountants initially record assets at acquisition cost and then allocate this amount to future periods as an expense. Changes in the fair value of most assets (except for use of the lower-of-cost-or-market method for inventories; the market value method for marketable securities and investments in securities; and impairments) do not appear in the accounting records. Similarly, using the market interest rate at the time of issue to account for bonds results in an initial liability equal to the amount of cash received and a subsequent liability that reflects amortization of this initial amount. Changes in the market value of bonds do not appear in the accounting records, unless a firm chooses the fair value option.

11.3 Applying the effective interest method using the historical market interest rate gives a constant amount of interest expense only if a firm initially issued bonds at face value. If a firm issued bonds at a discount or a premium to face value, then the amount of interest expense will change each period. A statement that applies to all bonds, whether issued at face value, a discount, or a premium, is that using the historical market interest rate in applying the effective interest method gives a constant rate of interest expense as a percentage of the liability at the beginning of the period. That constant rate is the historical market interest rate.

11.4 Firms repay a portion of the principal on serial bonds each period but repay all of the principal on coupon bonds at maturity. Thus, the amount of unpaid principal on serial bonds at any date prior to maturity is less than on coupon bonds, giving rise to less interest expense for serial bonds.

11.5 The initial issue prices will differ. Although the present value of the $1,000,000 face amount of these bonds will be the same for the two issues, the present value of the coupon payments will differ because the 9% coupon bonds require larger cash outflows each year than the 7% coupon bonds.

11.6   This statement is correct. Over the life of the bonds, the effect on net income before taxes is the difference between the cash received when the firm issued the bonds and the cash disbursed for interest and repayment of principal at maturity. Using the historical market interest rate or the current market interest rate to account for the bonds simply allocates this total income differently across the periods while the bonds are outstanding.

11.7   The statement is still correct. Instead of repaying the bonds at maturity, the firm repurchases them in the market. The amount paid to repurchase the bonds depends on market interest rates at the time, but that amount is independent of whether the firm used the historical market interest rate or the current market interest rate to account for the bonds while they were outstanding.

11.8   First, we give an example. Imagine the borrowing firm issues $1 million face value of zero coupon bonds maturing in 10 years when the market rate of interest at the time of issue is 4% compounded annually. You can see from Table 2, 10-period row, 4% column, that the borrowing firm will collect 67.556% of face value, $675,560 if the bonds have face value of $1 million. Imagine that one year later the market borrowing rate for this firm rises to 5% per year compounded annually. The zero coupon bond issue will have only nine years until maturity and Table 2, 9-period row, 5% column, reveals that its market value will drop to 64.461% of par, or $644,610 for the $1 million issue. If the borrowing firm were to repurchase the bonds—repay the borrowing, it would pay out only $644,610. It would record a gain on retirement of the bond issue of $30,950 (= $675,560 − $644,610).

The borrowing firm has enjoyed a gain from its borrowing activity. The gain results because it locked in for a 10-year period a borrowing of about $675,000 for an interest rate of 4%. When borrowing rates increase to 5% for this borrower, it has gained because its 10-year borrowing agreement allows it to pay back the lenders at 4% interest rate, whereas if it had borrowed at the start of the second year, it would have had to promise 5% interest rate. The borrowing firm was lucky or smart to have locked in the low borrowing rate just before borrowing rates increased.

In general, the borrowing firm will gain from its borrowing, not have overall loss or expense, when the market interest rate drops sufficiently after the bond issue so that the total cash needed to make debt service payments and to repay the bond is less than the cash collected at the start of the loan.

11.9   Old/current rules: The retailer will likely treat it as an operating lease. The minimum contractual lease payments do not include the rental based on sales. If sales are zero, the lease payment will be zero. Thus, the "minimum" payment is zero. The present value of the "small fixed amount" will not likely exceed 90% of the fair market value of the property. The 10-year lease is also likely less than 75% of the useful life of the building.

11.10   New/proposed rules: The present value of the minimum lease payments is the initial amount recorded in the capital lease. The lessee will report the monthly payments based on sales as expenses of the month of sales.

11.11   Under the current rules, the distinction depends upon which criteria of the lease made it a capital lease. The major difference is that at the end of a lease term the asset reverts to the lessor in a capital lease, whereas at the end of the installment payments, the asset belongs to the purchaser. The criteria for capitalizing a lease are such that the expected value of the asset when it reverts to the lessor is small. In most other respects, capital leases and installment purchases are similar in economic substance.

Under the new/proposed rules, the contractual payments under a lease and the contractual payments under an installment purchase are the same. At the end of the contractual term, the lessee may return the property to the lessor when the property has substantial potential value in use, so that the lessor bears risks and enjoys potential rewards of ownership that would have been the lessee's if the lease had no operating components

11.12   Disagree. Operating Lease: Rent revenue for the lessor will equal rent expense for the lessee on an operating lease, but lessor also has depreciation expense on leased assets. Capital Lease: Interest revenue for the lessor should equal interest expense for the lessee on a capital lease. The lessor recognizes its cost to acquire or manufacture the leased asset as cost of goods sold under a capital lease. The lessor also recognizes revenue under a capital lease equal to the "selling price" of the lease asset on the date of signing the lease.

11.13   Using the operating lease method for financial reporting permits the lessee to keep the lease liability off the balance sheet and report less cumulative expenses than the capital lease method. The lessee prefers the capital lease for income tax reporting because it reports more cumulative expenses than the operating lease method and therefore minimizes the present value of income tax payments.

11.14   Using the capital lease method for financial reporting permits the lessor to report a gross margin from the "sale" of the leased asset in the year the entities sign the lease and more cumulative revenue for interest than the operating lease method recognizes as rent revenue. The lessor prefers the operating lease method for income tax reporting because it excludes the gross margin from taxable income in the year of signing the lease and delays the recognition of rent revenue relative to the amount of interest revenue recognized under the capital lease method.

11.15   (Hagar Company; amortization schedule for note where stated interest rate differs from historical market rate of interest.) (amounts in US$)

a.   **Amortization Schedule for a Three-Year Note with a Maturity Value of $40,000, Calling for 6% Annual Interest Payments, Yield of 8% per Year**

Year	Carrying Value Start of Year	Interest Expense for Period	Payment	Interest Added to Carrying Value	Carrying Value End of Year
(1)	(2)	(3)a	(4)	(5)	(6)
1	$37,938	$3,035	$2,400	$635	$38,573
2	38,573	3,086	2,400	686	39,259
3	39,259	3,141	2,400	741	40,000

a(3) = (2) X 0.08.

b.   Computer.. 37,938
       Note Payable   37,938
     To record purchase of computer.

     Annual Journal Entry for Interest and Principal

     Interest Expense............   Amount in Col. (3)
         Cash ....   Amount in Col. (4)*
         Note Payable.............   Amount in Col. (5)*

     *In third year, the firm also debits Note Payable and credits Cash for $40,000.

11.16   (Computing the issue price of bonds.) (amounts in US$)

a. $10,000,000 X 0.20829[a] .... $ 2,082,900

[a]Present value of $1 for 40 periods at 4%.

b. $500,000 X 23.11477[a] .... $ 11,557,385

[a]Present value of annuity for 40 periods at 3%.

11.17   (Computing the issue price of bonds.) (amounts in US$)

a. $1,000,000 X 0.14205[a] .... $ 142,050

[a]Present value of $1 for 40 periods at 5%.

b. $50,000 X 23.11477[a] .... $ 1,155,739

[a]Present value of annuity for 40 periods at 3%.

c. $50,000 X 19.79277[a] .... $ 989,639
      $1,000,000 X 0.20829[b]   208,290
                                                                                     $ 1,197,929

[a]Present value of annuity for 40 periods at 4%.
[b]Present value of $1 for 40 periods at 4%.

d. $30,000 X 12.46221[a] .... $ 373,866
      $40,000 X 12.46221[a] X 0.37689[b]   187,875
      $1,000,000 X 0.14205[c]   142,050
                                                                                     $ 703,791

[a]Present value of annuity for 20 periods at 5%.
[b]Present value of $1 for 20 periods at 5%.
[c]Present value of $1 for 40 periods at 5%.

11.18   (Womack Company; amortization schedule for bonds.) (amounts in US$)

a. $100,000 X 0.67556[a] .... $ 67,556

     $5,000 X 8.11090[b]   40,555

        Issue Price .... $ 108,111

[a]Table 2, 4% column and 10-period row.

[b]Table 4, 4% column and 10-period row.

b.

Six-Month Period	Liability at Start of Period	Interest at 4% for Period	Cash Payment	Decrease in Carrying Value of Liability	Liability at End of Period
0					$ 108,111
1	$ 108,111	$ 4,324	$ 5,000	$ (676)	107,435
2	107,435	4,297	5,000	(703)	106,732
3	106,732	4,269	5,000	(731)	106,001
4	106,001	4,240	5,000	(760)	105,241
5	105,241	4,210	5,000	(790)	104,451
6	104,451	4,178	5,000	(822)	103,629
7	103,629	4,145	5,000	(855)	102,774
8	102,774	4,111	5,000	(889)	101,885
9	101,885	4,075	5,000	(925)	100,960
10	100,960	4,040[a]	5,000	(960)	100,000
Total....................		$ 41,889	$ 50,000	$(8,111)	

[a]Does not equal 0.04 X $100,960 due to rounding.

c.   Carrying Value of Bonds: $10,363. $\longrightarrow$ $10000 \, 1V \, (4\%)$ $PVA \, (4,4 \cdot)$
                                                    $+ \, 10000 \times 10 \times \frac{1}{2}$

     Bonds Payable... 10,363

        Gain on Bond Retirement...................................   63

        Cash   10,300

     To record retirement of bonds.

11.19   (Seward Corporation; amortization schedule for bonds.) (amounts in US$)

a. $100,000 X 0.74622[a] .... $ 74,622
      $4,000 X 5.07569[b] 20,303
         Issue Price .... $ 94,925

[a]Table 2, 5% column and 6-period row.
[b]Table 4, 5% column and 6-period row.

b.

Six-Month Period	Liability at Start of Period	Interest at 5% for Period	Cash Payment	Increase in Carrying Value of Liability	Liability at End of Period
1	$94,925	$ 4,746	$ 4,000	$ 746	$ 95,671
2	95,671	4,784	4,000	784	96,455
3	96,455	4,823	4,000	823	97,278
4	97,278	4,864	4,000	864	98,142
5	98,142	4,907	4,000	907	99,049
6	99,049	4,951[a]	4,000	951	100,000
Total..................		$ 29,075	$ 24,000	$ 5,075	

[a]Does not equal 0.05 X $99,049 due to rounding.

c.   **January 2, 2012**
      Cash... 94,925
         Bonds Payable   94,925
      To record issue of bonds.

      June 30, 2012
      Interest Expense.. 4,746
         Cash Payable   4,000
         Bonds Payable   746
      To record interest expense for first six months, the
      cash payment, and the increase in the liability for
      the difference.

11.19 c. continued.

December 31, 2012

Interest Expense.. 4,784

    Cash 4,000

    Bonds Payable 784

To record interest expense for the second six
months, the cash payment, and the increase in
the liability for the difference.

d. Bonds Payable (= 0.20 X $98,142) 19,628

   Loss on Retirement of Bonds.................................. 772

    Cash 20,400

11.20 (O'Brien Corporation; accounting for bonds using amortized cost
measurement based on the historical market interest rate.) (amounts in
US$)

a. $8,000,000 X 0.30656[a] .... $ 2,452,480

   $320,000 X 23.11477[b].. 7,396,726

   Issue Price .... $ 9,849,206

[a]Table 2, 3% column and 40-period row.
[b]Table 4, 3% column and 40-period row.

b. 0.03 X $9,849,206 = $295,476.

c. 0.03($9,849,206 + $295,476 – $320,000) = $294,740.

d. Carrying Value: ($9,849,206 + $295,476 – $320,000 +
$294,740 – $320,000) .... $ 9,799,422

e. $8,000,000 X 0.32523[a] .... $ 2,601,840

   $320,000 X 22.49246[b]... 7,197,587

   Present Value.. $ 9,799,427

[a]Table 2, 3% column and 38-period row.
[b]Table 4, 3% column and 38-period row.

The difference between the carrying value in Part *d.* and the present
value in Part *e.* results from rounding present value factors.

11.21   (Robinson Company; accounting for bonds using amortized cost measurement based on the historical market interest rate.) (amounts in US$)

a. $5,000,000 x 0.37689ᵃ .... $ 1,884,450
     $200,000 x 12.46221ᵇ 2,492,442
         Issue Price .... $ 4,376,892

     ᵃTable 2, 5% column and 20-period row.
     ᵇTable 4, 5% column and 20-period row.

b.   0.05 x $4,376,892 = $218,845.

c.   0.05($4,376,892 + $218,845 − $200,000) = $219,787.

d. $4,376,892 + $218,845 − $200,000 + $219,787 − $200,000 = $4,415,524.

e. $5,000,000 x 0.41552ᵃ .... $ 2,077,600
     $200,000 x 11.68959ᵇ 2,337,918
         Present Value .... $ 4,415,518

     ᵃTable 2, 5% column and 18-period row.
     ᵇTable 4, 5% column and 18-period row.

     The difference between the carrying value in Part *d.* and the present value in Part *e.* results from rounding present value factors.

11.22   (Huergo Dooley Corporation; accounting for bonds using amortized cost measurement based on the historical market interest rate.) (amounts in US$)

a. $2,000,000 x 0.61391ᵃ .... $ 1,227,820
     $80,000 x 7.72173ᵇ 617,738
                                                                                        $ 1,845,558

     ᵃPresent value of $1 for 10 periods at 5%.
     ᵇPresent value of an annuity for 10 periods at 5%.

Solutions

11.22 continued.

b. Interest Expense (= 0.05 X $1,845,558) 92,278
    Cash (= 0.04 X $2,000,000) 80,000
    Bonds Payable (Plug) 12,278

c. Interest Expense [= 0.05 X ($1,845,558 + $12,278)] 92,892
    Cash (= 0.04 X $2,000,000) 80,000
    Bonds Payable (Plug) 12,892

d. Bonds Payable [= 0.20 X ($1,845,558 + $12,278 +
    $12,892)] 374,146
    Loss on Repurchase of Bonds 53,933
    Cash 428,079

$2,000,000 X 0.78941[a] .... $ 1,578,820
$80,000 X 7.01969[b] 561,575
                                         $ 2,140,395
    Total .... X 0.20
    Purchase Price .... $ 428,079

[a]Present value of $1 for 8 periods at 3%.

[b]Present value of an annuity for 8 periods at 3%.

11.23   (Stroud Corporation; accounting for bonds using the fair value option based on the current market interest rate.) (amounts in US$)

a. **January 1, 2013:** The carrying value of these bonds is $10,000,000, their issue price. The issue price equals the face value because the coupon rate and the required market yield both equal 6%.

June 30, 2013:

$10,000,000 X 0.5598676[a] .... $ 5,598,676
$300,000 X 14.197818[b] 4,259,346
                                          $ 9,858,022

[a]Present value of $1 for 19 periods at 3.1%.

[b]Present value of an annuity for 19 periods at 3.1%.

11.23 a. continued.

December 31, 2013:

$10,000,000 x 0.557435[a] .... $ 5,574,350

$300,000 x 13.411061[b] 4,023,318

$ 9,597,668

[a]Present value of $1 for 18 periods at 3.3%.

[b]Present value of an annuity for 18 periods at 3.3%.

b. **First Six Months of 2013**

Debt Service Payment: 0.03 x $10,000,000 = $300,000.

Unrealized Gain: $141,978 (= $10,000,000 – $9,858,022).

Total interest expense plus holding gain for the first six months is –$158,022 = (–$300,000 + $141,978). That is, the firm has a net borrowing cost of $158,022. The debt service payment was partially offset by a holding gain on the bond, which resulted from an increase in market rates.

c. **Second Six Months of 2013**

Debt Service Payment:
Interest Expense: 0.03 x $10,000,000 = $300,000.

The fair value of the bonds at the end of the first six months was $9,858,022 and at the end of the second six months has declined to $9,597,668. This implies a holding gain of $260,354 (= $9,858,022 – $9,597,668).

The total of interest expense and holding gain for the six months' period is $39,646 = ($300,000 – $260,354).

11.24   (Restin Corporation; accounting for bonds using the fair value option based on the current market interest rate.) (amounts in US$)

a.   **January 1, 2014:**

$20,000,000 x 0.5025659[a] $10,051,318
$800,000 x 14.212403[b] 11,369,923
$21,421,241

[a]Present value of $1 for 20 periods at 3.5%.
[b]Present value of an annuity for 20 periods at 3.5%.

June 30, 2014:

$20,000,000 x 0.5297973[a] $10,595,946
$800,000 x 13.82949[b] 11,063,592
$21,659,538

[a]Present value of $1 for 19 periods at 3.4%.
[b]Present value of an annuity for 19 periods at 3.4%.

December 31, 2014:

$20,000,000 x 0.5672382[a] $11,344,763
$800,000 x 13.523807[b] 10,819,046
$22,163,809

[a]Present value of $1 for 18 periods at 3.2%.
[b]Present value of an annuity for 18 periods at 3.2%.

b.   **First Six Months**

Debt Service Payment: 0.04 x $20,000,000 = $800,000.

Unrealized Loss: $238,297 (= $21,659,538 – $21,421,241).

Total interest expense and holding loss is $1,038,297 = $800,000 + $238,297.

c.   **Second Six Months**

Debt Service Payment: 0.04 x $20,000,000 = $800,000.

Holding loss on bonds is $504,271 = $22,163,809 – 21,659,538.

Interest Expense plus holding loss totals $1,304,271 = $800,000 + $504,271.

11.25   (Boeing and United Airlines; applying the capital lease criteria under the current/old rules.) (amounts in US$)

   a.   This lease is a capital lease because the lease period of 20 years exceeds 75% of the expected life of the aircraft. The lease does not meet any other capital lease criteria. The aircraft reverts to Boeing at the end of 20 years. The present value of the lease payments when discounted at 10% is $51.1 million (= $6 million X 8.51356), which is less than $54 million (= 90% of the fair value of $60 million).

   b.   This lease is a capital lease because the present value of the lease payments of $54.8 million (= $7.2 million X 7.60608) exceeds 90% of the $60 million fair value of the aircraft.

   c.   The lease is not a capital lease. The present value of the required lease payments of $36.9 million (= $5.5 million X 6.71008) is less than $54 million (= 90% of the fair value of the aircraft). The life of the lease is less than 75% of the expected useful life of the aircraft. The purchase option price coupled with the rental payments provides Boeing with a present value of all cash flows exceeding $62.4 million [= ($5.5 million X 6.71008) + ($55 million X 0.46319)]. This amount exceeds the usual sales price of $60 million, so there does not appear to be a bargain purchase option.

   d.   This lease is not a capital lease. The present value of the minimum required lease payments is $50.9 million (= $6.2 million X 8.20141). The fee contingent on usage could be zero, so the calculations exclude it. The life of the lease is less than 75% of the useful life of the aircraft. The aircraft reverts to Boeing at the end of the lease period.

11.26   (Boeing and United Airlines; applying the new/current rules for leases.) (amounts in US$)

   a.   The present value of the lease payments when discounted at 10% is $51.1 million (= $6 million X 8.51356). United Airlines will record a leasehold asset for $51.1 million. Any cash payments it makes that exceed the expenses of a given period will be operating expenses for that period.

   b.   The present value of the lease payments is $54.8 million (= $7.2 million X 7.60608). United Airlines will record a leasehold asset for $54.8 million. Any cash payments it makes that exceed the expenses of a given period will be operating expenses for that period.

11.26 continued.

    c.   The present value of the required lease payments of $36.9 million (= $5.5 million X 6.71008) is less than $54 million (= 90% of the fair value of the aircraft). United Airlines will record a leasehold asset for $36.9 million. Any cash payments it makes that exceed the expenses of a given period will be operating expenses for that period.

    d.   The present value of the minimum required lease payments is $50.9 million (= $6.2 million X 8.20141). The fee contingent on usage could be zero, so the calculations exclude it. United Airlines will record a leasehold asset for $50.9 million. Any cash payments it makes that exceed the expenses of a given period will be operating expenses for that period.

11.27   (Sun Microsystems; preparing lessor's journal entries for an operating lease and a capital lease.) (amounts in US$)

    a.   This lease is a capital lease under the current/old rules. The life of the lease equals the expected useful life of the property. The present value of the lease payments of $12,000 [= $4,386.70 + ($4,386.70 X 1.73554)] equals the fair value of the leased asset.

    b.   **Beginning of Each Year**

Cash...	4,386.70	
Rental Fees Received in Advance.........................		4,386.70
To record cash received in advance from lessee.		

End of Each Year

Rental Fees Received in Advance............................	4,386.70	
Rent Revenue		4,386.70
To record rent revenue for each year.		

Depreciation Expense..	2,400.00	
Accumulated Depreciation....................................		2,400.00
To record annual depreciation (= $7,200/3).		

    c.   **January 1, 2013**

Cash...	4,386.70	
Lease Receivable (= $4,386.70 X 1.73554)	7,613.30	
Sales Revenue		12,000.00
To record "sale" of workstation.		

11.27 c. continued.

| Cost of Goods Sold | 7,200.00 | |
| Inventory | | 7,200.00 |

To record cost of workstation "sold."

December 31, 2013

| Lease Receivable (= 0.10 x $7,613.30) | 761.33 | |
| Interest Revenue | | 761.33 |

To record interest revenue for 2013.

January 1, 2014

| Cash | 4,386.70 | |
| Lease Receivable | | 4,386.70 |

To record cash received at the beginning of 2014. The carrying value of the receivable is now $3,987.93 (= $7,613.30 + $761.33 – $4,386.70).

December 31, 2014

| Lease Receivable (= 0.10 x $3,987.93) | 398.77 | |
| Interest Revenue | | 398.77 |

To record interest revenue for 2014. Interest revenue is slightly less than 0.10 x $3,987.93 due to rounding of present value factors. The carrying value of the receivable is now $4,386.70 (= $3,987.93 + $398.77).

January 1, 2015

| Cash | 4,386.70 | |
| Lease Receivable | | 4,386.70 |

To record cash received for 2015.

11.28 (Baldwin Products; preparing lessee's journal entries for an operating lease and a capital lease.) (amounts in US$)

a. This lease does not satisfy any of the criteria for a capital lease under the current/old rules, so it is an operating lease under those rules. The leased asset reverts to the lessor at the end of the lease period. The life of the lease (3 years) is less than 75% of the expected useful life of the leased asset (5 years). The present value of the lease payments of $25,771 (= $10,000 x 2.57710) is less than 90% of the fair value of the leased asset of $30,000.

11.28 continued.

   b. **December 31 of Each Year**

Rent Expense	10,000	
Cash		10,000

To record annual rent expense and cash payment.

   c. **January 2, 2013**

Leased Asset	25,771	
Lease Liability		25,771

To record capital lease.

December 31, 2013

Interest Expense (= 0.08 × $25,771)	2,062	
Lease Liability	7,938	
Cash		10,000

To record interest expense and cash payment for 2013. The carrying value of the lease liability is now $17,833 (= $25,771 − $7,938).

Depreciation Expense or Work-in-Process		
Inventory ($25,771/3)	8,590	
Accumulated Depreciation		8,590

To record depreciation expense for 2013.

December 31, 2014

Interest Expense (= 0.08 × $17,833)	1,427	
Lease Liability	8,573	
Cash		10,000

To record interest expense and cash payment for 2014. The carrying value of the lease liability is now $9,260 (= $17,833 − $8,573).

Depreciation Expense or Work-in-Process		
Inventory	8,590	
Accumulated Depreciation		8,590

To record depreciation expense for 2014.

11.28 c. continued.

December 31, 2015

Interest Expense (= 0.08 × $9,260)	740	
Lease Liability	9,260	
Cash		10,000

To record interest expense and cash payment for
2015. Interest expense does not precisely equal
0.08 × $9,260 due to rounding. Carrying value of
the liability is now zero.

Depreciation Expense or Work-in-Process		
Inventory	8,591	
Accumulated Depreciation		8,591

To record depreciation expense for 2015.

d. Operating Lease Method: Rent Expense (= $10,000 × 3).... $ 30,000
   Capital Lease Method: Interest Expense (= $2,062 +
     $1,427 + $740) .... $ 4,229
   Depreciation [= ($8,590 × 2) + $8,591]   25,771
     Total Expenses.. $ 30,000

11.29   (Aggarwal Corporation; accounting for long-term bonds.) (amounts in US$)

a. **Interest Expense**
  First Six Months: 0.05 × $301,512 = $15,076.
  Second Six Months: 0.05($301,512 + $15,076) = $15,829.
  Carrying value of bonds on December 31, 2013: $301,512 + $15,076 +
    $15,829 = $332,417.

b. **Carrying Value of Bonds on December 31, 2012**
  Interest:
    $35,000 × 8.11090 = $ 283,882   (Table 4, 10 periods and 4%)
  Principal:
   $1,000,000 × 0.67556 =   675,560   (Table 2, 10 periods and 4%)
    Total .... $ 959,442

Carrying Value of Bonds, December 31, 2012	$ 959,442
Add Interest Expense for 2013	x
Subtract Coupon Payments during 2013	(70,000)
Carrying Value of Bonds, December 31, 2013	$ 966,336

Interest expense for 2013 is $76,894.

11.29 continued.

   c. **Carrying Value of Bonds on July 1, 2013**

Carrying Value of Bonds, December 31, 2012 .... $ 1,305,832
Plus Interest Expense for First Six Months of 2013:
    0.03 × $1,305,832 39,175
Subtract Coupon Payment during First Six Months of
    2013 .... (45,000)
Carrying Value of Bonds, July 1, 2013............................. $ 1,300,007
Carrying Value of One-Half of Bonds................................ $ 650,004

July 1, 2013

Bonds Payable... 650,004		
Cash...	526,720	
Gain on Bonds Retirement	123,284	

   d. **Interest Expense for Second Six Months**
0.03 × $650,004 = $19,500.

11.30   (Time Warner, Inc.; accounting for zero coupon debt; see *The Wall Street Journal* for December 8, 1992.) (amounts in millions of US$)

   a. $483 million = $1,550 million/3.20714; see Table 1, 6% column, 20-period row. Alternatively, $483 million = $1,550 × 0.31180; see Table 2, 6% column, 20-period row.

   b. $5.82\% = (\$1,550/\$500)^{1/20} - 1 = 3.10^{1/20} - 1$. That is, for each dollar of the initial issue proceeds (of the $500 million), Time Warner must pay $3.10 (= $1,550/$500) at maturity of the notes. You can find the periodic interest rate to make $1.00 grow to $3.10 in 20 periods by trial and error or by using the exponential function on your computer or calculator. Note that you can state an equation to solve, as follows:

$$(1 + r)^{20} = 3.10; \text{ solve for } r.$$

You can see from Table 1 that 5.82% is approximately correct.

   c. $28 million = 0.07 × $400 million.

11.30 continued.

d. $101.4 million. Ask, first, what must the carrying value of the notes be at the end of 2031. Then, compute interest for the year on that amount. The carrying value of the notes at the end of 2031 must be $1,448.6 (= $1,550/1.07) million. Interest for one year at 7% on $1,448.6 million is $101.4 (= 0.07 × $1,448.6 = $1,550.0 – $1,448.6) million. You can check this approach to finding the answer by noting that:

$$\$1,448.6 \times 1.07 = \$1,550.0.$$

e. The carrying value of the $700 million face value of zero coupon bonds is $391 million (= $700 × 0.55839; see Table 2, 6% column and 10-period row). The market value of the $700 million face value of zero coupon bonds is $324 million (= $700 × 0.46319; see Table 2, 8% column and 10-period row). The journal entry to record the repurchase and retirement of the bonds is:

December 31, 2022

Bonds Payable..	391	
Cash...		324
Gain on Bonds Retirement		67

To record the repurchase and retirement of $700 million face value bonds.

11.31 (Understanding and using bond tables.)

a. The coupon rate on these bonds of 8% compounded semiannually equals the historical market interest rate of 8% compounded semiannually. The initial issue price therefore equals the face value. The carrying value increases each period for interest expense equal to 4% of the carrying value of the liability at the beginning of the period and decreases for 4% of the face value of the liability. Because the carrying value equals the face value throughout the life of the bonds, the carrying value remains at face value.

b. The coupon rate on these bonds is 8% compounded semiannually. When the historical market interest rate exceeds the coupon rate, the bonds will have a carrying value greater than face value. When the historical market interest rate is less than the coupon rate, the bonds will have a carrying value less than face value.

11.31 continued.

    c. Firms amortize any initial issue premium as a reduction in interest expense and a reduction in the bond liability over the life of the bonds. Firms amortize any initial issue discount as an increase in interest expense and an increase in the bond liability over the life of the bonds.

    d. $1,000,000 × 111.7278% = $1,117,278. Note that the rows indicate *years* to maturity, not the total number of periods.

    e. $1,000,000 × 110.6775% = $1,106,775.

    f.

Cash Payment for Debt Service	$ 80,000
Decrease in Carrying Value of Liability during 2013:	
$1,000,000 × (110.6775% – 110.4205%)	(2,570)
Interest Expense	$ 77,430
Interest Expense, First Six Months: 0.035 × ($1,000,000 × 110.6775%)	$ 38,737
Interest Expense, Second Six Months: 0.035 × ($1,000,000 × 110.5512%)	38,693
Interest Expense	$ 77,430

11.32 (Home Supply Company; interpreting disclosures of long-term debt.) (amounts in millions of US$)

    a. The likely explanation is that Home Supply Company issued these notes and bonds at face value and therefore has no discount or premium to amortize. Another possible explanation is that Home Supply Company issued these bonds for such a small discount or premium that the amount of any discount or premium disappears when rounding to the nearest million.

11.32 continued.

b.

Issue Date	Face Value	Term to Maturity at Issue Date	Issue Price	Coupon Interest Rate	Historical Market Interest Rate
October 2011	$500 Million	10 Years	$496 Million	5%	5.1%[a]
October 2011	$500 Million	30 Years	$492 Million	5.5%	5.61%[b]
October 2012	$550 Million	10 Years	$545.6 Million	5.4%	5.48%[c]
October 2012	$450 Million	30 Years	$445.6 Million	5.8%	5.87%[d]

[a]= PV(.0255,20,12500000, 500000000,0). 5.10% = 2.55% X 2.
[b]= PV(.02805,60,13750000,500000000,0). 5.61% = 2.805% X 2.
[c]= PV(.0274,20,14850000,550000000,0). 5.48% = 2.74% X 2
[d]= PV(.02935,60,13050000,450000000,0). 5.87% = 2.935% X 2.

c. Home Supply Company has amortized some of the initial issue discount, so that the carrying value on February 1, 2013, exceeds the issue price by the amount of discount amortized. The initial discounts are so small because the historical market interest rates are only slightly higher than the coupon rates.

d. Holders of the convertible notes receive a portion of their return in the value of the option to convert the notes into common stock. Thus, even though they bear more risk than more senior debt and require a higher return to compensate for the higher risk, they do not demand that return to be in the form of periodic cash payments.

e. The weighted-average historical market interest rate is higher than the weighted-average current market interest rate at each date because the carrying, or book, value is less than the current fair value.

11.33 (IBM and Adair Corporation; accounting for lease by lessor and lessee.) (amounts in US$)

a. **January 1, 2013**

Cash...	10,000	
Note Payable		10,000
Computer...	10,000	
Cash..		10,000

December 31, 2013

Depreciation Expense...	3,333	
Accumulated Depreciation...................................		3,333
Interest Expense (= 0.08 × $10,000)	800	
Note Payable (Plug)	3,080	
Cash (= $10,000/2.57710)		3,880

December 31, 2014

Depreciation Expense...	3,333	
Accumulated Depreciation...................................		3,333
Interest Expense [= 0.08 × ($10,000 – $3,080)].......	554	
Note Payable (Plug)	3,326	
Cash..		3,880

b. **January 1, 2013**
No entry.

December 31, 2013

Rent Expense..	3,810	
Cash..		3,810

December 31, 2014

Rent Expense..	3,810	
Cash..		3,810

c. **January 1, 2013**

Leased Asset...	10,000	
Lease Liability..		10,000

11.33 c. continued.

December 31, 2013

Depreciation Expense	3,333	
Accumulated Depreciation		3,333

Interest Expense (= 0.07 × $10,000)	700	
Lease Liability (Plug)	3,110	
Cash (= $10,000/2.62432)		3,810

December 31, 2014

Depreciation Expense	3,333	
Accumulated Depreciation		3,333

Interest Expense [= 0.07 × ($10,000 − $3,110)]	482	
Lease Liability (Plug)	3,328	
Cash		3,810

d. **January 1, 2013**

Cash	10,000	
Sales Revenue		10,000

Cost of Goods Sold	6,000	
Inventory		6,000

December 31, 2013 and 2014
No entries necessary.

e. **January 1, 2013**

Computer Equipment	6,000	
Inventory		6,000

December 31, 2013

Depreciation Expense	2,000	
Accumulated Depreciation		2,000

Cash	3,810	
Rent Revenue		3,810

11.33 e. continued.

December 31, 2014

Depreciation Expense...	2,000	
Accumulated Depreciation..................................		2,000

Cash..	3,810	
Rent Revenue		3,810

f. **January 1, 2013**

Lease Receivable..	10,000	
Sales Revenue		10,000

Cost of Goods Sold	6,000	
Inventory..		6,000

December 31, 2013

Cash..	3,810	
Interest Revenue (see Part *c.*)		700
Lease Receivable...		3,110

December 31, 2014

Cash..	3,810	
Interest Revenue (see Part *c.*)		482
Lease Receivable...		3,328

g. | **Lessee** | **2013** | **2014** | **2015** | **Total** |
|---|---|---|---|---|
| **Borrow and Purchase** | | | | |
| Depreciation Expense.... | $ 3,333 | $ 3,333 | $ 3,334 | $ 10,000 |
| Interest Expense .... | 800 | 554 | 286 | 1,640 |
| | $ 4,133 | $ 3,887 | $ 3,620 | $ 11,640 |
| | | | | |
| **Operating Lease** | | | | |
| Rent Expense .... | $ 3,810 | $ 3,810 | $ 3,810 | $ 11,430 |
| | | | | |
| **Capital Lease** | | | | |
| Depreciation Expense.... | $ 3,333 | $ 3,333 | $ 3,334 | $ 10,000 |
| Interest Expense .... | 700 | 482 | 248 | 1,430 |
| | $ 4,033 | $ 3,815 | $ 3,582 | $ 11,430 |

11.33 continued.

h. **Lessor** **Sale**	**2013**	**2014**	**2015**	**Total**
Sales Revenue................	$10,000	$ —	$ —	$ 10,000
Cost of Goods Sold.........	(6,000)	—	—	(6,000)
	$ 4,000	$ —	$ —	$ 4,000
Operating Lease				
Rent Revenue.................	$ 3,810	$ 3,810	$ 3,810	$ 11,430
Depreciation Expense....	(2,000)	(2,000)	(2,000)	(6,000)
	$ 1,810	$ 1,810	$ 1,810	$ 5,430
Capital Lease				
Sales Revenue................	$10,000	$ —	$ —	$ 10,000
Cost of Goods Sold.........	(6,000)	—	—	(6,000)
Interest Revenue............	700	482	248	1,430
	$ 4,700	$ 482	$ 248	$ 5,430

11.34 (Carom Sports Collectibles Shop; comparison of borrow/buy with operating and capital leases.) (amounts in US$)

a. $100,000/3.79079 = $26,379.725 = $26,380.

Carom Sports Collectibles Shop Amortization Schedule

Year	Start of Year Balance	Interest (10%)	Payment	Reduction	End of Year Balance
1	$ 100,000	$10,000	$26,380	$16,380	$83,620
2	83,620	8,362	26,380	18,018	65,602
3	65,602	6,560	26,380	19,820	45,782
4	45,782	4,578	26,380	21,802	23,980
5	23,980	2,398	26,380	23,982	(2)

11.34 continued.

   b. **Plan (1):**
       Asset—Cash.
       Asset—Computer System.
       Asset Contra—Accumulated Depreciation on Computer System.
       Liability—Bonds Payable and Interest Payable.

       Plan (2): Operating Lease Method: None.

       Plan (2): Capital Lease Method
       Asset—Cash.
       Asset—Leased Computer System.
       Asset Contra—Accumulated Depreciation.
       Liability—Lease Liability.

   c. $150,000 = $100,000 Depreciation + (0.10 × $100,000 × 5) Interest.

   d. (1) Operating Lease Method: $131,900 = $26,380 × 5.
       (2) Capital Lease Method: $131,900.

   e. The method of accounting for a lease affects only the timing of expenses, not their total. Expenses under plan (1) are larger because the firm borrows $100,000 for the entire five years, whereas under plan (2) it pays the loan with part of each lease payment; with smaller average borrowing, interest expense is smaller.

   f. (1) $30,000 = $20,000 depreciation + $10,000 bond interest.
       (2) Operating Lease Method: $26,380 rent.
            Capital Lease Method: $30,000 = $20,000 depreciation + $10,000 lease interest.

   g. (1) $30,000.
       (2) Operating Lease Method: $26,380 rent.
            Capital Lease Method: $22,400 (or $22,398) = $20,000 depreciation + $2,400 (or $2,398) interest.

11.34 g. continued.

CAROM SPORTS COLLECTIBLES SHOP SUMMARY
(Not Required)

	2013	2014	2015	2016	2017	Total
Plan 1						
Depreciation Expense	$20,000	$20,000	$20,000	$20,000	$20,000	$ 100,000
Interest Expense	10,000	10,000	10,000	10,000	10,000	50,000
Total	$30,000	$30,000	$30,000	$30,000	$30,000	$ 150,000
Plan 2 (Operating)						
Lease Expense	$26,380	$26,380	$26,380	$26,380	$26,380	$ 131,900
Plan 2 (Financing)						
Depreciation Expense	$20,000	$20,000	$20,000	$20,000	$20,000	$ 100,000
Interest Expense	10,000	8,362	6,560	4,578	2,400*	31,900
Total	$30,000	$28,362	$26,560	$24,578	$22,400	$ 131,900

*Plug to correct for rounding. By computation, this number is $2,398 = [$26,380 − ($26,380/1.10)].

11.35 (Northern Airlines; financial statement effects of capital and operating leases.) (amounts in millions of US$)

a. Capital Lease Liability, December 31, 2012 .... $ 1,088
    Plus Interest Expense (Plug).. 102
    Plus New Capital Leases Signed[a] 0
    Less Cash Payment on Capital Leases .... (263)
    Capital Lease Liability, December 31, 2013 .... $ 927

[a]A comparison of the commitments under capital leases on December 31, 2012 and December 31, 2013 indicates that Northern Airlines did not sign any new capital leases during 2013.

b. $102/$1,088 = 9.375%.

11.35 continued.

c.

Capitalized Leased Asset, December 31, 2012	$	1,019
Plus New Capital Leases Signed[a]		0
Less Depreciation on Capital Leases (Plug)........................		(154)
Capital Leased Asset, December 31, 2013	$	865

[a]See Footnote a to Part *a.* above.

d. **December 31, 2013**

Interest Expense..	102	
Lease Liability	161	
Cash		263

To record interest expense on capital leases, the
cash payment, and decrease in the capital lease
liability for the difference.

December 31, 2013

Depreciation Expense...	154	
Accumulated Depreciation		154

To recognize depreciation expense on capitalized
leased asset for 2013.

e. **December 31, 2013**

Rent Expense..	1,065	
Cash		1,065

To recognize rent expense on operating leases for
2013.

11.35 continued.

f. **Present Value of Operating Lease Commitment on December 31, 2012**

Year	Payments	Present Value Factor at 10.0%	Present Value
2013	$ 1,065	0.90909	$ 968
2014	1,039	0.82645	859
2015	973	0.75131	731
2016	872	0.68301	596
2017	815	0.62092	506
After			
2017	7,453[a]	5.81723[b] x 0.62092[c]	2,944
Total...			$ 6,604

[a]Assume that the firm pays the $7,453 at the rate of $815 a year for 9.145 (= $7,453/$815) periods at 10%.

[b]Factor for the present value of an annuity of $815 million for 9.145 periods at 10%.

[c]Factor for the present value of $1 for five periods at 10%.

11.35 f. continued.

Present Value of Operating Lease Commitment on December 31, 2013

Year	Payments	Present Value Factor at 10.0%	Present Value
2014	$ 1,098	0.90909	$ 998
2015	1,032	0.82645	853
2016	929	0.75131	698
2017	860	0.68301	587
2018	855	0.62092	531
After			
2018	6,710[a]	5.26685[b] x 0.62092[c]	2,796
Total			$ 6,463

[a]Assume that the firm pays the $6,710 at the rate of $855 a period for 7.848 (= $6,710/$855) periods.

[b]Factor for the present value of an annuity of $855 million for 7.848 periods at 10%.

[c]Factor for the present value of $1 for five periods at 10%.

g. **Long-Term Debt Ratio Based on Reported Amounts:**
   December 31, 2012: $13,456/$29,495 = 45.6%
   December 31, 2013: $12,041/$29,145 = 41.3%

h. **Long-Term Debt Ratio Including Capitalization of Operating Leases:**
   December 31, 2012: ($13,456 + $6,604 − $968)/($29,495 + $6,604) = 52.9%
   December 31, 2013: ($12,041 + $6,463 − $998)/($29,145 + $6,463) = 49.2%

i. Lessees prefer the operating lease treatment because the capital lease treatment leads the lessee to show more debt on its balance sheet and higher debt-equity ratios.

11.36   (GSB Corporation; measuring interest expense.)

The carrying value of a liability changes during a period as follows:

Beginning Balance + Interest Expense − Cash Payment = Ending Balance

Substituting the known information:
   $BB + 0.05BB - \$4,400 = \$110,000$

Solving for BB:
   $1.05BB = \$114,400$
   $BB = \$114,400/1.05$
   $BB = \$108,952$

Thus, interest expense for this last six-month period equals $5,447.62 (= 0.05 × \$108,952$).

This page is intentionally left blank

CHAPTER 12

LIABILITIES: OFF-BALANCE-SHEET FINANCING, RETIREMENT BENEFITS, AND INCOME TAXES

Questions, Exercises, and Problems: Answers and Solutions

12.1 See the text or the glossary at the end of the book.

12.2 Using an executory contract to achieve off-balance-sheet financing results in the recognition of neither an asset nor a liability on the balance sheet. Using an asset sale may result in either (i) a sale (an asset such as accounts receivable decreases and cash increases) or (ii) a collateralized loan (cash increases and a liability increases). Whether the transaction results in a sale or a loan depends on which entity enjoys the benefits and bears the risk of the asset sold. The fact that the seller of the assets will reimburse the buyer of the assets for any shortfall in collections from the purchased asset suggests that the seller bears the collection risk of the asset sold.

12.3 Executory contracts carry varying amounts of risk. For example, a firm might back out of a purchase commitment more easily than an employment contract or lease contract. Furthermore, the expected benefits might carry different degrees of risk. An employee might back out of an employment contract more easily than a lessor could demand return of a leased asset prior to the end of the lease. Users of the financial statements might assume that all rights and obligations under executory contracts are equally certain. A contrary view argues that assets and liabilities recognized on the balance sheet (for example, cash, inventory, equipment, goodwill) carry different degrees of uncertainty with respect to expected benefits and risks. Recognizing the benefits and obligations related to executory contracts provides information that firms disclose only in the notes to the financial statements. Recording them in the balance sheet increases their visibility.

12.4   The use of a special purpose entity or variable interest equity enhances the ability of a firm to demonstrate that it has transferred control of the receivables to the purchaser. Whether the transferor has in fact transferred control depends on its relation to the special purpose entity or variable interest entity and its rights and obligations related to the receivables. The special purpose entity or variable interest entity at least permits separation of the receivables from the transferring entity.

12.5   Accrual accounting recognizes a cost as an expense in the period when a firm uses, or consumes, goods and services. Employees provide labor services each period in return for both current compensation (for example, salary) and deferred compensation (for example, pensions, postretirement health care benefits). The absence of deferred compensation arrangements would presumably lead employees to demand higher current compensation to permit them to fund their own retirement plans. Thus, firms must recognize an expense during the current period for both compensation paid and the present value of deferred compensation.

12.6   Laws require firms to contribute funds to an independent trustee. The trustee manages the funds on behalf of employees. The employer cannot use these funds for its general corporate purposes (the assets are not assets of the employer).

12.7   The amounts that pension plans pay to retirees are based on the employer's contributions plus earnings from investments. Earnings from pension investments appear on the books of the pension plan. In theory, those earnings fund the increase in the pension obligation that results from the passage of time. Although expected earnings from investments and the interest cost on the pension obligation flow through net pension expense on the employer's books, in theory these amounts should perfectly offset—in which case pension expense will equal the employer's cash contribution to the pension plan.

12.8   Firms may have multiple pension plans for their different groups of employees (for example, domestic employees versus non-domestic employees). Some plans have assets that exceed liabilities (overfunded plans). Other plans have liabilities that exceed assets (underfunded plans). The employer, however, typically cannot use the assets of an overfunded plan to support an underfunded plan. Netting all pension plans results in loss of information about the mix of overfunded and underfunded plans.

12.9   U.S. GAAP allows firms to defer and amortize changes in prior service costs and actuarial gains and losses that occur during a period. The rationale is that a firm should take a long-term view of its pension plan. This long-term view permits firms to average out short-term changes in prior service costs and actuarial gains and losses over longer periods. These items affect other comprehensive income in the period when they originate. When firms amortize these items and include the amortization as an element of net pension expense, the firms remove the amount originally recognized in other comprehensive income and include it in net income.

12.10   U.S. GAAP requires firms to increase pension expense for the increase in the pension obligation that results from the passage of time (that is, the interest cost). Firms must generate earnings from investments sufficient to fund this increase. Earnings from pension investments offset the interest cost. This explains why U.S. GAAP requires a subtraction for earnings from investments.

12.11   Subtracting the expected return instead of the actual return on investments smoothes out variations between expected and actual rates of return and also enhances a long-term viewpoint appropriate for pension benefits.

12.12   Income tax expense equals income taxes currently payable plus (minus) the income taxes the firm expects to pay (save) in the future when revenues and expenses that appear in book income now appear in tax returns later.

12.13   This statement is incorrect. In order for deferred taxes to be a loan, there must be a receipt of cash or other goods or services at the inception of the loan and a disbursement of cash or other goods or services at the maturity date. The entries for a deferred tax liability are as follows:

When Timing Differences Originate:

Income Tax Expense   X
     Deferred Tax Liability   X

Assets	=	Liabilities	+	Shareholders' Equity	(Class.)
		+X		−X	IncSt → RE

12.13 continued.

When Timing Differences Reverse:

Deferred Tax Liability X
    Income Tax Expense X

Assets	=	Liabilities	+	Shareholders' Equity	(Class.)
		−X		+X	IncSt → RE

There are no cash or other asset flows involved and, therefore, no loan.

Another approach is to raise the question: How would cash flows have differed if a firm used the same methods of accounting for book as it used for tax? The response is that cash flows would have been the same even though there would be no deferred income taxes. Thus, recognizing or not recognizing deferred taxes has no incremental effect on cash or other asset flows and, therefore, cannot represent a loan.

12.14 Deferred tax assets (liabilities) arise when a firm recognizes either (i) revenue (expense) earlier for tax purposes than for book purposes or (ii) expenses (revenues) later for tax purposes than for book purposes. Deferred tax assets (liabilities) provide for lower (higher) taxable income in the future relative to book income and, therefore, future tax savings (costs).

12.15 When firms choose accounting methods that result in recognizing income earlier for book purposes than for tax purposes, they delay the payment of taxes. Income tax expense does not reflect the benefit of these delayed cash payments in that period because firms must include the delayed payment amount in both income tax expense and a deferred income tax liability. In the later period when taxable income exceeds book income, firms reduce income tax expense and the deferred income tax liability for the additional taxes paid. When firms recognize income earlier for tax purposes than for book purposes, they accelerate the payment of taxes. Income tax expense does not reflect the cost of the accelerated cash payment in that period because firms must include the accelerated payment amount as a reduction in income tax expense and a deferred income tax asset. In the later period when book income exceeds taxable income, firms increase income tax expense and reduce the deferred income tax asset for the taxes paid previously.

12.16 Analysts often forecast earnings and need to make some assumptions about a firm's average, or effective, tax rate in future periods. The information in the reconciliation helps analysts to estimate future effective tax rates.

12.17 Information on individual deferred tax assets and deferred tax liabilities provides information about a firm's operating, investing, and financing activities related to those individual items. For example, a continual increase in deferred tax liabilities for depreciation timing differences suggests a continuing increase in expenditures on depreciable assets. A decrease in deferred tax assets for warranties might suggest a reduction in sales of warranted products.

12.18 (Cypres Appliance Store; using accounts receivable to achieve off-balance-sheet financing.) (amounts in US$)

a. (i) **January 2, 2013**
Cash.. 92,593
　Bank Loan Payable...................................... 92,593

Assets	=	Liabilities	+	Shareholders' Equity	(Class.)
+92,593		+92,593			

To record bank loan.

December 31, 2013
Cash.. 100,000
　Accounts Receivable...................................... 100,000

Assets	=	Liabilities	+	Shareholders' Equity	(Class.)
+100,000					
−100,000					

To record collections from customers.

12.18 a. continued.

Interest Expense (= 0.08 × $92,593) 7,407
Bank Loan Payable 92,593
Cash 100,000

Assets	=	Liabilities	+	Shareholders' Equity	(Class.)
−100,000		−92,593		−7,407	IncSt → RE

To record interest expense on loan for 2013 and repayment of the loan.

(ii) Cash 92,593
Loss from Sale of Accounts Receivable 7,407
Accounts Receivable 100,000

Assets	=	Liabilities	+	Shareholders' Equity	(Class.)
+92,593				−7,407	IncSt → RE
−100,000					

To record sale of accounts receivable; an alternative title for the loss account is interest expense.

b. Both transactions result in an expense of $7,407 for 2013 for this financing. Both transactions result in an immediate increase in cash. Liabilities increase for the collateralized loan, whereas an asset decreases for the sale.

c. For the transaction to qualify as a sale for accounting purposes, Cypres Appliance Store must shift credit risk and interest rate risk to the bank. The bank should have no rights to demand additional receivables if interest rates increase or uncollectible accounts appear. Likewise, Cypres Appliance Store should have no rights to buy back the accounts receivable if interest rates decline. The bank will require different terms on the loan depending on the amount of risk it incurs.

12.19   (Lorimar Company; using inventory to achieve off-balance-sheet financing.) (amounts in US$)

a.   (i)   **January 2, 2013**

	Dr.	Cr.
Cash	300,000	
Bank Loan Payable		300,000

Assets	=	Liabilities	+	Shareholders' Equity	(Class.)
+300,000		+300,000			

To record bank loan.

December 31, 2013

	Dr.	Cr.
Interest Expense (= 0.1 x $300,000)	30,000	
Bank Loan Payable		30,000

Assets	=	Liabilities	+	Shareholders' Equity	(Class.)
		+30,000		−30,000	IncSt → RE

To record interest expense for 2013.

December 31, 2014

	Dr.	Cr.
Cash	363,000	
Sales Revenue		363,000

Assets	=	Liabilities	+	Shareholders' Equity	(Class.)
+363,000				+363,000	IncSt → RE

To record sale of tobacco inventory.

	Dr.	Cr.
Cost of Goods Sold	200,000	
Inventory		200,000

Assets	=	Liabilities	+	Shareholders' Equity	(Class.)
−200,000				−200,000	IncSt → RE

To record cost of tobacco inventory sold.

12.19 a. continued.

Interest Expense (= 0.10 x $330,000) 33,000
Bank Loan Payable 330,000
    Cash 363,000

Assets	=	Liabilities	+	Shareholders' Equity	(Class.)
−363,000		−330,000		−33,000	IncSt → RE

To record interest expense for 2014 and repayment of loan.

(ii) **January 2, 2013**
    Cash 300,000
        Sales Revenue 300,000

Assets	=	Liabilities	+	Shareholders' Equity	(Class.)
+300,000				+300,000	IncSt → RE

To record "sale" of tobacco to bank.

Cost of Goods Sold 200,000
    Inventory 200,000

Assets	=	Liabilities	+	Shareholders' Equity	(Class.)
−200,000				−200,000	IncSt → RE

To record cost of tobacco "sold."

b. Both transactions result in a total of $100,000 income for the two years combined. The collateralized loan shows $163,000 gross profit from the sale in 2014 and interest expense of $30,000 in 2013 and $33,000 in 2014. The "sale" results in $100,000 gross profit in 2013. Cash increases by $300,000 in both transactions. Liabilities increase for the collateralized loan, whereas an asset decreases for the "sale."

12.19 continued.

c.　For the transaction to qualify as a sale for accounting purposes, Lorimar Company must shift the risk of changes in storage costs for 2013 and 2014 and the risk of changes in the selling price for the tobacco at the end of 2014 to the bank. Lorimar should not guarantee a price or agree to cover insurance and other storage costs. The bank will require different terms for the loan depending on the risk it incurs.

12.20　(AirFlight; preparing journal entry for defined benefit plan.) (amounts in millions of US$)

2013

Pension Expense..	1,050	
Pension Asset ($46,203 – $45,582)................................	621	
Pension Liability ($45,183 – $43,484).........................	1,699	
Cash		526
Other Comprehensive Income (Actuarial Gains and Losses: $960 gain + $1,101 amortization)............		2,061
Other Comprehensive Income (Excess of Actual Return over Expected Return on Investments: $4,239 – $3,456)		783

Assets	=	Liabilities	+	Shareholders' Equity	(Class.)
+621		–1,699		–1,050	IncSt → RE
–526				+2,061	OCI → AOCI
				+783	OCI → AOCI

To record pension expense and pension funding for 2013, eliminate the net pension liability at the beginning of the year, recognize the net pension asset at the end of the year, and recognize other comprehensive income for the change in actuarial and performance gains and losses.

12.21   (Tasty Dish, Inc.; preparing a summary journal entry for a defined benefit plan.) (amounts in millions of US$)

2013

Pension Expense..	340
Pension Liability [($5,947 − $5,385) − ($5,771 − $5,086)]	123
Cash	19
Other Comprehensive Income (Actuarial Gains and Losses: $155 gain + $167 amortization)....	322
Other Comprehensive Income (Excess of Actual Return over Expected Return on Investments: $513 − $391)	122

Assets	=	Liabilities	+	Shareholders' Equity	(Class.)
−19	=	−123	+	−340	IncSt → RE
				+322	OCI → AOCI
				+122	OCI → AOCI

To record pension expense, pension funding, the increase in net pension liabilities, and other comprehensive income related to the change in actuarial and performance gains and losses.

12.22   (Reliance; preparing a summary journal entry for a health care plan.) (amounts in millions of euros)

2013

Health Care Expense	2,183
Health Care Liability [(€30,863 − €5,460) − (€39,274 − €6,497)]	7,374
Other Comprehensive Income (Actuarial Gains and Losses: €9,485 gain + €41 amortization)...	9,526
Other Comprehensive Income (Excess of Actual Return over Expected Return on Investments: €510 − €479)	31

12.22 continued.

Assets	=	Liabilities	+	Shareholders' Equity	(Class.)
		−7,374		−2,183	IncSt → RE
				+9,526	OCI → AOCI
				+31	OCI → AOCI

To record health care expense for 2013, the reduction in
the health care liability, and other comprehensive income
for the change in actuarial and performance gains and
losses.

12.23   (Fleet Sneaks; preparing journal entries for income tax expense.) (amounts
in millions of US$)

a.   **2011**

Income Tax Expense	504.4	
Income Tax Payable		495.4
Deferred Tax Liability		9.0

Assets	=	Liabilities	+	Shareholders' Equity	(Class.)
		+495.4		−504.4	IncSt → RE
		+9.0			

To record income tax expense, income tax payable,
and the change in deferred taxes for 2011.

2012

Income Tax Expense	648.2	
Income Tax Payable		622.8
Deferred Tax Liability		25.4

Assets	=	Liabilities	+	Shareholders' Equity	(Class.)
		+622.8		−648.2	IncSt → RE
		+25.4			

To record income tax expense, income tax payable,
and the change in deferred taxes for 2012.

12.23 a. continued.

2013

Income Tax Expense	749.6
Deferred Tax Liability...	26.0
Income Tax Payable	775.6

Assets	=	Liabilities	+	Shareholders' Equity	(Class.)
		−26.0		−749.6	IncSt → RE
		+775.6			

To record income tax expense, income tax payable,
and the change in deferred taxes for 2013.

b. Fleet Sneaks has overfunded retirement benefit plans, suggesting
that it has contributed more cash to the pension plan and, thereby,
received a tax deduction that it has expensed for financial reporting.
Fleet Sneaks recognized a deferred tax liability for this temporary
difference. The deferred tax liability increased in 2012 due to
increased overfunding. The deferred tax liability decreased in 2013
due to a decrease in the extent of overfunding.

12.24 (Marytown Energy; preparing journal entries for income tax expense.)
(amounts in millions of US$)

a. **2011**

Income Tax Expense	272
Income Tax Receivable...	96
Deferred Tax Liability..	368

Assets	=	Liabilities	+	Shareholders' Equity	(Class.)
+96		+368		−272	IncSt → RE

To record income tax expense, a claim for a refund in
taxes paid previously, and the increase in the deferred
tax liability for 2011.

12.24 a. continued.

2012

Income Tax Expense	341	
Deferred Tax Liability	74	
Income Tax Payable		415

Assets	=	Liabilities	+	Shareholders' Equity	(Class.)
		−74		−341	IncSt → RE
		+415			

To record income tax expense, income tax payable,
and the decrease in the deferred tax liability for 2012.

2013

Income Tax Expense	390	
Income Tax Payable		46
Deferred Tax Liability		344

Assets	=	Liabilities	+	Shareholders' Equity	(Class.)
		+46		−390	IncSt → RE
		+344			

To record income tax expense, income tax payable,
and the increase in the deferred tax liability for 2013.

12.24 continued.

b. Marytown Energy operated at a net taxable loss for 2011 and likely received a refund of taxes paid in previous years due to net operating loss carryforward provisions in the income tax law. The net taxable loss likely occurred because Marytown Energy acquired new equipment for which accelerated depreciation deductions for tax purposes exceeded straight-line depreciation for financial reporting. The increase in the deferred tax liability for 2011 supports this explanation. 2012 was a profitable year for both financial and tax reporting. The decrease in the deferred tax liability for temporary depreciation differences suggests that Marytown Energy reduced its capital expenditures sufficiently during 2012 to permit straight-line depreciation for financial reporting to exceed accelerated depreciation for tax reporting. 2013 was similar to 2011 except that accelerated depreciation for tax purposes resulted in low but positive taxable income and again led to an increase in the deferred tax liability. Income before taxes for financial reporting increased each year in line with the increase in income tax expense because of the stable effective tax rate.

12.25 (Pownall Company; deriving permanent and temporary differences from financial statement disclosures.) (amounts in US$)

a.

	Income Tax Expense	=	Income Taxes Currently Payable	+	Change in Deferred Tax Liability
	$156,000	=	$48,000	+	x
	x	=	$108,000		

Temporary Differences	=	Changes in Deferred Tax Liability/0.40
	=	$108,000/0.40
	=	$270,000

12.25 continued.

b. Because income tax expense exceeds income taxes payable, book income exceeded taxable income.

Taxable Income: $48,000/0.40	$ 120,000
Temporary Differences	270,000
Book Income Before Taxes Excluding Permanent Differences	$ 390,000
Permanent Differences (Plug)	72,000
Book Income Before Taxes (Given)	$ 318,000

12.26 (Lilly Company; reconstructing information about income taxes.) (amounts in euros [€])

LILLY COMPANY
Illustrations of Timing Differences and Permanent Differences

	Financial Statements	Type of Difference	Income Tax Return
Operating Income Except Depreciation	€427,800 (6)	—	€427,800 (4)
Depreciation	(322,800) (g)	Temporary	(358,800) (3)
Municipal Bond Interest	85,800 (5)	Permanent	—
Taxable Income	—		€ 69,000 (2)
Pretax Book Income	€190,800 (g)		
Income Taxes Payable at 40%			€ 27,600 (g)
Income Tax Expense at 40% of €105,000 = €427,800 − €322,800, Which Is Income Excluding Permanent Differences	(42,000) (g)		
Net Income	€148,800 (1)		

12.26 continued.

Order and derivation of computations:
  (g) Given.
  (1) €148,800 = €190,800 – €42,000.
  (2) €69,000 = €27,600/0.40.
  (3) Temporary difference for depreciation is (€42,000 – €27,600)/0.40 = €36,000. Because income taxes payable are less than income tax expense, depreciation deducted on tax return exceeds depreciation expense on financial statements. Thus, the depreciation deduction on the tax return is €358,800 = €322,800 + €36,000.
  (4) €427,800 = €358,800 + €69,000.
  (5) Taxable income on financial statements is €105,000 = €42,000/0.40. Total financial statement income before taxes, including permanent differences, is €190,800. Hence, permanent differences are €190,800 – €105,000 = €85,800.
  (6) €190,800 + €322,800 – €85,800 = €427,800. See also (4), for check.

12.27 (Woodward Corporation; effect of temporary differences on income taxes.) (amounts in US$)

a.

	2013	2014	2015	2016
Other Pre-Tax Income	$35,000	$35,000	$35,000	$35,000
Income Before Depreciation from Machine	25,000	25,000	25,000	25,000
Depreciation Deduction:				
0.33 × $50,000	(16,500)			
0.44 × $50,000		(22,000)		
0.15 × $50,000			(7,500)	
0.08 × $50,000				(4,000)
Taxable Income	$43,500	$38,000	$52,500	$56,000
Tax Rate	0.40	0.40	0.40	0.40
Income Taxes Payable	$17,400	$15,200	$21,000	$22,400

b.

Financial Reporting	2013	2014	2015	2016
Carrying Value, January 1	$50,000	$37,500	$25,000	$ 12,500
Depreciation Expense	(12,500)	(12,500)	(12,500)	(12,500)
Carrying Value, December 31	$37,500	$25,000	$12,500	$ —
Tax Reporting				
Tax Basis, January 1	$50,000	$33,500	$11,500	$ 4,000
Depreciation Deduction	(16,500)	(22,000)	(7,500)	(4,000)
Tax Basis, December 31	$33,500	$11,500	$ 4,000	$ —

12.27 continued.

c. **Financial Reporting**

	2013	2014	2015	2016
Income Before Depreciation.....	$60,000	$60,000	$60,000	$ 60,000
Depreciation Expense ($50,000/4)	(12,500)	(12,500)	(12,500)	(12,500)
Pretax Income	$47,500	$47,500	$47,500	$ 47,500
Income Tax Expense at 0.40	$19,000	$19,000	$19,000	$ 19,000

d.

	2013	2014	2015	2016
Income Tax Payable (from Part a.)—Cr.	$17,400	$ 15,200	$ 21,000	$22,400
Change in Deferred Tax Liability (Plug): Cr. if Positive, Dr. if Negative	1,600	3,800	(2,000)	(3,400)
Income Tax Expense—Dr.	$19,000	$ 19,000	$ 19,000	$19,000

2013

Income Tax Expense	19,000	
Cash or Income Tax Payable................................		17,400
Deferred Tax Liability...		1,600

Assets	=	Liabilities	+	Shareholders' Equity	(Class.)
−17,400		+1,600		−19,000	IncSt → RE

2014

Income Tax Expense	19,000	
Cash or Income Tax Payable................................		15,200
Deferred Tax Liability...		3,800

Assets	=	Liabilities	+	Shareholders' Equity	(Class.)
−15,200		+3,800		−19,000	IncSt → RE

12.27 d. continued.

2015

Income Tax Expense	19,000	
Deferred Tax Liability	2,000	
Cash or Income Tax Payable		21,000

Assets	=	Liabilities	+	Shareholders' Equity	(Class.)
−21,000		−2,000		−19,000	IncSt → RE

2016

Income Tax Expense	19,000	
Deferred Tax Liability	3,400	
Cash or Income Tax Payable		22,400

Assets	=	Liabilities	+	Shareholders' Equity	(Class.)
−22,400		−3,400		−19,000	IncSt → RE

12.28 (Federal Stores; interpreting disclosures regarding sales of receivables.)

a. 1. The credit card accounts and receivables are the possession and ownership of Community First.

2. Federal has not placed restrictions on the receivables that constrain Community First from doing what it pleases with the receivables.

3. Federal has no interest rate risk or credit risk associated with the receivables. Community First incurs interest rate risk and credit risk, controls which customers receive credit, and services the credit accounts.

b. Federal benefits from the increased sales revenue that the credit cards provide without incurring interest rate risk and credit risk. Federal also does not incur the administrative cost of the credit card operation. Federal loses control over which of its customers can obtain credit cards, perhaps losing sales it would otherwise obtain if Federal controlled the granting of credit.

12.29   (Lewis Corporation; interpreting note on off-balance-sheet financing.)

    1. The receivables are in the possession and ownership of the special purpose entity (SPE). Lewis has no control over the actions of the SPE. Neither Lewis nor its creditors have access to the assets of the SPE and creditors of the SPE have no access to Lewis' assets.

    2. Lewis has not placed restrictions on the receivables that constrain the SPE from doing what it pleases with the receivables.

    3. The SPE incurs interest rate risk and credit.

12.30   (Juicy-Juice; interpreting retirement plans disclosures.)   (amounts in millions of US$)

    a. Juicy-Juice increased the discount rate it used to compute the pension and health care obligations from 5.7% to 5.8%, thereby reducing the present value of these obligations and resulting in an actuarial gain. Also, Juicy-Juice reduced the initial health care cost trend rate from 10% to 9%, which reduced the health care obligation and resulted in an actuarial gain. Offsetting these two factors is a change in the assumed rate of compensation increases, which increases the pension obligation and offsets the actuarial gains from the preceding two factors. Juicy-Juice amortized an actuarial loss from previous years in computing its net pension expense and net health care expense. The question does not address this amortization but only the actuarial gain that arose in 2013.

    b. The actual return on investments (disclosed in the change in fair value of plan assets) exceeded the expected return on investments (disclosed in the computation of net pension expense) each year.

    c. Juicy-Juice contributed cash to the health care plan each year equal to the benefits paid. Thus, the health care plan has no assets to invest on which to generate a return. Common terminology refers to such funding arrangements as *pay as you go*.

    d.

Prior Service Cost, End of 2012	$ 5
Plus Increase in Prior Service Cost During 2013 from Plan Amendments	11
Less Amortization of Prior Service Cost During 2013.........	(3)
Prior Service Cost, End of 2013	$ 13

12.30 continued.

e. Net Actuarial Loss, End of 2012 .... $ 2,285
Less Decrease in Actuarial Loss During 2013 from
    Actuarial Gain in Pension Obligation .... (163)
Less Amortization of Actuarial Loss During 2013 .... (164)
Less Excess of Actual Return over Expected Return on
    Pension Investments ($513 – $391) .... (122)
Prior Service Credit, End of 2013 .... $ 1,836

f. Prior Service Credit, End of 2012 .... $ 114
Less Amortization of Prior Service Cost During 2013......... (13)
Prior Service Credit, End of 2013 .... $ 101

g. Net Actuarial Loss, End of 2012 .... $ 419
Less Decrease in Actuarial Loss from Actuarial Gain in
    Pension Obligation During 2013 .... (34)
Less Amortization of Actuarial Loss During 2013 .... (21)
Net Actuarial Loss, End of 2013 .... $ 364

h. **2013**
Pension Expense.. 340
Pension Liability (Noncurrent Liabilities: $2,753
    – $729).. 2,024
Other Comprehensive Income (Prior Service Cost:
    $13 – $5)... 8
Other ($7 – $3).. 4
    Cash... 19
    Pension Asset (Noncurrent Assets: $2,068 –
      $185)... 1,883
    Pension Liability (Current Liabilities:
      $25 – $0)... 25
    Other Comprehensive Income (Actuarial Loss:
      $2,285 – $1,836)... 449

Assets	= Liabilities	+	Shareholders' Equity	(Class.)
+4	–2,024		–340	IncSt → RE
–19	+25		–8	OCI → AOCI
–1,883			+449	OCI → AOCI

To record pension expense, pension funding, and the
change in balance sheet accounts relating to the pension plan for 2013.

12.30 continued.

   i.   **2013**

Health Care Expense	126	
Health Care Liability (Noncurrent Liabilities: $1,312 – $1,270)...	42	
Other Comprehensive Income (Prior Service Cost: $114 – $101)...	13	
Other..	49	
Cash...		75
Health Care Liability (Current Liabilities: $100 – $0)...		100
Other Comprehensive Income (Actuarial Loss: $419 – $364)...		55

Assets	=	Liabilities	+	Shareholders' Equity	(Class.)
+49		–42		–126	IncSt → RE
–75		+100		–13	OCI → AOCI
				+55	OCI → AOCI

To record health care expense, health care funding, and the change in balance sheet accounts relating to the health care plan for 2013.

12.31   (Treadaway, Inc.; interpreting retirement plan disclosures.) (amounts in millions of US$)

   a.   Pension plans measure the amount of interest cost using the present value of the pension obligation and the related discount rate. Pension plans measure the amount of the expected return on plan assets using the fair value of the pension assets and the assumed rate of return on investments. For Treadaway, the expected rate of return on investments exceeds the discount rate but the pension obligation exceeds pension assets. The amounts for interest cost and expected return on investments are a mixture of these four factors. The higher pension obligation exceeds the lower discount rate for 2011 and 2012 and results in interest cost exceeding the expected return on investments. The net effect of these four factors results in equal amounts for interest cost and expected return on investments for 2013, and is simply a coincidence.

12.31 continued.

b.   The decline in net health care expense results from a decline in interest cost, likely the result of decreases in the health care obligation that more than offset the effects of increases in the discount rate.

c.   Treadaway contributes sufficient cash each year to fund current benefits but no excess contributions to invest in assets.

d.   Treadaway increased the discount rate it uses to compute the pension obligation and health care obligation from 5.5% in 2012 to 5.75% in 2013. The increased discount rate reduces the obligations and results in an actuarial gain. In addition, Treadaway decreased the initial health care cost trend rate from 11.5% in 2012 to 11.2% in 2013, which reduces the health care obligation and results in an actuarial gain.

e.   Prior Service Cost, End of 2012 .... $ 314
Plus Increase in Prior Service Cost During 2013 from Plan
    Amendments   111
Less Amortization of Prior Service Cost During 2013..............   (59)
Prior Service Cost, End of 2013 .... $ 366

f.   Net Actuarial Loss, End of 2012 .... $ 1,646
Less Decrease in Actuarial Loss During 2013 from Actuarial
    Gain in Pension Obligation..   (120)
Less Amortization of Actuarial Loss During 2013...................   (91)
Less Excess of Actual Return over Expected Return on
    Pension Investments ($478 – $295) ....   (183)
Net Actuarial Loss, End of 2013 .... $ 1,252

g.   Prior Service Cost, End of 2012 .... $ 339
Plus Increase in Prior Service Cost During 2013 from Plan
    Amendments   1
Less Amortization of Prior Service Cost During 2013..............   (41)
Prior Service Cost, End of 2013 .... $ 299

h.   Net Actuarial Loss, End of 2012 .... $ 340
Less Decrease in Actuarial Loss During 2013 from Actuarial
    Gain in Health Care Obligation ....   (110)
Less Amortization of Actuarial Loss During 2013...................   (9)
Net Actuarial Loss, End of 2013 .... $ 221

12.31 continued.

i. **2013**

Pension Expense..	253	
Pension Liability (Noncurrent Liabilities: $736 – $19)	717	
Other Comprehensive Income (Prior Service Cost: $366 – $314)...	52	
Other..	20	
Cash..		567
Pension Liability (Noncurrent Liabilities: $1,348 – $1,267)..		81
Other Comprehensive Income (Actuarial Loss: $1,646 – $1,252)..		394

Assets	= Liabilities	+	Shareholders' Equity	(Class.)
+20	–717		–253	IncSt → RE
–567	+81		–52	OCI → AOCI
			+394	OCI → AOCI

To record pension expense, pension funding, and the change in balance sheet accounts relating to the pension plan for 2013.

j. **2013**

Health Care Expense	210	
Health Care Liability (Current Liabilities: $254 – $231)...	23	
Health Care Liability (Noncurrent Liabilities: $2,375 – $2,243)...	132	
Other..	27	
Cash..		233
Other Comprehensive Income (Prior Service Cost: $339 – $299)		40
Other Comprehensive Income (Actuarial Loss: $340 – $221).......................................		119

12.31 j. continued.

Assets	=	Liabilities	+	Shareholders' Equity	(Class.)
+27		−23		−210	IncSt → RE
−233		−132		+40	OCI → AOCI
				+119	OCI → AOCI

To record health care expense, health care funding, and the change in balance sheet accounts relating to the health care plan for 2013.

12.32 (Catiman Limited; interpreting income tax disclosures.) (amounts in millions of US$)

a. **2012**

Income Tax Expense	699	
Deferred Income Taxes	39	
Income Tax Payable		738

Assets	=	Liabilities	+	Shareholders' Equity	(Class.)
+39	or	−39		−699	IncSt → RE
		+738			

To record income tax expense, income tax payable, and a debit change in deferred income taxes for 2012.

b. **2013**

Income Tax Expense	742	
Income Tax Payable		736
Deferred Income Taxes		6

Assets	=	Liabilities	+	Shareholders' Equity	(Class.)
		+736		−742	IncSt → RE
−6	or	+6			

To record income tax expense, income tax payable, and the credit change in deferred income taxes for 2013.

12.32 continued.

c.   The first line of Catiman's tax reconciliation assumes that governmental entities tax income before income taxes at 35%, which is only the federal statutory rate. State and local taxes (net of any tax savings from subtracting state and local taxes in computing federal taxable income) increase the effective tax rate above 35%.

d.   Nondeductible items increase the effective tax rate, despite their appearing with other reconciling items with a negative sign in this case. The first line of the tax reconciliation assumes that all costs or expenses save income taxes at a 35% tax rate. If firms cannot deduct a particular cost or expense for tax purposes, the effective tax rate on income before income taxes increases.

e.   A recognized pension liability or health care liability suggests that Catiman has recognized more pension or health care expense than the firm has contributed cash. The contribution of cash gives rise to an income tax deduction. Thus, taxable income exceeds book income, resulting in a deferred tax asset for the higher taxes paid currently. A recognized prepaid pension asset suggests that Catiman has contributed more cash to the pension fund than it had recognized as pension expense. Thus, book income exceeds taxable income, resulting in a deferred tax liability for the delayed payment of taxes.

f.   Authoritative guidance requires firms using the accrual basis of accounting to recognize sales allowances as an expense in the period of sale, whereas firms cannot deduct sales allowances in computing taxable income until making actual expenditures. Thus, a growing firm will likely record higher taxable income than book income and recognize a deferred tax asset for the early payment of taxes.

g.   Catiman increased the deferred tax asset for expected benefits from tax loss and tax credit carryforwards. If Catiman is not yet profitable, uncertainty exists as to whether Catiman will benefit from the tax losses and tax credit carryforwards, creating the need for a deferred tax asset valuation allowance. Some of the other items in deferred tax assets may relate to the unprofitable entity, leading as well to uncertainty about the ability to realize those tax benefits.

Solutions

12.32 continued.

h. The decreasing amount of deferred tax liability for temporary depreciation differences suggests that book depreciation exceeds tax depreciation. The likely explanation is that Catiman reduced its expenditures on depreciable assets, resulting in more assets in the later years of their lives when straight-line depreciation for book purposes exceeds accelerated depreciation for tax purposes than assets in their early years when accelerated depreciation exceeds straight-line depreciation. Cumulative depreciation for tax purposes still exceeds cumulative depreciation for book purposes because this firm reports a deferred tax liability.

i. Catiman is the lessor. The reporting of a deferred tax liability indicates that cumulative book income exceeds cumulative taxable income. Catiman likely accounts for these leases as capital leases for financial reporting and operating leases for tax reporting. The capital lease method results in the lessor reporting a gain in the year the parties sign the lease, whereas the operating lease method spreads the income over the term of the lease.

12.33 (E-Drive; interpreting income tax disclosures.) (amounts in millions of euros)

a. **2012**

Income Tax Expense 4,232
Income Tax Payable 2,047
Deferred Income Taxes 2,185

Assets	=	Liabilities	+	Shareholders' Equity	(Class.)
		+2,047		–4,232	IncSt → RE
–2,185	or	+2,185			

To record income tax expense, income tax payable,
and the change in deferred income taxes for 2012.

12.33 continued.

b. **2013**

Income Tax Expense	3,901	
Income Tax Payable		2,177
Deferred Income Taxes		1,724

Assets	=	Liabilities	+	Shareholders' Equity	(Class.)
		+2,177		−3,901	IncSt → RE
−1,724	or	+1,724			

To record income tax expense, income tax payable, and the change in deferred income taxes for 2013.

c. The deferred tax amounts in Exhibit 12.23 relate not only to amounts affecting income tax expense of the current period but also to tax effects of items included in other balance sheet items. For example, when firms debit or credit other comprehensive income when initially recognizing or subsequently amortizing prior service costs and actuarial gains and losses of pension and health care plans, the firms must credit or debit other comprehensive income for the income tax effects of these items. The deferred tax amounts in Exhibit 12.23 include the tax effects of all temporary differences, not just those affecting income tax expense of the current period.

d. The first line of the tax reconciliation assumes that governmental entities tax income before income taxes at 35%, which is only the federal tax rate. Local taxes (net of any tax savings from subtracting local taxes in computing the relevant federal taxable income) increase the effective tax rate above 35%.

e. E-Drive recognizes a deferred tax asset for underfunded retirement plans and a deferred tax liability for overfunded retirement plans. IFRS requires firms to report underfunded retirement plans as liabilities and overfunded retirement plans as assets and not to net them. Similarly, IFRS requires firms to report the deferred tax assets and deferred tax liabilities related to these plans separately and not to net them.

12.33 continued.

f. A deferred tax asset for expenses suggests that E-Drive recognizes expenses earlier for financial reporting than for tax reporting. IFRS requires firms to recognize expenses for bad debts and warranties in the period of sale, whereas the income tax law does not permit a deduction for such items until actual uncollectible accounts receivable materialize and firms make warranty expenditures.

g. E-Drive is the lessor. The reporting of a deferred tax liability indicates that cumulative book income exceeds cumulative taxable income. E-Drive likely accounts for these leases as capital leases for financial reporting and operating leases for tax reporting. The capital lease method results in the lessor reporting a gain in the year the parties sign the lease, whereas the operating lease method spreads the income over the term of the lease.

h. A deferred tax liability for development costs suggests that E-Drive recognizes expenses earlier for tax reporting than for financial reporting. IFRS requires firms to capitalize as assets and subsequently amortize development costs incurred after the development project reaches the point of technological feasibility and the firm has the ability and intent to complete the project. For tax purposes, firms can deduct expenditures on development costs.

12.34 (Dime Store; interpreting income tax disclosures.) (amounts in millions of US$)

a. **2011**
Income Tax Expense 1,146
   Income Tax Payable 1,052
   Deferred Income Taxes 94

Assets	=	Liabilities	+	Shareholders' Equity	(Class.)
		+1,052		−1,146	IncSt → RE
−94	or	+94			

To record income tax expense, income tax payable,
and the change in deferred income taxes for 2011.

12.34 continued.

b. **2012**

Income Tax Expense 1,452
Deferred Income Taxes 122
   Income Tax Payable 1,574

Assets	=	Liabilities	+	Shareholders' Equity	(Class.)
−122	or	−122		−1,452	IncSt → RE
		+1,574			

To record income tax expense, income tax payable,
and the change in deferred income taxes for 2012.

c. **2013**

Income Tax Expense 1,710
Deferred Income Taxes 201
   Income Tax Payable 1,911

Assets	=	Liabilities	+	Shareholders' Equity	(Class.)
−201	or	−201		−1,710	IncSt → RE
		+1,911			

To record income tax expense, income tax payable,
and the change in deferred income taxes for 2013.

d. The deferred tax amounts in Exhibit 12.24 relate not only to amounts affecting income tax expense of the current period but also to tax effects of items included in other balance sheet items. For example, when firms debit or credit other comprehensive income when initially recognizing or subsequently amortizing prior service costs and actuarial gains and losses of pension and health care plans, the firms must credit or debit other comprehensive income for the income tax effects of these items. The deferred tax amounts in Exhibit 12.24 include the tax effects of all temporary differences, not just those affecting income tax expense of the current period.

12.34 continued.

    e.   The first line of Dime Store's tax reconciliation assumes that governmental entities tax income before income taxes at 35%, which is only the U.S. federal tax rate. State and local taxes (net of any tax savings from subtracting state and local taxes in computing U.S. federal taxable income) increase the effective tax rate above 35%.

    f.   The deferred tax asset for health care benefits suggests that Dime Store has an underfunded health care plan. Dime Store has recognized more health care expenses than it has contributed cash to the health care benefits plan. The cash contribution triggers an income tax deduction for computing taxable income. Dime Store has prepaid income taxes because health care expense for tax is less than book, giving rise to the deferred tax asset. The deferred tax liability for pension care benefits suggests that Dime Store has an overfunded pension plan. Dime Store has recognized less pension expenses than it has contributed cash to the pension benefits plan. The cash contribution triggers an income tax deduction for computing taxable income. Dime Store has delayed paying income taxes because pension expense for tax exceeds pension expense for book, giving rise to the deferred tax liability.

    g.   A steady deferred tax liability for temporary depreciation differences suggests that depreciation using the accelerated method for tax purposes approximately equals straight-line depreciation for book purposes. This equality generally occurs around the mid-point of assets' lives. The relatively flat deferred tax amount suggests that Dime Store replaces depreciable assets at approximately the same rate as they wear out.

    h.   Dime Store is profitable and more likely than not to realize the benefits of deferred tax assets.

12.35 (Equilibrium Company; behavior of deferred income tax account when a firm acquires new assets every year.) (amounts in euros)

TAX DEPRECIATION (MACRS)

Units Year	Acquired	Year 1	Year 2	Year 3	Year 4	Year 5	Year 6	Year 7
1	1	€2,400	€3,840	€2,280	€1,440	€1,320	€720	€0
2	1		2,400	3,840	2,280	1,440	1,320	720
3	1			2,400	3,840	2,280	1,440	1,320
4	1				2,400	3,840	2,280	1,440
5	1					2,400	3,840	2,280
6	1						2,400	3,840
7	1							2,400
a. Annual Depreciation		€2,400	€6,240	€8,520	€9,960	€11,280	€12,000	€12,000
b. Straight-Line Depreciation = €2,000 per Machine per Year		2,000	4,000	6,000	8,000	10,000	12,000	12,000
c. Difference		€400	€2,240	€2,520	€1,960	€1,280	€0	€0
d. Increase in Deferred Tax (40%)		€160	€896	€1,008	€784	€512	€0	€0
e. Balance of Deferred Income Taxes		€160	€1,056	€2,064	€2,848	€3,360	€3,360	€3,360

f. The Deferred Income Taxes account balance will remain constant at €3,360 so long as the firm continues this replacement policy. If asset prices increase or physical assets increase, or both, the Deferred Tax Liability will continue to grow.

Solutions

12.36   (Shiraz Company; attempts to achieve off-balance-sheet financing.)

[The chapter does not give sufficient information for the student to perform the analysis required by U.S. GAAP or IFRS. The six items are designed to generate discussion.]

Transfer of Receivables with Recourse Shiraz Company retains control of the future economic benefits of the receivables. If interest rates decrease, Shiraz can borrow funds at the lower interest rate and repurchase the receivables. Because the receivables carry a fixed-interest interest rate, Shiraz enjoys the benefit of the difference between the fixed interest return on the receivables and the lower borrowing cost. If interest rates increase, Shiraz will not repurchase the receivables. Credit Company bears the risk of interest rate increases because of the fixed interest return on the receivables. The right of Shiraz to repurchase the receivables restricts the ability of Credit Company to sell or exchange the receivables. The control of who benefits from interest rate changes and who bears the risk resides with Shiraz. Shiraz Company also bears credit risk in excess of the allowance. Shiraz Company should report the transaction as a collateralized loan.

Product Financing Arrangement Shiraz retains both the risk and the benefit of the inventory. Shiraz Company agrees to repurchase the inventory at a fixed price, thereby incurring the risk of changing prices. The purchase price formula includes a fixed interest rate, so Shiraz enjoys the benefits or incurs the risk of interest rate changes. Shiraz also controls the benefits and risk of changes in storage costs. Shiraz should treat this arrangement as a collateralized loan.

Purchase Contract U.S. GAAP provides specialized guidance that treats this type of purchase contract as an executory contract and does not require its recognition as a liability. There is a marked similarity between a product financing arrangement (involving inventory) and a purchase contract (involving a service). Shiraz Company must pay specified amounts each period regardless of whether it uses the shipping services. The wording of the problem makes it unclear as to whether the initial contract specifies a selling price (railroad bears risk of operating cost increases) or whether the selling price is the railroad's current charges for shipping services each period (Shiraz bears risk of operating cost increases). It seems unlikely that the railroad would accept a fixed price for all 10 years. Thus, it appears that Shiraz incurs a commitment to make highly probable

12.36 continued.

future cash payments in amounts that cover the railroad's operating and financing costs. This transaction has the economic characteristics of a collateralized loan, even though U.S. GAAP permits treatment as an executory contract.

Construction Joint Venture The construction loan will appear as a liability on the books of Chemical, the joint entity. Shiraz will recognize the fair value of its loan guarantee as a liability. Shiraz and Mission each own 50%, but Shiraz appears to have the residual claim because in return for guaranteeing the debt of Chemical, it can buy out Mission for a fixed cost-based price if the venture turns out well. It is possible that Shiraz controls Chemical and should consolidate it, thereby showing Chemical's assets and liabilities on the consolidated balance sheet. Chapter 14 discusses consolidation policy.

Research and Development Partnership Shiraz guarantees the bank loan in this case regardless of the outcome of the R & D effort and therefore must recognize a liability. It does not matter whether Shiraz has an option or an obligation to purchase the results of the R & D effort.

If Shiraz did not guarantee the bank loan, but instead has the option to purchase the results of the R & D work, it does not bear the risk of failure and need not recognize a liability. If Shiraz has the obligation to purchase the results, it recognizes a liability for the probable amount payable. The problem does not make it clear whether the amount payable includes the unpaid balance of the loan or merely the value of the R & D work (which could be zero). It seems unlikely that the bank would lend funds for the R & D work without some commitment or obligation by Shiraz to repay the loan.

Hotel Financing Shiraz Company will recognize a liability for the fair value of its guarantee, which is likely to be less than the amount of the loan. It appears in this case that the probability of Shiraz having to make payments under the loan guarantee is low. The hotel is profitable and probably generating positive cash flows. In addition, the bank can sell the hotel in the event of loan default to satisfy the unpaid balance of the loan. Thus, Shiraz's loan guarantee is a third level of defense against loan default. If default does occur and the first two lines of defense prove inadequate to repay the loan in full, then Shiraz would recognize a liability for the unpaid portion.

This page is intentionally left blank

CHAPTER 13

MARKETABLE SECURITIES AND DERIVATIVES

Questions, Exercises, and Problems: Answers and Solutions

13.1 See the text or the glossary at the end of the book.

13.2 a. Debt securities that a firm intends to hold to maturity and has the ability to hold to maturity appear as "held to maturity debt securities." Debt securities in the "available for sale" category include short-term investments that serve as a liquid investment of excess cash and short- and long-term investments in government debt securities and corporate debt securities that serve as sources of cash at a later date (for example, to pay debt coming due).

b. The classification "trading securities" implies a firm's active involvement in buying and selling securities for profit. The classification "available-for-sale securities" implies less frequent trading and usually relates to an operating purpose other than profit alone. For example, the firm might hold available-for-sale securities to generate income while a firm has temporarily excess cash.

c. Amortized cost equals the purchase price of debt securities plus or minus amortization of any difference between acquisition cost and maturity value. Amortized cost bears no necessary relation to the fair value of the debt security in periods after acquisition. The fair value of a debt security depends on the risk characteristics of the issuer, terms of the debt contract (e.g., interest rate, term to maturity), and general level of interest rates in the economy.

d. Unrealized gains and losses occur when the fair value of a security changes while the firm holds the security. The unrealized gain or loss on trading securities appears in the income statement each period. For available-for-sale securities, the unrealized gain or loss appears in Other Comprehensive Income, a shareholders' equity account that is closed to Accumulated Other Comprehensive Income, another shareholders' equity account.

13-1

Solutions

13.2 continued.

e. Realized gains and losses appear in the income statement when a firm sells a security. The realized gain or loss on trading securities equals the selling price minus the fair value of the security on the most recent balance sheet. The realized gain or loss on available-for-sale securities equals the selling price minus the acquisition cost of the security.

13.3 Firms acquire trading securities primarily for their short-term profit potential. Including the unrealized gain or loss in income provides the financial statement user with relevant information for assessing the performance of the trading activity. Firms acquire available-for-sale securities to support an operating activity (for example, investment of temporarily excess cash) rather than primarily for the profit potential of these securities. Deferring recognition in income of gains and losses until sale treats available-for-sale securities the same as inventories, equipment, and other assets. Excluding the unrealized gain or loss from earnings also reduces earnings volatility.

13.4 The required accounting does appear inconsistent. One explanation for this inconsistency is that the balance sheet and income statement serve different purposes. The balance sheet displays the resources of a firm and the claims on those users by creditors and owners. Fair values for securities are more relevant than acquisition cost or lower of cost or market for assessing the adequacy of resources to satisfy claims. The income statement reports the results of operating performance. One might argue that operating performance from investing in available-for-sale securities is not complete until the firm sells these securities. Another argument for excluding at least unrealized gains on available-for-sale securities from earnings is that delaying the income statement recognition of such gains until the securities are sold achieves consistency with the delayed recognition of unrealized gains on inventories, equipment, and other assets until those gains are realized.

As for earnings quality issues, the unrealized gains can be realized based on management decisions about the timing of sales of available-for-sale securities. This means management can bring the gains from accumulated other comprehensive income into net income. Management cannot manipulate other comprehensive income, only net income.

13.5   A derivative is an accounting hedge when the firm bears a risk (a variability in outcomes) such that the change in the value of the derivative offsets the change in the value of the hedged item as time passes. A derivative designated as an accounting hedge is required to be "highly effective" in offsetting the hedged risk. When the firm acquires a derivative that is ineffective as a hedge, for example, its changes in fair value are uncorrelated with changes in the value of the hedged item, the derivative would not qualify as an accounting hedge.

Under this interpretation, a derivative is not a hedge when changes in the fair value of the derivative do not at least partially offset changes in the fair value of a hedged item occurring at the same time.

If the firm chooses not to use hedge accounting when it could, the fluctuations in the fair value of the derivative appear in income. That is, they are not offset by the changes in fair value of the hedged item.

13.6   A *fair value hedge* is a hedge of an exposure to changes in the fair value of a recognized asset or liability or of an unrecognized firm commitment. A *cash flow hedge* is a hedge of an exposure to variability in the cash flows of a recognized asset or liability (such as variable interest rates) or of a forecasted transaction (such as expected future foreign sales).

13.7   Firms do not recognize the fair value of the commitment except to the extent that they recognize the fair value of the derivative that is hedging that commitment. Thus, firms recognize a portion of the commitment relating to the hedging activity but not the full fair value of that commitment. Firms also do not recognize the asset that the firm will receive when it satisfies the commitment.

13.8   The reason relates to matching. Under a fair value hedge, firms report recognized assets and liabilities at fair value and include unrealized gains and losses in net income. Firms also report associated derivatives at fair value and include unrealized gains and losses in net income. Thus, the treatment of the hedged asset or liabilities parallels the treatment of the derivative. Under a cash flow hedge, firms do not necessarily report the hedged asset or liability at fair value. Including unrealized gains and losses on the derivative in net income but not including the unrealized gains and losses on the hedged item in net income is inconsistent. The gains or loss on the hedged item usually affects net income when the firm receives or disburses cash. At that time, the firm transfers gains and losses on the associated derivative out of accumulated other comprehensive income and recognizes those gains and losses in net income.

13.9   To qualify for hedge accounting, there must be an expectation that the derivative will be effective in hedging a particular risk. Obtaining a derivative that will be highly effective in hedging a particular risk may be costly or impracticable. A firm might be satisfied with obtaining a derivative that will hedge a portion of the risk, accepting the likelihood that the derivative will not be highly effective and will not qualify for hedge accounting treatment. Another explanation is that the firm wishes to speculate on movements in interest rates, foreign exchange rates, or commodity prices. That is, firms acquire certain derivatives for trading gains and not to hedge a business risk.

13.10   This statement is correct. Firms would report all financial assets and financial liabilities at fair value and include unrealized gains and losses in net income.

13.11   (Classifying securities.)

   a.   Available-for-sale securities; current asset.

   b.   Held-to-maturity debt security; noncurrent asset.

   c.   Available-for-sale securities; current asset.

   d.   Available-for-sale securities; noncurrent asset.

   e.   Trading securities; current asset.

   f.   Available-for-sale securities; noncurrent asset (although a portion of these bonds might appear as a current asset).

13.12   (Accounting principles for marketable securities and derivatives).

   a.   (4)   The firm has option to use hedge accounting, deferring income effects until realization and reporting changes in fair value in periodic other comprehensive income, or to not use hedge accounting and reporting holding gains and losses, like trading securities gains and losses, in current period income.

   b.   (1)   This derivative is not an accounting hedge, so gains and losses appear in current income.

13.12 continued.

    c. (1) Because not both ability and intent to hold to maturity are present, it will appear at fair value. Because the firm trades securities such as this, the classification is as a trading security. If the firm were not a trader, then Treatment (3) would apply.

    d. (3) Standard treatment for available-for-sale securities.

13.13 (Murray Company; accounting for bonds held to maturity.) (amounts in US$)

    a. Present Value of Periodic Payments: $3,000 × 6.73274[a] = $ 20,198
        Present Value of Maturity Amount: $100,000 × 0.73069[b] =   73,069
        Total.. $ 93,267

    [a]Present value of an annuity for eight periods at 4%.

    [b]Present value of $1 for eight periods at 4%.

    b. See Schedule 13.1 below.

Schedule 13.1
Amortization Table for $100,000 Bonds with Interest
Paid Semiannually at 6% and Priced to Yield 8%
Compounded Semiannually
(Exercise 13)

Period	Balance at Beginning of Period	Interest Revenue for Period	Cash Received	Portion of Payment Increasing Carrying Value	Balance at End of Period
1	$93,267	$3,731	$3,000	$731	$ 93,998
2	$93,998	$3,760	$3,000	$760	$ 94,758
3	$94,758	$3,790	$3,000	$790	$ 95,548
4	$95,548	$3,822	$3,000	$822	$ 96,370
5	$96,370	$3,855	$3,000	$855	$ 97,225
6	$97,225	$3,889	$3,000	$889	$ 98,114
7	$98,114	$3,925	$3,000	$925	$ 99,039
8	$99,039	$3,961	$3,000	$961	$ 100,000

13.13 continued.

    c.   **January 1, 2013**

Marketable Debt Securities	93,267	
Cash..		93,267

       June 30, 2013

Cash..	3,000	
Marketable Debt Securities	731	
Interest Revenue...		3,731

       December 31, 2013

Cash..	3,000	
Marketable Debt Securities	760	
Interest Revenue...		3,760

    d.   **December 31, 2016**

Cash..	3,000	
Marketable Debt Securities	962	
Interest Revenue...		3,962

       December 31, 2016

Cash..	100,000	
Marketable Debt Securities		100,000

13.14   (Kelly Company, accounting for bonds held to maturity.) (amounts in US$)

    a.   Present Value of Periodic Payments: $17,500 X 5.41719[a] = $ 94,801

       Present Value of Maturity Amount: $500,000 X 0.83748[b] = 418,740

       Total... $ 513,541

      [a]Present value of an annuity for six periods at 3%.

      [b]Present value of $1 for six periods at 3%.

13.14 continued.

    b.   See Schedule 13.2 below.

Schedule 13.2
Amortization Table for $500,000 Bonds with Interest
Paid Semiannually at 7% and Priced to Yield 6%
Compounded Semiannually
(Exercise 14)

Period (1)	Balance at Beginning of Period (2)	Interest Revenue for Period (3)	Cash Received (4)	Portion of Payment Reducing Carrying Value (5)	Balance at End of Period (6)
1	$513,541	$15,406	$17,500	$(2,094)	$ 511,447
2	$511,447	$15,343	$17,500	$(2,157)	$ 509,291
3	$509,291	$15,279	$17,500	$(2,221)	$ 507,069
4	$507,069	$15,212	$17,500	$(2,288)	$ 504,781
5	$504,781	$15,143	$17,500	$(2,357)	$ 502,424
6	$502,424	$15,074[a]	$17,500	$(2,424)	$ 500,000

[a]Amount does not equal 3% of balance at the beginning of the period due to rounding.

    c. **January 1, 2013**

Marketable Debt Securities	513,541	
Cash		513,541

June 30, 2013

Cash	17,500	
Interest Revenue		15,406
Marketable Debt Securities		2,094

December 31, 2013

Cash	17,500	
Interest Revenue		15,343
Marketable Debt Securities		2,157

13.14 continued.

 d. **December 31, 2015**
  Cash.. 17,500
   Interest Revenue..   15,075
   Marketable Debt Securities   2,425

  December 31, 2016
  Cash.. 500,000
   Marketable Debt Securities   500,000

13.15 (Elston Corporation; accounting for available-for-sale securities.) (amounts in US$)

  10/15/2013
  Marketable Securities (Security A)............................ 28,000
   Cash   28,000
  To record acquisition of Security A.

  11/02/2013
  Marketable Securities (Security B)............................ 49,000
   Cash   49,000
  To record acquisition of Security B.

  12/31/2013
  Cash... 1,000
   Dividend Revenue   1,000
  To record dividend received from Security B.

  12/31/2013
  Unrealized Loss on Security A (Other Comprehensive
   Income) 3,000
    Marketable Securities (Security A)   3,000
  To record unrealized loss on Security A.

  12/31/2013
  Marketable Securities (Security B)............................ 6,000
   Unrealized Gain on Security B (Other
    Comprehensive Income)   6,000
  To record unrealized gain on Security B.

13.15 continued.

2/10/2014

Cash..	24,000	
Realized Loss on Sale of Available-for-Sale		
Securities (= $24,000 − $28,000)	4,000	
Marketable Securities (Security A)....................		25,000
Unrealized Loss on Security A (Accumulated		
Other Comprehensive Income)......................		3,000

To record sale of Security A including reclassifying
the unrealized loss from Accumulated Other
Comprehensive Income

12/31/2014

Cash..	1,200	
Dividend Revenue		1,200

To record dividend received from Security B.

12/31/2014

Unrealized Gain on Security B (Other Comprehensive		
Income)..	2,000	
Marketable Securities (Security B) (= $53,000		
− $55,000)		2,000

To remeasure Security B to fair value.

7/15/2015

Cash..	57,000	
Unrealized Gain on Security B (= $6,000 − $2,000)		
(Accumulated Other Comprehensive Income)	4,000	
Marketable Securities (Security B)		53,000
Realized Gain on Sale of Available-for-Sale		
Securities (= $57,000 − $49,000)....................		8,000

To record sale of Security B including reclassifying
the unrealized gain from Accumulated Other
Comprehensive Income.

13.16   (Simmons Corporation; accounting for available-for-sale securities.) (amounts in US$)

6/13/2013

Marketable Securities (Security S).............................	12,000	
Marketable Securities (Security T)............................	29,000	
Marketable Securities (Security U)	43,000	
Cash		84,000

To record acquisition of marketable equity securities.

10/11/2013

Cash...	39,000	
Realized Loss on Sale of Security U.............................	4,000	
Marketable Securities (Security U).........................		43,000

To record sale of Security U.

12/31/2013

Marketable Securities (Security S) (= $13,500 – $12,000)	1,500	
Unrealized Gain on Security S (Other Comprehensive Income)		1,500

To remeasure Security S to fair value.

12/31/2013

Unrealized Loss on Security T (Other Comprehensive Income)	2,800	
Marketable Securities (Security T) (= $26,200 – $29,000)		2,800

To remeasure Security T to fair value.

12/31/2014

Marketable Securities (Security S) (= $15,200 – $13,500)	1,700	
Unrealized Gain on Security S (Other Comprehensive Income)		1,700

To remeasure Security S to fair value.

13.16 continued.

12/31/2014

Marketable Securities (Security T) (= $31,700 – $26,200)	5,500	
Unrealized Loss on Security T (from 12/31/2013 Entry) (Other Comprehensive Income)		2,800
Unrealized Gain on Security T (Other Comprehensive Income)		2,700

To remeasure Security T to fair value.

2/15/2015

Cash...	14,900	
Unrealized Gain on Security S (= $1,500 + $1,700) (Accumulated Other Comprehensive Income)	3,200	
Marketable Securities (Security S)		15,200
Realized Gain on Sale of Security (= $14,900 – $12,000)		2,900

To record sale of Security S including reclassifying the unrealized gain from Accumulated Other Comprehensive Income.

8/22/2015

Cash...	28,500	
Unrealized Gain on Security T (Accumulated Other Comprehensive Income)..	2,700	
Realized Loss on Sale of Securities Available for Sale (Security T) (= $28,500 – $29,000)..........................	500	
Marketable Securities (Security T)...................		31,700

To record sale of Security T including reclassifying the unrealized gain from Accumulated Other Comprehensive Income.

13.17   (Fischer/Black Company; working backward from data on marketable securities transaction.) (amounts in US$)

a. $21,000 = $18,000 + $3,000.

b. $18,000, the amount credited to Marketable Securities in the journal entry which the student might think of as $21,000 acquisition cost, derived above, less $3,000 of Unrealized Loss.

c. $5,000 loss from the debit for Realized Loss.

13.18   (Canning/Werther; working backward from data on marketable securities transaction.) (amounts in US$)

a. $15,000 = $18,000 proceeds − $4,000 realized gain + $1,000 loss previously recognized because they are trading securities.

b. $14,000 = $18,000 proceeds − $4,000 realized gain, which is selling price less acquisition cost because they are available-for-sale securities.

13.19   (Reconstructing events from journal entries.) (amounts in US$)

a.   The fair value of a marketable security classified as available for sale is $4,000 less than its carrying value and the firm increases the Unrealized Loss account on the balance sheet.

b.   A firm sells marketable securities classified as either trading securities or as available-for-sale securities in the same period as it purchased the securities for an amount that is $200 (= $1,100 − $1,300) less than was originally paid for them.

c.   The fair value of marketable securities classified as available for sale is $750 more than its carrying value and the firm increases the Unrealized Gain account on the balance sheet.

d.   A firm sells marketable securities classified as either trading securities or available-for-sale securities in the same period that it purchased the securities for an amount that is $100 (= $1,800 − $1,700) more than was originally paid for them.

13.20   (Zeff Corporation; reconstructing transactions involving short-term available-for-sale securities.) (amounts in US$)

a.   Sale of marketable securities during 2013: Proceeds of $14,000; gain on sale is $4,000 = $14,000 − $10,000, so acquisition cost was $10,000.

b.   Carrying value at time of sale was $13,000, so unrealized gain at time of sale was $3,000 = $13,000 − $10,000.

13.20 continued.

  c. The ending balance of Net Unrealized Gains was $2,000 less ~~at the~~ end of 2013 than at the beginning, while the unrealized gain on the securities sold was $3,000. The sale reduced the balance by $3,000. Since the ending balance declined by only $2,000, the securities on hand must have increased during the year by $1,000, so the net decline is $2,000 = $3,000 − $1,000.

  d. The Marketable Securities account increased by $8,000 = $195,000 − $187,000 during 2013. The sale reduced the account by $13,000 and the unrealized gain on the securities held at the end of the year increased the balance by $1,000; see Part c. above. A net increase of $8,000 after a reduction of $12,000 means the cost of new securities is $20,000 = $8,000 + $12,000.

13.21 (Turner Corporation; accounting for forward currency contract as a fair value hedge.) (amounts in US$)

  a. The amount that Turner Corporation would receive if the contract were settled on December 31, 2013, is $1,020 (= $52,000 − $50,980). The present value of $1,020 discounted for six months at 8% per year is $981 (= $1,020 X 0.96154). Turner Corporation would report this amount as an asset.

  b. Turner Corporation would also report a commitment to purchase the equipment for $981. The firm would not report a liability for the full purchase price. The commitment is an executory contract. It recognizes the commitment only to the extent of the derivative on the asset side of the balance sheet.

  c. The fair value of the forward currency contract on June 30, 2014, just before settlement, is the amount of cash Turner Corporation will receive from the counterparty, which is $3,757 (= $54,737 − $50,980).

  d. **June 30, 2014**

Equipment	50,980	
Commitment to Purchase Equipment	3,757	
Cash		54,737

  e. **June 30, 2014**

Cash	3,757	
Forward Contract		3,757

13.22   (Biddle Corporation; accounting for forward currency contract as a cash flow hedge.) (amounts in US$)

a.   The amount that Biddle Corporation would receive if the contract were settled on December 31, 2013, is $1,200 (= $54,000 – $52,800). Biddle Corporation would report this amount as an asset.

b.   Biddle Corporation would report a payable to the supplier of $54,000 (40,000 X $1.35).

c.   The fair value of the forward contract on March 31, 2014, just before settlement is the amount of cash Biddle Corporation will receive from the counterparty, which is $3,200 (= $56,000 – $52,800).

d.   **March 31, 2014**

Note Payable	56,000	
Cash		56,000

e.   **March 31, 2014**

Cash	3,200	
Forward Contract		3,200

The carrying value of the equipment before recognizing any depreciation is $52,800. The net cash outflow is $52,800 (= $56,000 – $3,200). The gains in Accumulated Other Comprehensive Income from revaluing the forward contract of $3,200 exactly offset the losses from revaluing the Note Payable of $3,200. Thus, Biddle Corporation could make an entry clearing these amounts from Accumulated Other Comprehensive Income.

13.23   (Dostal Corporation; journal entries and financial statement presentation of short-term available-for-sale securities.) (amounts in US$)

a.   **2/05/2013**

Marketable Securities (Security A)	60,000	
Cash		60,000

8/12/2013

Marketable Securities (Security B)	25,000	
Cash		25,000

13.23 a. continued.

12/31/2013

Marketable Securities (Security A) (= $66,000 – $60,000)	6,000	
Unrealized Gain on Security A (Other Comprehensive Income)		6,000
Unrealized Loss on Security B (Other Comprehensive Income)	5,000	
Marketable Securities (Security B) (= $20,000 – $25,000)		5,000

1/22/2014

Marketable Securities (Security C)	82,000	
Cash		82,000

2/25/2014

Marketable Securities (Security D)	42,000	
Cash		42,000

3/25/2014

Marketable Securities (Security E)	75,000	
Cash		75,000

6/05/2014

Cash	72,000	
Unrealized Gain on Security A (Accumulated Other Comprehensive Income)	6,000	
Marketable Securities (Security A)		66,000
Realized Gain on Sale of Available-for-Sale Securities		12,000

6/05/2014

Cash	39,000	
Realized Loss on Sale of Available-for-Sale Securities	3,000	
Marketable Securities (Security D)		42,000

13.23 a. continued.

12/31/2014

Unrealized Loss on Security C (Other Comprehensive Income)	3,000	
Marketable Securities (Security C) (= $79,000 – $82,000)		3,000

12/31/2014

Marketable Securities (Security E) (= $80,000 – $75,000)	5,000	
Unrealized Gain on Security E (Other Comprehensive Income)		5,000

b. **Balance Sheet on December 31, 2013**

Marketable Securities at Fair Value.................................	$	86,000
Net Unrealized Gain on Available- for-Sale Securities ($6,000 – $5,000)...	$	1,000

Note

Marketable Securities on December 31, 2013, had an acquisition cost of $85,000 and a fair value of $86,000. Gross unrealized gains total $6,000 and gross unrealized losses total $5,000.

c. **Balance Sheet on December 31, 2014**

Marketable Securities at Fair Value.................................	$	179,000
Net Unrealized Loss on Available-for-Sale Securities........	$	(3,000)

Note

Marketable Securities on December 31, 2014, had an acquisition cost of $182,000 and a fair value of $179,000. Gross unrealized gains total $5,000, and gross unrealized losses total $8,000. Proceeds from sales of marketable securities totaled $111,000 during 2014. These sales resulted in gross realized gains of $12,000 and gross realized losses of $3,000. The net unrealized loss on securities available for sale changed as follows during 2014:

Balance, December 31, 2013...	$ 1,000	Cr.
Accumulated Other Comprehensive Income (Unrealized Gain on Securities Sold)	(6,000)	Dr.
Change in Net Unrealized Loss on Securities Held at Year End ($5,000 – $3,000)...	2,000	Cr.
Balance, December 31, 2014...	$ (3,000)	Dr.

13.24 (Rice Corporation; journal entries and financial statement presentation of long-term available-for-sale securities.) (amounts in US$)

a. **3/05/2013**

Investments in Securities (Security A).....................	40,000	
Cash...		40,000

5/12/2013

Investments in Securities (Security B)...................	80,000	
Cash...		80,000

12/31/2013

Investments in Securities (Security A) (= $45,000 – $40,000)	5,000	
Unrealized Gain on Security A (Other Comprehensive Income)		5,000

12/31/2013

Unrealized Loss on Security B (Other Comprehensive Income)	10,000	
Investments in Securities (Security B) (= $70,000 – $80,000).................................		10,000

3/22/2014

Investments in Securities (Security C)...................	32,000	
Cash...		32,000

5/25/2014

Investments in Securities (Security D)...................	17,000	
Cash...		17,000

5/25/2014

Investments in Securities (Security E)...................	63,000	
Cash...		63,000

10/05/2014

Cash..	52,000	
Unrealized Gain on Security A (Accumulated Other Comprehensive Income).............................	5,000	
Investments in Securities (Security A).............		45,000
Realized Gain on Sale of Available-for-Sale Securities...		12,000

13.24 a. continued.

10/05/2014

Cash...	16,000	
Realized Loss on Sale of Available-for-Sale Securities..	1,000	
Investments in Securities (Security D)............		17,000

12/31/2014

Investments in Securities (Security B) (= $83,000 − $70,000)	13,000	
Unrealized Loss on Security B (Other Comprehensive Income)		10,000
Unrealized Gain on Security B (Other Comprehensive Income)		3,000

12/31/2014

Unrealized Loss on Security C (Other Comprehensive Income) (= $27,000 − $32,000) ..	5,000	
Investments in Securities (Security C)............		5,000

12/31/2014

Investments in Securities (Security E) (= $67,000 − $63,000)	4,000	
Unrealized Gain on Security E (Other Comprehensive Income)		4,000

b. **Balance Sheet on December 31, 2013**

Investments in Securities at Fair Value.............................	$	115,000
Net Unrealized Loss on Available-for-Sale Securities (= $5,000 − $10,000)...	$	(5,000)

Note

Investments in Securities on December 31, 2013, had an acquisition cost of $120,000 and a fair value of $115,000. Gross unrealized gains total $5,000 and gross unrealized losses total $10,000.

13.24 continued.

c. **Balance Sheet on December 31, 2014**

Investments in Securities at Fair Value................................ $ 177,000

Net Unrealized Gain on Available-for-Sale Securities .... $ 2,000

Note

Investments in Securities on December 31, 2014, had an acquisition cost of $175,000 and a fair value of $177,000. Gross unrealized gains total $7,000 (= $3,000 + $4,000) and gross unrealized losses total $5,000. Proceeds from sales of investments in securities totaled $68,000 during 2014. These sales resulted in gross realized gains of $12,000 and gross realized losses of $1,000. The net unrealized loss on available-for-sale securities changed as follows during 2014:

Balance, December 31, 2013... $ (5,000) Dr.

Unrealized Gain on Securities Sold................................ (5,000) Dr.

Change in Net Unrealized Loss on Securities Held at
  Year End ($13,000 – $5,000 + $4,000) .... <u>12,000</u> Cr.

Balance, December 31, 2014... <u>$ 2,000</u> Cr.

13.25 (Moonlight Mining Company; analysis of financial statement disclosures for available-for-sale securities.) (amounts in thousands of US$)

a. $10,267 loss = $11,418 – $21,685.

b. $2,649 gain = $8,807 – $6,158.

c. $12,459 = $21,685 – $6,158 – $3,068.

d. None. The unrealized loss on current marketable securities of $2,466 (= $4,601 – $7,067) and the unrealized gain on noncurrent marketable securities of $2,649 (= $8,807 – $6,158) appear in Other Comprehensive Income, closed to the Accumulated Other Comprehensive Income account on the balance sheet.

13.26 (Callahan Corporation; effect of various methods of accounting for marketable equity securities.) (amounts in US$)

a. **Trading Securities**

	2013	2014
Income Statement:		
Dividend Revenue..	$ 3,300	$ 2,200
Unrealized Gain (Loss):		
($54,000 – $55,000)	(1,000)	—
($17,000 – $14,000)	—	3,000
Realized Gain (Loss) ($14,500 + $26,000) –		
($16,000 + $24,000)	—	500
Total...	$ 2,300	$ 5,700
Balance Sheet:		
Current Assets:		
Marketable Securities at Fair Value........	$54,000	$ 17,000

b. **Available-for-Sale Securities (Current Asset)**

	2013	2014
Income Statement:		
Dividend Revenue..	$ 3,300	$ 2,200
Realized Gain (Loss): [= $40,500 –		
($18,000 + $25,000)]	—	(2,500)
Total...	$ 3,300	$ (300)
Balance Sheet:		
Current Assets:		
Marketable Securities at Fair Value........	$54,000	$ 17,000
Shareholders' Equity:		
Net Unrealized Gain (Loss) on Available-for-		
Sale Securities (Part of Accumulated		
Other Comprehensive Income):		
($54,000 – $55,000)	(1,000)	—
($17,000 – $12,000)	—	5,000

c. Same as Part b. except that the securities appear as Investments in Securities in the noncurrent assets section of the balance sheet.

13.26 continued.

d.

| | Trading Securities | Available-for-Sale Securities | |
		Current Assets	Noncurrent Assets
2013	$ 2,300	$ 3,300	$ 3,300
2014	5,700	(300)	(300)
Total	$ 8,000	$ 3,000	$ 3,000

The unrealized gain on Security I of $5,000 (= $17,000 − $12,000) at the end of 2014 appears in income if these securities are trading securities but in a separate shareholders' equity account if these securities are available-for-sale securities (either a current asset or a noncurrent asset). Total shareholders' equity is the same. Retained earnings (pretax) are $5,000 larger if these securities are trading securities and the unrealized gain account is $5,000 larger if these securities are classified as available-for-sale securities.

13.27 (Analysis of financial statement disclosures related to marketable securities and quality of earnings.) (amounts in millions of US$)

a.
Cash	37,600	
Realized Loss on Sale of Available-for-Sale Securities	113	
Realized Gain on Available-for-Sale Securities		443
Marketable Securities		37,270[a]

[a]$14,075 + $37,163 − $13,968 = $37,270.

Marketable Securities	262	
Unrealized Loss on Available-for-Sale Securities (= $37,270 − $37,008) (Other Comprehensive Income)		262

b.
Balance, December 31, 2013 (= $957 − $510)	$ 447 Cr.	
Net Unrealized Loss on Securities Sold (from Part a.)	262 Cr.	
Increase in Net Unrealized Gain on Securities Held on December 31, 2014 (Plug)	518 Cr.	
Balance, December 31, 2014 (= $1,445 − $218)	$ 1,227 Cr.	

13.27 continued.

   c.   Interest and Dividend Revenue .... $ 1,081

       Net Realized Gain on Securities Sold from Market
          Price Changes Occurring during 2014:
          (= $37,600 – $37,008)... 592

       Net Unrealized Gain on Securities Held on December
          31, 2014 (from Part b.).. 518

       Total Income .... $ 2,191

   d.   The bank sold marketable securities during 2014, which had net unrealized losses of $262 million as of December 31, 2014. The sale of these securities at a gain suggests that the securities' market prices increased substantially ($592 million) during 2014. The substantial increase in the net unrealized gain of $518 lends support to this conclusion about market price increases. The bank could have increased its income still further by selecting securities for sale that had unrealized *gains* as of December 31, 2013. If prices continued to increase on such securities during 2014 prior to sale, the realized gain would have been even larger than the reported net realized gain of $330 million (= $443 – $113). Firms with available-for-sale securities with unrealized gains can manage net income, but not comprehensive income, by choosing which items to sell.

13.28   (Delmar; accounting for forward commodity price contract as a cash flow hedge.) (amounts in US$)

   a.   Delmar does not make an entry on October 31, 2013, because the forward commodity contract is a mutually unexecuted contract and requires no initial investment.

   b.   The fair value of the forward contract increases $100,000 [= 10,000 X ($320 – $310)].

December 31, 2013

Forward Commodity Contract............................... 100,000
   Other Comprehensive Income   100,000

The forward contract is an asset because the firm has the right to receive cash from the counterparty equal to the decline in the fair value of the inventory; $100,000 = [10,000 X ($320 – $310)].

13.28 continued.

c. The fair value of the inventory of approximately $310 per gallon exceeds its acquisition cost of $225 per gallon, so Delmar would not write down its inventory.

d. **March 31, 2014**
Forward Commodity Contract...................................... 400,000
   Other Comprehensive Income   400,000
$400,000 = 10,000 gallons × ($310 − $270).

e. **March 31, 2014**
Other Comprehensive Income 400,000
   Inventory...   400,000

f. **March 31, 2014**
Cash... 500,000
   Forward Commodity Contract............................   500,000
$500,000 = 10,000 gallons × ($320 − $270).

g. **March 31, 2014**
Cash.. 2,700,000
   Sales Revenue   2,700,000
$2,700,000 = 10,000 gallons × $270.

March 31, 2014
Accumulated Other Comprehensive Income 500,000
Cost of Goods Sold (Plug)....................................... 1,750,000
   Inventory...   2,250,000
Cost of Goods Sold (Plug) = $2,250,000 − $500,000
= $1,750,000

The balance in Accumulated Other Comprehensive Income before the entry above related to the forward contract is a credit of $500,000 (= $100,000 + $400,000). The gross margin on the sale is $950,000 (= $2,700,000 − $1,750,000). This is the same gross margin that Delmar would have reported if it had not obtained the forward contract and the market price for whiskey on March 31, 2014, had been Delmar's anticipated amount of $320 per gallon ($950,000 = $3,200,000 − $2,250,000). The forward contract shifted the risk of changes in the selling price to the counterparty.

13.28 continued.

    h.   Delmar would recognize changes in the fair value of both the inventory and the forward commodity contract and include the unrealized gains and losses in net income.

    i.   A justification for treating the forward commodity price contract as a fair value hedge is that the firm wanted to protect the gross margin on the sale of $950,000 against commodity price changes. A justification for treating the contract as a cash flow hedge is that it wanted to ensure that it received a net cash inflow of $3,200,000 on the sale of the whiskey.

13.29   (Owens Corporation; accounting for forward currency contract as a fair value hedge and a cash flow hedge.) (amounts in US$)

    a.   **July 1, 2013:** The purchase commitment and the forward foreign exchange contract are mutually unexecuted contracts as of July 1, 2013. U.S. GAAP and IFRS do not require firms to recognize mutually unexecuted contracts in the accounts.

December 31, 2013: The change in the value of the undiscounted cash flows related to the purchase commitment and the forward contract is $1,800 [= (60,000 × $1.35) − (60,000 × $1.32)]. The present value of $1,800 discounted at 8% for six months is $1,731 (= $1,800 × 0.96154).

December 31, 2013

Loss on Firm Commitment......................................	1,731	
Commitment to Purchase Equipment.................		1,731

To record a loss in net income on a previously un-recognized firm commitment because the U.S. dollar decreased in value relative to the euro.

December 31, 2013

Forward Contract	1,731	
Gain on Forward Contract		1,731

To measure the forward contract at fair value and recognize a gain in net income.

13.29 a. continued.

June 30, 2014

Interest Expense	69	
Commitment to Purchase Equipment		69

To recognize interest on the commitment because
of the passage of time: $69 = 0.04 \times \$1,731$.

June 30, 2014

Forward Contract	69	
Interest Revenue		69

To record interest on the forward contract because
of the passage of time: $69 = 0.04 \times \$1,731$.

The change in the value of the purchase commitment and the forward
contract due to exchange rate changes between December 31, 2013,
and June 30, 2014, is $3,000 [= (60,000 \times \$1.40) - (60,000 \times \$1.35)]$.

June 30, 2014

Loss on Firm Commitment	3,000	
Commitment to Purchase Equipment		3,000

To record a loss on the purchase commitment because the value of the U.S. dollar declined relative
to the euro.

June 30, 2014

Forward Contract	3,000	
Gain on Forward Contract		3,000

To record the increase in the fair value of the forward contract because the U.S. dollar declined in
value relative to the euro.

June 30, 2014

Equipment	79,200	
Commitment to Purchase Equipment	4,800	
Cash		84,000

To record the amount paid in U.S. dollars
[$84,000 = (\$60,000 \times \$1.4)]$, to eliminate the balance in the Commitment to Purchase Equipment
account of $4,800 (= \$1,731 + \$69 + \$3,000)$, and
to record the acquisition cost of the equipment for
$79,200.

13.29 a. continued.

June 30, 2014

Cash..	4,800	
Forward Contract..................................		4,800

To record cash received from the counterparty and eliminate the balance in the Forward Contract account of $4,800 (= $1,731 + $69 + $3,000).

b. Owens Corporation would not recognize changes in the value of the purchase commitment. The entries for changes in the fair value of the forward contract would affect other comprehensive income each period instead of net income. On June 30, 2014, Accumulated Other Comprehensive Income would have a balance of $4,800 (= $1,731 + $69 + $3,000). The entry on this date to purchase the equipment would involve a debit to Accumulated Other Comprehensive Income instead of the Commitment to Purchase Equipment account as shown in Part *a*. above.

c. To treat this hedge as a fair value hedge, Owens Corporation must intend to protect the value of the equipment. Perhaps Owens Corporation has committed to resell the equipment to a customer on June 30, 2014, for a fixed price in U.S. dollars and wants to protect its expected profit margin from the sale. To treat this hedge as a cash flow hedge, Owens Corporation must intend to protect the amount of cash it pays to the European supplier.

13.30 (Sandretto Corporation; accounting for interest rate swap as a fair value hedge.) (amounts in US$)

a. **January 1, 2013**

Equipment..	50,000	
Note Payable.......................................		50,000

To record the acquisition of equipment by giving a $50,000 note payable with a fixed interest rate of 6%.

December 31, 2013

Interest Expense....................................	3,000	
Cash..		3,000

To recognize interest expense and cash payment at the fixed interest rate of 6%: $3,000 = 0.06 × $50,000.

13.30 a. continued.

Interest rates increased during 2013. On December 31, the counterparty with whom Sandretto Corporation entered into the swap contract resets the interest rate for 2013 to 8%. Sandretto Corporation must restate the note payable to fair value and record the change in the fair value of the swap contract caused by the increase in the interest rate. The present value of the remaining cash flows on the note payable when discounted at 8% is:

Present Value of Interest Payments: $3,000 × 1.78326 = ... $ 5,350
Present Value of Principal: $50,000 × 0.85734 =................. 42,867
    Total Present Value .... $ 48,217

Sandretto Corporation makes the following entry to record the change in fair value:

December 31, 2013
Note Payable 1,783
    Gain on Revaluation of Note Payable.................. 1,783
To measure the note payable at fair value with cash flows discounted at 8%: $1,783 = $50,000 – $48,217. The gain is included in net income.

The increase in interest rate to 8% means that Sandretto Corporation must pay an additional $1,000 [= (0.08 – 0.06) × $50,000] each year in interest payments. The present value of a $1,000 annuity for two periods at 8% is $1,783 (= $1,000 × 1.78326). Thus, the fair value of the swap contract increased from zero at the beginning of 2013 to $1,783 at the end of 2013. Sandretto Corporation makes the following entry:

December 31, 2013
Loss on Revaluation of Swap Contract 1,783
    Swap Contract... 1,783
To measure the swap contract at fair value and recognize a liability on the balance sheet and a loss in net income.

13.30 a. continued.

December 31, 2014

Interest Expense	3,857	
Note Payable		857
Cash		3,000

To record interest expense at 8% of the carrying value of the note payable at the beginning of the year ($3,857 = 0.08 × $48,217), the cash payment at the contractual interest rate of 6% on the face amount of the note ($3,000 = 0.06 × $50,000), and the increase in the carrying value of the note payable for the difference.

December 31, 2014

Interest Expense	143	
Swap Contract		143

To record interest expense for the increase in the carrying value of the swap contract for the passage of time: $143 = 0.08 × $1,783.

December 31, 2014

Swap Contract	1,000	
Cash		1,000

To record cash paid to the counterparty because the interest rate increased from 6% to 8%.

Sandretto must revalue the note payable and the swap contract for changes in fair value. The bank resets the interest rate in the swap agreement to 4% for 2015. The present value of the remaining payments on the note at 4% is:

Present Value of Interest Payments: $3,000 × 0.96154 = ...	$ 2,885
Present Value of Principal: $50,000 × 0.96154 = ...	48,077
Total Present Value	$ 50,962

The carrying value of the note payable before revaluation is $49,074 (= $48,217 + $857). The entry to measure the note payable at fair value is:

13.30 a. continued.

December 31, 2014

Loss on Revaluation of Note Payable...................... 1,888

   Note Payable 1,888

To measure the note payable at fair value using
an interest rate of 4% to discount the remaining
cash flows to a present value: $1,888 = $50,962 –
$49,074. The loss is included in net income.

The fair value of the swap contract increases. Sandretto Corporation
will receive $1,000 at the end of 2015 because of the swap contract.
Thus, the swap contract becomes an asset instead of a liability. The
present value of $1,000 when discounted at 4% is $962 (= $1,000 x
0.96154). The carrying value of the swap contract before revaluation is
a liability of $926 (= $1,783 + $143 – $1,000). The entry to revalue the
swap contract is:

December 31, 2014

Swap Contract (Liability)... 926

Swap Contract (Asset) 962

   Gain on Revaluation of Swap Contract 1,888

To measure the swap contract at fair value using
a discount rate of 4% and recognize a gain in net
income from the increase in fair value.

At the end of 2014, the Note Payable account has a balance of $50,962
and the Swap Contract account has a debit balance of $962.

b. **January 1, 2015**

Note Payable 50,962

   Cash.. 50,000

   Swap Contract (Asset) 962

To repay note payable prior to maturity and close
out the swap contract.

c. The entries would be identical if Sandretto Corporation chose the fair
value option because the note payable and swap contract would be
measured at fair value and changes in fair value included in net income
under both the accounting for the derivative as a fair value hedge and
the accounting under the fair value option.

13.31 (Avery Corporation; accounting for an interest rate swap as a cash flow hedge.) (amounts in US$)

January 1, 2013

Equipment...	50,000	
Note Payable..		50,000

To record the acquisition of equipment by giving a $50,000 note payable with a variable interest rate of 6%.

December 31, 2013

Interest Expense..	3,000	
Cash		3,000

To recognize interest expense and cash payment at the variable interest rate of 6%: $3,000 = 0.06 \times $50,000.

The fair value of the swap agreement on December 31, 2013, after the counterparty resets the interest rate to 8% is $1,783 (= $1,000 \times 1.78326). This amount is the present value of the $1,000 that the counterparty will pay Avery Corporation on December 31 of 2014 and December 31 of 2015 if the interest rate remains at 8%.

December 31, 2013

Swap Contract..	1,783	
Gain on Revaluation of Swap Contract..................		1,783

To measure the swap contract at fair value and recognize an asset on the balance sheet and a gain in other comprehensive income.

December 31, 2014

Interest Expense..	4,000	
Cash		4,000

To recognize interest expense and cash payment at the variable interest rate: $4,000 = 0.08 \times $50,000.

Avery Corporation must also recognize interest on the swap contract because of the passage of time.

13.31 continued.

December 31, 2014

Swap Contract... 143

    Interest on Swap Contract 143

To record interest for the increase in the carrying
value of the swap contract for the passage of time:
$143 = 0.08 \times \$1,783$.

Avery Corporation receives from the counterparty the $1,000 [= $50,000 \times
(0.08 - 0.06)] required by the swap contract. The entry is:

December 31, 2014

Cash... 1,000

    Swap Contract 1,000

To record cash received from the counterparty because
the interest rate increased from 6% to 8%.

December 31, 2014

Accumulated Other Comprehensive Income 1,000

    Interest Expense 1,000

To reclassify a portion of accumulated other comprehensive income to net income for the hedged portion
of interest expense on the note payable.

At this point the swap contract account has a debit balance of $926
(= $1,783 + $143 − $1,000). Accumulated other comprehensive income
related to this transaction has a credit balance of $926.

    Resetting the interest rate on December 31, 2014, to 4% changes the
fair value of the swap contract from an asset to a liability. The present
value of the $1,000 that Avery Corporation will pay to the counterparty at
the end of 2015 when discounted at 4% is $962 (= $1,000 × 0.96154). The
entry to revalue the swap contract is:

December 31, 2014

Loss on Revaluation of Swap Contract 1,888

    Swap Contract (Asset) 926

    Swap Contract (Liability) 962

To measure the swap contract at fair value and recognize a liability on the balance sheet and a loss in
other comprehensive income.

13.31 continued.

December 31, 2015

Interest Expense..	2,000	
Cash		2,000

To recognize interest expense and cash payment at
the variable interest rate of 4%: $2,000 = 0.04 \times
$50,000.

December 31, 2015

Interest on Swap Contract...	38	
Swap Contract		38

To record interest for the increase in the carrying
value of the swap contract for the passage of time:
$38 = 0.04 \times $962.

December 31, 2015

Swap Contract...	1,000	
Cash		1,000

To record cash paid to the counterparty because the
interest rate decreased from 8% to 4%.

December 31, 2015

Interest Expense..	1,000	
Accumulated Other Comprehensive Income...........		1,000

To reclassify a portion of accumulated other comprehensive income to net income for the hedged portion
of interest expense on the note payable.

December 31, 2015

Note Payable..	50,000	
Cash		50,000

To record repayment of note payable at maturity.

The Swap Contract account has a balance of zero on December 31, 2015
(= $962 + $38 − $1,000). Thus, Avery Corporation makes no entry to close
out the Swap Contract account.

CHAPTER 14

INTERCORPORATE INVESTMENTS IN COMMON STOCK

Questions, Exercises, and Problems: Answers and Solutions

14.1   See the text or the glossary at the end of the book.

14.2   Control is present when one entity has the ability to make both strategic and operating decisions for another entity. The approach to determining control differs between U.S. GAAP and IFRS. Significant influence is present when one entity has sufficient ownership interest or contractual rights to influence those decisions but cannot unilaterally make those decisions. Ownership of more than 50% of the voting stock of another entity usually implies an ability to control that entity and the preparation of consolidated financial statements; control can exist with less than majority ownership under IFRS. Authoritative guidance specifies that ownership of 20% to 50% of the voting stock implies an ability to exert significant influence over another entity and the use of the equity method. Ownership of less than 20% may permit significant influence and ownership of greater than 20% may not permit significant influence, so firms must apply judgment in deciding on the appropriate accounting method.

14.3   Dividends represent revenues under the fair-value method, or represent a return of capital under the equity method, or are eliminated under the consolidation method.

14.4   Firms use over time the service potential of assets with a definite life. The depreciation and amortization allocate the acquisition cost of this service potential to the periods of benefit, whether the amount is in the Investments, Property, Plant, and Equipment, or some other account.

14.5   When control is present, a parent and a subsidiary operate as a single economic entity. Eliminating intercompany profit and loss in these cases reflects transactions of the economic entity with all other entities. When significant influence is present, the investor and investee operate as economic entity to a lesser extent than when control is present. Thus, the concept of operating as an economic entity, in part, justifies eliminating intercompany profit and loss on equity method investments. Also, the ability to exert significant influence places the firms in a related party arrangement where prices set on intercompany transactions may not reflect arms-length dealings.

14.6   The Investment account changes under the equity method with all changes in the shareholders' equity of the investee, whether those changes are from additional stock issues, treasury stock transactions, net income, other comprehensive income, or dividends.

14.7   Under the equity method, the change each period in the net assets, or shareholders' equity, of the subsidiary appears on the one line, Investment in Subsidiary, on the balance sheet. When the parent consolidates the subsidiary, changes in the individual assets and liabilities that comprise the net asset change appear in the individual consolidated assets and liabilities. Likewise, under the equity method, the investor's interest in the investee's earnings appears in one line on the income statement, Equity in Earnings of Unconsolidated Subsidiary. When the parent consolidates the subsidiary, the individual revenues and expenses of the subsidiary appear in consolidated revenues and expenses.

14.8   When the investor uses the equity method, total assets include the Investment in Subsidiary account. The investment account reflects the parent's interest in the *net* assets (assets minus liabilities) of the subsidiary. When the investor consolidates the subsidiary, total consolidated assets include all of the subsidiary's assets. Consolidated liabilities include the liabilities of the subsidiary. Thus, total assets on a consolidated basis exceed total assets when the investor uses the equity method.

14.9   A minority investor in an investee owns less than a controlling financial interest (for example, less than 50% of the voting shares). If a parent has a controlling financial interest, but less than 100% ownership, in an investee, the entities holding the remaining ownership interests in the investee are minority investors (also called noncontrolling investors). Their minority, or noncontrolling, interest appears on the consolidated balance sheet.

14.10 An economic entity is a group of companies under the control of a parent company. The parent company makes strategic and operating decisions with the interest of the group of companies, instead of the separate companies, foremost in mind. Thus, the economic entity operates as if it were a single company. Consolidated financial statements reflect the financial position and results of operations of the economic entity with all other entities and not the results of any one company within the consolidated group.

14.11 Failing to eliminate the Investment in Subsidiary account will result in double counting the net assets of the subsidiary in the consolidated balance sheet, once as the Investment account on the parent's books and once as the individual net assets on the subsidiary's books.

14.12 The noncontrolling interest in net income is an income statement account that shows the claim of the noncontrolling shareholders on the net income of certain less than wholly owned subsidiaries in the consolidated group. The noncontrolling interest in net assets is a balance sheet account that shows the claim of the noncontrolling shareholders on the net assets of certain less than wholly owned subsidiaries in a consolidated group. The noncontrolling shareholders' claim is limited to a claim on the net income and net assets of the particular subsidiary in which they have a noncontrolling ownership interest. Because the net income and net assets of the subsidiary merge with those of the parent and other subsidiaries in consolidated financial statements, the entire noncontrolling interest related to all the less than wholly owned subsidiaries appears as a single claim against consolidated net income and consolidated net assets.

14.13 Eliminating transactions between affiliated companies ensures that the consolidated financial statements: (1) reflect only transactions with outsiders and (2) reflect those outside transactions once and only once.

14.14 Contracts or other agreements might shift control of the entity from its owners to some other entity. For example, a court might control a subsidiary in bankruptcy even though a parent company owns 100% of the common stock. As another example, one entity might agree to cover all losses of another entity even though it owns none of the other entity's common stock. In addition, U.S. GAAP specifies a variable interest entity (VIE) as an entity for which control cannot be determined by analyzing voting interests.

14.15   (Cayman Company; equity method entries.) (amounts in US$)

Investment in Stock of Denver Company 550,000
    Cash   550,000

Assets	=	Liabilities	+	Shareholders' Equity	(Class.)
+550,000					
−550,000					

To record acquisition of common stock.

Investment in Stock of Denver Company 120,000
    Equity in Earnings of Denver Company   120,000

Assets	=	Liabilities	+	Shareholders' Equity	(Class.)
+120,000				+120,000	IncSt → RE

To accrue 100% share of Denver Company's earnings.

Cash or Dividends Receivable 30,000
    Investment in Stock of Denver Company   30,000

Assets	=	Liabilities	+	Shareholders' Equity	(Class.)
+30,000					
−30,000					

To accrue dividends received or receivable.

14.16   (Weber Corporation; equity method entries.) (amounts in millions of US$)

Investment in Stock of Albee Computer 100
    Cash   100

Assets	=	Liabilities	+	Shareholders' Equity	(Class.)
+100					
−100					

To record acquisition of shares of common stock.

14.16 continued.

Investment in Stock of Albee Computer 20
    Equity in Earnings of Albee Computer 20

Assets	=	Liabilities	+	Shareholders' Equity	(Class.)
+20				+20	IncSt → RE

To accrue Albee Computer's earnings for the year.

Cash (or Dividends Receivable) 6
    Investment in Stock of Albee Computer 6

Assets	=	Liabilities	+	Shareholders' Equity	(Class.)
+6					
−6					

To record dividends received or receivable.

Amortization Expense 1.6
    Investment in Stock of Albee Computer 1.6

Assets	=	Liabilities	+	Shareholders' Equity	(Class.)
+1.6				−1.6	IncSt → RE

To amortize patent; $1.6 = [0.20 \times (\$500 - \$420)/10]$.
Investment is now $112.4 = \$100 + \$20 - \$6 - \$1.6$.

14.17 (Wood Corporation; journal entries to apply the equity method of accounting for investments in securities.) (amounts in US$)

January 2
Investment in Securities (Knox) 350,000
Investment in Securities (Vachi) 196,000
Investment in Securities (Snow) 100,000
    Cash 646,000

Assets	=	Liabilities	+	Shareholders' Equity	(Class.)
+350,000					
+196,000					
+100,000					
−646,000					

14.17 continued.

December 31

Investment in Securities (Knox)	35,000	
Investment in Securities (Vachi)................................	12,000	
Investment in Securities (Snow)		4,800
Equity in Earnings of Affiliates		42,200

Assets	=	Liabilities	+	Shareholders' Equity	(Class.)
+35,000				+42,200	IncSt → RE
+12,000					
−4,800					

(0.50 × \$70,000) + (0.30 × \$40,000) − (0.20 × \$24,000) = \$42,200.

December 31

Cash...	19,500	
Investment in Securities (Knox)............................		15,000
Investment in Securities (Vachi)		4,500

Assets	=	Liabilities	+	Shareholders' Equity	(Class.)
+19,500					
−15,000					
−4,500					

(0.50 × \$30,000) + (0.30 × \$15,000) = \$19,500.

14.18 (Stebbins Corporation; journal entries to apply the equity method of accounting for investments in securities.) (amounts in US\$)

a. **January 1, 2013**

Investment in Securities (R)	250,000	
Investment in Securities (S)	325,000	
Investment in Securities (T)	475,000	
Cash...		1,050,000

Assets	=	Liabilities	+	Shareholders' Equity	(Class.)
+250,000					
+325,000					
+475,000					
−1,050,000					

14.18 a. continued.

December 31, 2013

Investment in Securities (R)	50,000		
Investment in Securities (S)	48,000		
Investment in Securities (T)		75,000	
Equity in Earnings of Affiliates		23,000	

Assets	=	Liabilities	+	Shareholders' Equity	(Class.)
+50,000				+23,000	IncSt → RE
+48,000					
−75,000					

(0.25 × $200,000) + (0.40 × $120,000) − (0.50 × $150,000)
= $23,000.

December 31, 2013

Cash	63,250		
Investment in Securities (R)		31,250	
Investment in Securities (S)		32,000	

Assets	=	Liabilities	+	Shareholders' Equity	(Class.)
+63,250					
−31,250					
−32,000					

(0.25 × $125,000) + (0.40 × $80,000) = $63,250.

December 31, 2013

Depreciation Expense	4,000		
Investment in Securities (R)		4,000	

Assets	=	Liabilities	+	Shareholders' Equity	(Class.)
−4,000				−4,000	IncSt → RE

The cost of the investment in Company R exceeds the carrying value of the net assets acquired by $50,000 [= $250,000 − (0.25 × $800,000)]. Stebbins Corporation attributes $40,000 of the excess to buildings and must depreciate $4,000 (= $40,000/10) each year. The firm attributes the remaining excess to goodwill, which it need not depreciate.

14-7

14.18 a. continued.

The cost of the investment in Company S exceeds its carrying value by $25,000 [= $325,000 − (0.40 X $750,000)]. Stebbins Corporation attributes this excess to goodwill. The acquisition cost of the investment in Security T equals the carrying value of the net assets acquired.

December 31, 2014

Investment in Securities (R)	56,250	
Investment in Securities (S)	30,000	
Investment in Securities (T)	25,000	
Equity in Earnings of Affiliates		111,250

Assets	=	Liabilities	+	Shareholders' Equity	(Class.)
+56,250				+111,250	IncSt → RE
+30,000					
+25,000					

(0.25 X $225,000) + (0.40 X $75,000) + (0.50 X $50,000) = $111,250.

December 31, 2014

Cash..	64,500	
Investment in Securities (R)		32,500
Investment in Securities (S)		32,000

Assets	=	Liabilities	+	Shareholders' Equity	(Class.)
+64,500					
−32,500					
−32,000					

(0.25 X $130,000) + (0.40 X $80,000).

December 31, 2014

Depreciation Expense..	4,000	
Investment in Securities (R)		4,000

Assets	=	Liabilities	+	Shareholders' Equity	(Class.)
−4,000				−4,000	IncSt → RE

14.18 continued.

    b. **January 1, 2015**

Cash...	275,000
Loss on Sale of Investments	9,500
Investment in Securities (R)	284,500

Assets	=	Liabilities	+	Shareholders' Equity	(Class.)
+275,000				–9,500	IncSt → RE
–284,500					

$250,000 + $50,000 – $31,250 – $4,000 + $56,250 – $32,500 – $4,000 = $284,500.

14.19   (Laesch Company; working backward to consolidation relations.) (amounts in US$)

    a. $70,000 = ($156,000 – $100,000)/0.80.

    b. 72.7% = ($156,000 – $100,000)/$77,000.

    c. $56,000 = ($156,000 – $100,000).

14.20   (Dealco Corporation; working backward from consolidated income statements.) (amounts in millions of US$)

    a. 40% = $56/$140.

    b. $42 = [0.40 X (1 – 0.25) X $140].

    c. 85% = [1 – ($42/$280)] = 1 – 0.15.

14.21   (CAR Corporation; consolidation policy and principal consolidation concepts.) (amounts in US$)

    a. CAR Corporation should consolidate Alexandre du France Software Systems and R Credit Corporation or, under exceptional circumstances, use the fair value method.

    b.

Charles Electronics	(0.75 X $120,000) =	$ 90,000
Alexandre du France Software Systems .	(0.80 X 60,000) =	48,000
R Credit Corporation	(0.90 X 144,000) =	129,600
Total Income from Subsidiaries		$ 267,600

14.21 continued.

c. Noncontrolling Interest shown under accounting assumed in problem:

Charles Electronics .... (0.25 X $120,000) = $30,000
Alexandre du France Software Systems ..   (None) =   —
R Credit Corporation ....   (None) =   ——
                                                                      $30,000

CAR Corporation subtracts the noncontrolling interest in computing net income.

d. Charles Electronics, no increase because already consolidated.

Alexandre du France Software Systems increase by 80% of net income less dividends:

$$0.80 \times (\$96,000 - \$60,000) = \$28,800.$$

R Credit Corporation, no increase because equity method results in the same income statement effects as do consolidated statements. Net income of CAR Corporation would be:

$1,228,800 = $1,200,000 (as reported) + $28,800 (increase).

e. Noncontrolling Interest shown if CAR Corporation consolidated all companies:

Charles Electronics .... (0.25 X $120,000) = $ 30,000
Alexandre du France Software Systems .   (0.20 X 96,000) =   19,200
R Credit Corporation .... (0.10 X 144,000) =   14,400
                                                                      $ 63,600

14.22 (Joyce Company and Vogel Company; equity method entries.) (amounts in US$)

Joyce Company's Books

(1) Investment in Stock of Vogel Company................... 420,000

    Cash...   420,000

Assets	=	Liabilities	+	Shareholders' Equity	(Class.)
+420,000					
−420,000					

To record acquisition of common stock.

(2) Accounts Receivable.. 29,000

    Sales Revenue   29,000

Assets	=	Liabilities	+	Shareholders' Equity	(Class.)
+29,000				+29,000	IncSt → RE

To record intercompany sales on account.

(2) Cost of Goods Sold.. 29,000

    Inventories   29,000

Assets	=	Liabilities	+	Shareholders' Equity	(Class.)
−29,000				−29,000	IncSt → RE

To record cost of intercompany sales.

(3) Advance to Vogel Company 6,000

    Cash...   6,000

Assets	=	Liabilities	+	Shareholders' Equity	(Class.)
+6,000					
−6,000					

To record advance to Vogel Company.

14.22 continued.

(4) Cash.. 16,000

    Accounts Receivable....................................... 16,000

Assets	=	Liabilities	+	Shareholders' Equity	(Class.)
+16,000					
−16,000					

To record collections on account from Vogel Company.

(5) Cash.. 4,000

    Advance to Vogel Company 4,000

Assets	=	Liabilities	+	Shareholders' Equity	(Class.)
+4,000					
−4,000					

To record collection of advance from Vogel Company.

(6) Cash.. 20,000

    Investment in Stock of Vogel Company.............. 20,000

Assets	=	Liabilities	+	Shareholders' Equity	(Class.)
+20,000					
−20,000					

To record dividend from Vogel Company.

(7) Investment in Stock of Vogel Company................... 30,000

    Equity in Earnings of Vogel Company................. 30,000

Assets	=	Liabilities	+	Shareholders' Equity	(Class.)
+30,000				+30,000	IncSt → RE

To accrue 100% share of Vogel Company's net income.

14.22 continued.

(8) Amortization Expense... 4,000
    Investment in Stock of Vogel Company...............   4,000

Assets	=	Liabilities	+	Shareholders' Equity	(Class.)
−4,000				−4,000	IncSt → RE

To record amortization of patent; $4,000 = ($420,000 − $380,000)/10.

Vogel Company's Books

(1) No entry.

(2) Inventories 29,000
    Accounts Payable   29,000

Assets	=	Liabilities	+	Shareholders' Equity	(Class.)
+29,000		+29,000			

To record intercompany purchase of materials on account.

(3) Cash... 6,000
    Advance from Joyce Company   6,000

Assets	=	Liabilities	+	Shareholders' Equity	(Class.)
+6,000		+6,000			

To record advance from Joyce Company.

(4) Accounts Payable 16,000
    Cash...   16,000

Assets	=	Liabilities	+	Shareholders' Equity	(Class.)
−16,000		−16,000			

To record payment for purchases on account.

14.22 continued.

(5) Advance from Joyce Company 4,000

    Cash... 4,000

Assets	=	Liabilities	+	Shareholders' Equity	(Class.)
−4,000		−4,000			

To record repayment of advance.

(6) Retained Earnings.. 20,000

    Cash... 20,000

Assets	=	Liabilities	+	Shareholders' Equity	(Class.)
−20,000				−20,000	RE

To record declaration and payment of dividend.

14.23 (Alpha/Omega; working backward from data that has eliminated intercompany transactions.) (amounts in US$)

a. $80,000 = $450,000 + $250,000 − $620,000.

b. $30,000 is Omega's cost; $20,000 is Alpha's cost; $20,000 original cost to Alpha.

Markup on the goods sold from Alpha to Omega, which remain in Omega's inventory, is $10,000 (= $60,000 + $50,000 − $100,000).
    Because Alpha priced the goods with markup 50% over its costs, the cost to Alpha to produce goods with markup of $10,000 is $20,000 and the total sales price from Alpha to Omega is $30,000 (= $10,000 + $20,000).

14.24 (Homer/Tonga; working backward from purchase data.) (amounts in US$)

a. $1,060,000 = $80,000 + $980,000.

b.

Carrying Value of Total Assets (from Part a.).....................	$1,060,000
Less Carrying Value of Current Assets	(210,000)
Less Carrying Value of Goodwill...	0
Carrying Value of Depreciable Assets	$ 850,000

14.25   (Effect of equity method versus consolidation.)

  a. (1) When Parent uses the equity method, it recognizes 80% of the net income of Sub. When Parent prepares consolidated financial statements with Sub, it recognizes 100% of the revenues, expenses, and net income of Sub and then subtracts the 20% noncontrolling interest share of net income. Thus, net income is the same whether Parent uses the equity method or consolidates Sub.

    (2) Liabilities in the numerator increase by the amount of the liabilities of Sub. Assets in the denominator decrease by the amount in the investment account and increase by the amount of Sub's assets. In this case where there is no excess purchase price, the denominator increases by the liabilities (= assets of Sub minus shareholders' equity) of Sub. Equal increases in the numerator and denominator of a ratio that is initially less than 1.0 result in an increase in the ratio.

  b. (1) The Parent or investor's share of Sub's net income declines, regardless of whether the amount appears on the single line, Equity in Earnings of Sub, or on multiple revenue and expense lines.

    (2) Total assets decrease when using the equity method because the investor invests less. Total assets do not decrease when preparing consolidated financial statements because Parent eliminates its Investment in Sub account and consolidates 100% of Sub's assets, regardless of its ownership percentage.

    (3) The liabilities of Sub do not appear on Parent's balance sheet when it uses the equity method, regardless of the ownership percentage.

    (4) Total liabilities do not change when preparing consolidated financial statements because Parent consolidates 100% of Sub's liabilities, regardless of its ownership percentage.

14.25 b. continued.

(5) Shareholders' equity decreases when using the equity method because Parent owns less of the net income, dividends, and shareholders' equity of Sub. The shareholders' equity on the consolidated balance sheet is the shareholders' equity of Parent only. Parent eliminates the shareholders' equity of Sub when preparing consolidated financial statements in its entry to eliminate the Investment in Sub account and recognize the noncontrolling interest.

(6) Assets and liabilities do not change with the decrease in ownership percentage because consolidated financial statements reflect 100% of Sub's assets and liabilities. The change in the ownership percentage affects the amount of the noncontrolling interest in Sub's net assets.

14.26 (Effect of errors on financial statements.)

	Assets	Liabilities	Shareholders' Equity	Net Income
a.	O/S	No	O/S	O/S
b.	O/S	No	O/S	O/S
c.	No	No	No	No
d.	O/S	O/S	No	No
e.	No	U/S	O/S	O/S

14.27 (Ely Company and Sims Company; preparing a consolidated balance sheet.) (amounts in US$)

	Ely Company	Sims Company	Consolidated
Assets			
Cash...	$ 12,000	$ 5,000	$ 17,000
Receivables............................	25,000	15,000	32,500
Investment in Sims Company..........................	78,000	—	—
Other Assets..........................	85,000	80,000	183,000
Total Assets	$ 200,000	$ 100,000	$ 232,500
Liabilities and Share-holders' Equity			
Current Liabilities.................	$ 45,000	$ 40,000	$ 77,500
Common Stock	50,000	10,000	50,000
Retained Earnings	105,000	50,000	105,000
Total Liabilities and Shareholders' Equity...	$ 200,000	$ 100,000	$ 232,500

The elimination entries (not required) are as follows:

Common Stock	10,000	
Retained Earnings	50,000	
Other Assets (Goodwill)...	18,000	
Investment in Sims Company................................		78,000

Assets	=	Liabilities	+	Shareholders' Equity	(Class.)
+18,000				–10,000	ContriCap
–78,000				–50,000	ContriCap

To eliminate investment account, the shareholders' equity of Sims Company, and recognize the excess price as an asset.

Current Liabilities..	7,500	
Receivables		7,500

Assets	=	Liabilities	+	Shareholders' Equity	(Class.)
–7,500		–7,500			IncSt → RE

To eliminate intercompany advances.

14.28 (Company P and Company S; preparing a consolidated balance sheet.) (amounts in US$)

a.

	Company P	Company S	Consolidated
Assets			
Cash..	$ 36,000	$ 26,000	$ 62,000
Accounts and Notes Receivable.....................	180,000	50,000	213,600
Inventories	440,000	250,000	690,000
Investment in Company S (Using the Equity Method).........................	726,000	—	—
Property, Plant, and Equipment (Net)..........	600,000	424,000	1,080,000
Total Assets..............	$ 1,982,000	$ 750,000	$ 2,045,600
Liabilities and Shareholders' Equity			
Accounts and Notes Payable	$ 110,000	$ 59,000	$ 152,600
Other Liabilities..............	286,000	21,000	307,000
Common Stock................	1,200,000	500,000	1,200,000
Additional Paid-In Capital..........................	—	100,000	—
Retained Earnings...........	386,000	70,000	386,000
Total Liabilities and Shareholders' Equity	$ 1,982,000	$ 750,000	$ 2,045,600

The elimination entries (not required) are as follows:

Common Stock..	500,000
Additional Paid-In Capital.....................................	100,000
Retained Earnings...	70,000
Property, Plant, and Equipment............................	56,000
Investment in Company S....................................	726,000

Assets	=	Liabilities	+	Shareholders' Equity	(Class.)
+56,000				−500,000	ContriCap
−726,000				−100,000	ContriCap
				−70,000	RE

To eliminate the investment account, the shareholders' equity accounts of Company S, and recognize the unamortized excess acquisition cost.

14.28 a. continued.

Accounts and Notes Payable...................................... 16,400
    Accounts and Notes Receivable........................... 16,400

Assets	=	Liabilities	+	Shareholders' Equity	(Class.)
−16,400		−16,400			IncSt → RE

To eliminate intercompany note.

b. The unamortized excess acquisition cost on December 31, 2014, is $56,000. With eight years remaining on the building's useful life, the annual depreciation is $7,000 (= $56,000/8). Thus, the excess acquisition on January 1, 2013, was $70,000 [= $56,000 + (2 × $7,000)]. The computation of the acquisition cost on January 1, 2013 is as follows:

Common Stock of Company S..	$ 500,000
Additional Paid-In Capital of Company S............................	100,000
Retained Earnings of Company S..	40,000
Excess Acquisition Cost...	70,000
Acquisition Cost...	$ 710,000

c.

Acquisition Cost on January 1, 2013	$ 710,000
Company P's Share of the Increase in Retained Earnings of Company S for 2013 and 2014; ($70,000 – $40,000)..	30,000
Less Amortization of Excess Acquisition Cost for 2013 and 2014	(14,000)
Carrying Value on December 31, 2014................................	$ 726,000

14.29 (Peak Company and Valley Company; equity method and consolidated financial statements.) (amounts in US$)

a. **January 1**

Investment in Valley Company............................... 50,000
    Cash... 50,000

Assets	=	Liabilities	+	Shareholders' Equity	(Class.)
+50,000					
−50,000					

To record acquisition of 100% of Valley Company.

14.29 a. continued.

December 31

Investment in Valley Company................................ 10,000

    Equity in Earnings of Valley Company............... 10,000

Assets	=	Liabilities	+	Shareholders' Equity	(Class.)
+10,000				+10,000	IncSt → RE

To recognize share of Valley Company's earnings.

December 31

Cash... 4,000

    Investment in Valley Company............................ 4,000

Assets	=	Liabilities	+	Shareholders' Equity	(Class.)
+4,000					
−4,000					

To recognize dividend received from Valley Company.

b.

	Peak Company	Valley Company	Consolidated
Assets			
Cash..................................	$ 33,000	$ 6,000	$ 39,000
Accounts Receivable........	42,000	20,000	54,000
Investment in Valley Company (Using the Equity Method)............	56,000	—	—
Other Assets.....................	123,000	85,000	208,000
Total Assets	$ 254,000	$ 111,000	$ 301,000
Liabilities and Shareholders' Equity			
Accounts Payable	$ 80,000	$ 25,000	$ 97,000
Bonds Payable..................	50,000	30,000	80,000
Common Stock..................	10,000	5,000	10,000
Retained Earnings...........	114,000	51,000	114,000
Total Liabilities and Shareholders' Equity	$ 254,000	$ 111,000	$ 301,000

14.29 b. continued.

Sales Revenue	$ 400,000	$ 125,000	$ 525,000
Equity in Earnings of			
Valley Company..........	10,000	—	—
Cost of Goods Sold...........	(320,000)	(90,000)	(410,000)
Selling and Administra-			
tive Expense.................	(44,000)	(20,000)	(64,000)
Income Tax Expense	(12,000)	(5,000)	(17,000)
Net Income......................	$ 34,000	$ 10,000	$ 34,000

The elimination entries (not required) are as follows:

Common Stock... 5,000
Retained Earnings... 51,000
   Investment in Valley Company........................... 56,000

Assets	=	Liabilities	+	Shareholders' Equity	(Class.)
−56,000				−5,000	ContriCap
				−51,000	RE

To eliminate the investment account and the shareholders' equity accounts of Valley Company.

An alternative elimination entry using amounts before closing entries
is as follows:

Common Stock... 5,000
Retained Earnings... 45,000
Equity in Earnings of Valley Company.................. 10,000
   Dividends Declared 4,000
   Investment in Valley Company........................... 56,000

Assets	=	Liabilities	+	Shareholders' Equity	(Class.)
−56,000				−5,000	ContriCap
				−45,000	RE
				−10,000	IncSt → RE
				+4,000	RE

To eliminate the investment account and the shareholders' equity accounts of Valley Company.

14.29 continued.

c. **January 1**
Investment in Valley Company................................... 70,000
    Cash...   70,000

Assets	=	Liabilities	+	Shareholders' Equity	(Class.)
+70,000					
−70,000					

To record acquisition of 100% of Valley Company.

December 31
Investment in Valley Company................................... 10,000
    Equity in Earnings of Valley Company...............   10,000

Assets	=	Liabilities	+	Shareholders' Equity	(Class.)
+10,000				+10,000	IncSt → RE

To recognize share of Valley Company's earnings.

December 31
Cash... 4,000
    Investment in Valley Company............................   4,000

Assets	=	Liabilities	+	Shareholders' Equity	(Class.)
+4,000					
−4,000					

To recognize dividend received from Valley Company.

December 31
Selling and Administrative Expenses..................... 2,000
    Investment in Valley Company............................   2,000

Assets	=	Liabilities	+	Shareholders' Equity	(Class.)
−2,000				−2,000	

To recognize acquisition of excess cost: $2,000 =$ $20,000/10.

14.29 continued.

	Peak Company	Valley Company	Consolidated
d. and e.			
Assets			
Cash......................................	$ 13,000	$ 6,000	$ 19,000
Accounts Receivable........	42,000	20,000	54,000
Investment in Valley Company (Using the Equity Method)............	74,000[a]	—	—
Other Assets....................	123,000	85,000	226,000
Total Assets	$ 252,000	$ 111,000	$ 299,000
Liabilities and Shareholders' Equity			
Accounts Payable	$ 80,000	$ 25,000	$ 97,000
Bonds Payable..................	50,000	30,000	80,000
Common Stock.................	10,000	5,000	10,000
Retained Earnings...........	112,000[b]	51,000	112,000
Total Liabilities and Shareholders' Equity	$ 252,000	$ 111,000	$ 299,000
Sales Revenue	$ 400,000	$ 125,000	$ 525,000
Equity in Earnings of Valley Company...........	10,000	—	—
Cost of Goods Sold............	(320,000)	(90,000)	(410,000)
Selling and Administrative Expense.................	(46,000)[c]	(20,000)	(66,000)
Income Tax Expense	(12,000)	(5,000)	(17,000)
Net Income......................	$ 32,000	$ 10,000	$ 32,000

[a]$74,000 = $70,000 + $10,000 - $4,000 - $2,000.

[b]$112,000 = $114,000 - $2,000 amortization.

[c]$46,000 = $44,000 + $2,000 amortization.

The elimination entry (not required) is as follows:

Common Stock..	5,000	
Retained Earnings...	51,000	
Other Assets..	18,000	
Investment in Valley Company............................		74,000

14.29 d. and e. continued.

Assets	=	Liabilities	+	Shareholders' Equity	(Class.)
+18,000				−5,000	ContriCap
−74,000				−51,000	RE

To eliminate the investment account and the shareholders' equity accounts of Valley Company.

Alternative elimination entries using amounts before closing entries are as follows:

Common Stock..	5,000	
Retained Earnings...	45,000	
Equity in Earnings of Valley Company	10,000	
Other Assets	18,000	
Dividends Declared		4,000
Investment in Valley Company		74,000

Assets	=	Liabilities	+	Shareholders' Equity	(Class.)
+18,000				−5,000	ContriCap
−74,000				−45,000	RE
				−10,000	IncSt → RE
				+4,000	RE

To eliminate the investment account and the shareholders' equity accounts of Valley Company.

Accounts Payable	8,000	
Accounts and Notes Receivable		8,000

Assets	=	Liabilities	+	Shareholders' Equity	(Class.)
−8,000		−8,000			

To eliminate intercompany advance.

14.30 (Parent Company and Sub Company; equity method and consolidated financial statements with noncontrolling interest.) (amounts in US$)

	Parent Company	Sub Company	Consolidated
Assets			
Cash...	$ 38,000	$ 12,000	$ 50,000
Accounts Receivable...............	63,000	32,000	95,000
Investment in Sub Company (Using Equity Method)	105,600	—	—
Other Assets............................	296,400	160,000	456,400
Total Assets	$503,000	$204,000	$601,400
Liabilities and Share- holders' Equity			
Accounts Payable	$ 85,000	$ 32,000	$117,000
Bonds Payable........................	150,000	40,000	190,000
Total Liabilities.................	$235,000	$ 72,000	$307,000
Noncontrolling Interest in Net Assets of Sub Company.....	$ —	$ —	$ 26,400
Common Stock	20,000	50,000	20,000
Retained Earnings	248,000	82,000	248,000
Total Shareholders' Equity	$268,000	$132,000	$294,400
Total Liabilities and Share- holders' Equity	$503,000	$204,000	$601,400
Sales Revenue	$800,000	$145,000	$945,000
Equity in Earnings of Sub Company	16,000	—	—
Cost of Goods Sold	(620,000)	(85,000)	(705,000)
Selling and Administrative Expense	(135,000)	(30,000)	(165,000)
Income Tax Expense...............	(24,000)	(10,000)	(34,000)
Net Income of Consolidated Entity..................................	$ 37,000	$ 20,000	$ 41,000
Noncontrolling Interest in Net Income of Sub Company.....	—	—	(4,000)
Net Income.............................	$ 37,000	$ 20,000	$ 37,000

14.30 continued.

The elimination and reclassification entry (not required) is as follows:

Common Stock 40,000
Retained Earnings 65,600
    Investment in Sub Company.....................................   105,600

Assets	=	Liabilities	+	Shareholders' Equity	(Class.)
−105,600				−40,000	ContriCap
				−65,600	RE

To eliminate investment account and Parent Company's
share of the shareholders' equity of Sub Company.

Alternative elimination entries using amounts before closing entries are as
follows:

Common Stock 40,000
Retained Earnings 56,000
Equity in Earnings of Sub Company 16,000
    Dividend Declared..   6,400
    Investment in Sub Company.....................................   105,600

Assets	=	Liabilities	+	Shareholders' Equity	(Class.)
−105,600				−40,000	ContriCap
				−56,000	RE
				−16,000	IncSt → RE
				+6,400	RE

To eliminate investment account and Parent Company's
share of the shareholders' equity of Sub Company.

14.30 continued.

		Common Stock	10,000	
		Retained Earnings	16,400	
		Noncontrolling Interest in Net Assets of Sub		
		Company		26,400

Assets	=	Liabilities	+	Shareholders' Equity	(Class.)
				−10,000	ContriCap
				−16,400	RE
				+26,400	Noncontrolling Interest

To recognize the noncontrolling interest in Sub Company.

An alternative elimination entry using amounts before closing entries is as follows:

		Common Stock	10,000	
		Retained Earnings	14,000	
		Noncontrolling Interest in Net Income of Sub		
		Company	4,000	
		Dividend Declared		1,600
		Noncontrolling Interest in Net Assets of Sub		
		Company		26,400

Assets	=	Liabilities	+	Shareholders' Equity	(Class.)
				−10,000	ContriCap
				−14,000	RE
				−4,000	IncSt → RE
				+1,600	RE
				+26,400	Noncontrolling Interest

To recognize the noncontrolling interest in Sub Company.

14.31   (Ganton; effect of intercorporate investment policies on financial statements.) (amounts in millions of US$)

a.   Ganton's acquisition cost of its investments in the bottlers exceeds the carrying value of the net assets of the bottlers. Ganton attributes the excess cost to long-term tangible or intangible assets. Note that consolidated Other Noncurrent Assets of $71,116 million exceeds the sum of the amounts on Ganton's books of $23,875 and the bottlers' books of $44,636 by $2,605 million. The portion attributable to Ganton's acquisition of bottlers is $785 million. The remainder of $1,820 (= $2,605 − $785) relates to the amount for the external interest in the bottlers. Thus, Ganton owns 30.134% (= $785/$2,605) of the bottlers and the external interest owns 69.9%. The amount for the noncontrolling interest in the net assets of the bottlers of $16,899 million comprises the following:

Noncontrolling Interest in Carrying Value of Bottlers Net Assets: 0.69866 × $21,583	$ 15,079
Excess of Fair Value over Carrying Value of Net Assets Attributed to the Noncontrolling Interest	1,820
Total Noncontrolling Interest	$ 16,899

b.   (1) **Equity Method**
       Liabilities to Assets Ratio: $21,525/$43,269 = 49.7%.
       Debt-Equity Ratio: $8,300/$21,744 = 38.2%

       (2) **Consolidation**
       Liabilities to Assets Ratio: $58,829/$97,472 = 60.4%.
       Debt-Equity Ratio: $31,674/$38,643 = 82.0%

c.   The bottlers have a heavier proportion of noncurrent assets and noncurrent liabilities than does Ganton. By owning less that 50% of the bottlers, Ganton does not have to consolidate them, resulting in lower debt ratios.

CHAPTER 15

SHAREHOLDERS' EQUITY: CAPITAL CONTRIBUTIONS AND DISTRIBUTIONS

Questions, Exercises, and Problems: Answers and Solutions

15.1 See the text or the glossary at the end of the book.

15.2 The two provisions provide different benefits and risks to the issuing firm, and the investor and should sell at different prices. Callable preferred stock should sell for less than convertible preferred stock. The issuing firm gains benefits with an option to call, or repurchase, the preferred stock and must thereby accept a lower issue price. The investor gains benefits with an option to convert into common stock and must pay a higher price.

15.3 Seniority means that, in the event of bankruptcy, the preferred shareholders are ahead of the common shareholders for claims on the firm's assets. A common claim that the preferred shareholders have, which is senior to any claim by common shareholders, is any declared but unpaid dividends.

15.4 All three items permit their holder to acquire shares of common stock at a set price. Their values depend on the difference between the market price and the exercise price on the exercise date and the length of the exercise period. Firms grant stock options to employees, grant stock rights to current shareholders and either sell stock warrants on the open market or attach them to a debt or preferred stock issue. The issuance of stock options and stock rights does not result in an immediate cash inflow, whereas the issuance of a stock warrant usually does. Accountants amortize the cost of stock options to expense over the expected period of benefit. Accountants credit the Additional Paid-In Capital (Stock Warrant) account if the value of the stock warrant is objectively measurable. At the time of exercise of all these items, the accountant records the cash proceeds as a capital contribution.

15.5   The greater the volatility of the stock price, the larger is the potential excess of the market price over the exercise price on the exercise date and the greater the benefit to the employee. The longer the time between the grant date and the exercise date, the more time that elapses for the market price to increase. Offsetting the value of this increased benefit element is the longer time to realize the benefit, which reduces the present value of the option. Stock option valuation models discount the expected benefit element in a stock option to a present value. The larger the discount rate, the smaller is the present value of the benefit.

15.6   The theoretical rationale is allocating the cost of employee compensation to the periods when the firm receives the benefits of employees' services.

15.7   The accounting for each of these transactions potentially involves transfers between contributed capital and retained earnings accounts and clouds the distinction between capital transactions and income transactions. The accounting for stock options results in a reduction in net income and retained earnings and an increase in contributed capital. The accounting for stock dividends results in a reduction in retained earnings and an increase in contributed capital. The purchase of treasury stock represents a reduction in both contributed capital and accumulated earnings. The reissuance of treasury stock at a "loss" may result in a debit to both contributed capital and retained earnings. Thus, the Common Stock and Additional Paid-In Capital accounts do not reflect just capital transactions and Retained Earnings does not reflect just income transactions.

15.8   In the case of a cash dividend, the shareholder now holds the investment in two parts—cash and stock certificates. The sum of the cash and the book value of the stock after the dividend declaration equals the book value of the stock before the firm declared the dividend. It is common to speak of a cash dividend as income, but it is merely the conversion of a portion of the shareholder's investment into a different form. In a sense, the shareholder earns income on the investment when the corporation earns its income. Because of the realization test for income recognition in accounting, however, the shareholders do not recognize income (except under the equity method) until the firm distributes cash. These comments for a cash dividend apply to a property dividend as well except that the shareholder holds a portion of the investment in a form less liquid than cash. A stock dividend does not even improve the marketability of the investment, although when a firm issues preferred shares to common shareholders or vice versa, shareholders may view the situation as being similar to a cash dividend. The stock dividend capitalizes a portion of retained earnings.

15.9 The managers of a firm have knowledge of the plans and risks of the firm that external investors may not possess. Although laws prevent firms from taking advantage of this "inside information," inclusion of gains from treasury stock transactions in net income might motivate firms to buy and sell treasury stock to improve reported earnings. Excluding these gains from net income removes this incentive. Also, the accounting for the acquisition of treasury stock (that is, a reduction from total shareholders' equity) has the same effect on shareholders' equity as a retirement of the capital stock. The reissue of the treasury stock for more than its acquisition cost does not result in a gain any more than the issue of common stock for more than par value represents a gain.

15.10 If a firm uses the constructive retirement method to account for treasury shares, this answer is correct. If, however, a firm uses the cost method, the repurchased shares do not disappear. Rather, the repurchased shares are held, at their acquisition cost, in an accounting called Treasury Shares. The firm may resell (that is, reissue) these treasury shares in the future.

15.11 (Carter, Inc.; issuing common stock.) (amounts in US$)

December 1, 2013

Cash (= 100,000 shares X $18 per share)....................	1,800,000	
Common Stock—Par Value		100,000
Additional Paid-In Capital		1,700,000

Assets	=	Liabilities	+	Shareholders' Equity	(Class.)
+1,800,000				+100,000	ContriCap
				+1,700,000	ContriCap

15.12 (Homing Corporation; issuing common stock.) (amounts in US$)

September 30, 2014

Cash (= 500,000 shares X $30 per share)....................	15,000,000	
Common Stock—Par Value		50,000
Additional Paid-In Capital		14,950,000

Assets	=	Liabilities	+	Shareholders' Equity	(Class.)
+15,000,000				+50,000	ContriCap
				+14,950,000	ContriCap

15.13 (Grable, Inc.; journal entries for dividends.) (amounts in US$)

a. Retained Earnings (Dividends Declared) 19,500
   Dividends Payable—Preferred Stock 19,500

Assets	=	Liabilities	+	Shareholders' Equity	(Class.)
		+19,500		−19,500	RE

Dividend of $1.50 per share on 13,000 shares.

b. Dividends Payable—Preferred Stock 19,500
   Cash 19,500

Assets	=	Liabilities	+	Shareholders' Equity	(Class.)
−19,500		−19,500			

c. Retained Earnings (Dividends Declared) 300,000
   Common Stock 300,000

Assets	=	Liabilities	+	Shareholders' Equity	(Class.)
				−300,000	RE
				+300,000	ContriCap

d. No entry.

15.14 (Watt Corporation; journal entries for dividends.) (amounts in US$)

a. **March 31, 2013**
   Retained Earnings (Dividends Declared) 10,000
   Dividends Payable 10,000

Assets	=	Liabilities	+	Shareholders' Equity	(Class.)
		+10,000		−10,000	RE

$10,000 = 20,000 x $0.50.

15.14 continued.

b. **April 15, 2013**

Dividends Payable... 10,000

    Cash..   10,000

Assets	=	Liabilities	+	Shareholders' Equity	(Class.)
−10,000		−10,000			

c. **June 30, 2013**

Retained Earnings (Dividends Declared) (= 2,000

    X $20) 40,000

        Common Stock (= 2,000 X $15)   30,000

        Additional Paid-In Capital................................   10,000

Assets	=	Liabilities	+	Shareholders' Equity	(Class.)
				−40,000	RE
				+30,000	ContriCap
				+10,000	ContriCap

d. **September 30, 2013**

Retained Earnings (Dividends Declared) 11,000

    Dividends Payable...   11,000

Assets	=	Liabilities	+	Shareholders' Equity	(Class.)
		+11,000		−11,000	RE

$11,000 = 22,000 shares X $0.50 per share.

e. **October 15, 2013**

Dividends Payable... 11,000

    Cash..   11,000

Assets	=	Liabilities	+	Shareholders' Equity	(Class.)
−11,000		−11,000			

15.14 continued.

    f. **December 31, 2013**

       Additional Paid-In Capital...................................... 165,000
          Common Stock (= 11,000 X $15)   165,000

Assets	=	Liabilities	+	Shareholders' Equity	(Class.)
				−165,000	ContriCap
				+165,000	ContriCap

15.15   (Danos Corporation; journal entries for treasury stock transactions.) (amounts in US$)

    a. Treasury Stock—Common 300,000
        Cash (= 10,000 X $30)   300,000

Assets	=	Liabilities	+	Shareholders' Equity	(Class.)
−300,000				−300,000	ContriCap

    b. Cash (= 6,000 X $32).. 192,000
       Additional Paid-In Capital (Common Stock
         Options) (= 6,000 X $6) 36,000
          Treasury Stock—Common (= 6,000 X $30)......   180,000
          Additional Paid-In Capital..............................   48,000

Assets	=	Liabilities	+	Shareholders' Equity	(Class.)
+192,000				−36,000	ContriCap
				+180,000	ContriCap
				+48,000	ContriCap

    c. Treasury Stock—Common 266,000
        Cash (= 7,000 X $38)   266,000

Assets	=	Liabilities	+	Shareholders' Equity	(Class.)
−266,000				−266,000	ContriCap

15.15 continued.

d. Land... 300,000
    Treasury Stock—Common [= (4,000 × $30) +
    (4,000 × $38)] 272,000
    Additional Paid-In Capital................................. 28,000

Assets	=	Liabilities	+	Shareholders' Equity	(Class.)
+300,000				+272,000	ContriCap
				+28,000	ContriCap

e. Cash (= 3,000 × $36)... 108,000
    Additional Paid-In Capital.................................... 6,000
    Treasury Stock—Common (= 3,000 × $38).......... 114,000

Assets	=	Liabilities	+	Shareholders' Equity	(Class.)
+108,000				−6,000	ContriCap
				+114,000	ContriCap

15.16 (Melissa Corporation; journal entries for treasury stock transactions.) (amounts in US$)

a. Treasury Stock—Common...................................... 120,000
    Cash (= 10,000 × $12) 120,000

Assets	=	Liabilities	+	Shareholders' Equity	(Class.)
−120,000				−120,000	ContriCap

b. Bonds Payable... 72,000
    Treasury Stock—Common (= 6,000 × $12).......... 72,000

Assets	=	Liabilities	+	Shareholders' Equity	(Class.)
		−72,000		+72,000	ContriCap

c. Treasury Stock—Common...................................... 300,000
    Cash (= 20,000 × $15) 300,000

Assets	=	Liabilities	+	Shareholders' Equity	(Class.)
−300,000				−300,000	ContriCap

15.16 continued.

   d. Land... 540,000
        Treasury Stock—Common [= (4,000 X $12) +
          (20,000 X $15)]   348,000
        Common Stock (= 6,000 X $5)   30,000
        Additional Paid-In Capital.................................   162,000

Assets	=	Liabilities	+	Shareholders' Equity	(Class.)
+540,000				+348,000	ContriCap
				+30,000	ContriCap
				+162,000	ContriCap

15.17   (Intelliant; accounting for stock options.) (amounts in US$)

The value of the stock options on January 1, 2013, is $142.434 (= 24.6 X $5.79) million. Intelliant amortizes this value as an expense of $47.478 (= $142.434/3) million for 2013, 2014, and 2015. Intelliant recognizes no additional expense when employees exercise their options in 2016.

15.18   (Morrissey Corporation; journal entries for employee stock options.) (amounts in US$)

December 31, 2013
No entry.

December 31, 2014 and December 31, 2015
Compensation Expense (= $400,000/2)........................ 200,000
    Additional Paid-In Capital (Stock Options)...........   200,000

Assets	=	Liabilities	+	Shareholders' Equity	(Class.)
				−200,000	IncSt → RE
				+200,000	ContriCap

15.18 continued.

June 30, 2016

Cash (= 30,000 X $60)	1,800,000	
Additional Paid-In Capital (Stock Options)		
[= (30,000/50,000) X $400,000]	240,000	
Common Stock (= 30,000 X $1)		30,000
Additional Paid-In Capital [= $240,000 +		
(30,000 X $59)]		2,010,000

Assets	=	Liabilities	+	Shareholders' Equity	(Class.)
+1,800,000				−240,000	ContriCap
				+30,000	ContriCap
				+2,010,000	ContriCap

November 15, 2016

Cash (= 20,000 X $60)	1,200,000	
Additional Paid-In Capital (Stock Options)		
[= (20,000/50,000) X $400,000]	160,000	
Common Stock (= 20,000 X $1)		20,000
Additional Paid-In Capital [= $160,000 +		
(20,000 X $59)]		1,340,000

Assets	=	Liabilities	+	Shareholders' Equity	(Class.)
+1,200,000				−160,000	ContriCap
				+20,000	ContriCap
				+1,340,000	ContriCap

15.19 (Watson Corporation; journal entries for employee stock options.) (amounts in US$)

December 31, 2014, 2015, and 2016

Compensation Expense (= $75,000/3)	25,000	
Additional Paid-In Capital (Stock Options)		25,000

Assets	=	Liabilities	+	Shareholders' Equity	(Class.)
				−25,000	IncSt → RE
				+25,000	ContriCap

15.19 continued.

April 30, 2017

Cash (= 15,000 × $25) 375,000	
Additional Paid-In Capital (Stock Options)	
[= (15,000/20,000) × $75,000].................................. 56,250	
Common Stock (= 15,000 × $10)	150,000
Additional Paid-In Capital [= $56,250 +	
(15,000 × $15)]	281,250

Assets	=	Liabilities	+	Shareholders' Equity	(Class.)
+375,000				−56,250	ContriCap
				+150,000	ContriCap
				+281,250	ContriCap

September 15, 2018

Cash (= 5,000 × $25) 125,000	
Additional Paid-In Capital (Stock Options) [= (5,000/	
20,000) × $75,000] 18,750	
Common Stock (= 5,000 × $10)	50,000
Additional Paid-In Capital [= $18,750 +	
(5,000 × $15)]	93,750

Assets	=	Liabilities	+	Shareholders' Equity	(Class.)
+125,000				−18,750	ContriCap
				+50,000	ContriCap
				+93,750	ContriCap

15.20 (Higgins Corporation; journal entries for convertible bonds.) (amounts in US$)

1/02/2013

Cash... 1,000,000	
Convertible Bonds Payable	1,000,000

Assets	=	Liabilities	+	Shareholders' Equity	(Class.)
+1,0000,000		+1,000,000			

To record the issue of convertible bonds.

15.20 continued.

1/02/2017

Convertible Bonds Payable 1,000,000	
Common Stock—$1 Par	40,000
Additional Paid-In Capital	960,000

Assets	=	Liabilities	+	Shareholders' Equity	(Class.)
	=	−1,000,000	+	+40,000	ContriCap
				+960,000	ContriCap

To record conversion using carrying value of bonds.

15.21   (Symantec; accounting for conversion of bonds.) (amounts in US$)

Carrying Value Method

Convertible Bonds Payable 10,255,000	
Common Stock (= 100,000 X $10)	1,000,000
Additional Paid-In Capital (Plug)	9,255,000

Assets	=	Liabilities	+	Shareholders' Equity	(Class.)
	=	−10,225,000	+	+1,000,000	ContriCap
				+9,255,000	ContriCap

Fair Value Method

Convertible Bonds Payable 10,255,000	
Loss on Conversion of Bonds (Plug) 245,000	
Common Stock (= 100,000 X $10)	1,000,000
Additional Paid-In Capital (= 100,000 X $95)........	9,500,000

Assets	=	Liabilities	+	Shareholders' Equity	(Class.)
	=	−10,255,000		−245,000	IncSt → RE
				+1,000,000	ContriCap
				+9,500,000	ContriCap

15.22   (Kiersten Corporation; journal entries for stock warrants.)   (amounts in US$)

February 26, 2013

Cash.. 240,000

     Additional Paid-In Capital (Common Stock

        Warrants) (= 60,000 x $4)...   240,000

Assets	=	Liabilities	+	Shareholders' Equity	(Class.)
+240,000				+240,000	ContriCap

June 6, 2015

Cash (= 40,000 x $30) 1,200,000

Additional Paid-In Capital (Common Stock

        Warrants) (= 40,000 x $4) 160,000

        Common Stock (= 40,000 x $10)   400,000

        Additional Paid-In Capital...............................   960,000

Assets	=	Liabilities	+	Shareholders' Equity	(Class.)
+1,200,000				−160,000	ContriCap
				+400,000	ContriCap
				+960,000	ContriCap

February 26, 2017

Additional Paid-In Capital (Common Stock

        Warrants) (= 20,000 x $4) 80,000

        Additional Paid-In Capital...............................   80,000

Assets	=	Liabilities	+	Shareholders' Equity	(Class.)
				−80,000	ContriCap
				+80,000	ContriCap

15.23   (Alpharm; journal entries for stock warrants.) (amounts in US$)

December 7, 2008

Cash... 46,180,000
    Convertible Preferred Stock....................................   43,450,000
    Additional Paid-In Capital (Stock Warrants).......   2,730,000

Assets	=	Liabilities	+	Shareholders' Equity	(Class.)
+46,180,000				+43,450,000	ContriCap
				+2,730,000	ContriCap

To record issuance of convertible preferred stock with stock warrants.

January 15, 2013

Convertible Preferred Stock 62,533,000
    Common Stock (5,269,705 X $0.01)   52,697
    Additional Paid-In Capital   62,480,303

Assets	=	Liabilities	+	Shareholders' Equity	(Class.)
				−62,533,000	ContriCap
				+52,697	ContriCap
				+62,480,303	ContriCap

To record conversion of preferred stock with accumulated dividends into common stock. $62,533,000 = $43,450,000 + $19,083,000.

15.24   (amounts in US$)

a.   Cash (= 50,000 X $30) 1,500,000
    Common Stock (= 50,000 X $5)   250,000
    Additional Paid-In Capital (= 50,000 X $25)   1,250,000

Assets	=	Liabilities	+	Shareholders' Equity	(Class.)
+1,500,000				+250,000	ContriCap
				+1,250,000	ContriCap

15.24 continued.

b. Cash (= 20,000 × $100) 2,000,000
    Preferred Stock..   2,000,000

Assets	=	Liabilities	+	Shareholders' Equity	(Class.)
+2,000,000				+2,000,000	ContriCap

c. Patent (= 16,000 × $15)... 240,000
    Common Stock (= 16,000 × $10)   160,000
    Additional Paid-In Capital (= 16,000 × $5).........   80,000

Assets	=	Liabilities	+	Shareholders' Equity	(Class.)
+240,000				+160,000	ContriCap
				+80,000	ContriCap

d. Convertible Preferred Stock.................................... 400,000
    Common Stock (= 25,000 × $1)   25,000
    Additional Paid-In Capital (= $400,000 –
    $25,000)   375,000

Assets	=	Liabilities	+	Shareholders' Equity	(Class.)
				–400,000	ContriCap
				+25,000	ContriCap
				+375,000	ContriCap

e. Compensation Expense (= 5,000 × $12) 60,000
    Common Stock (= 5,000 × $10)   50,000
    Additional Paid-In Capital (= 5,000 × $2)...........   10,000

Assets	=	Liabilities	+	Shareholders' Equity	(Class.)
				–60,000	IncSt → RE
				+50,000	ContriCap
				+10,000	ContriCap

15.25 (Journal entries for the issuance of common stocks.) (amounts in US$)

a. Inventory.. 175,000
    Land... 220,000
    Building.. 1,400,000
    Equipment... 405,000
        Common Stock (= 20,000 X $10)......................... 200,000
        Additional Paid-In Capital.................................. 2,000,000

Assets	=	Liabilities	+	Shareholders' Equity	(Class.)
+175,000				+200,000	ContriCap
+220,000				+2,000,000	ContriCap
+1,400,000					
+405,000					

b. Cash (= 10,000 X $100).. 1,000,000
        Preferred Stock... 1,000,000

Assets	=	Liabilities	+	Shareholders' Equity	(Class.)
+1,000,000				+1,000,000	

c. Cash (= 5,000 X $24).. 120,000
    Additional Paid-In Capital (Common Stock
        Warrants) (= 5,000 X $8)...................................... 40,000
        Common Stock (= 5,000 X $1)........................... 5,000
        Additional Paid-In Capital.................................. 155,000

Assets	=	Liabilities	+	Shareholders' Equity	(Class.)
+120,000				−40,000	ContriCap
				+5,000	ContriCap
				+155,000	ContriCap

d. Preferred Stock (= 10,000 X $50)........................... 500,000
        Common Stock (= 20,000 X $10)....................... 200,000
        Additional Paid-In Capital................................. 300,000

Assets	=	Liabilities	+	Shareholders' Equity	(Class.)
				−500,000	ContriCap
				+200,000	ContriCap
				+300,000	ContriCap

15.26   (Wilson Supply Company; transactions to incorporate and run a business.)
         (amounts in US$)

a. **1/02**
    Cash.. 9,000
        Common Stock—$30 Stated Value 9,000

Assets	=	Liabilities	+	Shareholders' Equity	(Class.)
+9,000				+9,000	ContriCap

300 shares X $30 = $9,000.

b. **1/06**
    Cash.. 60,000
        Common Stock—$30 Stated Value 60,000

Assets	=	Liabilities	+	Shareholders' Equity	(Class.)
+60,000				+60,000	ContriCap

2,000 shares X $30 = $60,000.

c. **1/08**
    Cash.. 400,000
        Preferred Stock—$100 Par Value 400,000

Assets	=	Liabilities	+	Shareholders' Equity	(Class.)
+400,000				+400,000	ContriCap

4,000 shares X $100 = $400,000.

d. **1/09**
    No entry.

15.26 continued.

e. **1/12**

Inventories	50,000
Land	80,000
Building	210,000
Equipment	120,000
Preferred Stock—$100 Par Value	100,000
Common Stock—$30 Stated Value	360,000

Assets	=	Liabilities	+	Shareholders' Equity	(Class.)
+50,000				+100,000	ContriCap
+80,000				+360,000	ContriCap
+210,000					
+120,000					

f. **7/03**

Retained Earnings (Dividends Declared)	20,000
Dividends Payable on Preferred Stock	20,000

Assets	=	Liabilities	+	Shareholders' Equity	(Class.)
		+20,000		−20,000	RE

$100 × (0.08/2) × (4,000 + 1,000) shares = $20,000.

g. **7/05**

Cash	825,000
Common Stock—$30 Stated Value	750,000
Additional Paid-In Capital	75,000

Assets	=	Liabilities	+	Shareholders' Equity	(Class.)
+825,000				+750,000	ContriCap
				+75,000	ContriCap

25,000 shares × $33 = $825,000.

15.26 continued.

h. **7/25**
Dividends Payable on Preferred Stock 20,000
   Cash 20,000

Assets	=	Liabilities	+	Shareholders' Equity	(Class.)
−20,000		−20,000			

i. **10/02**
Retained Earnings (Dividends Declared) 39,300
   Dividends Payable on Common Stock 39,300

Assets	=	Liabilities	+	Shareholders' Equity	(Class.)
		+39,300		−39,300	RE

$1 × (300 + 2,000 + 12,000 + 25,000) shares = $39,300.

j. **10/25**
Dividends Payable on Common Stock 39,300
   Cash 39,300

Assets	=	Liabilities	+	Shareholders' Equity	(Class.)
−39,300		−39,300			

15.27 (Fisher Company; reconstructing transactions involving shareholders' equity.) (amounts in US$)

a. $60,000 par value/$10 per share = 6,000 shares.

b. $7,200/360 = $20 per share.

c. 600 − 360 = 240 shares.

15.27 continued.

d. If the Additional Paid-In Capital is $31,440, then $30,000 [= 6,000 × ($15 − $10)] represents contributions in excess of par value on original issue of 6,000 shares. Then, $1,440 (= $31,440 − $30,000) represents the credit to Additional Paid-In Capital when it reissued the treasury shares.

The $1,440 represents 240 shares reissued times the excess of reissue price over acquisition price:

$$240(\$X - \$20) = \$1,440, \text{ or } X = \$26.$$

The shares were reissued for $26 each.

e. (1) Cash (= 6,000 × $15) 90,000
       Common Stock ($10 Par Value).................. 60,000
       Additional Paid-In Capital......................... 30,000

Assets	=	Liabilities	+	Shareholders' Equity	(Class.)
+90,000				+60,000	ContriCap
				+30,000	ContriCap

(2) Treasury Stock—Common 12,000
       Cash (= 600 × $20) 12,000

Assets	=	Liabilities	+	Shareholders' Equity	(Class.)
−12,000				−12,000	ContriCap

(3) Cash (= 240 × $26) 6,240
       Treasury Stock—Common (= 240 × $20)..... 4,800
       Additional Paid-In Capital......................... 1,440

Assets	=	Liabilities	+	Shareholders' Equity	(Class.)
+6,240				+4,800	ContriCap
				+1,440	ContriCap

15.27 e. continued.

(4a) Cash.. 10,000
    Securities Available for Sale 6,000
    Realized Gain on Sale of Securities
      Available for Sale..................................... 4,000

Assets	=	Liabilities	+	Shareholders' Equity	(Class.)
+10,000				+4,000	IncSt → RE
−6,000					

(4b) Securities Available for Sale 2,000
    Unrealized Gain on Securities Available
      for Sale (Accumulated Other
      Comprehensive Income) 2,000

Assets	=	Liabilities	+	Shareholders' Equity	(Class.)
+2,000				+2,000	OCI → AOCI

f. The realized gain appears in the income statement and the unrealized gain appears in a statement of other comprehensive income or in reconciliation of accumulated other comprehensive income.

15.28 (Shea Company; reconstructing transactions involving shareholders' equity.) (amounts in US$)

a. $100,000 par value/$5 per share = 20,000 shares.

b. $33,600/1,200 = $28 per share.

c. 2,000 − 1,200 = 800 shares.

d. If the Additional Paid-In Capital is $509,600, then $500,000 [= 20,000 X ($30 − $5)] represents contributions in excess of par value on original issue of 20,000 shares. Then, $9,600 (= $509,600 − $500,000) represents the credit to Additional Paid-In Capital when it reissued the treasury shares.

15.28 d. continued.

The $9,600 represents 800 shares reissued times the excess of reissue price over acquisition price:

$$800(\$X - \$28) = \$9{,}600, \text{ or } X = \$40.$$

The shares were reissued for $40 each.

e. (1) Cash.. 600,000
      Common Stock ($5 Par Value)....................   100,000
      Additional Paid-In Capital.........................   500,000

Assets	=	Liabilities	+	Shareholders' Equity	(Class.)
+600,000				+100,000	ContriCap
				+500,000	ContriCap

(2) Treasury Shares 56,000
      Cash..   56,000

Assets	=	Liabilities	+	Shareholders' Equity	(Class.)
−56,000				−56,000	ContriCap

2,000 X $28 = $56,000.

(3) Cash.. 32,000
      Treasury Shares   22,400
      Additional Paid-In Capital.........................   9,600

Assets	=	Liabilities	+	Shareholders' Equity	(Class.)
+32,000				+22,400	ContriCap
				+9,600	ContriCap

800 X $40 = $32,000.
800 X $28 = $22,400.

15.28 e. continued.

(4a) Cash... 12,000
    Realized Loss on Sale of Securities Available
        for Sale.. 2,000
        Securities Available for Sale 14,000

Assets	=	Liabilities	+	Shareholders' Equity	(Class.)
+12,000				−2,000	IncSt → RE
−14,000					

(4b) Unrealized Loss on Securities Available for
        Sale (Other Comprehensive Income) 7,000
        Securities Available for Sale 7,000

Assets	=	Liabilities	+	Shareholders' Equity	(Class.)
−7,000				−7,000	OCI → AOCI

Write down securities from $25,000 to $18,000.

f.   The realized loss appears in the income statement and the unrealized loss appears in a statement of other comprehensive income or in reconciliation of accumulated other comprehensive income.

15.29   (Lowen Corporation; accounting for stock options.) (amounts in US$)

Compensation expense reduces net income each year as follows:

2013: zero compensation because all benefits occur after the granting of the stock option.

2014:	0.5(5,000 X $2.40)	$	6,000
2015:	[0.5(5,000 X $2.40) + 0.5(6,000 X $3.00)]		15,000
2016:	[0.5(6,000 X $3.00) + 0.5(7,000 X $3.14)]		19,990
2017:	[0.5(7,000 X $3.14) + 0.5(8,000 X $3.25)]		23,990
	Total Compensation Expense	$	64,980

15.30   (Pramble Company; accounting for stock options.) (amounts in US$)

Compensation expense reduces net income each year as follows:

2014:   [0.5(35,759 X $10.99) + 0.5(40,866 X $12.50)] = $451,908.21
2015:   [0.5(40,866 X $12.50) + 0.5(29,100 X $14.34)] = $464,059.50
2016:   [0.5(29,100 X $14.34) + 0.5(33,904 X $16.30)] = $484,964.60
2017:   [0.5(33,904 X $16.30) + 0.5(33,091 X $17.29)] = $562,389.30

15.31   (Microtel Corporation; reconstructing transactions affecting shareholders' equity.) (amounts in millions of US$)

(1) Cash.. 6,783
       Common Stock and Additional Paid-In
         Capital..   6,783

Assets	=	Liabilities	+	Shareholders' Equity	(Class.)
+6,783				+6,783	ContriCap

To issue common stock for cash.

(2) Common Stock and Additional Paid-In Capital...   6,162
       Retained Earnings...   21,212
         Cash...   27,374

Assets	=	Liabilities	+	Shareholders' Equity	(Class.)
−27,374				−6,162	ContriCap
				−21,212	RE

To repurchase common stock for more than its initial issue price.

(3) Compensation Expense..   889
       Additional Paid-In Capital.................................   889

Assets	=	Liabilities	+	Shareholders' Equity	(Class.)
				−889	IncSt → RE
				+889	ContriCap

To record stock-based compensation expense.

15.31 continued.

(4) Revenues and Gains Net of Expenses and Losses ..   14,065
      Retained Earnings..   14,065

Assets	=	Liabilities	+	Shareholders' Equity	(Class.)
				−14,065	IncSt → RE
				+14,065	RE

To close revenues, gain, expense, and loss accounts to retained earnings.

(5) Retained Earnings...   3,837
      Cash..   3,837

Assets	=	Liabilities	+	Shareholders' Equity	(Class.)
−3,837				−3,837	RE

To declare and pay cash dividends.

(6) Marketable Securities   326
      Net Unrealized Gains and Losses on
        Marketable Securities   326

Assets	=	Liabilities	+	Shareholders' Equity	(Class.)
+326				+326	OCI → AOCI

To record net unrealized gains and losses for changes in fair value of marketable securities.

(7) Derivative Securities...   14
      Net Unrealized Gains and Losses on
        Derivatives   14

Assets	=	Liabilities	+	Shareholders' Equity	(Class.)
+14	or	−14		+14	OCI → AOCI

To record net unrealized gains and losses for changes in fair value derivatives.

15.32   (Sirens, Inc.; journal entries for changes in shareholders' equity.) (amounts in thousands of US$)

(1)   Cash... 82,941

      Common Stock—Par Value.................................... 22

      Additional Paid-In Capital................................. 82,919

Assets	=	Liabilities	+	Shareholders' Equity	(Class.)
+82,941				+22	ContriCap
				+82,919	ContriCap

To record the issuance of common stock to third parties for more than par value.

(2)   Cash... 19,246

      Common Stock—Par Value.................................... 4

      Additional Paid-In Capital................................. 19,242

Assets	=	Liabilities	+	Shareholders' Equity	(Class.)
+19,246				+4	ContriCap
				+19,242	ContriCap

To record the issuance of common stock to employees for more than par value.

(3)   Compensation Expense... 52,683

      Additional Paid-In Capital................................. 52,683

Assets	=	Liabilities	+	Shareholders' Equity	(Class.)
				−52,683	IncSt → RE
				+52,683	ContriCap

To record the amortized cost of employee stock options.

15.32 continued.

(4) Cash.. 3,532
     Common Stock—Par Value.................................   3
     Additional Paid-In Capital..................................   3,529

Assets	=	Liabilities	+	Shareholders' Equity	(Class.)
+3,532				+3	ContriCap
				+3,529	ContriCap

To record the sale of common stock associated with stock options.

(5) Additional Paid-In Capital....................................... 5
     Common Stock—Par Value.................................   5

Assets	=	Liabilities	+	Shareholders' Equity	(Class.)
				−5	ContriCap
				+5	ContriCap

To record exercise of common stock warrants and issuance of shares.

(6) Convertible Notes 3,184
     Common Stock—Par Value.............................   2
     Additional Paid-In Capital..................................   3,182

Assets	=	Liabilities	+	Shareholders' Equity	(Class.)
		−3,184		+2	ContriCap
				+3,182	ContriCap

To record conversion of notes into common stock.

15.33   (Busch Corporation; journal entries for changes in shareholders' equity.) (amounts in millions of US$)

(1) Cash.. 292.3

    Common Stock 8.8
    Additional Paid-In Capital................................   283.5

Assets	=	Liabilities	+	Shareholders' Equity	(Class.)
+292.3				+8.8	ContriCap
				+283.5	ContriCap

To record the issuance of common stock to employees under stock option plans.

(2) Compensation Expense.. 136.3

    Additional Paid-In Capital.................................   136.1
    Treasury Stock—Common...................................   0.2

Assets	=	Liabilities	+	Shareholders' Equity	(Class.)
				−136.3	IncSt → RE
				+136.1	ContriCap
				+0.2	ContriCap

To record the amortized cost of employees stock options. The reason for the credit to Treasury Stock is not explained by Busch.

(3) Revenues, Gains, Expenses, and Losses.................. 2,115.3

    Retained Earnings...   2,115.3

Assets	=	Liabilities	+	Shareholders' Equity	(Class.)
				−2,115.3	IncSt → RE
				+2,115.3	RE

To close revenue and expense accounts to retained earnings.

15.33 continued.

   (4) Retained Earnings...   932.4

         Cash...   932.4

Assets	=	Liabilities	+	Shareholders' Equity	(Class.)
−932.4				−932.4	RE

To record the declaration and payment of cash dividends.

   (5) Treasury Stock—Common.......................................   2,707.2

         Cash...   2,707.2

Assets	=	Liabilities	+	Shareholders' Equity	(Class.)
−2,707.2				−2,707.2	ContriCap

To record repurchase of common stock held as treasury stock.

   (6) Net Unrealized Gains and Losses on Marketable
        Securities..   0.3

         Marketable Securities.....................................   0.3

Assets	=	Liabilities	+	Shareholders' Equity	(Class.)
−0.3				−0.3	OCI → AOCI

To record net unrealized loss on marketable securities.

   (7) Net Unrealized Gains and Losses on Cash Flow
        Hedges..   2.0

         Derivative Securities......................................   2.0

Assets	=	Liabilities	+	Shareholders' Equity	(Class.)
−2.0	or	+2.0		−2.0	OCI → AOCI

To record net unrealized loss on cash flow hedges.

15.33 continued.

    (8) Pension Liability 205.2

            Pension Liability Adjustment 205.2

Assets	=	Liabilities	+	Shareholders' Equity	(Class.)
		+205.2		+205.2	OCI → AOCI

To reduce pension liability for a reduction in the mini-mum pension liability or for changes in actuarial as-sumptions, actuarial performance, or prior cost and increase in other comprehensive income.

15.34   (Monk Corporation; treasury shares and their effects on performance ratios.) (amounts in US$)

    a. (1) Cash 714.1

             Treasury Stock—Common 427.6

             Common Stock/Additional Paid-In Capital ...   286.5

Assets	=	Liabilities	+	Shareholders' Equity	(Class.)
+714.1				+427.6	ContriCap
				+286.5	ContriCap

The common shares were issued at an option price of $49.28 per share [= $714.1/(0.307 + 14.183)]. The treasury shares issued were purchased for $30.15 per share (= $427.6/14.183). The difference of $19.13 per share (= $49.28 − $30.15) was credited to Additional Paid-In Capital. This amount includes a debit to Additional Paid-In Capital for the cost of stock options previously amortized and a credit for the difference between the cash proceeds plus the cost of the stock options over the par value of the shares issued. The remaining credits to Common Stock and Additional Paid-In Capital were for the amounts received for the 0.307 common shares issued net of any amounts debited and credited to Additional Paid-In Capital as a result of recognizing the cost of the options in the accounts.

15.34 a. continued.

(2) Treasury Stock—Common 2,572.8
        Cash 2,572.8

Assets	=	Liabilities	+	Shareholders' Equity	(Class.)
−2,572.8				−2,572.8	ContriCap

These treasury shares were purchased for an average price of $93.75 per share (= $2,572.8/27.444).

	2013/2014	**2014/2015**
b.		
Net Income:		
[($3,870.5/$3,376.6) − 1]	+14.6%	
[($4,596.5/$3,870.5) − 1]		+18.8%
Earnings per Common Share:		
[($3.20/$2.70) − 1]	+18.5%	
[($3.83/$3.20) − 1]		+19.7%

Earnings per share increases faster than net income because Monk reduces the number of shares outstanding each year by repurchasing shares of treasury stock.

	2013	**2014**	**2015**
c.			
Book Value per Share:			
$11,735.7/(1,483.463 − 254.615) ...	$9.55		
$11,970.5/(1,483.619 − 277.017) ...		$9.92	
$12,613.5/(1,483.926 − 290.278) ...			$10.57
Percentage Change:			
[($9.92/$9.55) − 1]		+3.9%	
[($10.57/$9.92) − 1]			+6.6%

15.34 c. continued.

There are several reasons book value per share increases more slowly than net income and earnings per share. First, dividends reduce shareholders' equity but not net income. Second, the repurchases of treasury shares reduce the numerator proportionally more than they reduce the denominator. The average repurchase price during 2015 of $93.75 per share (see the answer to Part a.) had the effect of reducing book value per share. Book value per share increased overall in 2015 because of net income.

d.

	2013	2014	2015
[$3,376.6/(0.5[$11,139.0 + $11,735.7])]	29.5%		
[$3,870.5/(0.5[$11,735.7 + $11,970.5])]		32.7%	
[$4,596.5/(0.5[$11,970.5 + $12,613.5])]			37.4%

e. No. Monk has purchased considerably more treasury shares than are needed for its stock option plans. Treasury shares do not receive dividends, so Monk does conserve cash. Dividends have, however, grown at approximately the same growth rate as net income. One purpose might have been to increase the return on common shareholders' equity. Cash generally earns a return of approximately 4% each year after taxes. By eliminating this low-yielding asset from the balance sheet, Monk's overall rate of return on common shareholders' equity increases. The market often interprets stock repurchases as a positive signal that management has inside information and thinks that the stock is undervalued. The positive signal results in an increase in the stock price. One can estimate the increase in market price by observing the average price at which Monk repurchased its shares each year:

2013: $1,570.9/33.377 = $47.07
2014: $2,493.3/38.384 = $64.96
2015: $2,572.8/27.444 = $93.75

Thus, the stock price doubled during the three-year period, whereas earnings increased by approximately 36% [= ($4,596.5/$3,376.6) − 1].

This page is intentionally left blank

CHAPTER 16

STATEMENT OF CASH FLOWS: ANOTHER LOOK

Problems and Cases: Answers and Solutions

16.1   (Effects of transactions on statement of cash flows.) (amounts in US$)

a. The journal entry to record this transaction is:

Retained Earnings.. 15,000
   Dividends Payable...   3,000
   Cash..   12,000

	ΔCash	=	ΔL	+	ΔSE	–	ΔN$A
Financing	–$12,000	=	$3,000	+	–$15,000	–	$0

The credit to the Cash account reduces Line (11) by $12,000. Paying dividends is a financing activity, so Line (10) increases by $12,000.

b. The journal entry to record this transaction is:

Cash... 75,000
   Bank Loan Payable   75,000

	ΔCash	=	ΔL	+	ΔSE	–	ΔN$A
Financing	+$75,000	=	$75,000	+	$0	–	$0

The debit to the Cash account increases Line (11) by $75,000. Borrowing is a financing activity so Line (8) increases by $75,000.

16.1 continued.

c. The journal entry to record this transaction is:

Cash... 20,000
Accumulated Depreciation................................ 35,000
    Machinery.. 40,000
    Gain on Sale of Machinery............................ 15,000

	ΔCash	=	ΔL +	ΔSE −	ΔN$A
Investing	$20,000	=	$0 +	$15,000 −	−$5,000

The debit to the Cash account results in an increase in Line (11) of $20,000. Selling machinery is an investing activity so Line (6) increases by $20,000. The gain on the sale increases net income on Line (3) by $15,000. Because the full cash proceeds is an investing activity, Line (5) increases by $15,000 to subtract from net income a revenue that did not provide an operating source of cash.

d. The journal entry for this transaction is:

Rent Expense.. 28,000
    Cash.. 28,000

	ΔCash	=	ΔL +	ΔSE −	ΔN$A
Operations	−$28,000	=	$0 +	−$28,000 −	$0

The credit to the Cash account reduces Line (11) by $28,000. The recognition of rent expense reduces net income on Line (3) by $28,000. Expenditure matched the expense, so Line (2) shows an increase in the amount subtracted of $28,000.

e. The journal entry to record this transaction is:

Marketable Securities 39,000
    Cash.. 39,000

	ΔCash	=	ΔL +	ΔSE −	ΔN$A
Investing	−$39,000	=	$0 +	$0 −	$39,000

The credit to the Cash account reduces Line (11) by $39,000. Purchasing marketable securities is an investing transaction so Line (7) increases by $39,000.

16.1 continued.

f. The journal entry to record this transaction is:

Accumulated Depreciation..................................... 14,000
    Truck.. 14,000

ΔCash	=	ΔL	+	ΔSE	–	ΔN$A
$0	=	$0	+	$0	–	$0

Because this transaction affects neither the Cash account nor net income, it does not appear on the statement of cash flows.

g. The journal entry to record this event is:

Unrealized Holding Loss of Marketable
    Securities (Other Comprehensive Income)....... 8,000
        Marketable Securities 8,000

ΔCash	=	ΔL	+	ΔSE	–	ΔN$A
$0	=	$0	+	–$8,000	–	–$8,000

Because this entry does not affect either the Cash account or net income, it does not appear on the statement of cash flows. The firm discloses in a supplementary schedule or note the write down of marketable equity securities totaling $8,000.

h. The journal entry to record this transaction is:

Interest Expense.. 15,000
    Bonds Payable.. 500
    Cash.. 14,500

	ΔCash	=	ΔL	+	ΔSE	–	ΔN$A
Operations	–$14,500	=	$500	+	–$15,000	–	$0

The credit to the Cash account results in a decrease in Line (11) of $14,500. The recognition of interest expense reduces net income on Line (3) by $15,000. Because the firm used only $14,500 of cash for this expense, Line (4) increases by $500 for the portion of the expense that did not use cash. Line (2) increased the amount to be subtracted by the amount of the expense paid in cash, $14,500.

16.1 continued.

i. The journal entry for this event is:

Goodwill Impairment Loss	22,000	
Goodwill		22,000

ΔCash	=	ΔL	+	ΔSE	–	ΔN$A
$0	=	$0	+	–$22,000	–	–$22,000

This entry does not involve the Cash account so Line (11) does not change. The recognition of the impairment loss reduces net income on Line (3) by $22,000. Because this loss requires no cash outflow, Line (4) increases by $22,000 to convert net income to cash flow from operations.

16.2 (Effects of transactions on statement of cash flows.) (amounts in US$)

a. The journal entry to record this transaction is:

Building	400,000	
Note Payable		360,000
Cash		40,000

	ΔCash	=	ΔL	+	ΔSE	–	ΔN$A
Investing	–$40,000	= $360,000	+		$0	–	$400,000

The credit to the Cash account reduces Line (11) by $40,000. Acquiring a building is an investing transaction so Line (7) increases by $40,000. The firm discloses in a supplementary schedule or note the acquisition of a building costing $400,000, by paying cash and assuming a mortgage for $360,000.

b. The journal entry for this event is:

Bad Debt Expense	32,000	
Allowance for Uncollectible Accounts		32,000

ΔCash	=	ΔL	+	ΔSE	–	ΔN$A
$0	=	$0	+	–$32,000	–	–$32,000

16.2 b. continued.

This entry does not involve the Cash account so Line (11) does not change. The recognition of bad debt expense reduces net income on Line (3) by $32,000. Because this expense does not use cash, Line (4) increases by $32,000 to convert net income to cash flow from operations.

c. The journal entry for this event is:

Allowance for Uncollectible Accounts................... 28,000
   Accounts Receivable... 28,000

	ΔCash	=	ΔL	+	ΔSE	–	ΔN$A
	$0	=	$0	+	$0	–	$0

This event does not affect the Cash account so Line (11) does not change. The event also does not affect net income so Line (3) does not change. Thus, the event would not normally appear in the statement of cash flows. An alternative acceptable answer is Line (4) increases by $28,000 and Line (5) increases by $28,000.

d. The journal entry to record this transaction is:

Cash... 15,000
   Equity in Earnings of Affiliate.......................... 12,000
   Investment in Securities.................................... 3,000

	ΔCash	=	ΔL	+	ΔSE	–	ΔN$A
Investing	$15,000	=	$0	+	$12,000	–	–$3,000

The debit to the Cash account results in an increase in Line (11) of $15,000. Line (1) increases by $15,000 for the dividend received. The caption "Cash Receipt from Customers" needs expanding to include "and from Investments." The recognition of equity in earnings increases net income on Line (3) by $12,000. Because the firm received $3,000 more cash than its equity in earnings, Line (4) increases by $3,000 when converting net income to cash flow from operations. An alternative acceptable answer for the increase in Line (4) of $3,000 is that Line (4) increases by $15,000 for the dividend received and Line (5) increases by $12,000 to subtract the equity in earnings.

16.2 continued.

e. The journal entries to record this transaction are:

Cash.. 22,000
Realized Loss on Sale of Marketable Securities .. 3,000
   Marketable Securities 25,000

Marketable Securities 2,000
   Unrealized Holding Loss on Marketable
     Securities.. 2,000

	ΔCash	=	ΔL +	ΔSE –	ΔN$A
Investing	+$22,000	=	$0 +	–$1,000 –	–$23,000

The debit to the Cash account results in an increase in Line (11) of $22,000. Selling marketable securities is an investing transaction so Line (6) increases by $22,000. The recognition of a realized loss on the sale reduces net income on Line (3) by $3,000. Because the loss does not use cash, Line (4) increases by $3,000 to add back the loss to net income when converting net income to cash flow from operations.

f. The journal entry to record this transaction is:

Preferred Stock... 10,000
   Common Stock 2,000
   Additional Paid-In Capital............................... 8,000

	ΔCash	=	ΔL +	ΔSE –	ΔN$A
	$0	=	$0 +	$0 –	$0

This transaction affects neither the Cash account [Line (11)] nor net income [Line (3)]. Thus, it would not appear on the statement of cash flows. The firm discloses in a supplementary schedule or note the conversion of preferred stock into common stock totaling $10,000.

16.2 continued.

g. The journal entry to record this transaction is:

Legal Expense.. 5,000
   Land..   5,000

ΔCash	=	ΔL	+	ΔSE	–	ΔN\$A
\$0	=	\$0	+	–\$5,000	–	–\$5,000

The transaction does not affect the Cash account so Line (11) does not change. The recognition of legal expense reduces net income on Line (3) by \$5,000. Because this expense does not use cash, Line (4) increases by \$5,000 to convert net income to cash flow from operations.

h. The journal entry for this transaction is:

Rental Fees Received in Advance.......................... 8,000
   Rent Revenue..   8,000

ΔCash	=	ΔL	+	ΔSE	–	ΔN\$A
\$0	=	–\$8,000	+	\$8,000	–	\$0

This entry does not affect the Cash account so Line (11) does not change. The recognition of rent revenue increases net income on Line (3) by \$8,000. Because this revenue does not increase cash during the current period, Line (5) increases by \$8,000 to convert net income to cash flow from operations.

i. The journal entry to record this event is:

Long-Term Debt 30,000
   Current Portion of Long-Term Debt   30,000

ΔCash	=	ΔL	+	ΔSE	–	ΔN\$A
\$0	=	\$0	+	\$0	–	\$0

This entry affects neither the Cash account [Line (11)] nor net income [Line (3)] and would, therefore, not appear on the statement of cash flows.

16.3   (Effects of transactions on statement of cash flows.) (amounts in US$)

a.   The journal entry to record this event is:

Contracts in Process... 15,000
    Contract Revenue...   15,000

ΔCash	=	ΔL +	ΔSE –	ΔN$A
$0	=	$0 +	$15,000 –	$15,000

This entry does not affect the Cash account so Line (11) does not change. The recognition of contract revenue increases net income on Line (3) by $15,000. Because this revenue does not result in a change in cash, Line (5) increases by $15,000 to convert net income to cash flow from operations.

b.   The journal entry to record this transaction is:

Land... 50,000
    Donated Capital...   50,000

ΔCash	=	ΔL +	ΔSE –	ΔN$A
$0	=	$0 +	$50,000 –	$50,000

This transaction affects neither the Cash account [Line (11)] nor net income [Line (3)] and, therefore, does not appear on the statement of cash flows. The firm discloses in a supplementary schedule or note the donation of land by a governmental agency totaling $50,000.

c.   The journal entry to record this event is:

Unrealized Holding Loss on Investments in
    Securities (Other Comprehensive Income)....... 8,000
        Investments in Securities.............................   8,000

ΔCash	=	ΔL +	ΔSE –	ΔN$A
$0	=	$0 +	–$8,000 –	–$8,000

This transaction affects neither the Cash account [Line (11)] nor net income [Line (3)] so would not appear on the statement of cash flows. The firm discloses in a supplementary schedule or note the write down of marketable equity investments totaling $8,000.

16.3 continued.

d. The journal entry to record the recognition of depreciation is:

Inventories 60,000
  Accumulated Depreciation................................   60,000

The journal entry to record the sale of the inventory items is:

Cost of Goods Sold... 60,000
  Inventories   60,000

ΔCash	=	ΔL	+	ΔSE	−	ΔN$A
$0	=	$0	+	−$60,000	−	−$60,000

These entries do not affect the Cash account so Line (11) does not change. The recognition of cost of goods sold containing depreciation reduces net income on Line (3) by $60,000. Because this expense does not use cash, Line (4) increases by $60,000 to convert net income to cash flow from operations.

e. The journal entry to record this transaction is:

Warranty Expense... 35,000
  Estimated Warranty Liability   35,000

ΔCash	=	ΔL	+	ΔSE	−	ΔN$A
$0	=	$35,000	+	−$35,000	−	$0

This entry does not affect the Cash account so Line (11) does not change. The recognition of warranty expense reduces net income on Line (3) by $35,000. Because this expense does not use cash, Line (4) increases by $35,000 to convert net income to cash flow from operations.

f. The journal entry to record this transaction is:

Estimated Warranty Liability 28,000
  Cash...   28,000

	ΔCash	=	ΔL	+	ΔSE	−	ΔN$A
Operations	−$28,000	=	−$28,000	+	$0	−	$0

16-9

16.3 f. continued.

The credit to the Cash account reduces Line (11) by $28,000. Honoring warranties is an operating item so Line (2) increases the amount to be subtracted. This entry does not affect net income on Line (3) this period. Thus, Line (5) increases by $28,000 to convert net income to cash flow from operations.

g. The journal entry to record this event is:

Income Tax Expense	80,000	
Deferred Tax Liability	20,000	
Cash		100,000

	ΔCash	=	ΔL	+	ΔSE	–	ΔN\$A
Operations	–$100,000	= –$20,000	+	–$80,000	–		$0

The credit to the Cash account results in a reduction in Line (11) of $100,000. Line (2) increases the amount to be subtracted by $100,000. The recognition of income tax expense reduces net income on Line (3) by $80,000. Because the firm used more cash this period than the amount of income tax expense, Line (5) increases by $20,000 when converting net income to cash flow from operations.

h. The journal entry to record this event is:

Loss from Writedown of Inventories	18,000	
Inventories		18,000

	ΔCash	=	ΔL	+	ΔSE	–	ΔN\$A
	$0	=	$0	+	–$18,000	–	–$18,000

This entry does not affect the Cash account so Line (11) does not change. The recognition of the writedown reduces net income on Line (3) by $18,000. Because the writedown did not use cash, Line (4) increases by $18,000 to convert net income to cash flow from operations.

16.4 (Metals Company; working backward from statement of cash flows.) (amounts in millions of US$)

(2) Cash (Operations—Depreciation Expense
      Addback).. 664.0
        Accumulated Depreciation............................ 664.0

(3) Cash (Operations—Deferred Tax Addback).......... 82.0
        Deferred Income Tax Liability 82.0

(4) Investment in Affiliates...................................... 47.1
        Cash (Operations—Equity in Undistributed
        Earnings Subtraction) 47.1

(5) Cash (Investing—Sale of Marketable
  &   Securities)... 49.8
(11)   Cash (Operations—Gain on Sale of
          Marketable Securities Subtraction)........ 20.8
        Marketable Securities 29.0

(6) Cash (Operations—Decrease in Accounts
      Receivable) 74.6
        Accounts Receivable..................................... 74.6

(7) Inventories... 198.9
        Cash (Operations—Increase in Inventories) 198.9

(8) Prepayments 40.3
        Cash (Operations—Increase in Prepayments).. 40.3

(9) Cash (Operations—Increase in Accounts
      Payable).. 33.9
        Accounts Payable 33.9

(10) Other Current Liabilities....................................... 110.8
        Cash (Operations—Decrease in Other Current
        Liabilities).. 110.8

(12) Marketable Securities 73.2
        Cash (Investing—Acquisition of Marketable
        Securities)... 73.2

16.4 continued.

| (13) | Property, Plant, and Equipment | 875.7 | |
| | Cash (Investing—Acquisition of Property, Plant, and Equipment) | | 875.7 |

| (14) | Investments in Securities | 44.5 | |
| | Cash (Investing—Acquisition of Subsidiaries) | | 44.5 |

| (15) | Cash (Financing—Common Stock Issued to Employees) | 34.4 | |
| | Common Stock | | 34.4 |

| (16) | Treasury Stock | 100.9 | |
| | Cash (Financing—Repurchase of Common Stock) | | 100.9 |

| (17) | Retained Earnings | 242.9 | |
| | Cash (Financing—Dividends Paid to Shareholders) | | 242.9 |

| (18) | Cash (Financing—Additions to Short-Term Borrowing) | 127.6 | |
| | Notes Payable | | 127.6 |

| (19) | Cash (Financing—Additions to Long-Term Borrowing) | 121.6 | |
| | Bonds Payable | | 121.6 |

| (20) | Bonds Payable | 476.4 | |
| | Cash (Financing—Payments to Long-Term Borrowing) | | 476.4 |

| (21) | Property, Plant, and Equipment | 76.9 | |
| | Mortgage Payable | | 76.9 |

| (22) | Property, Plant, and Equipment | 98.2 | |
| | Capitalized Lease Obligation | | 98.2 |

| (23) | Convertible Bonds Payable | 47.8 | |
| | Common Stock | | 47.8 |

16.5 (Metals Company deriving direct method presentation of cash flow from operations using data from T-account work sheet.) (amounts in millions of US$)

(a) (The letters here correspond to the column header letters in the exhibit below.) Copy Income Statement and Cash Flow from Operations

(b) Copy Information from T-Account Work Sheet Next to Related Income Statement Item

(c)–(d) Sum Across Rows to Derive Direct Receipts and Expenditures

Operations	(a)	Indirect Method (b)	Changes in Related Balance Sheet Accounts from T-Account Work Sheet (c)	Direct Method (d)	From Operations: Receipts Less Expenditures
Sales Revenues	$20,465.0	$74.6	= Accounts Receivable Decrease	20,539.6	Receipts from Customers
Gain on Sale of Marketable Equity Securities	20.8	(20.8)	Gain Produces No Operating Cash	—	
Equity in Earnings of Affiliates	214.0	(47.1)	Metals Company's Share of Earnings Retained by Affiliates	166.9	Receipts for Equity Method Investments
Cost of Goods Sold	(9,963.3)	664.0	Depreciation on Manufacturing Facilities	(9,464.3)	Payments for Inventory
		33.9	= Accounts Payable Increase		
		(1 98.9)	= Increase in Inventories		
General and Administrative Expenses	(5,570.2)	(40.3)	= Prepayments Increase	(5,721.3)	Payments for General and Administrative Services
		(1 10.8)	= Decrease in Other Current Liabilities		
Interest Expense	(2,887.3)	—		(2,887.3)	Payments for Interest
Income Tax Expense	(911.6)	82.0	Deferred Income Taxes Uses no Cash this Period	(829.6)	Payment for Income Taxes
Net Income	= $1,367.4	= 1,367.4	Totals	$1,804.0	= Cash Flow from Operations Derived via Direct Method

$1,804.0 = Cash Flow from Operations Derived via Indirect Method

16.6   (Ingers Company; working backward from the statement of cash flows.)
        (amounts in millions of US$)

(2)	Cash (Operations—Depreciation Expense Addback)...	179.4	
	Accumulated Depreciation...............................		179.4
(3) & (12)	Cash (Investing—Sale of Property, Plant, and Equipment)..	26.5	
	Property, Plant, and Equipment (Net)		22.9
	Cash (Operations—Gain on Sale Subtraction)..		3.6
(4)	Investment in Securities	41.5	
	Cash (Operations—Equity in Earnings Subtraction)..		41.5
(5)	Cash (Operations—Deferred Taxes Addback)......	15.1	
	Deferred Income Taxes		15.1
(6)	Cash (Operations—Decrease in Accounts Receivable)	50.9	
	Accounts Receivable..		50.9
(7)	Inventories	15.2	
	Cash (Operations—Increase in Inventories)		15.2
(8)	Other Current Assets..	33.1	
	Cash (Operations—Increase in Other Current Assets)...		33.1
(9)	Accounts Payable	37.9	
	Cash (Operations—Decrease in Accounts Payable)..		37.9
(10)	Cash (Operations—Increase in Other Current Liabilities)...	19.2	
	Other Current Liabilities....................................		19.2
(11)	Property, Plant, and Equipment...........................	211.7	
	Cash (Investing—Acquisition of Property, Plant, and Equipment).......................................		211.7

16.6 continued.

(13) Marketable Securities 4.6

     Cash (Investing—Acquisition of Marketable

     Securities).. 4.6

(14) Cash (Investing—Advances from Equity

     Companies)... 18.4

     Investment in Equity Companies 18.4

(15) Short-Term Debt 81.5

     Cash (Financing—Repayment of Short-

     Term Debt) 81.5

(16) Cash (Financing—Issue of Long-Term Debt) 147.6

     Long-Term Debt Payable 147.6

(17) Long-Term Debt Payable 129.7

     Cash (Financing—Repayment of Long-Term

     Debt) 129.7

(18) Cash (Financing—Issue of Common Stock

     Under Option Plan) 47.9

     Common Stock, Additional Paid-In Capital . 47.9

(19) Cash (Financing—Sale of Treasury Stock) 59.3

     Treasury Stock, Additional Paid-In Capital 59.3

(20) Retained Earnings.. 78.5

     Cash (Financing—Dividends Paid) 78.5

(21) Leasehold Asset 147.9

     Capitalized Lease Obligation........................... 147.9

(22) Preferred Stock... 62.0

     Common Stock, Additional Paid-In Capital 62.0

(23) Investments in Securities 94.3

     Common Stock, Additional Paid-In Capital 94.3

16.7   (Warren Corporation; preparing a statement of cash flows.) (amounts in US$)

a.

		Cash			
	√ 223,200				

Operations

Net Income	(5)	234,000	
Loss on Sale of Machinery	(1b)	15,600	
Amortize Patent	(2b)	5,040	
Decrease in Accounts Receivable	(7)	18,000	
Bad Debt Expense	(8)	2,400	
Decrease in Inventories	(9)	66,000	
Depreciation Expense	(11)	106,800	
Amortize Leasehold Improvements	(12)	10,800	
Increase in Accounts Payable	(13)	153,360	

Investing

Sale of Machinery	(1b)	57,600	463,200	(1a)	Acquisition of Machinery
			2,400	(2a)	Payment for Patent Defense
			180,000	(10)	Acquisition of Securities

Financing

13,200	(3)	Retirement of Preferred Stock	
60,000	(15)	Provision for Current Portion of Serial Bonds	

√ 174,000		

16.7 a. continued.

Accounts Receivable				Allowance for Uncollectible Accounts				Inventory		
√	327,600					20,400	√	√ 645,600		
		3,600	(6)	(6) 3,600		2,400	(8)		66,000	(9)
		18,000	(7)							
√	306,000					19,200	√	√ 579,600		

Securities Held for Plant Expansion				Machinery and Equipment (Cost)				Accumulated Depreciation		
√	-0-			√ 776,400					446,400	√
(10)	180,000			(1a) 463,200		127,200	(1b)	(1b) 54,000	106,800	(11)
√	180,000			√ 1,112,400					499,200	√

Leasehold Improvements				Allowance for Amortization				Patents		
√	104,400					58,800	√	√ 36,000		
						10,800	(12)	(2a) 2,400	5,040	(2b)
√	104,400					69,600	√	√ 33,360		

Accounts Payable				Dividends Payable				Bonds Payable (Current)		
		126,000	√			—	√		60,000	√
		153,360	(13)			48,000	(4)	(15) 60,000	60,000	(14)
		279,360	√			48,000	√		60,000	√

6% Serial Bonds Payable				Preferred Stock				Common Stock		
		360,000	√			120,000	√		600,000	√
(14) 60,000				(3) 12,000						
		300,000	√			108,000	√		600,000	√

Retained Earnings			
		321,600	√
(4) & (5) 48,000		234,000	(5)
(3) 1,200			
		506,400	√

16.7 continued.

b.

WARREN CORPORATION
Statement of Cash Flows
For the Year Ending June 30, 2014

Operations:

Net Income	$ 234,000	
Loss on Sale of Machinery	15,600	
Depreciation	106,800	
Amortization of Leasehold Improvements....	10,800	
Amortization of Patents	5,040	
Bad Debt Expense	2,400	
Decrease in Accounts Receivable	18,000	
Decrease in Inventories	66,000	
Increase in Accounts Payable	153,360	
Cash Flow from Operations		$ 612,000
Investing:		
Sale of Machinery	$ 57,600	
Payment of Legal Fee for Patent Defense	(2,400)	
Acquisition of Securities for Plant		
Expansion	(180,000)	
Acquisition of Machinery	(463,200)	
Cash Flow from Investing		(588,000)
Financing:		
Retirement of Serial Bonds	$ (60,000)	
Retirement of Preferred Stock	(13,200)	
Cash Flow from Financing		(73,200)
Net Change in Cash		$ (49,200)
Cash, January 1, 2014		223,200
Cash, June 30, 2014		$ 174,000

16.8 (Roth Company; preparing a statement of cash flows.) (amounts in US$)

a.

	Cash		
	√ 37,950		

Operations

Net Income	(1)	95,847	3,600	(2)	Gain on Sale of Marketable
Bond Discount					Securities
Amortization	(6)	225			
Depreciation	(10)	1,875	16,050	(4)	Gain on Condemnation
Increase in Income					of Land
Taxes Payable	(14)	51,924			
Deferred Taxes	(15)	504	37,500	(8)	Increase in Accounts Receivable
			26,250	(9)	Increase in Inventories
			8,640	(11)	Equity in Earnings
			5,835	(12)	Decrease in Accounts Payable

Investing

Sale of Marketable			122,250	(5)	Acquisition of
Securities	(2)	17,400			Equipment
Proceeds from					
Condemnation					
of Land	(4)	48,000			

Financing

Issuance of Bonds	(7)	97,500			
	√	131,100			

Marketable Securities		Accounts Receivable		Inventory	
√ 24,000		√ 36,480		√ 46,635	
	13,800 (2)	(8) 37,500		(9) 26,250	
√ 10;200		√ 73,980		√ 72,885	

16.8 a. continued.

Land		Building		Equipment	
√ 60,000		√ 375,000		√ -0-	
	31,950 (4)			(5) 122,250	
√ 28,050		√ 375,000		√ 122,250	

Accumulated Depreciation		Investment in 30% Owned Company		Other Assets	
	22,500 √	√ 91,830		√ 22,650	
	1,875(10)	(11) 8,640			
	24,375 √	√ 100,470		√ 22,650	

Accounts Payable		Dividends Payable		Income Taxes Payable	
	31,830 √		-0- √		-0- √
(12) 5,835			12,000(13)		51,924(14)
	25,995 √		12,000 √		51,924 √

Other Liabilities		Bonds Payable		Deferred Income Taxes	
	279,000 √		71,550 √		765 √
			225 (6)		504(15)
			97,500 (7)		
	279,000 √		169,275 √		1,269 √

Preferred Stock		Common Stock		Unrealized Holding Loss on Marketable Securities	
	45,000 √		120,000 √	√ 750	
(3) 45,000			45,000 (3)		
	-0- √		165,000 √	√ 750	

Retained Earnings	
	124,650 √
(13)12,000	95,847 (1)
	208,497 √

16.8 continued.

b.
ROTH COMPANY
Statement of Cash Flows
For the Three Months Ended March 31, 2014

Operations:

Net Income	$ 95,847	
Bond Discount Amortization	225	
Depreciation	1,875	
Deferred Income Taxes	504	
Increase in Income Taxes Payable	51,924	
Gain on Sale of Marketable Securities	(3,600)	
Gain on Condemnation of Land	(16,050)	
Equity in Earnings	(8,640)	
Increase in Accounts Receivable	(37,500)	
Increase in Inventories	(26,250)	
Decrease in Accounts Payable	(5,835)	
Cash Flow from Operations		$ 52,500
Investing:		
Proceeds from Sale of Marketable Securities	$ 17,400	
Proceeds from Condemnation of Land	48,000	
Acquisition of Equipment	(122,250)	
Cash Flow from Investing		(56,850)
Financing:		
Issue of Bonds	$ 97,500	
Cash Flow from Financing		97,500
Net Change in Cash		$ 93,150
Cash, January 1 2014		37,950
Cash, March 31, 2014		$ 131,100

Supplementary Information

Holders of the firm's preferred stock converted shares with a carrying value of $45,000 into shares of common stock.

Solutions

16.8 continued.

c. Roth deriving direct method cash flow from operations using data from T-account work sheet.

(a) (The letters correspond to the column headers in the exhibit below.) Copy Income Statement and Cash Flow from Operations

(b) Copy Information from T-Account Work Sheet Next to Related Income Statement Item

(c) – (d) Sum Across Rows to Derive Direct Receipts and Expenditures

Operations	(a)	Indirect Method (b)	Changes in Related Balance Sheet Accounts from T-Account Work Sheet (c)	Direct Method (d)	From Operations: Receipts Less Expenditures
Sales	$364,212	$(37,500)	= Accounts Receivable Increase	326,712	Receipts from Customers
Gain on Sale of Marketable Equity Securities	3,600	(3,600)	Gain Produces No Operating Cash		
Equity in Earnings of 30% Owned Company	8,640	(8,640)	Roth's Share of Earnings Retained by Affiliates		Receipts for Equity Method Investments
Gain on Condemnation of Land	16,050	(16,050)		—	Proceeds of Land Condemnation
Cost of Sales	(207,612)	(5,835) (26,250)	Depreciation on Manufacturing Facilities = Accounts Payable Increase = Increase in Inventories	(239,697)	Payments for Inventory
General and Administrative Expenses	(33,015)		= Prepayments Increase = Decrease in Other Current Liabilities	(33,015)	Payments for Selling and Administrative Services
Depreciation	(1,875)	1,875			
Interest Expense	(1,725)	225	Bond Discount Amortization Uses No Cash this Period	(1,500)	Payments for Interest
Income Tax Expense	(52,428)	504 51,924	Deferred Income Taxes Uses no Cash this Period = Increase in Income Taxes Payable		Payment for Income Taxes
Net Income	$95,847	= 95,847		$52,500	= Cash Flow from Operations Derived via Direct Method

Totals .... $52,500 = Cash Flow from Operations Derived via Indirect Method

16.9 (Biddle Corporation; preparing a statement of cash flows.) (amounts in US$)

a.

Cash							
√	45,000						

Operations

Income from Continuing Operations	(14)	60,500	6,000	(3)	Gain on Retirement of Bonds Net of Income Taxes
Loss on Sale of Equipment	(4)	2,000	35,000	(7)	Increase in Accounts Receivable
Depreciation	(9)	10,000			
Amortization	(10)	1,500	20,000	(8)	Increase in Inventories
Increase in Accounts Payable	(11)	30,000			
Deferred Income Taxes	(13)	20,000	5,000	(12)	Decrease in Accrued Liabilities

Investing

Sale of Equipment	(4)	9,500	42,500	(6)	Acquisition of Land

Financing

			19,000	(3)	Retirement of Bonds, Including Income Taxes
			1,000	(5)	Dividends
√	50,000					

Accounts Receivable—Net		Inventories		Land	
√ 70,000		√ 110,000		√ 100,000	
(7) 35,000		(8) 20,000		(2) 20,000	
				(6) 42,500	
√ 105,000		√ 130,000		√ 162,500	

16.9 a. continued.

	Plant and Equipment	
√	316,500	
		26,500 (4)
√	290,000	

	Accumulated Depreciation		
		50,000	√
(4) 15,000		10,000	(9)
		45,000	√

	Patents	
√	16,500	
		1,500 (10)
√	15,000	

	Accounts Payable	
	100,000	√
	30,000	(11)
	130,000	√

	Accrued Liabilities	
		105,000 √
(12) 5,000		
		100,000 √

	Deferred Income Taxes	
	50,000	√
	20,000	(13)
	70,000	√

	Long-Term Bonds	
		90,000 √
(3) 25,000		
		65,000 √

	Common Stock	
		105,000 √
		10,500 (1)
		9,500 (2)
		125,000 √

	Additional Paid-In Capital	
	85,000	√
	21,000	(1)
	10,500	(2)
	116,500	√

	Retained Earnings	
		73,000 √
(1) 31,500		60,500 (14)
(5) 1,000		
		101,000 √

16.9 continued.

b.
BIDDLE CORPORATION
Statement of Cash Flows
For the Year Ended December, 2014

Operations:

Net Income	$ 60,500	
Subtract Gain on Sale of Repurchase of Bonds	(6,000)	
Add Back Loss on Sale of Equipment	2,000	
Depreciation	10,000	
Amortization	1,500	
Deferred Income Taxes	20,000	
Increase in Accounts Payable	30,000	
Increase in Accounts Receivable	(35,000)	
Increase in Inventories	(20,000)	
Decrease in Accrued Liabilities	(5,000)	
Cash Flow from Operations		$ 58,000
Investing:		
Sale of Equipment	$ 9,500	
Acquisition of Land	(42,500)	
Cash Flow from Investing		(33,000)
Financing:		
Retirement of Bonds	$ (19,000)	
Dividends	(1,000)	
Cash Flow from Financing		(20,000)
Net Change in Cash		$ 5,000
Cash, January 1, 2014		45,000
Cash, December 31, 2014		$ 50,000

Supplementary Information

During 2014, Biddle Corporation issued common stock with a market value of $20,000 in the acquisition of land.

16.10   (Plainview Corporation; preparing a statement of cash flows.) (amounts in US$)

a.

	Cash	
	√ 165,300	

Operations

Net Income	(1)	236,580	17,000	(5)	Gain on Sale of Marketable Securities
Loss from Fire	(6)	35,000			
Equity in Loss	(9)	17,920			
Decrease in Accounts Receivable—Net	(11)	59,000	131,100	(12)	Increase in Inventories
Depreciation	(15)	79,900	1,400	(13)	Increase in Prepayments
Increase in Accounts Payable	(16)	24,800	1,500	(18)	Decrease in Accrued Payables
Increase in Income Taxes Payable	(19)	66,500	500	(20)	Deferred Taxes
Loss on Retirement of Bonds	(21)	5,000			

Investing

Sale of Marketable Securities	(5)	127,000	28,000	(8)	Acquisition of Machinery
Building Sold	(7)	4,000	103,400	(10)	Acquisition of Marketable Securities
Bond Sinking Funds Used	(14)	63,000			

Financing

Reissue of Treasury Stock	(3)	6,000	130,000	(2)	Dividends
Issuance of Debentures	(22)	125,000	145,000	(17)	Payment of Note Payable— Current
			315,000	(21)	Retirement of Bonds

	√ 142,100	

16.10 a. continued.

Marketable Securities			Accounts Receivable—Net			Inventories	
√	129,200		√	371,200		√	124,100
(10) 103,400		110,000 (5)			59,000 (11)	(12) 131,100	
√	122,600		√	312,200		√	255,200

Prepayments			Bond Sinking Fund			Investment in Subsidiary	
√	22,000		√	63,000		√	152,000
(13) 1,400					63,000 (14)		17,920 (9)
√	23,400		√	-0-		√	134,080

Plant and Equipment—Net			Accounts Payable			Notes Payable—Current	
√ 1,534,600				213,300	√	145,000	√
(6) 65,000		100,000 (6)		24,800 (16)		(17) 145,000	
(8) 28,000		4,000 (7)					
		79,900 (15)					
√ 1,443,700				238,100	√	-0-	√

Accrued Payables			Income Taxes Payable			Deferred Income Taxes	
		18,000 √			31,000 √		128,400 √
(18) 1,500					66,500 (19)	(20) 500	
		16,500 √			97,500 √		127,900 √

6% Mortgage Bonds			8% Debentures			Common Stock	
		310,000 √			-0- √		950,000 √
(21) 310,000					125,000 (22)		83,500(4)*
		-0- √			125,000 √		1,033,500 √

Additional Paid-In Capital			Unrealized Holding Gain on Marketable Securities			Retained Earnings	
		51,000 √			2,500 √		755,700 √
		16,700 (4)*				(2) 130,000	236,580 (1)
						(3) 3,000	
						(4)* 100,200	
		67,700 √			2,500 √		759,080 √

Treasury Stock	
√ 43,500	
	9,000 (3)
√ 34,500	

*(4) 83,500 = 1,033,500 − 950,000
*(4) 16,700 = 67,700 − 51,000
*(4) 100,200 = 83,500 + 16,700

16.10 continued.

b.

PLAINVIEW CORPORATION
Statement of Cash Flows
For the Year Ended December, 2014

Operations:

Net Income	$ 236,580	
Loss from Fire	35,000	
Equity in Loss of Subsidiary	17,920	
Loss on Retirement of Bonds	5,000	
Depreciation	79,900	
Gain on Sale of Marketable Securities	(17,000)	
Deferred Income Taxes	(500)	
Decrease in Accounts Receivable—Net	59,000	
Increase in Accounts Payable	24,800	
Increase in Income Taxes Payable	66,500	
Increase in Inventories	(131,100)	
Increase in Prepayments	(1,400)	
Decrease in Accrued Payables	(1,500)	
Cash Flow from Operations		$ 373,200
Investing:		
Marketable Securities Sold	$ 127,000	
Building Sold	4,000	
Bond Sinking Funds Used	63,000	
Acquisition of Marketable Securities	(103,400)	
Acquisition of Machinery	(28,000)	
Cash Flow from Investing		62,600
Financing:		
Reissue of Treasury Stock	$ 6,000	
Issue of Debentures	125,000	
Dividends	(130,000)	
Retirement of Bonds	(315,000)	
Payment of Short-Term Note	(145,000)	
Cash Flow from Financing		(459,000)
Net Change in Cash		$ (23,200)
Cash, January 1, 2014		165,300
Cash, December 31, 2014		$ 142,100

16.11 (Airlines Corporation; preparing and interpreting the statement of cash flows.) (amounts in millions of US$)

a. T-account work sheet for 2013.

Cash

√ 1,087

Operations

(1)	324	106	(4)
(3)	517	147	(7)
(11)	56	39	(8)
(15)	42	67	(9)
(17)	12	49	(16)

Investing

(4)	1,199	1,568	(2)
(10)	40	957	(6)

Financing

(12)	325	110	(13)
(18)	4	98	(19)

√ 465

Marketable Securities		Accounts Receivable		Inventories	
√	—	√	741	√	210
(5)	85	(7)	147	(8)	39
(6)	957				
√	1,042	√	888	√	249

Prepayments		Property, Plant, and Equipment			Accumulated Depreciation			
√	112	√	7,710				3,769	√
(9)	67	(2)	1,568	1,574 (4)	(4)	481	517	(3)
√	179	√	7,704				3,805	√

16.11 a. continued.

Other Assets		Accounts Payable		Short-Term Borrowing	
√ 610			540 √		121 √
	40 (10)		56 (11)		325 (12)
√ 570			596 √		446 √

Current Portion Long-Term Debt		Advances from Customers		Other Current Liabilities	
	110 √		619 √		1,485 √
(13) 110	84 (14)		42 (15)	(16) 49	
	84 √		661 √		1,436 √

Long-Term Debt		Deferred Tax Liability		Other Noncurrent Liabilities	
	1,418 √		352 √		715 √
(14) 84			12 (17)		4 (18)
	1,334 √		364 √		719 √

Common Stock		Unrealized Holding Gain on Marketable Securities		Retained Earnings	
	119 √		— √		1,188 √
			85 (5)		324 (1)
	119 √		85 √		1,512 √

Additional Paid-In Capital		Treasury Stock	
	48 √	√ 14	
		(19) 98	
	48 √	√ 112	

16.11 a. continued.

a. T-account work sheet for 2014.

<table>
<tr><td colspan="2"></td><td colspan="2">Cash</td></tr>
<tr><td></td><td>√</td><td>465</td><td></td></tr>
</table>

Operations

(1)	101	286	(4)
(3)	560	25	(7)
(15)	182	74	(8)
(16)	390	30	(9)
(18)	4	44	(11)

Investing

(4)	1,697	2,821	(2)
		17	(6)
		35	(10)

Financing

(12)	1	84	(13)
(17)	230		
(19)	2		
(20)	5		
√	221		

Marketable Securities		Accounts Receivable		Inventories	
√	1,042	√	888	√	249
(5)	7	(7)	25	(8)	74
(6)	17				
√	1,066	√	913	√	323

Prepayments		Property, Plant, and Equipment			Accumulated Depreciation		
√	179	√	7,704			3,805	√
(9)	30	(2)	2,821	1,938 (4)	(4)	527	560 (3)
√	209	√	8,587			3,838	√

16.11 a. continued.

Other Assets		Accounts Payable		Short-Term Borrowing	
√ 570			596 √		446 √
(10) 35		(11) 44			1(12)
√ 605			552 √		447 √

Current Portion Long-Term Debt		Advances from Customers		Other Current Liabilities	
	84 √		661 √		1,436 √
(13) 84	89(14)		182(15)		390(16)
	89 √		843 √		1,826 √

Long-Term Debt		Deferred Tax Liability		Other Noncurrent Liabilities	
	1,334 √		364 √		719 √
(14) 89	230(17)		4(18)		2(19)
	1,475 √		368 √		721 √

Common Stock		Additional Paid-In Capital		Unrealized Holding Gain on Marketable Securities	
	119 √		48 √		85 √
	1(20)		4(20)		7 (5)
	120 √		52 √		92 √

Retained Earnings		Treasury Stock	
	1,512 √	√ 112	
	101 (1)		
	1,613 √	√ 112	

16.11 continued.

b. **Comparative Statement of Cash Flows for Airlines Corporation
(amounts in millions of US$)**

	2014	2013
Operations:		
Net Income	$ 101	$ 324
Depreciation Expense	560	517
Deferred Income Taxes	4	12
Gain on Sale of Property, Plant, and Equipment	(286)	(106)
(Increase) Decrease in Accounts Receivable	(25)	(147)
(Increase) Decrease in Inventories	(74)	(39)
(Increase) Decrease in Prepayments	(30)	(67)
Increase (Decrease) in Accounts Payable	(44)	56
Increase (Decrease) in Advances from Customers	182	42
Increase (Decrease) in Other Current Liabilities	390	(49)
Cash Flow from Operations	$ 778	$ 543
Investing:		
Sale of Property, Plant, and Equipment	$ 1,697	$ 1,199
Acquisition of Property, Plant, and Equipment	(2,821)	(1,568)
Acquisition of Marketable Securities	(17)	(957)
(Increase) Decrease in Other Noncurrent Assets	(35)	40
Cash Flow from Investing	$(1,176)	$ (1,286)
Financing:		
Increase in Short-Term Borrowing	$ 1	$ 325
Increase in Long-Term Borrowing	230	—
Increase in Common Stock	5	—
Decrease in Long-Term Borrowing	(84)	(110)
Acquisition of Treasury Stock	—	(98)
Increase in Other Noncurrent Liabilities	2	4
Cash Flow from Financing	$ 154	$ 121
Net Change in Cash	$ (244)	$ (622)
Cash, January 1	465	1,087
Cash, December 31	$ 221	$ 465

16.11 continued.

c. During 2013, cash flow from operations exceeded net income primarily because of the non-cash expense for depreciation. Cash flows from operations and from the sale of property, plant, and equipment were sufficient to finance capital expenditures. Airlines Corporation used the excess cash flow as well as cash from additional short-term borrowing to repay long-term debt and reacquire treasury stock. It invested the remaining excess cash flow in short-term marketable securities. Although the balance in the cash account declined during 2013, the combined balance in cash and marketable securities actually increased.

Net income declined in 2014 relative to 2013 but cash flow from operations increased. The increase occurred because Airlines Corporation received increased cash advances from customers and stretched its other current liabilities. Cash flow from operations and from the sale of property, plant, and equipment were insufficient to finance capital expenditures. Airlines Corporation increased long-term borrowing and decreased the balance in its cash account to finance these capital expenditures.

One additional item to note for Airlines Corporation is the significant turnover of aircraft each year. The airline sold older aircraft at a gain and replaced them with newer aircraft.

16.12 (Irish Paper Company; preparing and interpreting the statement of cash flows.) (amounts in millions of US$)

a. T-account work sheet for 2012.

		Cash		
√	374			

		Operations		
(1)	376	221	(7)
(6)	306	31	(8)
(9)[1]	2	112	(10)
(12)	54	59	(11)
(14)	72	5	(17)
(18)	87		

		Investing		
(7)	5	92	(3)
(13)	8	775	(4)

		Financing		
(5)	449	59	(2)
		129	(16)
		201	(19)

√	49	

[1]OK to classify this as (Dis)investing source of cash.

16.12 a. continued.

Accounts Receivable			Inventories			Prepayments		
√	611		√	522		√	108	
(10)	112		(11)	59				54(12)
√	723		√	581		√	54	

Investments in Affiliates			Property, Plant, and Equipment			Accumulated Depreciation		
√	254		√	5,272			2,160	√
(3)	92	2 (9p)	(4)	775	78 (7)	(7)	74	306 (6)
(8)	31							
√	375		√	5,969			2,392	√

Other Assets			Accounts Payable			Current Portion Long-Term Debt		
√	175			920	√		129	√
(7)	220	8(13)		72(14)		(16)	129	221(15)
√	387			992	√		221	√

Other Current Liabilities			Long-Term Debt			Deferred Income Taxes		
	98	√		1,450	√		607	√
(17)	5		(15)	221	449 (5)		87(18)	
	93	√		1,678	√		694	√

Common Stock			Retained Earnings			Treasury Stock		
	629	√		1,331	√	√	15	
(19)	201		(2)	59	376 (1)			
	428	√		1,648	√	√	15	

16.12 a. continued.

a. T-account work sheet for 2013.

		Cash		
	√	49		

	Operations			
(1)	169	19	(8)
(7)	346	38	(9)
(10)[1]	5	106	(11)
(14)	186	154	(12)
		10	(17)
		26	(18)

	Investing			
(3)	86	931	(4)
(8)	21	78	(13)

	Financing			
(5)	890	59	(2)
(19)	4	221	(16)
√	114		

[1]OK to classify this as (Dis)investing source of cash.

Accounts Receivable		Inventories		Prepayments	
√	723	√	581	√	54
(11)	106	(12)	154		
√	829	√	735	√	54

Investments in Affiliates				Property, Plant, and Equipment				Accumulated Depreciation			
√	375			√	5,969					2,392	√
(9)	38	86	(3)	(4)	931	42	(8)	(8)	40	346	(7)
		5	(10p)	(6)	221						
√	322			√	7,079					2,698	√

16.12 a. continued.

Other Assets			Accounts Payable		Current Portion Long-Term Debt		
√	387			992 √			221 √
(13)	78			186(14)	(16)	221	334(15)
√	465			1,178 √			334 √

Other Current Liabilities			Long-Term Debt		Deferred Income Taxes		
		93 √		1,678 √			694 √
(17)	10		(15) 334	890 (5)	(18)	26	
				221 (6)			
		83 √		2,455 √			668 √

Common Stock		Retained Earnings			Treasury Stock	
	428 √		1,648 √	√	15	
	4(19)	(2) 59	169 (1)			
	432 √		1,758 √	√	15	

16.12 a. continued.

a. T-account work sheet for 2014.

Cash

		√	114		

Operations

(6)	353		142	(1)
(7)	34		30	(8)
(9)	32		2	(12)
(10)	159		45	(17)
(11)	164		7	(18)
(14)	136			

Investing

(7)	114		13	(3)
			315	(4)
			19	(13)

Financing

(5)	36		59	(2)
(19)	8		334	(16)
√	184			

Accounts Receivable			Inventories			Prepayments		
√	829		√	735		√	54	
		159 (10)			164 (11)	(12)	2	
√	670		√	571		√	56	

Investments in Affiliates			Property, Plant, and Equipment			Accumulated Depreciation		
√	322		√	7,079				2,698 √
(3)	13	32 (9)	(4)	315	222 (7)	(7)	74	353 (6)
(8)	30							
√	333		√	7,172				2,977 √

16.12 a. continued.

Other Assets				Accounts Payable					Current Portion Long-Term Debt		
√	465					1,178	√			334	√
(13)	19					136 (14)		(16)	334	158 (15)	
√	484					1,314	√			158	√

Other Current Liabilities				Long-Term Debt					Deferred Income Taxes		
		83	√			2,455	√			668	√
(17)	45			(15)	158	36	(5)	(18)	7		
		38	√			2,333	√			661	√

Common Stock				Retained Earnings					Treasury Stock		
		432	√			1,758	√	√	15		
		7 (19)		(1)	142						1 (19)
				(2)	59						
		439	√			1,557	√	√	14		

16.12 continued.

b.

IRISH PAPER COMPANY
Statement of Cash Flows
(amounts in millions of US$)

	2012	2013	2014
Operations:			
Net Income (Loss)	$ 376	$ 169	$ (142)
Depreciation Expense	306	346	353
Loss (Gain) on Sale of Property, Plant, and Equipment	(221)	(19)	34
Equity in Undistributed Earnings of Affiliates	(29)	(33)	2
Increase (Decrease) in Deferred Income Taxes	87	(26)	(7)
(Increase) Decrease in Accounts Receivable	(112)	(106)	159
(Increase) Decrease in Inventories	(59)	(154)	164
(Increase) Decrease in Prepayments	54	—	(2)
Increase (Decrease) in Accounts Payable	72	186	136
Increase (Decrease) in Other Current Liabilities	(5)	(10)	(45)
Cash Flow from Operations	**$ 469**	**$ 353**	**$ 652**
Investing:			
Sale of Property, Plant, and Equipment	$ 5	$ 21	$ 114
Acquisition of Property, Plant, and Equipment	(775)	(931)	(315)
(Increase) Decrease in Investments in Affiliates	(92)	86	(13)
(Increase) Decrease in Other Assets	8	(78)	(19)
Cash Flow from Investing	**$(854)**	**$(902)**	**$ (233)**

16.12 b. continued.

Financing:			
Issue of Long-Term Debt	$ 449	$ 890	$ 36
Issue of Common Stock or Treasury Stock	—	4	8
Redemption of Long-Term Debt	(129)	(221)	(334)
Redemption of Common Stock Warrants	(201)	—	—
Dividends	(59)	(59)	(59)
Cash Flow from Financing	$ 60	$ 614	$ (349)
Net Change in Cash	$(325)	$ 65	$ 70
Cash, January 1	374	49	114
Cash, December 31	$ 49	$ 114	$ 184

Supplementary Information

During 2013, Irish Paper Company assumed a mortgage payable of $221 million in the acquisition of property, plant, and equipment.

c. The pattern of cash flows for 2012 is typical of a growing, capital-intensive firm. Cash flow from operations exceeds net income because of the addback of depreciation expense. Book income before taxes exceeds taxable income, resulting in a deferral of taxes payable. Accounts receivable and inventories increased to support the growth, while accounts payable increased to finance the increased inventories. Irish made significant capital expenditures during the year for which it had to rely in part on external debt financing.

The pattern of cash flows for 2013 is similar to that for 2012, again typical of a growing firm. In this case, however, cash flow from operations declines relative to 2012 because of reduced net income. The reduced net income occurs in part because of a smaller gain on sale of property, plant, and equipment and in part because of larger depreciation and administrative expenses. Irish financed its increased capital expenditures with additional long-term borrowing.

The pattern of cash flows for 2014 is typical of a firm that stopped growing. Sales and net income declined, the result of underutilizing manufacturing capacity. Cash flow from operations increased, however, because Irish collected receivables and decreased its investment in inventories. It also stretched its accounts payable. Cash flow from operations was more than sufficient to finance a reduced level of capital expenditures and repay long-term debt.

16.13   (Breda Enterprises, Inc.; preparing a statement of cash flows.) (amounts in US$)

BREDA ENTERPRISES, INC.
Statement of Cash Flows
For the Year Ended December 31, 2014

Operations:		
Net Income (1)	$ 90,000	
Adjustments for Non-cash Transactions:		
Decrease in Merchandise Inventory (3)	4,000	
Increase in Accounts Payable (3)	12,000	
Loss on Sale of Equipment (4)	13,000	
Depreciation Expense (4)	42,000	
Amortization of Leasehold Asset (5)	5,000	
Loss on Conversion of Bonds (8)	15,000	
Increase in Accounts Receivable (Net) (2)	(10,600)	
Increase in Notes Receivable (2)	(15,000)	
Increase in Interest Receivable (2) [(0.08 × $15,000) × (1/6)]	(200)	
Decrease in Advances from Customers (2)	(2,700)	
Realized Gain on Marketable Securities (7)	(4,600)	
Interest Expense Greater than Cash Paid for Interest = Amortization of Bond Premium (8)	(1,500)	
Cash Flow from Operations		$ 146,400
Investing:		
Sale of Equipment (4)	$ 25,000	
Sale of Marketable Securities (7)	9,100	
Purchase of Equipment (4) ($31,000 + $38,000 − $26,000)	(43,000)	
Cash Flow from Investing		(8,900)
Financing:		
Reduction of Lease Liability (5)	$ (2,400)	
Dividends (6)	(24,000)	
Cash Flow from Financing		(26,400)
Change in Cash		$ 111,100

16.14   (Gear Locker; interpreting the statement of cash flows.)

a.   The rate of increase in net income suggests that Gear Locker grew rapidly during the three-year period. Increased investments in accounts receivable and inventories used operating cash flow. Increases in supplier credit did not fully finance the increased working capital investments, resulting in negative cash flow from operations.

b.   During 2012, Gear Locker sold marketable securities and borrowed short term to finance the negative cash flow from operations. Accounts receivable and inventories convert into cash within one year, so short-term financing is appropriate. Selling marketable securities to help finance these working capital investments suggests that the revenue from these securities was less than the cost of additional short-term borrowing.

During 2013, Gear Locker relied on short-term borrowing to finance its working capital needs, matching the term structure of its financing with the term structure of its assets.

During 2014, Gear Locker issued additional common stock to finance its working capital needs. Several explanations for this switch in financing are possible. First, the proportion of debt in the capital structure may have reached a point after the borrowing in 2013 that lenders considered the firm unduly risky, thereby raising the cost of additional borrowing. Second, Gear Locker may have expected continuing rapid growth and wished to infuse a more permanent form of capital than short-term debt into the capital structure. Third, short-term borrowing rates might have increased significantly relative to long-term rates and Gear Locker chose to access longer-term sources of capital.

c.   Gear Locker is growing rapidly, so that new capacity additions exceed depreciation recognized on existing capacity.

d.   Gear Locker is not capital intensive. The firm uses independent manufacturers in East Asia and markets its products through independent retailers. Thus, its property, plant, and equipment serves primarily its administrative needs.

e.   Gear Locker has few fixed assets that might serve as collateral for such borrowing. The principal collateral is short-term, so lenders likely prefer to extend short-term financing.

16.15   (Canned Soup Company; interpreting the statement of cash flows.)

a.   Canned uses suppliers and other creditors to finance its working capital needs. Consumer foods is a mature industry in the United States, so Canned's modest growth rate does not require large incremental investments in accounts receivable and inventories.

b.   (1) Capital expenditures have declined slightly each year, suggesting little need to add productive capacity.

(2) Depreciation expense is a growing percentage of acquisitions of property, plant, and equipment, suggesting slower growth in manufacturing capacity.

(3) Canned trades a substantial amount of marketable securities each year. Mature, profitable firms tend to accumulate cash beyond their operating needs and invest in marketable securities until they need cash.

(4) Canned acquired another business in 2013. Firms in mature industries grow by acquiring other firms. Canned financed this acquisition in part by selling marketable securities.

c.   (1) Increases in long-term debt approximately equal repayments of long-term debt, particularly for 2012 and 2013. Mature firms tend to roll over debt as long as they remain in the no-growth phase.

(2) Canned repurchased a portion of its common stock with excess cash.

(3) Dividends have grown in line with increases in net income and represent approximately a 37% payout rate relative to net income.

16.16   (Prime Contracting Services; interpreting the statement of cash flows.)

a.   The firm reduced expenditures on fixed assets beginning in 2012. It sold fixed assets in 2014 and 2015. The firm repaid debt under equipment loans and capital leases, probably because the firm sold or returned fixed assets that served as collateral for this debt. The increase in Other Current Liabilities indicates the heavier use of employees in providing services.

16.16 continued.

b. Net income declined between 2011 and 2013 as the firm attempted to build its new people-based service business. It collected accounts receivable from the previous asset-based service contracts. The continually increasing sales suggest that the firm collects receivables from its new people-based services more quickly than from its previous asset-based services contracts. Thus, the increase in accounts receivable declined each year. The firm also stretched payments to employees, providing cash. Note that the increase in depreciation did not provide cash. The increased depreciation charge reduced net income and the addback merely offsets the reduction. The increased depreciation charge results from expenditures made on fixed assets in 2011 and 2012.

c. The people-based service business began to grow, leading to increasing net income. The firm also sold off fixed assets at a gain during 2014 and 2015, increasing net income. The cash proceeds from sale of the fixed assets appear in the Investing section, not cash flow from operations. The firm experienced increased accounts receivable from this growing business in 2014, which required cash. Additional increases in net income in 2015 coupled with decreases in accounts receivable helped cash flow from operations in that year.

d. Net income has increased and long-term borrowing has decreased, reducing the firm's risk. Offsetting these changes, however, is a significant increase in short-term borrowing in 2015.

16.17 (Cypress Corporation; interpreting the statement of cash flows.)

a. Although net income increased between 2011 and 2013, the firm increased accounts receivable and inventories to support this growth. It stretched its creditors somewhat to finance the buildup of accounts receivable and inventories, but not sufficiently to keep cash from operations from decreasing.

b. The principal factors causing cash flow from operations to increase in 2013 is an increase in net income. Inventories decreased and the firm stretched its payable somewhat as well. The principal factors causing the increased cash flow from operations in 2015 are increased and decreased accounts receivable and decreased inventories, partially offset by decreases in accounts payable and other liabilities.

16.17 continued.

   c. The firm has repaid both short- and long-term debt, likely reducing its debt service payments. It invested excess cash in marketable securities. It also substantially increased its dividend. Even with these actions, cash on the balance sheet increased significantly, particularly in 2015.

16.18   (LKR Company; deriving cash flows from financial statement data; comprehensive review, including other comprehensive income.) (amounts in US$)

Cash Flow from Operations...............	$ 181,500	[9]	Plug $181,500
Investing/Disinvesting:			
Purchase of Securities Available			
for Sale	(9,000)	[8]	
Proceeds of Sale of Securities			
Available for Sale	7,300	[7]	
Purchase of Land............................	(11,000)	[6]	
Sale of Old Buildings and			
Equipment.................................	53,000	[5]	See below
Purchase of New Buildings and			
Equipment.................................	(108,000)	[4]	Increase in B&E (Cost) + Cost of B&E Sold
Financing:			
Increase (Decrease) in Long-Term			
Debt	(2,000)	[3]	
Increase (Decrease) in Common			
Shares...	7,000	[2]	
Cash Dividends	(105,800)	[1]	= Income – Increase in Retained Earnings
Net Change in Cash	$ 13,000	[0]	$13,000

16.18 continued.

Depreciation Charge	$	54,000
Less Increase in Accumulated Depreciation		(44,000)
Accumulated Depreciation on Asset Sold	$	10,000
Cost of Asset Sold	$	40,000
Less Accumulated Depreciation on Asset Sold		(10,000)
Basis of Asset Sold	$	30,000
Gain on Sale		23,000
Sale Proceeds	$	53,000

a. $53,000; see above.

b. $7,300 = $4,000 [cost] + $3,300 [gain].

c. $9,000 = $80,000 [EB] – $68,000 [BB] – $7,000 [OCI] + $4,000 [cost].

d. $10,300 increase = $7,000 [OCI] + $3,300 [gain].

e. $900 = $1,600 [Inc St] – ($13,700 [EB] – $13,000 [BB]).

f. $11,000 = $1,100 [Min Int Inc St]/0.10 (= 100.0% minus Ownership %).

g. $34,000 [Warranty Expense, as BS liability did not change].

h. $123,000 = $125,000 – ($43,000 – $41,000)   (2nd term is also $800/0.40] [Bad Debt expense less increase in Allowance].

i. $60,000 = $54,000 [expense] + [($34,400 – $32,000)/0.40].   Second term in the parentheses is increase in Deferred Tax Liability.

j. $105,800 = $141,800 – ($236,000 – $200,000) [Income less increase in Retained Earnings].

k. –$100,800 = –$105,800 [dividends, see above] – $2,000 [debt payoff] + $7,000 [stock issue].

16.18 continued.

   l.   –$67,000 = –$9,000 (purchase of securities; see Part *c*.) + $7,300 (see [7]) + $53,000 (derivation above in schedule preceding Part *a*.) – $108,000 (see [4]) – $11,000 (see [6]).

   m. $181,500 = $13,000 + $100,800 + $67,700 = increase in cash plus outflows for financing + outflows for investing. [Derived as plug.]

   n. $1,356,000 = $1,500,000 – ($154,000 – $143,000) + ($6,000 – $14,000) – $125,000 = Sales less increase in Accounts Receivable, net plus increase in Advance from Customers less Bad Debt Expense. In this problem, Advances from Customer decreased, so the arithmetic effect is a subtraction of $8,000.

   o.   Expenditure of $794,000 = ($212,000 – $58,000) – ($192,000 – $50,000) + $788,000 – ($5,000 – $4,000) – ($141,000 – $136,000) = increase in Inventory plus Cost of Goods Sold – increase in Advances to Suppliers of Inventory plus increase in Accounts Payable for Inventory.

   p.   –$53,400 = expenditures of $53,400 = $90,400 – $18,000 – $19,000 Income Tax Expense (Current) less decrease in Prepaid Income Taxes less increase in Income Taxes Payable.

   q.   LIFO [see balance sheet subtraction for adjustment from FIFO to LIFO].

   r. $8,000 larger = $58,000 – $50,000 increase in Allowance to Reduce LIFO Valuation for the year.

   s. $58,000 [EB of Allowance].

   t.   [e], but holding gains on inventory will become part of net income when U.S. GAAP and IFRS allow or require fair value to be the balance sheet basis for inventory.

This page is intentionally left blank

CHAPTER 17

SYNTHESIS AND EXTENSIONS

Exercises and Problems: Answers and Solutions

17.1   (Identifying accounting principles.)

   a.   FIFO cost flow assumption.

   b.   Allowance method.

   c.   Equity method.

   d.   Capital or financing lease method.

   e.   Weighted-average cost-flow assumption.

   f.   Effective interest method.

   g.   Cash flow hedge.

   h.   Market value method.

   i.   Percentage-of-completion method.

   j.   Allowance method.

   k.   Fair value hedge.

   l.   Operating lease method.

   m.   FIFO cost-flow assumption.

   n.   Market value method for securities available for sale.

   o.   Straight-line method.

17.1 continued.

    p.   FIFO cost-flow assumption.

    q.   Operating lease method.

    r.   LIFO cost-flow assumption.

    s.   Capital or financing lease method.

    t.   LIFO cost-flow assumption.

17.2   (Identifying accounting principles.)

    a.   Fair value method of accounting for either marketable securities or long-term investments in securities classified as available for sale.

        Receipt of a dividend in cash.

    b.   Fair value method for marketable securities classified as available for sale.

        Recording an unrealized loss.

    c.   Equity method of accounting for long-term investments.

        Receipt of dividend from an investee.

    d.   Allowance method of accounting for uncollectible accounts.

        Recognition of bad debt expense associated with uncollectible accounts.

    e.   Operating method of accounting for leases by lessee.

        Payment of rent for this period.

    f.   Equity method of accounting for long-term investments.

        Accrual of investor's share of investee's earnings.

    g.   Allowance method of accounting for uncollectible accounts.

        Write-off of an uncollectible account.

17.2 continued.

    h. Lower-of-cost-or-market valuation basis for inventories. In most cases, this is included in cost of goods sold.

        Write-down of inventories to market value.

    i. Capital lease method of accounting for long-term leases by lessee.

        Payment of cash for interest and for reduction in principal of lease liability.

    j. Cost method of accounting for treasury stock.

        Purchase of treasury stock for cash.

    k. Remeasurement to reflect change in fair value of derivative accounted for as a fair value hedge.

        Remeasurement of swap contract to fair value.

17.3   (Campbell Incorporated; calculating earnings per share.) (amounts in thousands of US$)

    a. Basic earnings per share:

        2012: $1.75 per share = $1,200,472/687,910

        2013: $2.07 per share = $1,456,091/702,987

    b. Diluted earnings per share:

        2012: $1.72 per share = $1,200,472/699,012

        2013: $2.04 per share = $1,456,091/713,456

    c. Diluted earnings per share are smaller than basic earnings per share because the diluted number of shares exceeds the number of basic shares.

17.4   (Hatchet Limited; calculating earnings per share.) (amounts in US$)

    a. Net income, 2012 = $3.16 per share × 112.7 million shares = $356.1 million.

17.4 continued.

    b. Weighted-average number of shares outstanding, basic, 2012 = $356.1 million (Part *a*.)/$3.02 per share = 117.9 million shares.

    c. Net income, 2013 = $4.13 per share X 103.4 shares = $427.0 million.

    d. Weighted-average number of shares outstanding, diluted, 2013 = $427.0 million (Part *c*.)/$4.01 per share = 106.5 million shares.

17.5   (Kennett Corporation; calculating weighted-average shares outstanding.)

Period	Shares Outstanding	Fraction of Year	Product
January–March	214.6	25.00%	53.7
April–August	250.8 (= 214.6 + 36.2)	41.67%	104.5
September–December	278.2 (= 250.8 + 27.4)	33.33%	92.7
Weighted Average Outstanding		100.00%	**250.9**

    a. Kennett had 278.2 million common shares outstanding as of December 31, 2013.

    b. Kennett's weighted-average number of common shares is 250.9 million, calculated above.

17.6   (Boslan Group; calculating weighted-average shares outstanding.)

Period	Shares Outstanding	Fraction of Year	Product
January–February	89.1	16.67%	14.9
March–July	114.2 (= 89.1 + 25.1)	41.67%	47.6
August–October	92.0 (= 114.2 − 22.2)	25.00%	23.0
November–December	89.1 (= 92.0 − 2.9)	16.67%	14.9
Weighted Average Outstanding		100.00%	110.4

    a. Boslan had 89.1 million common shares outstanding as of December 31, 2013 (the same number of common shares outstanding as of the beginning of the year).

    b. Boslan's weighted-average number of common shares is 92.9 million, calculated above.

17.7   (Company A/Company B; interpreting changes in earnings per share.)
(amounts in US$)

a. **Company A Earnings
    Per Share:**

2012 .... $\dfrac{\$100,000}{100,000 \text{ Shares}} = \$1 \text{ per Share}$

2013 .... $\dfrac{\$100,000}{100,000 \text{ Shares}} = \$1 \text{ per Share}$

**Company B Earnings
    Per Share:**

2012 .... $\dfrac{\$100,000}{100,000 \text{ Shares}} = \$1 \text{ per Share}$

2013 .... $\dfrac{\$110,000}{100,000 \text{ Shares}} = \$1.10 \text{ per Share}$

b. Company A: No growth [= ($1.00/$1.00) – 1.0].
    Company B: 10% [= ($1.10/$1.00) – 1.0] annual growth.

c. Company B: This result is misleading. Comparisons of growth in
    earnings per share are valid only if firms employ equal amounts of
    assets in the business. The rates of return both on assets and on
    shareholders' equity are better measures of growth performance.
    Earnings per share results do not, in general (as in this problem), take
    earnings retention into account.

d. The problem states that both Company A and Company B earned a
    ROE of 10% each year. Thus, using the change in ROE as the
    performance criterion, both companies performed the same.
    Specifically, both Company A and Company B had no change in ROE
    between 2012 and 2013.

17.8   (Gen/Dyn; treatment of accounting errors, changes in accounting principles,
and changes in accounting estimates.) (amounts in US$)

1. **Accounting Error:**
    2012: $1,100 (= $1,500 – $400)
    2013: $1,800

17.8 continued.

2. **Change in Accounting Principle:**
2012: $1,100 (= $1,500 − $400)
2013: $1,800

3. **Change in Accounting Estimate:**
2012: $1,500
2013: $1,800

17.9 (Union Cable Company; journal entries to correct errors and adjust for changes in estimates.) (amounts in US$)

a. Retained Earnings.. 12,000
    Patent (or Accumulated Amortization)..............   12,000

Assets	=	Liabilities	+	Shareholders' Equity	(Class.)
−12,000				−12,000	RE

To correct error from neglecting to amortize patent during previous year.

b. Accumulated Depreciation....................................... 7,000
    Retained Earnings...   4,000
    Retained Earnings...   3,000

Assets	=	Liabilities	+	Shareholders' Equity	(Class.)
+7,000				+4,000	RE
				+3,000	RE

To correct error in recording the sale of a machine by eliminating the balance in accumulated depreciation relating to the machine sold and converting a $4,000 loss on the sale to a $3,000 gain. (The two credits to Retained Earnings could be netted to form a single $7,000 credit to Retained Earnings.)

17.9 continued.

c. Depreciation Expense... 50,000
    Accumulated Depreciation................................. 50,000

Assets	=	Liabilities	+	Shareholders' Equity	(Class.)
–50,000				–50,000	IncSt → RE

To record depreciation expense for 2012. Carrying
value on January 1, 2012 is $1,600,00 [= $2,400,000 –
($80,000 X 10)]. The revised annual depreciation is
$50,000 (= $1,600,000/32).

d. Bad Debt Expense 10,000
    Allowance for Uncollectible Accounts................. 10,000

Assets	=	Liabilities	+	Shareholders' Equity	(Class.)
–10,000				–10,000	IncSt → RE

To adjust the balance in the allowance account to the
amount needed to cover estimated uncollectibles.

17.10 (Chicago Corporation; comprehensive review problem.) (amounts in US$)

a.
Balance, December 31, 2012...................................	$ 100,000
Provision for 2013	120,000
Less Balance, December 31, 2013	(160,000)
Write-Offs During 2013	$ 60,000

b.
	LIFO	FIFO
Beginning Inventory	$ 1,500,000	$ 1,800,000
Purchases...	5,300,000	5,300,000
Available for Sale...	$ 6,800,000	$ 7,100,000
Less Ending Inventory.................................	(1,800,000)	(1,700,000)
Cost of Goods Sold.......................................	$ 5,000,000	$ 5,400,000
Net Sales	$ 13,920,000	$ 13,920,000
Less Cost of Goods Sold..............................	(5,000,000)	(5,400,000)
Gross Profit..	$ 8,920,000	$ 8,520,000

c. The quantity of inventory increased because the LIFO ending
inventory is larger than the LIFO beginning inventory. The acquisition
costs of the inventory items decreased because the FIFO ending
inventory is less than the FIFO beginning inventory despite an
increase in quantity during the year.

17.10 continued.

d. None of the companies declared dividends during 2013 because the changes (increases) in the investment accounts equal the amounts recognized as Chicago Corporation's equity in the earnings of these companies.

e.

Investment in Chicago Finance Corporation	1,800,000	
Investment in Rosenwald Company	125,000	
Investment in Hutchinson Company	75,000	
Equity in Earnings of Chicago Finance Corporation		1,800,000
Equity in Earnings of Rosenwald Company		125,000
Equity in Earnings of Hutchinson Company		75,000

Assets	=	Liabilities	+	Shareholders' Equity	(Class.)
+1,800,000				+1,800,000	IncSt → RE
+125,000				+125,000	IncSt → RE
+75,000				+75,000	IncSt → RE

f. $4,000,000/40 = $100,000.

g.

Cash	400,000	
Accumulated Depreciation	800,000	
Machinery and Equipment		1,000,000
Gain on Sale of Machinery and Equipment		200,000

Assets	=	Liabilities	+	Shareholders' Equity	(Class.)
+400,000				+200,000	IncSt → RE
+800,000					
−1,000,000					

h.

Interest Expense	288,000	
Bonds Payable (= $3,648,000 − $3,600,000)		48,000
Cash (= 0.06 X $4,000,000)		240,000

Assets	=	Liabilities	+	Shareholders' Equity	(Class.)
−240,000		+48,000		−288,000	IncSt → RE

17.10 continued.

i. Effective interest rate × $3,600,000 = $288,000. The effective interest rate = 8%. Chicago Corporation issued these bonds for less than their face value because the coupon rate of 6% is less than the market interest rate at the time of issue of 8%.

j. Difference between book and taxable depreciation = $150,000/0.30 = $500,000.

Because the Deferred Tax Liability account increased, tax depreciation must be $500,000 larger than depreciation for financial reporting.

k. Cash.. 1,000,000
    Treasury Shares.. 400,000
    Additional Paid-In Capital 600,000

Assets	=	Liabilities	+	Shareholders' Equity	(Class.)
+1,000,000				+400,000	ContriCap
				+600,000	ContriCap

l. Acquisition Cost.. $1,250,000
   Less Carrying Value .... (750,000)
   Accumulated Amortization... $ 500,000

Because the patent is being amortized at the rate of $125,000 per year, the patent was acquired four years before the balance sheet date (= $500,000/$125,000).

m. If Chicago Corporation owns less than 20% of the common stock of Hutchinson Company, it will record the investment at fair value. Chicago Corporation would show the Investment in Hutchinson account at its fair value of $125,000 (= $100,000 + $25,000) and show a $25,000 amount in the Unrealized Gain on Investment in Securities account in Accumulated Other Comprehensive Income in the shareholders' equity section of the balance sheet. Hutchinson Company did not declare dividends during the year. Thus, net income of Chicago Corporation would decrease by the $75,000 equity in Hutchinson Company's earnings during 2013 recognized under the equity method. Consolidated retained earnings would, therefore, be $75,000 less than as now stated. In the statement of cash flows, there

17.10 m. continued.

would be $75,000 smaller net income and no subtraction of $75,000 for the equity in earnings of Hutchinson Company.

n. Capitalized Lease Obligation ($1,100,000 –
       $1,020,000) 80,000
    Interest Expense.. 90,000
          Cash 170,000

Assets	=	Liabilities	+	Shareholders' Equity	(Class.)
–170,000		–80,000		–90,000	IncSt → RE

Amortization of Leased Property Rights 150,000
       Accumulated Amortization 150,000

Assets	=	Liabilities	+	Shareholders' Equity	(Class.)
–150,000				–150,000	IncSt → RE

Total expense would be $240,000 (= $90,000 + $150,000).

o. The income statement would show a $200,000 loss from the price decline, and retained earnings would be $200,000 less than as shown. The Inventories account would be shown at $1,600,000 instead of $1,800,000. There would be an addback for the loss on the statement of cash flows because the loss did not use cash.

p. Basic earnings per share = ($4,400,000 – $120,000)/1,600,000 = $2.675.

Fully diluted earnings per share = $4,400,000/(1,600,000 + ?) = $2.20.

The number of common shares that would be issued is 400,000.

17.10 continued.

q.

Cash

√	200,000				

Operations

(1)	4,400,000	100,000	(3)	
(11)	1,000,000	300,000	(4)	
(12)	125,000	1,800,000	(5)	
(13)	150,000	125,000	(6)	
(15)	60,000	75,000	(7)	
(16)	130,000	200,000	(9)	
(17)	50,000	20,000	(14)	
(18)	260,000			
(19)	48,000			
(22)	170,000			

Investing

(9)	400,000	100,000	(8)
		1,700,000	(10)

Financing

(23)	1,000,000	2,200,000	(2)
		968,000	(20)
		80,000	(21)
√	325,000		

Accounts Receivable			Merchandise Inventory		
√	500,000		√	1,500,000	
(3)	100,000		(4)	300,000	
√	600,000		√	1,800,000	

Prepayments			Investments in Chicago Finance Corporation		
√	200,000		√	2,200,000	
			(5)	1,800,000	
√	200,000		√	4,000,000	

17.10 q. continued.

Investment in Rosenwald Corporation		
√	900,000	
(6)	125,000	
√	1,025,000	

Investment in Hutchinson Corporation		
√	100,000	
(7)	75,000	
√	175,000	

Land		
√	400,000	
(8)	100,000	
√	500,000	

Building		
√	4,000,000	
√	4,000,000	

Merchandise and Equipment			
√	7,300,000		
(10)	1,700,000	1,000,000	(9)
√	8,000,000		

Property Rights Under Lease		
√	1,500,000	
√	1,500,000	

Accumulated Depreciation and Amortization			
		3,800,000	√
(9)	800,000	1,000,000	(11)
		4,000,000	√

Patent			
√	875,000		
		125,000	(12)
√	750,000		

Goodwill		
√	1,125,000	
√	1,125,000	

Accounts Payable		
	400,000	√
	150,000	(13)
	550,000	√

Advances from Customers		
	660,000	√
(14)	20,000	
	640,000	√

Salaries Payable		
	240,000	√
	60,000	(15)
	300,000	√

17.10 q. continued.

Income Taxes Payable		
	300,000	√
	130,000	(16)
	430,000	√

Rent Received in Advance		
	0	√
	50,000	(17)
	50,000	√

Other Current Liabilities		
	200,000	√
	260,000	(18)
	460,000	√

Bonds Payable		
	3,600,000	√
	48,000	(19)
	3,648,000	√

Equipment Mortgage Payable			
		1,300,000	√
(20)	968,000		
		332,000	√

Capitalized Lease Obligation			
		1,100,000	√
(21)	80,000		
		1,020,000	√

Deferred Tax Liability		
	1,400,000	√
	170,000	(22)
	1,570,000	√

Convertible Preferred Stock		
	2,000,000	√
	2,000,000	√

Common Stock		
	2,000,000	√
	2,000,000	√

Additional Paid-In Capital		
	2,400,000	√
	600,000	(23)
	3,000,000	√

Retained Earnings			
		2,800,000	√
(2)	2,200,000	4,400,000	(1)
		5,000,000	√

Treasury Stock			
√	1,400,000		
		400,000	(23)
√	1,000,000		

17.11   (Tuck Corporation; comprehensive review problem.) (amounts in US$)

a. Balance in Marketable Equity Securities on December 31,
    2012 .... $ 125,000
    Less Cost of Marketable Equity Securities Sold .... (35,000)
    Plus Decrease in Unrealized Loss on Marketable
    Securities 4,000
    Plus Cost of Marketable Equity Securities Purchased .... ?
    Balance in Marketable Equity Securities on December 31,
    2013 .... $ 141,000

The cost of marketable equity securities purchased is $47,000.

b. Cost of Marketable Equity Securities Sold .... $ 35,000
    Less Loss on Sale of Marketable Equity Securities .... (8,000)
    Sales Proceeds .... $ 27,000

c. Balance in Allowance Account on December 31, 2012 .... $ 128,800
    Plus Provision for Estimated Uncollectible Accounts .... ?
    Less Write-Offs of Specific Customers' Accounts .... (63,000)
    Balance in Allowance Account on December 31, 2013 .... $ 210,400

The provision for estimated uncollectibles is $144,600.

d.   LIFO   Difference   FIFO
    Beginning Inventory .... $1,257,261 $ 430,000 $1,687,261
    Purchases............................   2,848,054   —   2,848,054
    Available .... $4,105,315 $ 430,000 $4,535,315
    Less Ending Inventory......... (1,525,315)   (410,000)   (1,935,315)
    Cost of Goods Sold............... $2,580,000 $ 20,000 $2,600,000

e. Unrealized Loss on Investments in Securities 5,000
        Investments in Securities   5,000

Assets	= Liabilities +	Shareholders' Equity	(Class.)
−5,000		−5,000	OCI → AOCI

To recognize unrealized loss on investments in securities.

f. Dividend revenue of $8,000. The unrealized loss of $5,000 (see Part e.)
    is not included in the calculation of net income for 2013.

17.11 continued.

g. Investment in Davis Corporation 87,000
    Equity in Earnings of Affiliates......................... 87,000

Assets	=	Liabilities	+	Shareholders' Equity	(Class.)
+87,000				+87,000	IncSt → RE

To recognize share of Davis Corporation's earnings in 2013; 0.40 × $217,500 = $87,000.

Cash.. 24,000
    Investment in Davis Corporation...................... 24,000

Assets	=	Liabilities	+	Shareholders' Equity	(Class.)
+24,000					
−24,000					

To recognize dividend received from Davis Corporation; 0.40 × $60,000 = $24,000.

Investment in Davis Corporation 20,000
    Cash 20,000

Assets	=	Liabilities	+	Shareholders' Equity	(Class.)
+20,000					
−20,000					

To record additional investment in Davis Corporation.

h. Cash.. 7,000
    Accumulated Depreciation...................................... 19,000
    Equipment.. 23,000
    Gain on Sale of Equipment................................. 3,000

Assets	=	Liabilities	+	Shareholders' Equity	(Class.)
+7,000				+3,000	IncSt → RE
+19,000					
−23,000					

17.11 continued.

i. Present Value of Lease Payment at Signing .... $ 10,000
Present Value of 19 Lease Payments Due on January 2 of
    Each Subsequent Year at 8%; $10,000 × 9.6036 96,036
Total.. $ 106,036

j. Balance in Rental Fees Received in Advance on December
    31, 2012 .... $ 46,000
Plus Cash Received for Rentals During 2013 .... ?
Less Rental Fees Earned During 2013............................... (240,000)
Balance in Rental Fees Received in Advance on December
    31, 2013 .... $ 58,000

Cash received during 2013 totaled $252,000.

k. Balance in Estimated Warranty Liability on December
    31, 2012 .... $75,200
Plus Estimated Warranty Cost Provision for 2013 46,800
Less Cost of Actual Warranty Services............................... (?)
Balance in Estimated Warranty Liability on December
    31, 2013 .:... $78,600

Warranty costs incurred during 2013 totaled $43,400.

l. First 6 Months: 0.025 × $1,104,650.00 .... $27,616.25
Second 6 Months: 0.025 × $1,102,266.25ᵃ 27,556.66
    Total Interest Expense... $55,172.91

ᵃ$1,104,650.00 − ($30,000.00 − $27,616.25) = $1,102,266.25.

m. Interest Expense.. 20,996
Mortgage Payable 19,004
    Cash 40,000

Assets	=	Liabilities	+	Shareholders' Equity	(Class.)
−40,000		−19,004		−20,996	IncSt → RE

To record mortgage interest and principal payment;
$20,996 = 0.07 × ($262,564 + $37,383).

17.11 continued.

n.

Present Value of Payment on January 1, 2013......................	$10,000
Present Value of Seven Remaining Lease Payments	
($10,000 X 5.20637)..	52,064
Total	$62,064

o.

Capitalized Lease Obligation, December 31, 2012	$62,064
Lease Payment on January 1, 2013	(10,000)
Interest Expense for 2013 (0.08 X $52,064)	4,165
Total ($10,000 + $46,229)...	$56,229

p.

Income Tax Expense	150,000	
Income Tax Payable		135,000
Deferred Tax Liability ($145,000 – $130,000) ..		15,000

Assets	=	Liabilities	+	Shareholders' Equity	(Class.)
		+135,000		–150,000	IncSt → RE
		+15,000			

q.

Income Tax Payable—Current, December 31, 2012	$ 140,000
Provision for Current Taxes Payable (See Part p.)	135,000
Less Cash Payments Made During 2013...............................	(?)
Income Tax Payable—Current, December 31, 2013	$ 160,000

Cash payments for income taxes during 2013 were $115,000.

r.

$$\frac{\text{Deferred Tax Expense Relating to Depreciation}}{\text{Income Tax Rate}} = \frac{\$12,000}{0.30} = \$40,000$$

s.

Convertible Preferred Stock (5,000 X $100)	500,000	
Common Stock (25,000 X $10)............................		250,000
Additional Paid-In Capital		250,000

Assets	=	Liabilities	+	Shareholders' Equity	(Class.)
				–500,000	ContriCap
				+250,000	ContriCap
				+250,000	ContriCap

To record conversion of preferred into common stock.

17.11 continued.

t. Treasury Stock 8,800
    Cash 8,800

Assets	=	Liabilities	+	Shareholders' Equity	(Class.)
−8,800				−8,800	ContriCap

To record purchases of treasury stock.

Cash.. 25,200
    Treasury Stock .... 21,600[a]
    Additional Paid-In Capital .... 3,600[b]

Assets	=	Liabilities	+	Shareholders' Equity	(Class.)
+25,200				+21,600	ContriCap
				+3,600	ContriCap

To record the sale of treasury stock.

[a]1,800 shares × $12 = $21,600.

[b]Additional Paid-In Capital on December 31, 2012............ $ 130,000
Plus Amount Arising from Conversion of Preferred
  Stock.. 250,000
Plus Amount Arising from Issue of Common Stock........... 200,000
Plus Amount Arising from Sale of Treasury Stock............ ?
Additional Paid-In Capital on December 31, 2013............ $ 583,600

The additional paid-in capital arising from the treasury stock sales is $3,600.

17.12 (Layton Ball Corporation; case introducing earnings-per-share calculations for a complex capital structure.) (amounts in US$)

a. $\dfrac{\$9,500}{2,500} = \$3.80$ per share.

17.12 continued.

b. 1,000 options × \$15 = \$15,000 cash raised.

$$\frac{\$15,000 \text{ new cash}}{\$25 \text{ per share}} = 600 \text{ shares assumed purchased.}$$

Total number of shares increases by 400 (= 1,000 – 600).

$$\frac{\$9,500}{2,500 + 400} = \$3.276 \text{ per share.}$$

c. 2,000 warrants × \$30 = \$60,000 cash raised.

$$\frac{\$60,000 \text{ new cash}}{\$25 \text{ per share}} = 2,400 \text{ shares purchased.}$$

Total number of shares decreases by 400 (= 2,000 – 2,400).

$$\frac{\$9,500}{2,500 - 400} = \$4.524 \text{ per share.}$$

d. Before taxes, each converted bond saves \$40 in annual interest expense. After taxes, the savings in expense and increase in income is only \$24 [= (1 – 0.40) × \$40].

There are 100 bonds outstanding; each is convertible into 10 shares. Thus, the new earnings per share figure is

$$\frac{\$9,500 + \$24 \text{ savings per bond} \times 100 \text{ bonds}}{2,500 + 10 \text{ shares per bond} \times 100 \text{ bonds}} = \frac{\$11,900}{3,500 \text{ shares}} =$$

\$3.40 per share.

e. The warrants are antidilutive and should be ignored if we seek the maximum possible dilution of earnings per share.

$$\frac{\$9,500 + \$2,400 \text{ (increase from interest savings)}}{2,500 + 1,000 \text{ (bond conversion)} + 400 \text{ (option exercise)}} = \frac{\$11,900}{3,900} =$$

\$3.05 per share.

17.12 continued.

    f.   Probably financial publications should use the earnings per share that results in the maximum possible dilution. They should ignore antidilutive securities. Do not conclude from the presentation in this problem that one can check the dilution characteristics of potentially dilutive securities one by one and know for sure which combination of assumed exercise and conversions leads to the minimum earnings per share figure.

APPENDIX

TIME VALUE OF CASH FLOWS: COMPOUND INTEREST CONCEPTS AND APPLICATIONS

Questions, Exercises, and Problems: Answers and Solutions

A.1   See the text or the glossary at the end of the book.

A.2   The value of cash flows differs over time because cash can earn interest. Extracting, or discounting, the interest element in a future cash flow permits expressing that future cash flow in terms of an equivalent present cash flow.

A.3   In simple interest, only the principal sum earns interest. In compound interest, interest is earned on the principal plus amounts of interest not paid or withdrawn.

A.4   There is no difference; these items refer to the same thing.

A.5   The timing of the first payment for an annuity due is *now* (at the beginning of the first period), whereas that for an ordinary annuity is at the *end* of the first period. The future value of an annuity due is computed as of one year after the final payment, but for an ordinary annuity is computed as of the time of the last payment.

A.6   The discount rate that sets the net present value of a stream of payments equal to zero is the implicit rate for that stream. Excel® provides a procedure to solve for the implicit interest rate. One can also solve for implicit interest rate by trial and error.

(1) Guess a rate.

(2) Compute the net present values of the cash flows using the current guess.

A.6 continued.

        (3) If the net present value in (2) is less than zero, then increase the rate guessed and go to Step (2).

        (4) If the net present value in (2) is greater than zero, then reduce the rate guessed and go to Step (2).

        (5) Otherwise, the current guess is the implicit rate of return.

        The process will converge to the right answer only if one is systematic with the guesses, narrowing the range successively.

A.7   Present values increase when interest rates decrease, and present values decrease when interest rates increase, regardless of the time period.

A.8   6%. The present value will be larger the smaller the discount rate.

A.9   The formula assumes that the growth [represented by the parameter g in the formula $1/(r - g)$] continues forever. That is a long time. The formula assumes also that the discount and growth rates remain constant. In our experience, more harm results from assuming the growth persists forever than from the other assumptions.

A.10   a. $5,000 X 3.20714 X 1.06 = $16,998.

        b. $5,000 X 10.06266 X 1.25971 = $63,380.

A.11   a. $150,000 X 0.62741 = $94,112.

        b. $150,000 X 0.54027 = $81,041.

A.12   a. $4,000 X 6.97532 = $27,901.

        b. $4,000 X 7.33593 = $29,344.

A.13   a. ¥45,000,000/10.63663 = ¥4.23 million.

        b. ¥45,000,000/12.29969 = ¥3.66 million.

A.14   a. €90,000 X 14.20679 X 1.05 = €90,000 X (15.91713 − 1.0) = €1,342,542.

        b. €90,000 X 18.53117 X 1.10 = €90,000 X (21.38428 − 1.0) = €1,834,585.

A.15 a. £145,000/4.62288 = £31,366.

     b. £145,000/4.11141 = £35,268.

A.16 a. (10) $5,000 × $T(1, 21, 6)$.

         (11) $150,000 × $T(2, 8, 6)$.

         (12) $4,000 × $T(3, 6, 6)$.

         (13) ¥45,000,000/$T(3, 8, 8)$.

         (14) €90,000 × $T(3, 11, 5)$ × 1.05 = €90,000 × $[T(3, 12, 5) - 1.0]$.

         (15) £145,000/$T(4, 6, 8)$.

     b. Asking questions about compound interest calculations on examinations presents a difficult logistical problem to teachers. They may want the students to use compound interest tables, but not wish to incur the costs of reproducing them in sufficient numbers for each student to have a copy. They may not wish to give an open book test. This device is useful for posing test questions about compound interest.

        The device is based on the fact that teachers of accounting are not particularly interested in testing their students' ability to do arithmetic. Teachers want to be sure that students know how to use the tables and calculating devices efficiently in combination. Such a combination suggests that the humans do the thinking and the calculators do the multiplications and divisions.

A.17 (Effective interest rates.)

     a. 12% per period; 5 periods.

     b. 6% per period; 10 periods.

     c. 3% per period; 20 periods.

     d. 1% per period; 60 periods.

A.18   (amounts in US$)

    a. $100 × 1.21665 = $121.67.

    b. $500 × 1.34587 = $672.94.

    c. $200 × 1.26899 = $253.80.

    d. $2,500 × (1.74102 × 1.74102) = $7,577.88.

        $(1.02)^{56} = (1.02)^{28} × (1.02)^{28}$.

    e. $600 × 1.43077 = $858.46.

A.19   (amounts in US$)

    a. $100 × 0.30832 = $30.83.

    b. $250 × 0.53063 = $132.66.

    c. $1,000 × 0.78757 = $787.57.

A.20   (amounts in US$)

    a. $100 × 13.80933 = $1,380.93.

    b. $850 × 9.89747 = $8,412.85.

    c. $400 × 49.96758 = $19,987.03.

A.21   (amounts in US$)

    a. $1,000(1.00 + 0.94340) + $2,000(4.21236 − 0.94340) + $2,500(6.80169 − 4.21236) = $14,955.

    b. $1,000(1.00 + 0.92593) + $2,000(3.99271 − 0.92593) + $2,500(6.24689 − 3.99271) = $13,695.

    c. $1,000(1.00 + 0.90909) + $2,000(3.79079 − 0.90909) + $2,500(5.75902 − 3.79079) = $12,593.

A.22   (amounts in US$)

    a. $3,000 + ($3,000/0.06) = $53,000.

    b. $3,000 + ($3,000/0.08) = $40,500.

A.23   (amounts in US$)

    a. $3,000/(0.06 − 0.02) = $75,000.

    b. $3,000/(0.08 − 0.02) = $50,000.

    c.   [$3,000/(0.06 − 0.02)] × 0.79209 = $59,406.75.

    d.   [$3,000/(0.08 − 0.02)] × 0.73503 = $36,751.50.

A.24   (amounts in US$)

    a. $60,000 + ($60,000/0.1664) = $420,577. $(1.08)^2 − 1 = 0.1664.$

    b. $60,000 + ($60,000/0.2544) = $295,850. $(1.12)^2 − 1 = 0.2544.$

A.25   (amounts in US$)

7.00%. Note that $100,000/$55,307 = 1.80809. See Appendix Table 4, 2-period row and observe 1.80809 in the 7% column.

A.26   (amounts in US$)

12% = $($140,493/$100,000)^{1/3} − 1.$

A.27   (amounts in US$)

    a.   16% = $($67,280/$50,000)^{1/2} − 1.$

    b.

Year (1)	Carrying Value Start of Year (2)	Interest for Year = (2) × 0.16 (3)	Amount (Reducing) Increasing Carrying Value (4)	Carrying Value End of Year = (2) + (3) + (4) (5)
1	$ 50,000	$ 8,000		$ 58,000
2	58,000	9,280	$ (67,280)	-0-

A.28   (Berman Company; find implicit interest rate; construct amortization schedule.) (amounts in US$)

a.   14.0%.

$$\text{Let } x = \frac{\$8,000}{(1+r)} + \frac{\$8,000}{(1+r)^2} + \frac{\$8,000}{(1+r)^3} + \frac{\$100,000}{(1+r)^3} = \$86,000.$$

If $r = 14.0\%$, then $x = \$18,573 + \$67,497 - \$86,000 = \$70$.

If $r = 14.1\%$, then $x = \$18,542 + \$67,320 - \$86,000 = \$138$.

b.

Year (1)	Carrying Value Start of Year (2)	Interest for Year = (2) x 0.14 (3)	Payment End of Year (Given) (4)	Amount (Reducing) Increasing Carrying Value = (3) – (4) (5)	Carrying Value End of Year = (2) + (5) (6)
1	$ 86,000	$ 12,040	$ 8,000	$ 4,040	$ 90,040
2	90,040	12,605	8,000	4,605	94,645
3	94,645	13,250*	108,000	(94,750)	(105)
OR 3	94,645	13,355*	108,000	(94,645)	-0-

*Interest would actually be recorded at $13,355 (= $108,000 – $94,645) so that the carrying value of the note reduces to zero at its maturity.

A.29   (Find equivalent annual rate offered for purchase discounts.) (amounts in US$)

a.   Terms of sale of 2/10, net/30 on a $100 gross invoice price, for example, mean that the interest rate is 2/98 for a 20-day period, because if the discount is not taken, a charge of $2 is levied for the use of $98. The $98 is used for 20 days (= 30 – 10), so the number of compounding periods in a year is 365/20 = 18.25. The expression for the exact rate of interest implied by 2/10, net 30 is $(1 + 2/98)^{(365/20)} - 1 = 1.020408^{18.25} - 1 = 44.59\%$.

b.   Appendix Table 1 can be used. Use the 2% column and the 18-period row to see that the rate implied by 2/10, net 30 must be at least 42.825% (= 1.42825 – 1).

A.30   (amounts in US$)

$30,000 + ($10,000/0.01) = $1,030,000.

A.31   (amounts in US$)

Present value of future proceeds = 0.85282 x $30,000 + C = $30,000; where C represents the present value of the foregone interest payments. Appendix Table 2, 16-period row, 1% column = 0.85282.

C = $30,000 − $25,585 = $4,415.

A.32   (amounts in US$)

a.   Will: $24,000 + $24,000(3.31213) = $103,491.12 (Preferred).

Dower Option: $300,000/3 = $100,000.

b.   Will: $24,000 + $24,000(3.03735) = $96,896.40.

Dower Option: $300,000/3 = $100,000 (Preferred).

A.33   (amounts in US$)

Present value of deposit = $3.00.

Present value of $3.00, recorded 20 periods, have discounted at 0.50% per period = $3.00 x 0.90506 = $2.72.

Loss of $0.28 (= $3.00 − $2.72) in foregone interest vs. Loss of $1.20 in price.

Net advantage of returnables is $0.92.

A.34   (General Electric.) (amounts in US$)

$1.00(1.00 + 0.92456 + 0.85480 + 0.79031 + 0.73069) = $1.00 x 4.30036 = $4.30.

$4.30 − $3.50 = $0.80.

A.35   (Oberweis Dairy.) (amounts in US$)

$1,800/12 = $150 saved per month. $6,000/$150 = 40.0.

Present value of annuity of $1 discounted at 1% for 50 periods = 39.19612.

The present value of the annuity is $40 when the annuity lasts between 51 and 52 periods. Oberweis Dairy will recoup its investment in about 52 months, a bit more than four years.

A.36   (Levi Strauss; calculating impairment.) (amounts in US$)

a. $ 3,000,000 X 7.46944 = $ 22,408,320

b. $ 3,000,000 X 7.36578 = $ 22,097,340
         500,000 X 1.69005 =   845,025
                                $ 22,942,365

c. $ 2,000,000 X 7.36578 = $ 14,731,560
       1,000,000 X 2.40183 =   2,401,830
         500,000 X 1.69005 =   845,025
                                $ 17,978,415

d. $17,978,410 X 0.20   = $ 3,595,682

A.37   (Friendly Loan Company; finding implicit interest rates; truth-in-lending laws reduce the type of deception suggested by this problem.) (amounts in US$)

The effective interest rate is 19.86% and must be found by trial and error. The time line for this problem is

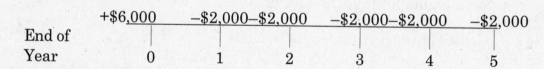

A.37 continued.

Dividing every number in the above time line by 2,000, we get a time line that is equivalent, at least in terms of the implied interest rate, to

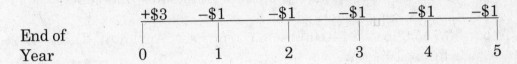

	+$3	−$1	−$1	−$1	−$1	−$1
End of						
Year	0	1	2	3	4	5

Scanning Appendix Table 4, 5-period column, one finds the factor 2.99061, which is approximately 3.00, in the 20% column, so one can easily see that the implied interest rate is about 20% per year. The 3.00 is the +$3 cash inflow shown in the above time line for End of Year 0.

A.38 (Black & Decker Company; deriving net present value of cash flows for decision to dispose of asset.) (amounts in US$)

$40,698. The $100,000 is gone and an economic loss of $50,000 was suffered because of the bad purchase. The issue now is do we want to swap a larger current tax loss and smaller future depreciation charges for no tax loss now and larger future depreciation charges.

The new machine will lead to depreciation charges lower by $10,000 per year than the "old" machine and, hence, income taxes larger by $4,000. The present value of the larger taxes is $4,000 × 3.60478 (Appendix Table 4, 12%, 5 periods). Let S denote the proceeds from selling the old machine. The new current "outlay" to acquire the new machine is $50,000 − S − $0.40(\$100,000 − S)$ or $\$10,000 − 0.60S$, so that for the new machine to be worthwhile:

$$\$10,000 − 0.60S < −\$14,419$$

OR

$$0.6S > \$24,419$$

OR

$$S > \$40,698.$$

Solutions

A.39   (Lynch Company/Bages Company; computation of present value of cash flows; untaxed acquisition, no change in tax basis of assets.) (amounts in US$)

a. $440,000 = $390,000 + $50,000 = $700,000 – $260,000.

b. $3,745,966 = $440,000 × 8.51356; see Appendix Table 4, 20-period column, 10% row.

A.40   (Lynch Company/Bages Company; computation of present value of cash flows; taxable acquisition, changing tax basis of assets.) (amounts in US$)

$4,258,199. If the merger is taxable, then the value of the firm V satisfies:

(1) $$\begin{aligned} V &= 8.51356 \times [\$700,000 - 0.40(\$700,000 - V/20)] \\ V &= \$5,959,492 - \$2,383,797 + 0.17027V, \text{ or} \\ 0.83972V &= \$3,575,695, \text{ so} \\ V &= \$4,258,199. \end{aligned}$$

To understand (1), observe that:

$V =$	Value of firm
$V/20 =$	New depreciation charge
$\$700,000 - V/20 =$	New taxable income
$0.40(\$700,000 - V/20) =$	New income tax payable, so
$\$700,000 - 0.40(\$700,000 - V/20) =$	New after-tax cash flow to be capitalized at 10% for 20 years using present value factor 8.51356.

A.41 (American Basketball Association/National Basketball Association; valuation of intangibles with perpetuity formulas.) (amounts in millions of US$)

a. $50 million = $4 million/0.08.

b. Increase.

c. $68 million = ($4 million X 1.02)/(0.08 − 0.02) = $4.08 million/(0.08 − 0.02).

d. Increase.

e. Decrease.

A.42 (Ragazze; analysis of benefits of acquisition of long-term assets.) (amounts in US$)

a. $270,831.

Dec. 31 Year	Cash Inflows Operating Receipts (1)	Salvage (2)	Cash Outflows Maintenance (3)	Test Runs (4)	Total (1) + (2) − (3) − (4) (5)	Present Values at 12% Factor (6)	Cash Flow (7)
0 = 2013							
1 = 2014				$20,000	$ (20,000)	0.89286	$ (17,857)
2 = 2015	$130,000		$ 60,000		70,000	0.79719	55,803
3 = 2016	130,000		60,000		70,000	0.71178	49,825
4 = 2017	130,000		60,000		70,000	0.63552	44,486
5 = 2018	130,000		60,000		70,000	0.56743	39,720
6 = 2019	130,000		100,000		30,000	0.50663	15,199
7 = 2020	130,000		100,000		30,000	0.45235	13,571
8 = 2021	130,000		100,000		30,000	0.40388	12,116
9 = 2022	130,000	$ 30,000			160,000	0.36061	57,968
							$ 270,831

(7) = (5) x (6).

b. $78,868 = $250,000/3.16987.

A.43 (Gulf Coast Manufacturing; choosing between investment alternatives.) (amounts in US$)

Basic Data Repeated from Problem

	Lexus	Mercedes-Benz	Factor	Source [B]	Lexus	Mercedes-Benz
Initial Cost at the Start of 2013	$60,000	$45,000	1.00000		$ 60,000	$ 45,000
Initial Cost at the Start of 2016		48,000	0.75131	T[2, 3, 0.10]		36,063
Trade-in Value						
End of 2015		23,000	0.75131	T[2, 3, 0.10]		(17,280)
End of 2018 [A]	16,000	24,500	0.56447	T[2, 6, 0.10]	(9,032)	(13,830)
Estimated Annual Cash Operating Costs, Except Major Servicing	4,000	4,500	4.35526	T[4, 6, 0.10]	17,421	19,599
Estimated Cash Cost of Major Servicing						
End of 2016	6,500		0.68301	T[2, 4, 0.10]		
End of 2014 and End of 2017		2,500	0.82645	T[2, 2, 0.10]	4,440	2,066
			0.62092	T[2, 5, 0.10]		1,552
Sum of Present Values of All Costs					$72,829	$73,170

[A] At this time, Lexus is 6 years old; second Mercedes-Benz is 3 years old.

[B] $T[i,j,r]$ means Table i (= Appendix Table 2 or Appendix Table 4), row j, interest rate r.

a. Strategy L, buying one Lexus has lower present value of costs, but the difference is so small that we'd encourage the CEO to go with his whim, whatever it may be. Also, the relatively new theory of real options will likely prefer Strategy M because it gives the owner more choices at the end of the third year.

b. Depreciation plays no role, so long as we ignore income taxes. Only cash flows matter.

A.44   (Fast Growth Start-Up Company; valuation involving perpetuity growth model assumptions.) (amounts in millions of US$)

We find the answer with trial and error, starting with five years of fast growth.

Growth Rate for Early Years of Fast Growth:	25%
Growth Rate for Steady State, Terminal Value:	4%
Discount Rate:	15%
Number of Years of Fast Growth:	5

	End of Year		Free Cash Flow	Discount Factors from Table 2	Present Value End of Year 0
	0	$	100	1.00000	$ 100.0
	1		125	0.86957	108.7
	2		156	0.75614	118.1
	3		195	0.65752	128.4
	4		244	0.57175	139.6
	5		305	0.49718	151.7
Terminal Value	5		2,885	0.49718	1,434.5
$305 × 1.04/(0.15 − 0.04)					
			Total Valuation...............................		$ 2,181.1

Growth Rate for Early Years of Fast Growth:	25%
Growth Rate for Steady State, Terminal Value:	4%
Discount Rate:	15%
Number of Years of Fast Growth:	6

A.44 continued.

End of Year		Free Cash Flow	Discount Factors from Table 2	Present Value End of Year 0
0	$	100	1.00000	$ 100.0
1		125	0.86957	108.7
2		156	0.75614	118.1
3		195	0.65752	128.4
4		244	0.57175	139.6
5		305	0.49718	151.7
6		381	0.43233	164.9
Terminal Value 6		3,607	0.43233	1,559.2

$381 X 1.04/(0.15 – 0.04)

Total Valuation............................... $ 2,470.7

Growth Rate for Early Years of Fast Growth: 25%
Growth Rate for Steady State, Terminal Value: 4%
Discount Rate: 15%
Number of Years of Fast Growth: 7

End of Year		Free Cash Flow	Discount Factors from Table 2	Present Value End of Year 0
0	$	100	1.00000	$ 100.0
1		125	0.86957	108.7
2		156	0.75614	118.1
3		195	0.65752	128.4
4		244	0.57175	139.6
5		305	0.49718	151.7
6		381	0.43233	164.9
7		477	0.37594	179.3
Terminal Value 7		4,508	0.37594	1,694.8

$477 X 1.04/(0.15 – 0.04)

Total Valuation............................... $ 2,785.6

We see that assuming a bit more than six years of fast growth, followed by the steady state justifies a market valuation (the so-called market cap) of $2.5 billion.

This page is intentionally left blank

This page is intentionally left blank

This page is intentionally left blank